The Global
Etiquette Guide
to Europe

11/2000

Judson —
A pleasure to be able to
present these books to you.
(Here's to all our work
together!
Best always,
— Dean Foster

The Global Etiquette Guide to Europe

Everything You Need to Know for Business and Travel Success

Dean Foster

John Wiley & Sons, Inc.

New York • Chichester • Weinheim • Brisbane • Singapore • Toronto

This book is dedicated to my parents, Joseph and Sylvia, who first showed me the world

Published by John Wiley & Sons, Inc.
Published simultaneously in Canada

This publication is designed to provide accurate and authoritative information in regard to the subject matter covered. It is sold with the understanding that the publisher is not engaged in rendering professional services. If professional advice or other expert assistance is required, the services of a competent professional person should be sought.

Library of Congress Cataloging-in-Publication Data:

Foster, Dean.
    The global etiquette guide to Europe : everything you need to know for business and travel success / Dean Foster.
       p. cm.
    Includes index.
    ISBN 0-471-31866-3 (paper : alk. paper)
       1. Etiquette—Europe—Handbooks, manuals, etc. 2. Europe—Social life and customs—Handbooks, manuals, etc. I. Title.

    BJ1838.F673   2000
    395'.094—dc21   99-054688

Printed in the United States of America

10 9 8 7 6 5 4 3 2 1

Contents

Preface

The idea for this series emerged out of the work that my staff and I, and literally thousands of people from around the world that we work with, have been doing for almost two decades: assisting businesspeople and travelers to better understand their colleagues in other cultures. This work has primarily focused on international business and has taken many forms: helping to prepare families of employees adjust to an overseas assignment; assisting individual businesspeople in their negotiations with colleagues abroad; and helping global organizations to build more effective global teams. As business has globalized, the need for cross-cultural information has grown.

But globalization hasn't affected only the businessperson. While most of the work in the cross-cultural field has developed in response to international business needs, the need for cross-cultural information for the nonbusiness international traveler (both actual and of the armchair variety!) has also grown. Unfortunately, the amount of useful, objective, and applicable information, adapted to the needs of the more casual international explorer, has been limited. In most cases, what information was available usually took the form of anecdotal war stories, overgeneralized stereotypes (always interesting, but of dubious veracity), or theoretical statements about culture that were too removed from the day-to-day adventures of the international traveler. As the gap between useful cultural information for international businesspeople and international travelers grew, so did the need to bridge it. Hence, the idea for the Global Etiquette Guides series.

Correction: I embarked on this project at first with the goal of writing one book. But the world, as it turned out, was simply too big, and so was the book. Given my work, I for one should not have been surprised at this development, but at first was concerned about how to handle the dilemma. Nevertheless, under the kind and careful guidance of my editor, publisher, and agent, we expanded the original concept into a series. And I am glad we did. For one thing, it gave me the breathing room to explore all cultures to the degree that was necessary for the reader; for another, it gave me the opportunity to experience just how fine a team I was working with.

My editor, Tom Miller, did double duty, providing patience and insight, through both the serialization of the original book and the actual editorial review of the material. His input, despite my occasional and always incorrect misgivings, gave me focus, pause to rethink when it was important to do so, and perhaps most importantly, impetus and space to keep going in the face of demanding schedules and unpredictable events. A good editor provides the professional expertise to fine-tune the work. A great editor also provides faith. Tom never failed to offer both.

Jane Dystel is everything an author can ask for in an agent. On many levels, this series would not have happened without her. She is always available, always on my side, and equally able to manage scrupulously the details of a particular project while helping me to put the pieces in place for the bigger career; I am very grateful to have her support. This is the second time we have worked together on a project, and I look forward to many more.

Bob Stein is the lawyer behind the scenes. Lawyers are, no doubt, overlooked far too often, and easily forgotten once their job is done. Here I have probably been more neglectful than most, for Bob is also a dear and longtime friend who has never failed to support me, even in my most ridiculous moments, and I fear I have taken advantage of that. Forgive me, Bob, and thank you . . . again.

I also want to thank all the professionals in the cross-cultural field with whom I have had the pleasure to work over the years. They have all contributed in important ways to these books. To my colleagues at Berlitz International and at Windham International, who, around the world, have given me opportunities to play a leading role in the cross-cultural field, I am eternally grateful. To the many professionals in both competing and supporting organizations whom I have learned from, and worked and played with, many, many thanks. Finally, to the diverse thousands of individuals around the globe, of all cultures and backgrounds, who, in their work with me and my staff, have provided us with the joy and opportunity to learn about their unique part of the world, my very heartfelt thanks. Without your perspectives, experiences, and input, my work, and ultimately these books, would never have been possible.

When exploring cultural differences, one quickly observes that there are some cultures that "work to live," and others that "live to work." Balancing these two perspectives is a constant challenge for both cultures and individuals, and my world would surely be quite unbalanced without the love and support of my wife, Sheryl. She has been my constant, both the wind literally beneath my wings and my tether to the shore. I know this has not been easy, as she must also balance her own professional demands with our personal life. That she has done both is a testament to her strength and love. These books, as with so much else in my life, could not have occurred without her.

Leah, my daughter, plays a great role in these books. As I've watched her grow into the intelligent and caring young woman she is today, she serves as a constant reminder that the prize we work so hard for should truly be worth something. It needs to be created in love, based on justice, and worth the struggle. As I hope I have given meaning to her life, she continues to give meaning to mine. We have been growing up together all her life, and although she is now "all grown-up," I have no intention of stopping.

Finally, after crediting all these worthy folks for their kind and important contributions, I must now credit myself: all the shortcomings of these books are mine. If I overstated a culture too broadly, overlooked an important cultural consideration, or in any way misrepresented or misjudged a particular way of life, the error is mine and no one else's. I only ask that the reader please consider the cause as the "anthropologist's dilemma": that is, the impossibility of describing a culture objectively, due to the fact that the "describer" is always viewing the culture being observed in reference to his or her own (in my case, the United States). For some, this unfortunate natural law of the social sciences may be an added bonus (for other Americans, perhaps). For others, this may cause some serious and legitimate misgivings. I hear you both. Please take solace in the fact that every effort has been made to minimize the negative effects of this phenomenon whenever and wherever possible. No doubt I have not succeeded completely.

Why Getting It Right around the World Is So Important

Apparently, the world is getting smaller and smaller every day. We can't make it through a twenty-four hour period without the media informing us of something happening in a distant land, without our local bank accounts being affected by a foreign stock market, without our schools having to make decisions about bilingual education, and without the possibility that our friends, co-workers, neighbors, and possibly family, will have come from somewhere else, speak a language we barely understand, and have a perspective on life that may be radically different from our own. As English speakers, isn't it unnecessary that we learn another language . . . or become familiar with other cultures? After all, isn't technology spreading the English language and American pop culture so globally that we're all going to understand one another through the medium of Coca-Cola and rock 'n' roll anyway? The answer to all of the above, as anyone who steps off a plane in a foreign land will learn, is a resounding "No."

I like to think that the world is getting bigger, not smaller; that world cultures, perhaps unique among many aspects of life that are indeed being homogenized, will not be, and that cultures more deeply rooted and with far longer histories than that of the American pop culture, along with their languages, will still be with us long after Coca-Cola becomes their favorite soft drink and rock their favorite form of music.

There is no doubt that cultures are in contact with one another to a degree never before experienced in human history. The vastness of human experience, which is the world, is suddenly in our respective faces as never before. Each of us is experiencing not the smallness of the world, but the very bigness of it. For most of us, this is not an easy thing to do. For a variety of reasons, such as the economics of globalization, the development of technology, and the evolution (or devolution, depending upon your point of view) of current political forms, the need to recognize and understand differences in cultures has probably never been more critical than it is today.

Businesspeople traveling the world are learning to appreciate the consequences of the misunderstood gesture, the ill-placed word, the uninformed judgment; workers down the hall are required to communicate effectively with co-workers who may or may not speak their language or understand their ways; world travelers, from tourists to diplomats, evaluate the success of their sojourns more and more according to their ability to understand and appreciate the differences that exist between themselves and their new foreign hosts. Understanding, managing, appreciating, and maximizing the benefits of cultural differences, in fact, have become the most critical factors in the success of the global businessperson, the international diplomat, the manager of a multicultural office, or simply the continent-hopping tourist seeking a vacation of reward and richness. No, the world is not getting smaller—but we *are* being required to act much bigger in order to make sense of it all.

This book can help us to do that. There is no doubt that those forces of economics, politics, and technology that are bringing us in closer contact with one another foster, in some measure, a sense of unity. However, the degree to which understanding is developed simply as a result of cultural contact is questionable. Unfortunately, history provides us with evidence that when cultures collide, through whatever forces and for whatever reasons, the initial results are often disastrous. There is nothing inherent in cultural contact that automatically leads to understanding, homogeneity, peace, love, justice, and universal brotherhood. In fact, the reverse, at least in the short run, has been true. Over time, and only when specific structures such as democratic political forms, legal systems, and economic opportunities are in place, can cultures that once did not understand one another begin to accept one another. All one needs to do to better appreciate this sobering fact is to read the international headlines of any major newspaper any day of the week.

Nevertheless, if we are bound, as we apparently are, to hurtle headlong into one another's cultures, the least we can do is prepare ourselves to understand the other a little better. The forces of globalization carry information that both informs and misinforms one culture about the other. So we cannot depend for truth on what Hollywood tells us about Japan, what Joe Smith relates to us over drinks about his recent trip to China, or what our coworker Jacqueline from Paris tells us about how the French think. Neither the global businessperson nor the casual tourist can afford to make mistakes when abroad, to misunderstand the intent of his or her foreign hosts, or to risk inadvertently offending someone. If we are all now working, living, loving, growing, and having to not only survive but thrive in a universe far larger and more complex than anything we were prepared to handle, it's time, to say the least, to get prepared. And that's the purpose of this book.

What This Book Is . . . and Is Not

This book is one of several in the series of Global Etiquette Guides, each of which focuses on a major world region. Each book follows the same format and structure, so whether you are beginning the series with this book or have already read one of the others, you will recognize a structure that makes the reading fun and provides you with the information you need about the countries in the region quickly and easily.

However, no one book can provide you with everything you've ever wanted to know about any particular culture, let alone the major cultures of even one particular world region. People make lifelong careers out of studying one particular culture, and there are sections in most libraries with many books focused solely on one aspect of one culture. Nor can one book provide you with everything you need to know to do business successfully in those cultures. But this book will look at most major cultures in Europe, those with which most people will have some contact or be influenced by in their lifetimes. It will provide important information about the basic day-to-day behaviors in those countries that enable the inhabitants to pursue what they believe to be the best way to live their lives, achieve their goals, and solve their problems; in short, the day-to-day customs, etiquette, and protocols of these cultures that make them what they are and, perhaps, different from our own.

The information provided about business issues, practical "do's and don'ts" for all travelers, and the underlying values and belief systems of the various cultures will be useful for global businesspeople, casual international travelers, and cultural researchers. Most important, this information will address the one issue we all have in common in the face of our amazing diversity: our need to create a day-to-day modus operandi for living, for dealing with other people, and for communicating our needs and desires. *The Global Etiquette Guide to Europe* is intended to be a practical and relatively thorough guide to the protocol, etiquette, and customs that are the ways of life in one of the world's most important cultural regions.

What Do We Mean by "Culture"?

Culture is the normative way in which groups of people behave and the belief systems that they develop to justify and explain these behaviors. These behaviors can differ between groups, generally as a result of the unique experiences that disparate groups have had. In turn, these experiences are usually a combination of history, geography, economics, and other factors, which vary from group to group. What makes all cultures similar, however, are the essentially universal problems of life that we all must address, as individuals and as societies. The problems and questions are the same everywhere, but the answers we come up with as societies can be different. This is what defines our individual cultures. Geert Hofstede, one of the seminal researchers in the field of culture, says, "If the mind is the hardware, then culture is the software," meaning that we are all hardwired pretty much the same, but the programs that we run on can be quite dissimilar. Culture is human software, and the challenge is to make the programs compatible.

I also want to emphasize the normative and group aspects of culture. I am constantly amazed at how from person to person we all seem so much alike, and yet from society to society we can be so very different. Culture reveals itself mainly in the group dynamics of the major institutions of society, and not necessarily in the interpersonal behaviors of individuals. In any particular culture, therefore, you may run into people who behave very differently from the way we describe the culture; in these cases, these individuals are behaving outside the norm. Culture is not a predictor of individual behavior, so when we discuss any cultural protocol, we are talking about general tendencies, expectations, and normative preferences. As someone foreign to a culture, you may be very far from its norm; for that very reason, it is important to know what that norm is, respect it, and adjust to it.

This issue of norms also reminds us that the statements we make about any given culture are generalizations. There are certainly situations, individuals, and conditions that would reveal contradictory behaviors within the same culture. When we make a cultural statement, at least in this book, we are speaking of *primary* tendencies; in no way is this meant to imply that contradictory behaviors will not exist. In fact, it is the delicious complexity of cultures that makes them so fascinating and challenging to work with. In most cases, we are usually also referring to situations between strangers, for once personal relationships are established, many formalities fall by the wayside.

So how important is it really to "go native"? The answer: not very. The goal of this book, and the goal of all cultural understanding, is not to prescribe behaviors for you—behaviors that may be uncomfortable or unnatural to your own culture (many no doubt will be). Rather, the goal of this book is to explain unfamiliar behaviors so that you can come to understand them and why they exist, appreciate the benefits they bring to their culture, and adjust to them to the degree that you are comfortable in order to make someone from that culture equally comfortable with you. No one, however, can be someone he or she is not, and the worst thing you can do is to act inauthentically. There is no greater offense than an awkward and uncomfortable North American, for example, giving his Russian colleague a bear hug and a kiss for the first time, simply because he read in a book that he should. The greater benefit from such information comes when the American understands the meaning of the Russian embrace, is prepared for it, and does not respond to it in a way that offends the Russian. Wherever you are, be yourself and be true to your own culture, but be true as an enlightened, informed, and respectful cultural being.

How the Book Is Organized

When you approach a world region, such as Europe, from a cultural perspective, there are first megacultures, and to varying degrees, variations on these megacultural themes, which are usually grouped geographically within the region. For example, there is the megacultural category of Slavic cultures, which can be found in the eastern European region. Within this category are countries such as Russia, Slovakia, Bulgaria, Serbia, and Poland. The list is quite extensive, and all of these countries are, in many key ways, more similar to one another than they are to countries within a different megacategory—such as, for example, the Anglo-Celtic cultures. Much of what is said about the protocols and etiquette of any one Slavic culture will also be true for most other Slavic cultures; nevertheless, there can also be many differences between them (no two countries, for example, could be more different than Poland and Bulgaria, and yet both are Slavic cultures). And since the protocol and etiquette *topics* that are discussed for any one country are generally the same for all countries, the European cultures are organized according to these main European megacultural or regional groups.

Each group begins with a discussion of those cultures that provide the foundations for all the countries within the group, followed by further explorations of the countries within that cultural region and how they differ from one another. This has been done in order to highlight the distinctions that make each country within a cultural region unique and different without having to repeat information that is common to all the countries. Nevertheless, many readers will probably want to dip into the book country by country, rather than read it as a whole. If that's your style, rest assured that important cultural behaviors and facts are repeated country by country when necessary, so you won't miss too much if you want to read about only one country without referring to others in the same region. To make finding specific countries easy, the contents page lists each country, so you can go straight to the page listed for information on that country's protocol and etiquette if you so desire.

The topics explored for every country are generally the same. Each chapter begins with "Some Introductory Background" on the culture and "Some Historical Context," followed by a quick "Area Briefing," which usually talks about politics and government, schools and education, and religion and demographics. This should give you an appreciation for the forces that have shaped the culture. "Fundamental Cultural Orientations" explores the belief systems that justify the behaviors people reveal to one another on a day-to-day basis, giving you an understanding of why the protocols and etiquette exist as they do. The rest of the chapter takes an in-depth look at the actual customs of the country: greetings and verbal and nonverbal communication styles; protocol in public; dress; dining and drinking; how to be a good guest or host; gift giving; how to celebrate the major holidays; and important aspects of the business culture. For each of these topics, there are subtopics that explore aspects of the culture in relation to men and women, younger and older generations, and both business and social circumstances.

This book does not look at all nations and all cultures within Europe. The world is a dynamic and changing place, and one of the difficulties about writing about culture at this point in world history is the fact that countries and cultures do not necessarily line up. While there is no one country representing the distinct Basque culture, for example, there is most definitely a Basque culture in Europe. And while Moldova is an independent European country, the degree to which we need to know about and the degree to which there are in fact significant cultural differences between it and Romania and Ukraine are debatable. For these, and other thorny reasons, the book explores only those countries in the region that are, in the judgment of the author, distinguishably different from one another and of greatest interest to the reader. My apologies if I have not included a country or a culture of interest: it is not out of disrespect or malice, but merely because of space, knowledge, and time limitations.

The Meaning of the Information

In order to understand why the protocol, manners, and etiquette of any particular country are as they are, it is critically important to understand the belief systems and fundamental values that are at the heart of the culture. This is why every country includes a brief discussion of "Fundamental Cultural Orientations." These orientations, of course, change country by country, but the categories themselves remain the same. For example, it is essential to arrive at a business meeting in Germany at the stated time. It would not be correct to arrive five minutes late, or even five minutes early. This protocol is based on a more fundamental cultural orientation in Germany around the issue of time. In Italy, it might be appropriate to arrive at a meeting five minutes late; this different protocol results from a different fundamental cultural orientation in Italy around the same issue, time. Of course, it's important to remember that Germans *can* be late and Italians *can* be on time; it's just that there is, from a cultural point of view, a difference in the concept of what constitutes timeliness. Therefore, let's briefly explore those fundamental orientation issues around which all cultures can differ, because we will be referring to them again and again with each country we visit.

As the example stated earlier illustrated, cultural orientations revolve around some very basic concerns shared by all cultures:

1. What's the Best Way for People to Relate to One Another?

Societies are all about people, and how we organize ourselves in relation to one another is an issue that every culture must sort out for itself. Cultures might insist on honoring a societal hierarchy, structure, and organization, and they do so with all sorts of perks: titles, rank, different signs of respect, different roles for men and women, and so on. Other cultures deemphasize the importance of such things, preferring to treat everyone as equals. So we have cultures that are *hierarchy* and *organization* oriented, and on the opposite end of the spectrum, cultures that are *egality* oriented. Some cultures might reward individuals for standing out, empowering them to make decisions on their own, while other cultures insist that individuals fit into the group, making sure that no one does anything without the consent and support of others. So we have cultures that are *other-independent*, and on the opposite end of the spectrum, cultures that are *other-dependent*. A culture might place a value on devising systems for organizing life, creating interconnected rules and regulations that must apply universally to all, while another culture might place more emphasis on the personal relationships that exist among people as the determinant of how to do things. So we have cultures that are *rule* oriented, and others that are *relationship* oriented. All of these orientations have to do with what a culture believes to be the best ways by which people can relate to one another.

2. What's the Best Way to View Time?

All societies have to handle moving through time, creating a way of understanding and simultaneously managing the flow of things. Cultures might place a great deal of importance on managing and controlling time. For these *monochronic* cultures, clocks, agendas, calendars, and deadlines determine what and when things are done, and time is a limited commodity that must be carefully managed. For other cultures, time exists, but it is not the determinant of people's actions. For these *polychronic* cultures, time stands in the background; there is usually plenty of it, and relationships and immediate needs usually determine what and when things are done. Some cultures might move quickly with a limited amount of information, while other cultures need a great deal of information in order to make even a small decision. Therefore, cultures may be *risk-taking* or *risk-averse*. Finally, do the people put more of their energy into maintaining what they already have, or do they value change for change's sake? A culture may be *past* oriented (and often more fatalistic), while another may be more *future* oriented (and often more controlling).

3. What's the Best Way for Society to Work with the World at Large?

All societies must make decisions about how they fit into, process, and deal with the larger world. Essentially, this means that a culture communicates, thinks, and plans. Some cultures might create, analyze, and communicate information very directly; they depend upon the meaning of the word, and don't embed information in the larger context of the situation. These cultures often place a high value on confrontation and absolute truth: they are *low-context* communicators. However, other cultures value the importance of communicating indirectly—with actions, not words—and have subtle systems in place for exchanging information appropriate to the situation and the environment, through nonverbal behavior. These cultures place a high value on the maintenance of smooth interpersonal relationships; they are *high-context* communicators. One culture might place the greater emphasis on the process by which goals are achieved, while another culture places the greater emphasis on the goal itself, regardless of how it's achieved. Therefore, cultures can be *process* oriented (relying often on deductive logic) or *results* oriented (relying often on inductive logic). In addition, cultures may be more associative in their thought processing; that is, they do things based on the way they know things always have been done, or how they are already being done in a similar situation. Finally, cultures might value the formal, established, reliable, and in some cases almost ritualized way of doing things, while other cultures might value change, informality, and spontaneity. Therefore, cultures may be *formal* or *informal* in their general orientation toward protocol itself.

It's important to remember that very few cultures are either absolutely one way or the other in their orientation. Most fall somewhere in between, and are simply more or less inclined to one way than the other. It's also important to remember that any one culture is a profile made up of all of these orientations, so be careful not to prejudge what one culture's orientation might be in one area just because of its orientation in another: you might be very surprised at the diversity and complexity of the combinations that exist when we tour the European region! All world regions, Europe included, provide us with the opportunity to explore an enormous diversity of cultural behaviors; the range, especially in what is considered correct and incorrect, is staggering. Remember, the only constancy is change and the only absolute is complexity. What is correct in one culture may be incorrect in another, and what works in one can be a disaster in the other. As the old saying goes, "When in Rome, do as the Romans," and when in Paris we must also do as the French, in Frankfurt as the Germans, in Moscow as the Russians . . .

PART ONE

Western Europe

No Elbows or American Cheese, Please!

An Introduction to the Region

There is an old joke that Europeans are fond of, which goes something like this: Heaven is where the cops are English, the cooks are French, the mechanics are German, the lovers are Italian, and it's all run by the Swiss. Hell, of course, is where the cops are German, the cooks are English, the mechanics are French, the lovers are Swiss, and it's all run by the Italians. Nowhere is there a more complex mix of cultures and lifestyles than in Europe, especially the Europe of today. Depending upon your geographical criteria, for example, there are around fifty sovereign states on what amounts to a western peninsula of Asia. Then, if you look at the cultural distinctions within those sovereign states, you can about double that number to reflect the number of cultures on the European continent. At one time, European nations ruled much of the rest of the world, and the effect of European culture, including language, economics, politics, philosophy, and art, on the rest of the world, for good and bad, is profound. Today, curiously, the Continent claims its place as the crucible (perhaps along with China) for determining what the twenty-first century might look like. Currently, the western half of the Continent is attempting to do what has never been done before: create a twenty-first-century geopolitical form that goes beyond the nation-state (specifically, the Economic Union, or EU), while cultures in the eastern half of the Continent are still struggling to resolve seventeenth-century questions of how to constitute themselves into nation-states. The original, and hence most entrenched, cultures of the post-Columbian Americas, both north and south of the Rio Grande, had their origins in Europe, and Europe is still where most Americans look to find their roots, backgrounds, cousins, religions, and language. We begin our exploration of the world's great cultures in this Global Etiquette Guides series, therefore, with the cultures of Europe, this first part being devoted to what is commonly referred to as western Europe.

Getting Oriented

Get more than two people together to discuss the question of defining macro-cultural groups, and there will be all sorts of differing opinions, based on each individual's unique perspective. With apologies to all who might disagree for whatever reason, western Europe, for our purposes, consists of the following macrocultural groups:

The Anglo-Celtic cultures: England, Scotland, Wales, and Ireland
The Frankish cultures: France, Monaco, and the French areas of Switzerland
    and Belgium
The Germanic cultures: Germany, Austria, Liechtenstein, and Switzerland
The Benelux cultures: Belgium, Luxembourg, and the Netherlands
The Nordic cultures: Scandinavia (Sweden, Norway, and Denmark), Finland,
    and Iceland
The Baltic cultures: Estonia, Latvia, and Lithuania

One way of approaching the cultures of Europe is to superimpose a cross onto the entire Continent. The horizontal line cuts across the Continent roughly from west to east through the Alps, and the vertical line divides the Continent north to south from the eastern portion of Germany down into the Balkans. The coincidence of macro-European cultures generally falling within the quadrants resulting from the superimposed cross is more than symbolic. South of the horizontal line we have the Latin cultures of Iberia and Italy, parts of Switzerland, and other areas. North of the horizontal line we have the Protestant reformist cultures of Germany, the Nordic states, the United Kingdom, and others. East of the vertical line we have the Eastern Orthodox cultures of the Slavic world, while those cultures west of the vertical line are generally Roman Catholic and/ or Protestant in origin. Of course, there are exceptions and complexities within this model: Roman Catholic Ireland and Poland; the Muslim Balkans; the global influence of Jews, North Africans, Romanies, and other cultural groups. But, in general, it's a neat way of getting our hands around the single major root cause of European cultural differences today: over a thousand years of religious conflict, which has divided the continent into mainly Catholic, Protestant, and Orthodox camps (generally reflected respectively in the cultures of Latin, northern, and Slavic Europe). The following chapters will treat each major western European country separately, presented according to the macrocultural groups within which each country falls. Let's begin with the Anglo-Celtic cultures of England, Ireland, Scotland, and Wales.

<table>
<tr><td>

**CHAPTER
ONE**

</td><td>

The Anglo-Celtic Cultures:
England

</td></tr>
</table>

Some Introductory Background on England and the English

Living in Britain, for many non-British English speakers (and this does include Americans!), can be a surprisingly difficult and challenging experience. This unanticipated surprise results from the assumption of similarity, due to history and language, which unfortunately masks some real cultural differences. While there are not as many cultural differences between the United States and Britain as there are, say, between the United States and China, Americans expect the differences they encounter in China, but are usually surprised and confused at the fewer, but very real, differences they encounter in Britain. Cultures in which the language is similar and whose histories may have intertwined can be uniquely challenging because both sides need to overcome the expectation that there are no significant differences when, in fact, there often are. Indeed, on some key measures, there are no two cultures more different than the United States and the United Kingdom. The United States is, for example, a horizontal culture, while Britain is a vertical culture; that is, the United States was created by a revolution against precisely those things, like kings and queens and royalty and inherited privilege, that are still hallmarks of British culture. Therefore, while no doubt sharing many things in common, there is much that is different between us. George Bernard Shaw said that "Americans and Britons are cousins separated by a common language," and that about sums up the subtle yet profound difficulties encountered when American and British culture bump into each other. Whether it's driving on different sides of the road (Americans drive on the right precisely because the British drove on the left), eating differently with utensils (Americans switch their knives and forks precisely because the British did not), or spelling words differently (Americans omit the letter *u*, for example, in words like *colour* and *behaviour* precisely because the British spell them that way!), Britons and Americans, and other English speakers, have taken cultural pains to differentiate themselves from each other. Over and over again, we will see that our hidden differences have as profound an impact on our mutual behavio(u)rs and reactions to each other, as do the more obvious similarities. (By the way, the term *Brit,* used in place of *Briton,* is generally acceptable, but only if used affectionately.)

The similarities that blind us to our differences, however, are overwhelming. After all, the first Europeans to settle permanently in what was to become the United States were British: the Pilgrims, to be exact. It is important to remember that the Pilgrims were the traveling arm of the Puritans: those radical religious fundamentalists of their day for whom the Anglican Church of England (as created by Henry VIII) was still too papist and Catholic for their taste. The Anglican establishment wasn't too fond of Puritans, either, and while eventually having quite a say in the future development of Britain—due to, among other things, a civil war and a religious bloodletting known as the War of the Roses—Protestants also sought safer ground abroad: some in the Netherlands and some in the northern part of the New World, in what was to become the United States. Today, Britain is a complex culture constantly struggling to hold these two fundamentally different traditions in balance: the aristocratic, hierarchical, monarchic Anglican traditions and the reformist, democratic, egalitarian Puritan traditions, out of which formative American values emerged. Both have deep historical roots in Britain and are very much at work today: the ancient monarchy is now one of the few active monarchies still left in the world, and democratic traditions go as far back as 1215 when, with the signing of the Magna Carta, the people forced the king to devolve some of his powers by creating a Parliament. When modern Americans and Britons get along, it is because they are sharing in those behaviors, beliefs, and activities that are fundamentally rooted in the common ideas of the democratic Protestant Reformation (individualism, equality, progress, change, etc.); and when modern Americans and Britons have difficulties, it is because those reformist Puritan ideas, which are at the heart of American culture, are running up against the traditional Anglican, aristocratic, monarchical traditions that Americans rebelled against (hierarchy, privilege, status quo, etc.).

Some Historical Context

Look at the map of Britain, and you begin to understand a critical feature of British culture. Most important, it is an island. The island fortress of Britain has served to help Britons distinguish themselves from their European neighbors (a headline in the London *Times* of the early twentieth century read, "Heavy Fog Over Channel, Continent Cut Off")—indeed, to help themselves against their occasional Continental enemies. Even today, there is a strong trend among the British to identify themselves as a people separate from the Continent, and it is evident in many areas: from the reticence of many Britons to join up with the policies of the Economic Union (EU) to the skepticism surrounding the benefits of the "Chunnel" (the tunnel that now connects Britain to France and the rest of the Continent). A second important feature is the weather and climate. It is always perfectly all right to talk about the weather in Britain: everyone does it, and although it is usually just a way of maintaining small talk (and Britons are marvelously skilled at this, as a means of avoiding confrontation), it is a key aspect of British life. Basically, the country has a rough and challenging climate; it allows for a "man versus nature" approach to life, promoting everything from a preference for "sensible" clothes, to a reverence for the never-quite-finished sheltering and cozy home and hearth, to the Industrial Revolution (which began, appropriately enough, in England). A small island nation, short on natural resources, densely populated by a people created from waves of invasions over eons, resulting in a people of strong, insular identity and conviction.

The modern Briton is an amalgam of many other cultures. The first organized post-Neolithic indigenous culture of Britain was created by the Celtic peoples who migrated to Britain and Ireland in approximately 300 B.C. The Romans followed, then the Vikings, then the Normans (from the north of France), and finally the Anglo-Saxons—those peoples from the Saxony area of Germany, and those from the nearby geographic area formed by the "right angle" created where the peninsula of Denmark meets Germany (hence the term *Anglo-*). The result was, among other things, the creation of the modern English language and culture and the subjugation of the indigenous Celtic cultures. Today, the modern variants of the Celtic culture are mainly found in the Scots (never Scotch, that's a whiskey), the Irish, and the Welsh. All inhabitants of the island of Britain are British (or Britons); therefore, the Scots, the Welsh, and the English are all, technically, British. However, the English are not Scots, nor Welsh, nor Irish. It is very important, therefore, to identify Britons carefully; offense is easily taken in mistaking one for the other. Complicating the issue, of course, is the fact that the English also subjugated the Irish on their own island, resulting in the political division into Northern Ireland in the north and the Republic of Ireland in the south. Due to those major European religious divisions referred to earlier, these cultural groups also distinguished themselves along religious and political lines, so that Northern Ireland is predominantly Protestant with a Catholic minority, while the Republic of Ireland is mainly Catholic. *Great Britain* is a political term, referring to the union of the Kingdoms of Scotland and England, the principality of Wales, assorted minor entities (such as the Isle of Man and the Jersey Islands), and Northern Ireland (sometimes referred to incorrectly as Ulster by Protestants in the north; Ulster actually is larger than the six counties that make up Northern Ireland). North-ern Irish Protestants sometimes prefer to call themselves Britons rather than Irish. Be especially careful in the terms you use to refer to your colleagues from these Anglo-Celtic isles. Since we have a separate section on Celtic Ireland, Scotland, and Wales, for our purposes here we will be referring exclusively to the English.

An Area Briefing

Politics and Government

Britain is a constitutional monarchy; there is no written constitution, in that the laws of the land (made by Parliament), in combination with the stability of the monarchy and the traditions that have built up over the years, all constitute the political and legal way of life in Britain. The Parliament, or representative government in Britain, is made up of two houses: the House of Commons (popularly elected) and the House of Lords (currently changing, but in the past assigned according to peerage). The Parliament is technically subordinate to the king or queen, but in fact determines the political life of the country, and the monarchy is severely limited to its role as the stabilizing, figurehead embodiment of the state. The elected government is based on the parliamentary system, wherein the prime minister represents the ruling party in the House of Commons; should the majority in the Commons change, the prime minister would also need to reflect this, and new elections would be called. Currently, there are two major parties: Labour (predecessors: the Whigs), generally representing a more socially active approach to government; and Conservative (predecessors: the Tories), generally representing a more restricted approach to government.

Schools and Education

"Public" schools are really privately run schools that are open to the public (a reference to the time when schooling was available only through tutors and the church); today, such schools usually provide an elite education (through the "Oxbridge" university system representing schools such as Oxford and Cambridge or secondary schools such as Eton); it can be costly, and usually requires excellent academics, but is not legally restricted only to one particular class. Typically, though, education for the masses is available through the state-run school system, which prepares students, at the postsecondary level, either for an academic or professional career through state-run universities and colleges, or for a trade and vocational career through trade/vocational and community colleges. There used to be an "Eleven Plus" exam that determined the course of secondary study lower-school students would take, but that has been replaced with a more sophisticated process for assigning future course study to students. Once secondary school has been completed, students take their "GCSE" exam (formerly known as "O" levels exam), which determines either university/ college or trade/vocational study after secondary school; additionally, if the university course is taken, a second exam ("A" levels) is usually required to further determine the school and course of study.

Religion and Demographics

Officially, the Church of England (or the Anglican Church) is the state church. Nevertheless, many other religions are represented in England today, including Catholicism, Judaism, Islam, and so on. In addition, while the Anglican Church is perhaps the closest of all non-Catholic denominations to Rome, most Anglicans in Britain today are secular Christians. Nevertheless, the traditions of the church, particularly as they affect other institutions (and the observance of holidays, such as Christmas), are well maintained.

Fundamental Cultural Orientations

1. What's the Best Way for People to Relate to One Another?

OTHER-INDEPENDENT OR OTHER-DEPENDENT? The English value the individualist; that is, someone who develops his or her unique identity within the group, within the borders. Americans value individualism; that is, the idea that one should separate him- or herself from the group and strike out on one's own. This allows for acceptance in Britain of the "eccentric," while in the United States, the true hero is someone who achieves on his or her own and in his or her own way, without the benefit of, and sometimes in defiance of, others and their rules. The U.S. tradition is, in part, the result of a successful revolution against the British "rule makers," while the British tradition is the result of a long history of Anglicanism, monarchism, and of many culturally diverse peoples having to live together on a very small island. What this means today is that there is a keen sense of how one's actions in Britain play out with others, and a distrust in standing apart. Britons can find American individualism too strong, "over the top," naive, and unrealistic. Americans, in turn, can find British reticence frustrating, unproductive, and too self-effacing for no apparent good.

HIERARCHY-ORIENTED OR EGALITY-ORIENTED? Here, too, we see an existence, side by side, of the two contradictory traditions in Britain. There is what has become known as the "great and the good": that combination in Britain of civil servants (from the "right" families and schools), aristocrats, church leaders, and wealthy scions of industry who, in effect, determine how society runs. The direct result is a class system that is still rigid and distinct by most standards, membership in any one class being identified by such factors as occupation, speech, dress, and taste. The belief that this system has value is so strong that it is often considered wrong or "bad form" to act as if one wanted out of one's class and into another, no matter what class one starts out in. This runs smack against the American glorification of the poor little lad who grew up in a log cabin to become president, or of Horatio Alger's rags-to-riches stories. Remember, in feudal England, the landlord had everything and never had to work for it; the serf worked all his life and never had anything to show for it. Effort, or striving, has, in this tradition a distinctly negative connotation, for it is associated with the serf; the remarkable formula of "Effort Equals Reward" is a revolutionary Puritan notion (coming out of the Protestant idea that individuals can demonstrate their worthiness directly to God) adopted by Americans and revolutionary Englishmen. This situation has resulted in, among other things, a management class that was, at least until very recently, very distant from the workers; a disbelief in the rewards of hard work; managers who were distinguished by their ability to withhold information; and the need to have personal relationships with particular individuals in order to get certain things done. It also results in a subtle disrespect for anything that is "achieved," as the greater glory is in being able to humbly demonstrate innate (i.e., ascribed) ability. In Britain, about the only places where all classes were equal on a day-to-day basis were, and are, the queue and the pub. The pub has been known as the great equalizer, for it is where all citizens have equal access to all others (that's assuming, of course, that all classes will patronize the same pub, which they don't).

RULE-ORIENTED OR RELATIONSHIP-ORIENTED? A curious blend of the two opposing traditions here: the aristocratic, Anglican, monarchist tradition emphasizes the importance of individual relationships, which is tied to class and who one is and who one knows. However, the democratic reformist tradition is very powerful in Britain today, and the British are sometimes seen as real sticklers for doing things by the book—no matter who, no matter what. Here again, which tradition has the upper hand depends upon whom one is with and the circumstances. If the "particular" tradition holds the cards, you can be sure the American will ultimately be rubbed the wrong way, feeling snubbed and disregarded. Americans in Britain will consistently be confounded by requirements that are applied to all, while seeing, at a distance, clear evidence that many are exempt from the same strictures.

2. What's the Best Way to View Time?

MONOCHRONIC OR POLYCHRONIC? The English are primarily monochronic, believing in the value of organizing one's time carefully. Business and life are conducted best when done so in an orderly, progressive way. This leads to all sorts of uniquely British phenomena—from what some might term obsessive queuing at most any given opportunity, to the reliance on business agendas, memoranda, follow-ups, and the observance of schedules and timetables.

RISK-TAKING OR RISK-AVERSE? Here again we have the curious mix of two opposing ideas: England is a conservative culture that approaches new ideas cautiously and skeptically, yet the British can equally feel very confident and comfortable in the most remarkably threatening and "risky" situations. Perhaps it is the universalism of the British and their reliance on their rules and ways of doing things that gives them their remarkable confidence in dealing with uncertain or chaotic conditions. After all, these are the same people who, to paraphrase Noel Coward, were mad enough to go out in the noonday sun and sip their tea at four o'clock, no matter where on earth they may actually have been. Risk-taking, yes; but as we see below, change-oriented, no.

PAST-ORIENTED OR FUTURE-ORIENTED? The British culture is a "controlling-oriented" one: the belief that the individual can, with enough will, resources, luck, and stamina, push their way through is widespread. "Muddling through," "carrying on," "keeping a stiff upper lip," "mustn't grumble": these are all hallmarks of the unstoppable and unflappable English. This means that you will have to work uphill as well as "prove your stuff" in order to get things done, especially if what you are attempting to do with the English requires that they do things differently from the way they always have. And here is where the past plays a great role in England. There is no guarantee, for example, that tomorrow will be any better than today: in fact, English history is mainly the story of their great struggle in order simply to keep what they already have. Therefore, *precedence,* or the way that things have already been done successfully, is the main reason why they do what they do, even into the future. Optimistic, risk-taking Americans may have a hard time convincing the British to try a new way. Unless there is a very good reason to throw out that tattered, cracked-leather chair in the corner, they'll keep it, thank you very much.

3. What's the Best Way for Society to Work with the World at Large?

LOW-CONTEXT DIRECT OR HIGH-CONTEXT INDIRECT COMMUNICATORS? English understatement, American overstatement: this is one of the key communication differences between the two cultures. English communication patterns emphasize the unstated, the implied, and the qualified as opposed to the American orientation toward clear, frank, and direct speech. There is a preference for the use of qualifiers: "perhaps," "could/should," and the brilliantly evasive "quite," "nice," and "indeed." English humor is extremely dry, reserved, self-effacing, clever, and based on a playful use of double and opposite meanings. Traditionally, the English have been portrayed as being extremely polite with strangers while being cuttingly direct and forthright within their peer group or with those with whom relationships have been long-standing. There is perhaps no greater example of this preoccupation with public politeness than the excessive apology to the stranger on the street when accidentally bumped into, the self-conscious avoidance of eye contact on a crowded "tube," or the constant use of sayings, aphorisms, and proverbs to say what cannot be said directly.

PROCESS-ORIENTED OR RESULT-ORIENTED? Perhaps precisely because the British have managed to devise a culture in which two so opposite traditions can still live and thrive side by side, it should not be surprising that the dominant thought orientation is one of inductive experience based on precedent, not a search for Platonic ideals or philosophical correctness. What appeals to the English is what has worked in the past: precedence. There is neither the (French) orientation to logical form, nor the (German) orientation to provable method; rather, practical past empirical success, however achieved, is the reason for doing things a certain way. The English are practical, empirical, and results oriented; therefore, no newer logic or better result sways them on its own if they are already satisfied with the results they have painstakingly achieved and currently enjoy.

Greetings and Introductions

Language and Basic Vocabulary

British and American English (or Australian, Canadian, Indian, Caribbean, African, and other versions, for that matter) can be very different. The language alone, much less the communication style preferences discussed above, provides numerous opportunities for misunderstanding. Here's a short dictionary of some important British/American English minefields:

British	American	British	American
lift	elevator	*flat*	apartment
block of flats	apartment house	*spanner*	wrench
typist	clerk	*roundabout*	traffic circle
kipping	taking a nap	*pram*	baby carriage
tram	trolley car	*char*	cleaning lady
biro	ballpoint pen	*dinner jacket*	tuxedo
jumper	sweater	*lounge*	living room
serviette	napkin	*napkin*	diaper
toilet/WC/loo	restroom	*pardon?*	come again?
full stop	period	*bonus issue*	dividend
	(at sentence end)	*crisps*	potato chips
chips	french fries	*vest*	(men's) jacket
biscuit	cookie	*knickers*	(women's) underwear
waistcoat	vest	*trousers*	pants

pants	(men's) underwear	*fanny*	female genitalia
braces	suspenders	*scone*	biscuit
lorry	truck	*fag*	cigarette
rubbers	pencil erasers	*dustman*	garbageman
kiosk	telephone booth	*hoarding*	billboard
tube	the metro	*subway*	underground walkway
goods train	freight train	*way out*	exit

- In England, double or triple numbers (e.g., "77" or "000") on the telephone are usually referred to as "double seven" or "triple zero," and you "ring" someone up, instead of "call" someone up.

- British English refers to groups of individuals in the plural ("Cambridge play Oxford").

- There are many spelling differences between British and U.S. English, but here are some important ones:

colour	cheque
honour	gaol
centre	kerb
theatre	pyjama
criticise	storey (floor of a building)
agonise	tyre
travelled	aluminium
travelling	grey
defence	whisky (but Irish whiskey)
pretence	manoeuvre
licence	waggon
practise	carburretor

Here are some common, seriously misunderstood phrases:

To knock up: to ring up, to wake up, to be exhausted

To shag: to encounter sexually

To table something: to bring something forward for discussion

To strike out: to go after an opportunity

A fortnight: a two-week period

A bomb: a dazzling success

A davenport: a small writing desk

Surgery: a doctor's office or practice

Honorifics for Men, Women, and Children

Mr/Mrs/Miss is preferred for the overwhelmingly (95 percent by some estimates) middle-class Briton today; the term *Ms* is ever so slowly gathering common usage (please note that in written form, "Mr," "Mrs," and "Ms" do not have periods—"full stops" in British English—after them: they are words in and of themselves and not abbreviations). If someone holds a degree or title (e.g., Ph.D., Doctor, Lord, or Lady), it should be used while addressing him or her, even though the holder of such a title never uses it when referring to him-

or herself (however, such titles and degrees may be written on stationery and business cards). Please note: surgeons are referred to as "Mr.," not "Doctor." Occasionally, titled aristocracy might present a card with a line hand-drawn across their title: it is an indication that you may refer to them without their title in casual conversation. Nobility use their title *plus* first name, not family name, when being addressed (the correct form for addressing peerage is complex, and can be researched in books specifically addressing this issue). Children in Britain are another matter: they have been traditionally viewed as incomplete adults; as such, the British childhood is often suffered, and children are endured. If introduced to a child, use whatever name or honorific is used by the adult. Children in Britain, in turn, are expected to be respectful and not overly conversational when speaking with adults, and must always use honorifics when referring to adults. Pets, however (especially dogs), are still another matter: they are adored, perhaps because there is no risk of their talking back, and referred to endearingly with the most amazing names (by the way, in England, black cats are considered lucky).

The What, When, and How of Introducing People

Always wait to be introduced to strangers before taking that responsibility upon yourself. Depending upon your familiarity with the situation or others, it may not be appropriate to introduce yourself. Britons are most comfortable with a third-party introduction whenever possible. Try to ensure that for yourself ahead of time. Do not presume to seat yourself at a gathering: if possible, wait to be told where to sit. With whom, when, and how you are introduced is a key to understanding how you are perceived and how the British are going to "fit you in" within their world. Pay close attention. This is especially important if you believe you will be interacting with individuals from a different strata or class. Shake hands with everyone individually in a group before departing: the American group wave is *not* appreciated. Avoid ending the conversation with the American expression "Have a nice day": it sounds controlling and insincere to the English.

Physical Greeting Styles

The handshake is common, but perhaps not as "gripping and pumping" as the American version (the spoken introduction is the cue to let go). Introductions such as "Pleased to meet you" and "How do you do" are most common; any introductory phrase that is posed in question format (e.g., "How do you do?") does *not* require an answer: merely repeat the phrase back. Smiling and other nonverbal forms of communication need not accompany the handshake. A man should wait until the woman extends her hand before reaching for it, and a woman may take the lead in extending her hand or not. A man must remove his gloves when shaking hands with a woman, but a woman need not remove her gloves when shaking hands with a man. Bows and curtsies are quite old-fashioned and not common, except in formal occasions, usually with royalty. It is a nontouching culture, which means that men do not slap each other on the back or hug when greeting; women who know each other may kiss each other on the cheek once, but rarely will men and women do so, unless they know each other particularly well. When being introduced, make immediate eye contact, then quickly look away: eye contact is minimal during conversation in Britain, unless a very specific point with a specific speaker is being made—in that case, eye contact is usually very direct.

Communication Styles

Okay Topics / Not Okay Topics

Okay: the weather, animals and pets, anything that is a universal pain in the neck (griping is an apparent pastime), the economy. *Not okay:* politics (especially "the royals," the "Irish," and the associated "Troubles"), religion (although the Anglican Church is the official Church of England, few Britons today find their spiritual renewal there: it is a very secular culture), sex (Britons are very private about this, which is probably why the tabloids rely on it daily to sell their papers: sex is always a scandal), and British food (it is really quite good, especially nowadays). In addition, avoid references to the British "setting sun" (the end of the empire). Do not inquire about a person's occupation in casual conversation. Americans often begin a conversation with "So, what do you do?"; this is too personal in England, and assumes that one "does" something in the first place (not the occupation of a lord, remember). Do not volunteer your own personal family history, or ask about others'.

Tone, Volume, and Speed

In most formal situations (excluding the home and family-style restaurants), understatement is the driver: therefore, the volume is almost always turned down, almost to mumbling; the tone is respectful and humbling; but the speed can vary, depending upon the situation (class).

Use of Silence

The need to avoid confrontation is so strong at times that silence or withdrawal may occasionally be employed to avoid a direct battle. Do not confuse avoidance of confrontation with lack of directness: if no confrontation is anticipated, Britons are usually remarkably direct (especially in business).

Physical Gestures and Facial Expressions

The basic rule is to minimize physicality: it is seen as childlike and representative of ill-breeding. Touching one's nose indicates "keep this a secret" or "this is between us"; in addition, the "V for Victory" sign must be done with palm facing outward. In most English-speaking countries (with the exception of the United States, where we must, because of our revolutionary experience with Britain, apparently do everything differently from them), making this sign with the palm inward is a vulgar gesture of defiance (it comes from the British demonstrating at the battle of Agincourt to the French that they still had two fingers left with which to pull the archer's bow). Upon first meeting, facial expressions are kept to a minimum; therefore, feelings may be hard to read from the face.

Waving and Counting

The index finger is one; the thumb is five. Pointing is usually done with the head or chin, and not with the fingers: it is considered unseemly. The wave is generally the same as in the United States.

Physicality and Physical Space

When possible, a small distance between speakers is preferred, although given the density of the highly urbanized England of today, this is not often possible. Never speak with your hands in your pockets: keep them always firmly to your side, stand straight, and sit with feet planted flat on the floor. If men and women must cross their legs, it must never be ankle over knee, and for women, it is most preferable to cross ankle over ankle.

Eye Contact

Contradictory behaviors here: in casual conversation, especially between people who are not (or do not want to become) that familiar with each other, eye contact is minimal, beginning with a meeting of the eyes, and then a looking away. This is true for social as well as business conversation. However, when important points are being made, interest is being shown, or a relationship desired, maintaining direct eye contact is very important. Do not stare at people in public. Once eye contact is made with an individual, no other individual can intrude on the conversation until the conversation is completed. Avoiding eye contact is a very common way of saying, "I want my privacy," and the English can be a very private people, even in public.

Emotive Orientation

Avoid backslapping, shouting, or calling attention to oneself (especially in public), and broad behavior. Polite, self-possessed behavior is the norm. Keep your hands to your sides, and avoid emphasizing the spoken word with gestures. The essence of British humor is the not-stating of what is obvious, or implying the opposite of what is said. It is therefore what is not done that may be more important than what is: this leads to a reticence of emotive expression, especially in more formal situations.

Protocol in Public

Walking Styles and Waiting in Lines

Queuing is a national pastime: never break a queue, and if there is a queue, go to the back of it and wait, no matter how long it takes. Queues develop at all public facilities, and then some. People walk on the left in public, drive on the left, and pass on the right: this is true on escalators and moving walkways, as well as roads and streets. Remember also that you usually have the right of way as a pedestrian only in a "zebra" walkway (the stripes painted at a crosswalk): cars must stop as soon as you step into the zebra (pronounced with the "e" as in "egg"); nevertheless, be careful!

Behavior in Public Places: Airports, Terminals, and the Market

Americans find British customer service an oxymoron. Someone once stated that they thought the British television series *Fawlty Towers* was a comedy until they went to Britain and realized it was really a documentary. As in many European countries, mass marketing and customer orientation is a new idea in a culture with roots in artisanal quality and bourgeois production. Store hours are typically not built around customer convenience (many stores are closed on weekends and most evenings—except Thursdays, usually), and getting served in a store or restaurant can be an exercise in patience: it's one person at a time, thank you, and you are often not acknowledged as waiting until the sales agent is ready for you. Typically, the customers are invisible to the salesclerk until eye contact is made, and it can be maddeningly difficult for customers to get the clerk's attention at times. In food markets, if you touch the produce, you buy it; in goods stores, it may be difficult for you to return a product unless there is a flaw in it. Smoking in public places is on the decline.

Coins are still accepted at some public telephones, but there are many that only take telecards: get them at local newsstands, kiosks, and so on.

Bus / Metro / Taxi / Car

Never break a queue for a bus, train, or taxi; on public transportation, it is polite to surrender your seat to the elderly, parents with babies, or the handicapped, but men need not do so for women of the approximate same age. Enter a taxi in the back on the opposite side of the driver; when leaving the taxi, go round to the driver's window first before paying the fare.

Tipping

Usually 10 to 15 percent; more is considered nouveau and gauche. This is true for restaurants and taxis. Porters and hotel help get a pound per service rendered, theater and bathroom attendants usually 20 to 50 pence (p.).

Dress

There is a distinctly British version of casualness that is creeping into dress in England these days, although "casual Fridays" have certainly not arrived (except, perhaps, in certain specific industries). Going to the theater, for example, need not be dress-up (in fact, the ease with which theater tickets can be purchased in London, for example, promotes "off-the-street" attendance)—except for theater openings (very formal)—and business attire on the street is usually generational. That traditional bowler hat, for example, is definitely out, even in The City (the London financial district). Office attire, however, is still the business suit or jacket and tie for men, and dress or skirt and blouse for women. British men's shirts typically do not have pockets; if they do, they should remain empty. British businesspeople do not wear loafer-type shoes: lace-ups are preferred. However, because English aristocratic life revolves around the country estate (this is different on the Continent, where the aristocracy took a decidedly urban and refined identity), there has always been an acceptance of the "squired" look for men, even for those in business: the tweedy jacket, the slightly too short pants, the argyle socks, and the solid—slightly scuffed—walking shoes have always had their place (usually in informal social gatherings); in business, the business suit can be worn either of two ways: very well-styled (bespoke and influenced by Savoy Row) and, with equal acceptance, slightly rumpled, even a bit worn (after all, well-made is well-served).

Seasonal Variations

There are four distinct seasons, and one dresses accordingly; summers can be surprisingly warm in the south (although showers can still pop up at any time), and winters can be bone-chillingly damp and cold (there is little snow, however); spring and autumn are both soft and swift, transitioning quickly between winter and summer.

Colors

The country estate look always had muted, natural colors: the fabric is the key, while dark, sophisticated colors rule with the high-tailored look. The high-tailored look can also include some surprisingly (for Americans) "loud" statements: very broad stripes, for example, and a bright color-coordinated tie for men or an equally bright scarf for women. In England, men who attended public schools, or were members of specific military units, would traditionally wear their "school ties" or "military ties": these were usually of a special diagonal striped design. American men should refrain from wearing striped ties in England, as they suggest this English tradition (although the stripes are usually going in the opposite direction!).

Styles

Traditionally, formal in England has meant "white tie and tails." American "formal" in England is usually "black tie" (tuxedo in America); and informal or casual in England has always meant tie and jacket (not necessarily suit). About the only time men wear casual, American-type clothes (sports shirts, jeans, sneakers, etc.) is at home, on the street on weekends, or at nonexclusive sporting events.

Accessories / Jewelry / Makeup

Women typically do not accessorize much for business, and the very high-powered look for women at work is not common.

Dining and Drinking

Mealtimes and Typical Foods

Breakfast is typically a large, important meal, and can be held anytime, usually from 7 to 9 A.M. An authentic English breakfast consists of white toast (in addition to croissants, or any other breads and pastries), juice, cereal, bacon, sausages ("bangers"), fried potatoes, sauteed mushrooms and tomatoes, and so on.

A real specialty that may be included is kippers (smoked herring), although this has its roots in Scottish cuisine. Drinks can be tea or coffee (tea is taken usually with milk or cream, although the aristocratic tradition in England emphasizes tea with lemon and no cream).

Lunch is served from noon to 1 or 2 P.M., and usually consists of sandwiches, salads, pub specials, and the like. Drinks are beer, sodas, or "squash" (different fruit concentrates plus water or soda water; you might see colored bottles of syrups set out: these are fruit concentrates to be poured into glasses of water or seltzer as a flavoring). On Sunday, the main meal of the day is supper, which is usually served beginning at lunchtime, but includes real dinner dishes, and mainly always a roast.

Formal dinner is served from 7:30 to 8:30 P.M., with 8 P.M. the customary time. It usually begins with an alcoholic drink (sherry, gin, or a whiskey), plus nuts and such. The appetizer is usually soup or prawns, followed by fish or meat and vegetables. Dessert includes sweet puddings (as opposed to savory, non-dessert puddings) and trifles, and can also include cheese and crackers. Wine is usually served with dinner, and the English have a real love for dessert wines: especially ports and liqueurs. Dinner parties usually end at around 11:30 P.M. to midnight.

Tea is a special tradition in England. There are two different forms: "tea" and "high tea." High tea is really a substitute for dinner, and is taken around 5 P.M.: it consists of a hot dish (a savory pie, for example) plus all the other ingredients of regular tea. Regular tea usually consists of savory finger sandwiches, then cakes and sweets, all washed down with many cups of tea. Making a proper pot of tea is an important skill. After "putting the kettle on" (heating the hot water on the stove up to and just over the boiling point), one pours the scalding water into the teapot (a ceramic vessel containing the tea leaves), and lets the tea steep for about five minutes. Be sure that the teapot is very near the teakettle when you are ready to pour in the hot water: walking too far from the stove with a hot kettle is not good for the tea (and probably dangerous, as well!). Additional hot water may be added to the teapot as needed until the tea has given all it can.

Regional Differences

Well-known regional foods include crumpets (similar to English muffins—which, by the way, don't exist in Britain, except for those imported from the United States), a Midlands dish; pasties (meat and savory pies), a typical Cornish dish; steak and kidney pie (East Anglia); pudding (usually a savory pudding made from congealed meat drippings and other ingredients), from Yorkshire; and fool and trifle (sweet custardlike puddings served at the end of the meal with jams, fruit conserves, cream, etc.). Be sure to try clotted cream from the lake country: it's a rich, buttery cream that goes well with crumpets and scones. There are many other dishes with remarkable names: bangers and mash (sausage and mashed potatoes), toad-in-the-hole (similar to cocktail franks wrapped in pastry), spotted dick (custard with raisins—sultanas, in Britain), and others. Beans on toast is a common English lunchtime favorite, as is the ploughman's lunch (usually some fine English cheese, bread, and pickles); and no English child made it through childhood without porridge (actually a Scottish invention) and Marmite (a salty, yeasty bread spread; definitely an acquired taste). The British are very fond of their sweets and chocolates: you can find them everywhere.

Typical Drinks and Toasting

Mixed drinks before dinner are not as common as in the States, although martinis and such are growing in popularity (ask for the American martini if a gin or vodka martini is what you want; if you ask for a "martini," you will get a Martini and Rossi vermouth, which is very common). Preprandials include a short whisky (Scottish whisky mainly, and spelled without the "e"; Irish whiskey is spelled with the "e"; in either case, it is usually drunk neat or with water, never over ice), some dry sherry, a gin and tonic, or vermouth. Red and white wines (often French; the British refer to red Burgundies as clarets) during the meal are common, and port or a sweet sherry at the end of the meal is perfect. Less formal meals, especially at lunch, are washed down with English beer, of which there are dozens of fine examples. English beer is not warm; it is merely served at room temperature. If you want a chilled beer, ask for a lager. Common English beers come usually in the following varieties, from the strongest on down: ale, stout, bitter, and lager. Beer usually comes in pints (almost two full glasses) or half-pints (women usually do not order pints, and a "ladylike" beer is often lager and lime—with a lime or lime juice added to the beer). The alcohol content of most English beers can be higher than American beers, so measure yourself accordingly.

The most common toast is cheers, or to your health. Sometimes there is a toast at the end of a very formal meal to the queen, the king, or the royal family; otherwise, with all other toasts, one typically does not toast anyone older or more senior than oneself.

There is a tradition in many Commonwealth countries to order rounds (or "shouts") of drinks for friends: it is a taking of turns in the buying of drinks for all in the group.

Tea is usually served separately at tea and for breakfast; after lunch and dinner, coffee is the usual drink.

Table Manners and the Use of Utensils

The most important difference is that the English do not switch knives and forks, as Americans do. When both are to be used, the knife remains in the right hand, and the fork remains in the left. When the meal is finished, the knife and fork are laid parallel to each other across the right side of the plate. If you put both utensils down on the plate for any real amount of time, it is a sign to the waitstaff that you are finished, and your plate may be taken away from you. In addition, the fork is often held tines down, so that food is scooped up onto the backside of the fork; do this after much practice, or with foods that can stick to the back of the fork (like mashed potatoes and peas). There are often many additional pieces of cutlery, and the cutlery is often substantial. The knife above the plate is used for butter; otherwise, if you're unsure of which utensil to use, always start from the outside and work your way in, course by course. Hands are expected, when not holding utensils, to be in one's lap at the dinner table (this is the reverse of the practice on the Continent, which is to keep the hands above the table). At the table, pass all dishes to your left.

Seating Plans

The most honored position is at the head of the table, with individuals of greatest importance seated first to the left and then the right of the head of the table; if there is a hosting couple, one will be at one end of the table, the other at the opposite end. As on the Continent, men and women are seated next to each other, and couples are often broken up and seated next to people they may not have previously known. This is done in the interest of conversation. Men typically rise when women enter the room, and continue to hold doors for women and allow them to enter a room first.

Refills and Seconds

If you do not want more food, leave a bit on your plate; unlike in some other cultures, however, you may not be offered additional food if you finish your plate, as the course offered was the course offered. You may always have additional beverages; drink enough to cause your cup or glass to be less than half full, and it will automatically be refilled. As on the Continent, portions are generally smaller than in the United States, but there are generally more courses than in the States.

At Home, in a Restaurant, or at Work

Restaurants usually stop serving around 11 P.M., and dinner is usually served at 8 P.M., so there aren't too many seatings in the course of an evening. Be sure to make reservations (and confirm them) in the most exclusive restaurants; this is not necessary, however, in traditional British family restaurants, or those of the more informal "fish-and-chips" style. Indian and Chinese take-away restaurants are very common these days. Pub hours were traditionally set by law at 11:30 A.M. to 3 P.M., and 5 to 11 P.M., Monday through Saturday, and from noon to 3 P.M. and 7 to 10:30 P.M. on Sunday; however, these times are changing, and many pubs, as "private clubs," stay open much longer hours (you may be required to pay a small membership fee to join the club, which is sometimes not even stated, but merely included in your bill). In informal restaurants, you may be required to share a table; if so, do not force conversation—act as if you are seated at a private table. Waitstaff may be summoned by making eye contact; waving or calling their name is very impolite. Business breakfasts are really quite uncommon in Britain, although the business lunch or dinner is acceptable: it is perfectly fine to discuss business at these times. The business lunch can often be at the pub. More upscale business dining would involve lunch or dinner at a French or Italian restaurant. During the workday, tea breaks are common, and the tea trolley (loaded with tea, coffee, and pastries) that makes its rounds in the office is usually eagerly awaited. Smoking is becoming less and less common everywhere: ask permission before lighting up, except at formal occasions where women still do withdraw into another room (the traditional drawing room), leaving the men to light up their cigars and sip their port.

Being a Good Guest or Host

Paying the Bill

Usually the one who issues the invitation pays the bill, although the guest is expected to make an effort to pay. Sometimes other circumstances determine the payer (such as rank). Making payment arrangements ahead of time so that no exchange occurs at the table is a very classy way to host.

When to Arrive / Chores to Do

If invited to a private home, offer to help with the chores if there is no waitstaff present; however, your offer will probably be rejected, and you should not expect to visit the kitchen. If you are at a dinner party in a private home, do not move from room to room unless and until the host offers to show you around. Spouses are often included in business dinners (most commonly if there are spouses on both sides), and you are more likely to be invited to a dinner party at home in England than you would be in any other European country.

Gift Giving

In general, gift giving is simply not done in Britain for business purposes; it is best not to send a gift at any time, including the holidays, unless you receive one first from your business associate. However, holiday cards are very appropriate, particularly as a thank-you for your business in the previous year, and should be mailed in time to be received the week before Christmas. Gifts are expected for social events, especially as thank-yous for private dinner parties. The best gift in this case is flowers—and it is best to have them sent ahead of time on the day of the dinner. Never send chrysanthemums (as on the Continent, they are used primarily as funeral flowers) or red roses (these may signify romantic intent), and always be sure the bouquet is in odd numbers (an old European tradition). If you must bring flowers with you to the dinner party, be sure to unwrap them before presenting them. Other good gifts would be chocolates or a bottle of champagne (avoid wine, as it may present the hosts with the dilemma of whether it should be brought to the table, especially when they have already selected the wine for the meal; champagne, however, is always appropriate, as it can serve as an aperitif or an after dinner drink, or can be enjoyed by the hosts at a later date). In addition to the gift (and certainly necessary if you did not send or bring one), be sure to send a handwritten thank-you note on a card the very next day after the dinner party; it is best if it is messengered and not mailed. If you are staying with a family, an appropriate thank-you gift would be something from your country that is of high quality and difficult to get in England: gourmet foodstuffs (maple syrup, pralines, lobsters, etc.), coffee-table books about America, or anything that reflects your host's personal tastes and is representative of America (a cap bearing the logo of a famous American team for the football-playing son of the family, for example) is appropriate. Gifts are often opened in the presence of the giver. Holiday (Christmas and New Year's) cards are customarily sent to good clients, customers, and friends.

Special Holidays and Celebrations

Major Holidays

New Year's Day (Hogmanay in Scotland) is increasingly a major celebration throughout the United Kingdom. Many English celebrate New Year's Eve and New Year's Day in Scotland. Good Friday and Easter Sunday are official holidays, as is May Day (the first Monday in May); there is also an official Spring Bank Holiday—the last Monday in May—which makes May, as is the case on the Continent, a holiday-filled month. The last Monday in August is the Summer Bank Holiday, and there is Christmas Day and Boxing Day (the day after Christmas). Virtually no business is conducted during the weeks before Christmas and between Christmas and New Year's. Boxing Day derives its tradition as the day that household servants would have off to compensate them for their service on Christmas Day, and employers would often give them Christmas boxes (hence the name) as gifts. Christmas Day is celebrated with a fine Christmas dinner, usually a goose and lots of pudding, with all the associated trimmings before, during, and after the meal, and Christmas crackers as well (each guest receives a "cracker"—a gift-wrapped vessel containing little presents—which makes a popping noise when pulled open from either end). Guy Fawkes Day is an unofficial holiday (November 5), commemorating the foiled attempt by Mr. Fawkes to blow up Parliament in 1605: he was captured, and today the anniversary is celebrated with fireworks and burned effigies of Guy throughout the land—a real excuse for mischief (related, no doubt, to the Celtic harvest festivals and Halloween). If you can, avoid initiating new business during the high summer, from late June through the end of August, as this is traditionally vacation ("holiday") time.

Business Culture

Daily Office Protocols

In general, the business day is usually more carefully defined in Britain: it begins at 9 A.M. and ends at 5 P.M., with senior managers perhaps staying in their offices until 6 P.M. or so. It is not uncommon to socialize in the local pub after the workday for an hour or so with one's office colleagues. The pub is a place to wind down, where ceremony and differentials in rank disappear. When first arriving in the office, greet each person you know with a "Good morning," but there is no need to shake hands. Shake hands with someone new in the office when you meet, but there is no need to greet or shake hands again with anyone you've previously greeted in the course of a business day (the American habit of greeting the same people again and again in the course of the day is a source of mystery to most Europeans, Britons included). Women and men of equal rank generally are treated equally.

Management Styles

Among individuals of the same rank, regardless of gender, there is much direct and informal communication; among individuals of different rank, there can be restrained and indirect communication, postponed decision making, and a tendency to wait for direction from above while not offering suggestions to superiors. Individuals have considerable freedom to achieve goals on their own, as long as directions have been carefully provided from above, and there is periodic review of progress. English workers expect to be rewarded for jobs well done, but not necessarily publicly, and do not expect unsolicited praise. Traditionally, the most powerful jobs in the large British business organization have been those responsible for financial control, and people with such responsibility typically used their position to police or monitor the financial situation of the company.

Boss-Subordinate Relations

Until recently, there was a very rigid separation between the ranks in British business: the management class, usually from the "great and the good," often was brought into an organization laterally (managers did not come up through the ranks, but rather were moved about in the stratosphere from one organization to another). Moreover, rank had its privileges: separate dining rooms, separate floors, separate corporate events. Business life today is singularly more fluid, although the degree to which this change has occurred is industry-specific; in most cases, those larger industries that have emerged out of previously state-run essentials, such as telecommunications, transportation, energy, and heavy manufacturing, are still, in many ways, the most conservative. In more traditional businesses, the boss, therefore, is regarded more formally, and distinguishes him- or herself as the decision maker, separate and apart from subordinates. Subordinates, in turn, do not volunteer opinions, recommendations, or thoughts openly, and their relationships with their superiors can be formal, with indirect and circumscribed patterns of communication.

Conducting a Meeting or Presentation

At meetings of peers, there can be open communication and sharing of ideas: meetings can, in fact, be information-sharing and decision-making forums where all individuals are expected to contribute. In more formal, conservative organizations, meetings are often gatherings of nonpeers, where decision makers have clearly called the forum together in order to gather information from below, clarify goals, and formulate action plans. In these cases, individuals often do not share ideas and are not expected to contribute to mutual problem solving.

Negotiation Styles

Once relationships have been established, and there is clearly a mutual benefit to working together, Britons can be blunt, direct, and very clear about what's on their minds. However, until such time, during the relationship-building phase of the negotiation, it is important to allow Britons the necessary time to size up your company, your proposal, and you. Direct questions may not result in direct responses. In general, Britons are motivated by precedent; therefore, your proposal stands a better chance the closer it conforms to the way Britons have done things in the past. Remember that precedent need not have a logical base, but it often does have an empirical, experiential history that they will eagerly recall to you as reasons why they can or cannot agree with your proposal.

Planning a Project

Don't push for the decision: if the British are keenly interested (or not) they will tell you; otherwise, try not to appear too pushy and develop some patience. Remember also that Britons can be very restrained in their attitudes, so do not expect emotional demonstrations of support: cool, detached, and businesslike approaches are the most appreciated. It is very important to avoid the hard sell, or denigrating another company's product or service: this will only reduce their interest in you and your product (remember, there is more concern for self-apology than for self-aggrandizement: this is often the reverse for the American).

Written Correspondence

Time is usually written in military time. Use the word "Dear" plus title or family name to open a correspondence, and end the correspondence with the following appropriate closings:

Yours faithfully   (when you do not have a name: a "Dear Sir" letter)

Yours sincerely   (when you do have a name: "Dear Mr Smith")

Best regards,   (when you know the recipient personally)
   or *Kind regards*

Cheers   (*very* informal; use *only* when you know the
               recipient very well or in personal notes)

The Anglo-Celtic Cultures: Ireland, Scotland, and Wales

CHAPTER TWO

IRELAND

Some Introductory Background on Ireland and the Irish

Unique among western European nations, the Irish culture is a mixture of the three Cs: the influence of being Celtic, Catholic, and colonized. The only Roman Catholic culture in the Anglo-Celtic isles, Irish behavior is also strongly influenced by more pagan Celtic forces; layered onto these two religious roots is the colonial legacy of the Anglo-Saxons (English) in Ireland. The confluence of these three factors creates the Irish character: a blend of opposites, and an amalgam of struggling contradictions. The Irish are known as a people who

- will fight against all odds, but have deeply believed their power is limited and their fate ultimately only in God's hands
- value human relationships above all else, but blame inherited human sin and failure for the faults of the world (and the source of their misery)
- value conformity and respectability, yet praise the rebel, the artist, and the eccentric
- value fighters and visionaries, yet can be compliant in the face of authority
- place great stock in loyalty to one's own, but can withhold emotion and information in their relationships
- have a great sense of responsibility, yet tend to project blame outward to others
- appear to take great risks, make elaborate plans, and seem eternally optimistic, yet be resistant to following details, see the unrealism in others and not themselves, and assume things will not work out and always fall apart
- demand evidence and proof before doing certain things, but take other things completely on faith

It took a great Irish poet to declare that the Irish were quite mad, that theirs was the land of "happy wars and sad love songs"; Freud declared that the only people who would never benefit from psychoanalysis were the Irish.

It is important for Americans to remember that their conception of the Irish American experience (like the Italian American experience) reflects an image of the Irish of a particular time (turn of the century) and place (generally the northeast United States and rural Ireland) that is not reflective of the Irish of Ireland today. In fact, for a variety of reasons, such as the high level and relative success of schooling of most of the Irish population, the natural use of English, and the influence of the Economic Union (resulting in Ireland being a rather inexpensive place for European manufacturers to set up shop) Ireland today has the fastest growing economy in Europe, and is one of the world's high-tech centers. Perhaps nowhere else in Europe does the younger generation have so much rapidly developing opportunity. And yet the culture, while being on the brink of rapid change, is in many ways resistant to the modern world. Perhaps there is something important we can learn about how to live in the modern world from the Irish today.

Some Historical Context

The Irish were the seafaring and agrarian Celtic peoples of the island who thrived before the Romans, the Normans, and the Anglo-Saxons arrived. When Christianity came to the Anglo-Celtic isles, it was the neo-Roman Saint Patrick who brought it to Ireland, and made it stick by incorporating many of the indigenous pagan Celtic elements into the religion. These Celtic, pre-Christian practices (and underlying views of the world) are still practiced and believed in today (join the festivities in Ireland during the midsummer eve, June 21, or on All Saints' Day, November 1, and see how pre-Christian Celtic festivals have been interwoven into the daily Catholic life of the Irish today). Contrary to the Roman monks who brought Christianity to England by eliminating original beliefs and forcing the people to accept Roman Catholicism as a replacement for pagan ritual, Catholicism in Ireland was welcomed because it provided a greater opportunity for celebrating the Celtic way of life in the face of the English influence. By the time the now converted Anglican English expanded their already consolidated power in Britain into Ireland and began the subjugation of the Irish people, Roman Catholicism was deeply entrenched in Ireland, and the colonial oppression of the Irish people took a decidedly Anglo-Saxon versus Celtic tone, ultimately to be redefined in the secular and republican twentieth century as a struggle between Catholics and Protestants, between republican revolutionaries and aristocratic monarchists. Today, while the prospects for peace between the two groups seems more possible than in times past (due perhaps to the recent economic success of Ireland), the ancient hostility between Celtic people and invading Anglo-Saxons is still a very real cultural conflict, and probably will continue to be, at least under the surface.

An Area Briefing

Politics and Government

The national government is headed by the prime minister (the *Taoiseach*), who is appointed by the president (elected directly by popular vote for a term of seven years) based on the support they have in the lower house (the Dáil) of the bicameral legislature or parliament (the Oireachtas). The Upper House of the

Oireachtas is the Senad (Senate). There are, of course, ministers who assist the *Taoiseach,* and approximately four to five major political parties, representing the political spectrum from left to right, including the Irish liberation movement (struggling for the liberation of Northern Ireland from the British and its incorporation into the Irish Republic).

Schools and Education

Most primary schools in Ireland are run by the Catholic or Protestant churches (the National Schools). Around the age of twelve or thirteen, children move on to secondary education, which is usually less denominational. The secondary education typically takes the form of either of two tracks: vocational (preparing children for a nonprofessional work life) or secondary (preparing children for further academic study and university). At the age of fifteen, students take the Junior Certificate exam; if they pass, they may leave school for the workforce, or they also may stay and continue their secondary education for an additional two years. At the age of seventeen, students take the Leaving Certificate, which entitles them to enter the workforce or, depending upon their course of study, attend university (either state-run or private).

Religion and Demographics

The majority of the people in Ireland are Roman Catholic, some of whom live in the predominantly Protestant north, as well. There are few Protestants (and other religions) in the country. Ireland is demographically an extremely young nation today, and while still primarily an agrarian culture with agrarian traditions, much of the population (especially younger) is based in and around the urban centers of Dublin, Belfast, and Cork. Women have a particularly difficult time achieving levels of authority in Irish business or the Irish workforce, as the traditional nurturing roles of women in Irish society are strongly reinforced by the three *C*s.

Fundamental Cultural Orientations

1. What's the Best Way for People to Relate to One Another?

OTHER-INDEPENDENT OR OTHER-DEPENDENT? There is a very strong need for others: their approval, their support, their camaraderie, and sometimes their scorn. Catholicism and its group orientation, the need to rely on a strong family in the face of a society that often did not provide the basics for survival, and the need to unite against foreign foes all provide strong reasons for the powerful sense of other-dependency in Ireland. We see this in the way the Irish socialize, relate to others within the family, and work together: the approval and support of others is ultimately vital to the success of any project and the well-being of any individual. This is not to say that eccentric individualists are not valued: they are, for they provide in Irish society, a barometer against which the Irish can measure themselves and a figure in need who they can adopt and assist. The loner is never an outsider in Irish society; only foreigners are true outsiders.

HIERARCHY-ORIENTED OR EGALITY-ORIENTED? Most Irish share the same position in regard to each other: they are people of the sod, farmers, or people who are just emerging from the older agrarian traditions. There were, of course, pagan Celtic kings and an ancient Celtic aristocracy, similar to the landed gentry of Scotland, but it was never as rigid or strong in Ireland, and was quickly disassembled when Christianity took over. Therefore, those at the top of whatever hierarchy there was were often outside occupiers (colonizing English who reinforced the importance of hierarchy and structure by the very fact that they represented and imposed a religion and a way of life that opposed the rigid and hierarchical Catholic Church), while the rest of the people were pretty much of the same level. This has resulted in a dual orientation: an expectation of and respect for hierarchy and authority, and a dismissal of authoritarian power and a seeking of ways around it. Women and men are separated by gender in terms of their societal roles; this is changing somewhat in the Ireland of today, but women are still revered as mothers and nurturers, and men are entitled to struggle with the issues of work and politics (there is much comment by either sex about the other's performance of these roles).

RULE-ORIENTED OR RELATIONSHIP-ORIENTED? The relationships one has determine most of what happens in the Irish world. Who and what you know, and one's position and how one is regarded by others, are maintained primarily by one's actions and relationships and not by the rules that one follows.

2. What's the Best Way to View Time?

MONOCHRONIC OR POLYCHRONIC? More often than not, the Irish are extremely polychronic. You can (actually should) arrive late at a dinner party by about five or ten minutes; you can expect your business associate to be late for the meeting during the day; events start and stop based on the requirements of the moment and the status of the people involved. Partly because of the orientation toward relationships, partly because hardships required them to work in the immediate now, partly because traditionally agrarian peoples are dependent upon events that occurred according to the dictates of nature and not of men— for all these reasons and more, the Irish put time in the background. As a people, they are deeply aware of the power of the past; they refer to it, love it, and use it as the reason to explain the sometimes inexplicable nature of Irishness. The ancient Celtic millennia are alive and well on every street corner, inside every church, and in every kitchen in Ireland.

RISK-TAKING OR RISK-AVERSE? Here again we have the curious mix of two opposing ideas, as with the British, but for different reasons. The Irish had to take risks, sometimes extraordinary ones, just to stay alive. As is the case with most colonized cultures, the Irish have displayed, from time to time, the mentality that all can be sacrificed for the struggle; therefore, risk-taking, and the ability to throw everything to the wind for the sake of something dear, becomes possible. Whether fighting the British in one of the "happy rebellions," or risking all to emigrate to a new land and a new life, the Irish could leave everything behind when there was no reason any more to hold on or stay. Essentially, though, the Irish are deeply conservative, and know how important it is to hold

on to what one has, to be cautious, clever, and careful in an otherwise dangerous and uncharitable world. When there is nothing left to lose (and they judge
this in more than materialist terms), they, like all colonized peoples, will take
great risk. Day to day, they are cautious and require security, support, information, and, most important, trust before taking action.

PAST-ORIENTED OR FUTURE-ORIENTED? The Irish generally look to their
past for their strength, and see the complexity of their roots as a source for
judging the present and the future. There is a strong belief that only God knows
what the future will hold, that their ability to control events and change the
course of things is ultimately doomed. The Irish duality is especially striking
now, for during this time of rapid change from an agrarian/industrial society to
an information-based society, Ireland is succeeding and many of the young people feel empowered in a way the Irish never have before.

3. What's the Best Way for Society to Work with the World at Large?

LOW-CONTEXT DIRECT OR HIGH-CONTEXT INDIRECT COMMUNICATORS?
High-context communicators . . . par excellence. The Irish have a well-deserved
reputation for the art of declamation. They don't just say what needs to be said:
they appreciate the ability of the average person to say something in a way that
is witty, clever, artful, beautiful, interesting, or philosophical. Everyday statements can suddenly take on implications much greater than the obvious. Listen
closely: much may be said beyond what is being stated. The Irish can be direct,
but usually only if it is yet another device to enhance the overall cleverness and
effectiveness of what is being said; directness for directness's sake is usually
avoided. Someone once said that if there was a longer way to say anything, the
Irish will say it. Language—both their native Gaelic (a Celtic language, now
only spoken on a daily basis by about one-third of the country in the southwest), and their adopted English—is dear to the Irish, perhaps because it can
sometimes become such a powerful source of identity for a colonized society.
Language is loved both in speech and in literature: some of the world's greatest
authors and poets are Irish, and the Irish, in their daily life, live with and know
their bards.

PROCESS-ORIENTED OR RESULT-ORIENTED? The Irish are both deductive
and associative: the way things are done—with whom, when, how, and why—is
all much more important, generally, than the result. This state of mind does not
necessarily exist because the process determines the outcome (as we will see
with the French), but rather because in and of itself, it can have more merit than
the final achievement. The journey, not the end, is the focus. The way, the why,
and the how are often more valued than the what.

FORMAL OR INFORMAL? Ireland has perhaps the most informal culture of all
western Europe. Ceremony and formality, while they exist, are not part of daily
life to any great degree—and non-Irish are completely exempt from having to
follow any of these forms anyway. The Irish, of course, are exceedingly polite
and warm, but never in a ceremonial or ritualized way. Relax and enjoy.

Greetings and Introductions

Language and Basic Vocabulary

As stated above, the Irish love their language, their speech, their literary heritage, to a person. Enjoy the remarkable fun and skill even the average Irish person displays in his or her everyday speech, and the beautifully lilting Irish accent that is applied to the spoken English. English is the lingua franca, although the native Gaelic is one of the two official languages; the latter is taught in all schools, and spoken in the southwest (the Gaeltacht region), with its use being the subject of much debate (there is an official policy of bilingualism, and you will see signage in both languages). When English is used, many of the linguistic rules stated for England are applied (please refer to the language section for England).

American English is much appreciated, but American misunderstanding of the way Irish use language is not. Get used to lots of "slagging" and "craics." A "crack" (*craic,* in Gaelic), or "having a good crack," is having fun with the language—making jokes, being witty, fooling around, embedded as an essential part of every conversation. (Note: "crack" does not in any way refer to drugs.) Having a good *craic* is usually done at someone else's expense: this is, in most circumstances, done good-humoredly and with the intention of a good time for all. If you're the "slaggee" (the point of the mild derision), you are expected to be a good sport and put up with it; ideally, you are supposed to join in the fun, and slag back, and this back-and-forth poking fun at each other usually goes on until the topic changes, everyone has seen that both parties have had a good shot at each other, or one party clearly is the loser and it's best to stop. The victor in a slag, if there is one, usually buys the next round (yes, this is *the* sport in the pub).

On the telephone, double or triple numbers (e.g., 77 or 000) are usually referred to as "double seven" or "triple zero," and you "ring" someone up, instead of "call" someone up.

Here are some basic Gaelic terms and their English meanings:

dia dhuit	hello	*slan*	good-bye
oiche mhaith	good night	*le do thoil*	please
go rabh maith agat	thank you	*slainte!*	cheers!
ta failte romhat	you're welcome	*gam pardun*	excuse me
Ca bhuil an . . . ?	Where is the . . . ?		

And here follows an Irish-English "mini-dictionary":

"A cup of tea in your hand": This phrase is used by a friend who invites you over for a cup of tea but realizes that you can't stay because you are too busy (the invasion of the modern world on this essentially agrarian-based culture). It means you are free to go ahead and slurp down your tea quickly.

"A soft day": This is a statement of the average Irish meteorological condition; it describes the uniquely Irish weather that is somewhere between mist and rain, and often much admired.

"Below": Refers to the position of something in relation to the speaker; it is usually somewhere north of where the speaker is.

"Blow-in": Someone who has moved into a neighborhood recently, has no roots there, and is likely to be moving on shortly.

"Boreen": A country path or road.

"Bowsie": Someone who is always involved in fights and scrapes.

"Chancer": Someone who always seems to be pushing the envelope—taking unnecessary chances, deliberately breaking minor laws, etc.

"Chipper": A shop where fish and chips is sold.

"Chiseller": A young person; an adolescent.

"Compass points": The directionals north, south, east, and west are often used in Ireland to describe where people and things are; for example, Kathleen O'Donnell North describes the woman who lives in the north of the village as opposed to the Kathleen O'Donnell who lives in the south of the village.

"Culchie": A country person, a simple naive person, unused to the city.

"Eejit": A fool.

"Evening": Any time from about 2 P.M. onward; especially outside of the cities, people often greet each other in the afternoon on with "Good evening" or "Good night."

"Gaelic": When used in common speech, it is probably referring to the uniquely Irish version of rugby (football) invented by the Gaelic League earlier this century.

"Giving out": Talking extremely loud, or pushing a slag beyond what is appropriate.

"Good luck": More often, this is a way of saying "good-bye."

"Grind": A private institution, a school, a business.

"Hippy": This is an insulting term of derision applied to anyone who dresses weirdly and lives a strange lifestyle outside the norm in Irish society.

"Jackeen": This refers to anyone from Dublin.

"Jar": Several drinks.

"Louser": A mean and nasty, unforgiving person.

"Mizzling": Softly raining.

"Now," or "So . . .": This is a way of moving on in the conversation. It is best translated as "right," "okay, so let's move on," etc.

"Over": The place (usually the United Kingdom) to which one travels often (e.g., "Do you go over to visit your friends often?").

"Pishougue": A fairy, a leprechaun (be careful: the Irish intensely dislike foreigners viewing them as leprechauns or cute little people).

"Press": Refers to a kind of cupboard or storage cabinet, a wardrobe, etc.

"Scoroichting" (pronounced as "screerting"): This term describes any occasion in which men gather together, usually to discuss politics.

"The divil a much": "I don't believe that!"

"There's good eating in that": "That's really good to eat!"

"Thundergub": A loud and obnoxious person.

"Till": This word roughly means "in order to . . ." (e.g., "Please lend me your kettle till I can put tea up").

"Wain": A child.

"Will ya wisht": "Please be quiet."

"Yerrah": This term is used as an exclamation, but more often to declaim disbelief (used like the English word, *indeed*).

"Yoke": Anything that is modern, technical, mechanical, or beyond simple and rural.

Honorifics for Men, Women, and Children

Mr, Mrs, and Miss are preferred today; the term *Ms* is ever so slowly gathering common usage (please note that in written form, Mr, Mrs, and Ms do not have periods—"full stops" in British/Irish English—after them: they are words in and of themselves and not abbreviations). If someone holds a degree or title (e.g., Ph.D., Doctor, Lord or Lady, etc.) it should be used while addressing them, but the holder of that title never uses it when referring to him- or herself (however, such titles and degrees may be written on stationery and business cards). *Please note:* surgeons are referred to as "Mr," not "Doctor." If introduced to a child, use whatever name or honorific is used by the adult, usually the first name of the child. Children in Ireland, in turn, are expected to be respectful and not overly conversational when speaking with adults, and must *always* use honorifics when referring to adults. If you or someone with you is referred to as "plain," don't be offended: it means you are the salt of the earth, one of the Irish, and not a derogatory term describing your looks.

The What, When, and How of Introducing People

Always wait to be introduced to strangers before taking that responsibility upon yourself. You will not have to wait long for the introduction; however, if the circumstances are casual, it will probably be perfectly all right to introduce yourself. Do not presume to seat yourself at a gathering: if possible, wait to be told where to sit. Shake hands with everyone individually in a group before departing: the American group wave is not appreciated. Avoid ending the conversation with the American expression "Have a nice day": it sounds controlling and insincere.

Physical Greeting Styles

The handshake is common, but perhaps not with as much gripping and pumping as the American form (the spoken introduction is the cue to let go). Introductions such as "Pleased to meet you" and "How do you do" are most common. Any introductory phrase that is posed in question format (e.g., "How do you do?") does not require an answer; merely repeat the phrase back. Smiling and other nonverbal forms of communication need not accompany the handshake. Men should wait until a woman extends her hand before reaching for it, and women may take the lead in extending their hand or not. It is a physical and touching culture, especially once people know each other: until that moment, however (which may come very quickly; you will know it when the Irish become more physical with you) men do not slap each other on the back or hug when greeting; women who know each other may kiss each other on the cheek once, but rarely will men and women do so, unless they know each other particularly well. When being introduced, make immediate eye contact, and maintain it. The more interested the Irish are, the more directly they will make and maintain eye contact.

Communication Styles

Okay Topics / Not Okay Topics

Okay: the weather (the ubiquitous soft rain and mist is not viewed negatively, as it may be in other parts of the Anglo-Celtic isles, and negative comments are not necessarily appreciated), animals and pets, anything that is a universal pain in the neck, the economy (and its remarkable growth), the beauty of Ireland, Irish literature and arts, anything Gaelic, your own Irish ancestry, and drink. *Not okay:* politics and "the Troubles": the United Kingdom, the English, the issue of Protestants and Catholics, Americans and the Irish (there are strong feelings about Irish Americans and their "free ride" relative to conditions in Ireland), sex (remember the Roman Catholic Church), and the roles of women and men.

Tone, Volume, and Speed

In most situations (at home or in family restaurants excluded), understatement and wit is the driver; therefore, volume is almost always turned down with people from the outside. The tone is almost always more emotional and louder in circumstances in which the people know each other.

Use of Silence

Usually never. If there is silence, you can be sure something very serious has occurred, or that the situation is very awkward and uncomfortable.

Physical Gestures and Facial Expressions

Not very many, and similar to what we've said about Britain. You may be more physical, if that is the behavior of your Irish colleagues (but this is usually only between individuals of the same gender or family). Touching one's nose indicates "keep this a secret" or "this is between us"; in addition, the "V for Victory" sign must be done with the palm facing outward. In most English-speaking countries, making this sign with the palm inward is a vulgar gesture of defiance. Facial expressions, with the out-group, are kept to a minimum; with the in-group, the face can be much more expressive.

Waving and Counting

The index finger is one; the thumb is five. Pointing is usually done with the head or chin, and not with the fingers. The wave is done generally the same way as in the United States.

Physicality and Physical Space

When possible, distance between speakers is usually less than between other northern Europeans. Avoid speaking with your hands in your pockets: always keep them firmly at your side. Stand straight and sit with feet planted flat on the floor. If men and women must cross their legs, it must never be ankle over knee; for women, the preferred style is to cross ankle over ankle.

Eye Contact

Contradictory behaviors are the rule here: in casual conversation, especially with people you are not (or do not want to become) familiar with, eye contact is minimal, beginning with a meeting of the eyes, and then a looking away. This is true for social as well as business conversation. However, when important points are being made, interest is being shown, or a relationship is desired, maintaining direct eye contact is very important. Do not stare at people in public. Coming into someone's line of sight is a way of including oneself in an ongoing activity or conversation, and the group orientation of the Irish compels them to include you when this occurs.

Emotive Orientation

There can be much emotiveness: body expression and a sophisticated, almost poetic, use of words in daily speech are valued.

Protocol in Public

Walking Styles and Waiting in Lines

Queuing is important. Queues develop at all public facilities. Never break a queue; go to the back of the line and wait, no matter how long it takes. People walk on the left in public, drive on the left, and pass on the right: this is true on escalators and moving walkways, as well as roads and streets. (The same left-hand rules of the road apply in Ireland as in Britain.)

Behavior in Public Places: Airports, Terminals, and the Market

Build personal relationships, for that is what will get you the attention you need in public places; in most cases, the Irish are delightful in service, and are especially proud to serve outsiders who show respect and friendliness to them. In food markets, if you touch the produce, you buy it; in goods stores, it may be difficult for you to return a product unless there is a flaw in it.

Public telephones are mainly coin-operated. Drop a few coins in from the top, and any that are not used (if your call takes less time than you paid for) will be returned to you after you hang up.

Bus / Metro / Taxi / Car

Never break a queue for a bus, a train, or a taxi. On public transportation, it is polite to surrender your seat to the elderly, parents with babies, or the handicapped. Men are expected to yield their seats to women (of any age, except the young). Enter taxis in the back on the opposite side of the driver; when leaving a cab, go round to the driver's window first before paying the fare.

Tipping

Tips are usually 10 to 15 percent; in restaurants, the tip is usually included on the bill (double-check with the establishment if you are unsure). Unusually good service may be rewarded with a few extra coins, but this is not necessary. Taxis require fifty pence for a short trip, and about an extra Irish pound as a tip for long trips (about one-half hour or more). Porters and hotel help get a pound per service rendered, theater and bathroom attendants usually twenty pence.

Dress

Irish dress codes are, for the most part, similar to those covered in the section on Britain, but with these additional concerns:

- You must always carry a raincoat, (and perhaps a "brolly"—umbrella); there is more rainfall in Ireland than in Britain, and it is even more unpredictable.
- Dinners, in restaurants and at private parties, usually do not require jackets and ties for men. Clothes can be more casual and informal than in Britain (but no sneakers and jeans). Formal wear in Ireland usually means dinner jackets, as it does in the rest of Europe, and is much more dressy than in the United States.

Dining and Drinking

Mealtimes and Typical Foods

Breakfast is typically a large, important meal: it can be held anytime from 7 to 10 A.M., and usually consists of cereal (hot), juice, and a "fry-up" (fried eggs, bacon, potatoes, and sometimes fish, tomatoes, etc.). Drinks can be tea or coffee (tea is taken either with milk or cream or lemon). It's important to note that toast is usually served with marmalades and jams after the fry-up, not during.

Lunch is served from noon to 1 or 2 P.M., and can consist of sandwiches, salads, or hot dishes, such as corned beef and cabbage, savory pies, and roast pork with cooked vegetables and potatoes. Drinks are beer, sodas, or "squash" (different fruit concentrates mixed with water or soda water: you might see the colored bottles of liquid set out).

On Sunday, the main meal of the day is the Sunday supper, which is usually served beginning at lunchtime, but consists of real dinner meals. Dinner is served from 5 to 8 P.M., with 7 to 7:30 P.M. the customary time to start dinner parties. If the daily main meal at home is lunch, dinner may consist of just another fry-up-style meal. If a dinner is given to entertain business colleagues, it usually begins with an alcoholic drink (sherry, gin, or a whiskey), and moves on to a soup or fish dish, and then a meat course (usually a roast with both mashed and roasted potatoes), plus cooked vegetables. There is usually no salad. There may or may not be dessert: in most cases, after the meat course, cheese and crackers are served with port or a dessert wine, followed by coffee. The drinks served with dinner are usually wine or beer (depending upon the formality and the type of roast). Dinner parties usually end at around 11 or 11:30 P.M.

Tea is a special tradition in both England and Ireland. There are two different kinds: "tea" and "high tea." High tea is really a substitute for dinner, and is taken around 4 to 6 P.M. It consists of a hot dish (a savory pie, for example) plus all the other ingredients of regular tea. Regular tea usually consists of savory finger sandwiches, then cakes and sweets, all washed down with many cups of tea.

Making a proper pot of tea is an important skill. After "putting the kettle on" (heating the hot water on the stove up to and just over the boiling point), one pours the scalding water into the teapot (a ceramic vessel containing the tea leaves), and lets the tea steep for about five minutes. Be sure that the teapot is very near the teakettle when you are ready to pour in the hot water: walking too far from the stove with a hot kettle is not good for the tea (and probably dangerous, as well!). Additional hot water may be added to the teapot as needed until the tea has given all it can.

Regional Differences

Ireland has many of the same specialties found in English cooking, with these additions:

- mixed coddle: boiled bacon and sausages (U.S.-style bacon is known as "rashers"; Irish bacon is really boiled pork)
- corned beef and cabbage: cooked cabbage and potted and spiced beef
- colcannon: a mixture of cabbage and potatoes
- Irish smoked salmon (as opposed to Scotch, Norwegian, or Icelandic)
- Irish lamb, prepared usually in a stew with cooked vegetables
- seafood and fish from the western coast (oysters, plaice, etc.)
- Irish fish and chips (which is eaten more with mayonnaise and less with vinegar—the English way)

Typical Drinks and Toasting

Mixed drinks before dinner are not as common as in the States, although martinis are growing in popularity (ask for the American martini if a gin or vodka martini is what you want; if you just ask for a "martini," you will get a Martini and Rossi vermouth, which is very common). Whiskey (spelled with an *e*) means Irish whiskey, and, as with Scotch whisky (spelled without the *e*), you need to name your brand in a pub since there usually will be a huge selection. Whiskey is usually drunk neat or with water, never over ice. Other preprandials include dry sherry, gin, or vermouth. Red and white wines are not uncommon at business meals, and port or a sweet sherry at the end of the meal is perfect.

Less formal meals, especially at lunch, are washed down with beer, of which there are dozens of fine examples, the most notable being Guinness. Guinness is *the* national drink; it is a stout (very hearty, rich, and dark), and usually served cool, as opposed to most other beers, which will be served at room temperature (if you want a chilled non-stout beer, ask for a lager). The Guinness served in Ireland, by the way, is different from the Guinness in the United States: be sure to try it. Beer usually comes in pints (almost two full glasses) or half-pints (in pubs, women almost always order half-pints and men order pints; don't mix up the two—it will be noticed and commented upon), and a "pint of plain" is a pint of Guinness. The alcohol content of most Irish beers can be higher than American beers, so measure yourself accordingly. Another popular drink is the "shandy": beer and lemonade.

The custom in a pub is to take turns ordering rounds of drinks for friends or colleagues. Never fail to buy your round (but women do not buy rounds when men are present). The pub is the great social hall of Ireland; it usually has two sections, a bar and a lounge. Drinks are usually a bit more expensive in the lounge; there is often service, and meals can be taken there as well. At the bar, light snacks are usually available. Pub hours vary, so be sure you know when the local house is open (especially on weekends). Drinks are usually not served with ice; if you want it, you'll need to ask, and then you'll usually get only one cube. If you want another cube, you will need to ask again. Be sure to join in the slagging and craicking at the pub: you'll enjoy it. Refusing a drink, either in the pub or a restaurant, or in someone's home, is a real offense: Ireland is a drinking culture, so be sure to give a very good reason for not drinking with others ("doctor's orders" is usually the only reason that will work). Getting drunk, though, while occasionally expected, is not admired.

The most common toast is *slainte!* meaning cheers!, or to your health!

Table Manners and the Use of Utensils

The Irish do not switch knives and forks, as Americans do. When both are used, the knife remains in the right hand, and the fork remains in the left. When the meal is finished, the knife and fork are laid parallel to each other across the right side of the plate. If you put both utensils down on the plate for any real amount of time, it is a sign to the waitstaff that you are finished, and your plate may be taken away from you. In addition, the fork is often held tines down, so that food is "scooped" up onto its back side; do this after much practice, or with foods that can stick to the back of the fork (like mashed potatoes and peas). The knife above the plate is used for butter. If you're unsure of which utensil to use, always start from the outside and work your way in, course by course.

Bread is usually not served at the dinner party, and the little plate next to the big plate is the place to put the peelings from your boiled potatoes. The proper technique involves holding the potato down with your fork in one hand, and peel the skin with your knife in the other. Hands are expected to be in one's lap when not holding utensils at the dinner table (this is the reverse of the custom on the Continent, which is to keep hands above the table). At the table, pass all dishes to your left. Portions are usually enormous (in homes and even in restaurants), so don't worry about seconds, and do try to eat everything on your plate. After a dinner party at someone's home, everyone is expected to participate in the entertainment, which usually means singing and sometimes dancing.

Seating Plans

The most honored position is at the head of the table, with the most important guests seated first to the left and then the right of the head of the table. If there is a hosting couple, one will be at each end of the table. Sometimes, but not always, men and women are seated next to one another, and couples may be broken up and seated next to people they may not have previously known. This is done in the interest of conversation. Men typically rise when women enter the room, and continue to hold doors for women and allow them to enter a room first.

In restaurants, waitstaff may be summoned by making eye contact; waving or calling their names is very impolite. Business breakfasts are really quite uncommon, although the business lunch or dinner is very acceptable. The business lunch can often be at the pub. During the workday, office tea breaks are common, and the tea trolley (loaded with tea, coffee, and pastries) is eagerly awaited. Smoking is common everywhere—in the pubs, between courses at home, and on the top deck of double-decker buses—although the nonsmoking movement has had an impact.

Being a Good Guest or Host

Paying the Bill

Usually the one who does the inviting pays the bill, although the guest is expected to make an effort to pay. Sometimes other circumstances determine the payee (such as rank). Making payment arrangements ahead of time so that no exchange occurs at the table is a very classy way to host.

When to Arrive / Chores to Do

If invited to a dinner party at a private home, offer to help with the chores if there is no waitstaff present; it will be appreciated, and you may be invited to help. Do not move from room to room in a private home unless and until the host offers to show you around. Spouses are often included at business dinners (most commonly if both business associates bring their partners). You may expect to be invited fairly quickly to a dinner party with the family at your colleague's home in Ireland. Go, by all means.

Gift Giving

In general, gift giving is not expected for business purposes; it is best not to send a business gift at any time, including the holidays, unless you receive one first from your colleagues. However, holiday cards are very appropriate, particularly as a thank-you for their business during the previous year, and should be mailed in time to be received the week before Christmas.

Gifts are expected for social events, or in celebration of a special event with an individual or their family with whom you have built a good relationship. Gifts are also required as thank-yous for private dinner parties. In all cases, it is important to remember that gifts must not be ostentatious, too obviously expensive (e.g., fine champagne), or over the top. Simple and tasteful is best. The best gift for a dinner party is a good bottle of wine, a nice box of chocolates, or a simple arrangement of flowers that you can bring with you when you arrive. Don't worry about the type of flowers as much as you would on the Continent (just avoid the red roses and funereal lilies).

It is not necessary to send a handwritten thank-you note on a card the day after the dinner party unless it was truly a formal event. If you are staying with a family, an appropriate thank-you gift need only be a small token of your gratitude (simple or unique American foodstuffs, some table napkins, another table item, etc.). Gifts should be opened in the presence of the giver.

Special Holidays and Celebrations

Major Holidays

Do not attempt to do any real business during August—this is traditionally vacation ("holiday") time. Things begin to close up in Ireland from the middle of December right on through the first week of the New Year. Holy Week (between Palm Sunday and Easter Sunday) is also an extremely slow time of the year for business. Finally, May is a time for business fairs, and businesspeople may not be available (especially during the first half of the month).

January 1	New Year's Day
March 17	Saint Patrick's Day (usually a somber, churchgoing celebration; people often dress up and wear shamrocks in their lapels)
March/April	Easter
May 1	Labour Day
First Monday in June	Bank holiday
First Monday in August	Bank holiday
December 25	Christmas
December 26	Saint Stephen's Day (a common custom is for bands of children to dress up in costumes and go from house to house banging on pot lids and such, asking for coins)

Business Culture

Daily Office Protocols

In general, the business day is usually more carefully defined in Ireland, although keeping to these times is less important: it begins at 9 A.M. and ends at 5 P.M., with senior managers perhaps staying in their offices until 6 P.M. or so. After the workday, it is not uncommon to socialize for an hour or so in the local pub with one's office colleagues. The pub is a place to wind down, a place where ceremony and differentials in rank disappear. When first arriving in the office, greet each individual you know with a "good morning," but there is no need to shake hands. Shake hands with someone new in the office when you meet, but there is no need to greet or shake hands again with anyone you've previously greeted in the course of a business day. Women and men of equal rank generally are treated equally. Business cards, even between newly introduced associates, are not that common, but have a supply handy; more often than not, you will present your card to the secretary, and not necessarily to the individual with whom you are meeting. Real interest is often indicated when your Irish colleague asks for your card at the end of the meeting.

Management Styles

Among individuals of the same rank, regardless of gender, there is much direct and informal communication; among individuals of different rank, there can be restrained and indirect communication, postponed decision making, and a tendency to wait for direction from above and not quickly offering suggestions to superiors. Individuals in larger, more traditional organizations usually do not take initiative until instructed to do so from above, but then will usually do so eagerly. Irish workers expect to be rewarded for jobs well done, but not necessarily publicly, and do not expect unsolicited praise.

Boss-Subordinate Relations

Most Irish businesses are small, family-run organizations, so there is usually clear communication; the few very large businesses usually rigidly separate management from staff, although an atmosphere of informal communication is worked at. Business life today is singularly more fluid, although the degree to which this change has occurred is industry specific; in most cases, those larger industries that have emerged out of previously state-run essentials, such as telecommunications, transportation, energy, agriculture, and heavy manufacturing, are still, in many ways, the most conservative. In more traditional businesses, the boss, therefore, is regarded more formally, and distinguishes him- or herself as the decision maker, separate and apart from the rank and file. Subordinates, in turn, do not volunteer opinions, recommendations, or thoughts openly, and relationships are indirect, with circumscribed patterns of communication.

Conducting a Meeting or Presentation

At meetings of peers, there can be open communication and sharing of ideas; in fact, these sessions can be information-sharing and decision-making forums in which all individuals are expected to contribute. In more formal, conservative organizations, meetings are often gatherings of nonpeers, clearly called together by decision makers in order to gather information from below, clarify goals, and formulate action plans. In these cases, individuals may be less inclined to share ideas and are not expected to contribute to mutual problem solving.

Negotiation Styles

Once a relationship has been established, and there is clearly a mutual benefit to working together, the Irish can be direct and very clear about what's on their minds, but never blunt and rarely confrontational. However, until such time, during the relationship-building phase of the negotiation, it is important to allow the Irish the time they need to size up you, your company, and your proposal. Direct questions may not result in direct responses. In general, the Irish are motivated by personal relationships and trust; therefore, your proposal stands a better chance the more it makes your Irish colleagues feel comfortable with you and your attitudes toward them and Ireland (the details of the project, may in fact, be secondary to these concerns).

Planning a Project

Don't push for the decision: if the Irish are keenly interested (or not) you will eventually know, and any effort to obtain direct information or force a faster decision will only sour your relationship and hurt your proposal's chances. Try not to appear too pushy and develop some patience. It is very important to avoid the hard sell, or denigrating another's product or service: this will only reduce their interest in you and your product.

Written Correspondence

Use the word *dear* plus title or family name to open a correspondence, and end the correspondence with the following appropriate closings:

Yours faithfully	(when you do not have a name: a "Dear Sir" letter)
Yours sincerely	(when you do have a name: "Dear Mr Smith")
Best regards (or *Kind regards*)	(when you know the recipient personally)
Cheers	(*very* informal; use *only* when you know the recipient very well or in personal notes)

SCOTLAND AND WALES

Both of these regions, being Celtic in origin, share similar behaviors, world-views, and protocols with Ireland and England, yet also have some individual characteristics important to mention separately from both. Here are some critical considerations:

• Both are singularly rural, even though they are on the island of Britain. This proximity to England is what, in many ways, makes both regions more similar to England than Ireland (which is separated from England by the Irish Sea). In addition, Scotland retains more of its clannish Celtic traditions than perhaps either region.

• Scotland is a kingdom (like England) and Wales is technically a principality (hence the title, the Prince of Wales); do not confuse the two.

• While the Welsh and the Scots share similar Celtic roots, do not confuse the two. Welsh are Welsh (do not refer to the slanderous English term *welching*), and Scots are Scots (not scotch: that's a whisky).

• Never ask what Scots wear under the kilts, or joke in any way about Scottish culture: they are extremely proud and serious about it, as are the Welsh about theirs, perhaps because they feel they need to be so protective and defensive of it in the face of the English majority. There are very strong literary traditions in both Scotland and Wales.

• Wales is going through an industrial renaissance, while much of northern England and Scotland is struggling to emerge from the shackles of the dying heavy manufacturing "rust belt" industries. Wales is becoming a major center for trading and modern manufacturing. High-tech industries are becoming entrenched in both areas.

• In Scotland, eggs and bacon are not regularly served during the weekly breakfast, and usually show up on Sunday menus. Porridge is common for breakfast in both Scotland and Wales.

• As in Ireland, main meals in both Scotland or Wales can either be in the middle of the day or the evening: if the main meal is lunch, a tea around 4 P.M. with sandwiches, eggs, and sweets is common, with a light supper later in the evening. Yes, Welsh rarebit (not rabbit) is served in Wales. A light dinner around five or six in the evening is very common in Wales, accompanied mainly by tea (beer is reserved for after dinner and during lunch). In contrast to the huge Irish food portions, in Scotland and Wales you will see smaller portions, following English patterns.

• Contrary to patterns in Ireland, in Scotland and Wales, it is more important to be punctual at work and in social situations; arrive on time if invited to a dinner party at someone's home, for example.

• The lounge section in the pub in Scotland and Wales is more often referred to as the saloon: it is, as in Ireland, the place where women feel more comfortable (while women often go to pubs alone in England, they don't do so as often in Ireland, Scotland, or Wales).

• Food specialties in Scotland include haggis (a sheep's stomach stuffed with a mixture of vegetables, meats, oats, and seasonings) and suet (a sweet dessert made from animal fats and sugar)—both are eaten ceremonially on New Year's Eve (referred to as Hogmanay) and Robert Burns's Night (January 25) along with black bun (Scottish fruitcake) on Hogmanay; bannocks (oat griddle cakes); crowdie (a mixture of cottage cream and double cream, usually served with oatcakes and butter at teatime); cock-a-leekie soup (leeks and chicken soup); and cullen skink (fish soup). And don't overlook Scottish smoked salmon and trout, often cooked fresh from the stream! Hogmanay is a major event in Scotland (and increasingly so for all of Britain: many people travel to Scotland for New Year's celebrations, which usually last all night into the wee hours). The morning of New Year's Day is celebrated as the "First Footing," where celebrants—traditionally male—go from house to house carrying a piece of coal, a black bun, and a bottle of whisky. The coal, black bun, and whisky represent, respectively, wishes for a new year filled with warmth, sustenance, and happiness. Once the man who calls on you is invited in (and he should be the first person to enter the home on the morning of the first day of the year), he pours a toast to the master or mistress of the house. Later in the day, friends and relatives usually gather in someone's home to express New Year's greetings, and exchange small, useful gifts. If invited to a New Year's Day afternoon gathering, inquire ahead of time how many people will be in attendance, and bring a little something for everyone as a gift (simply wrapped, if at all).

• Welsh food specialties include Glamorgan sausage (deep-fried egg, batter, and cheese in the shape of a sausage), seafood, and faggots (small meatballs made of mixed meats, bread crumbs, and spices served either hot or cold).

CHAPTER THREE

The Frankish Cultures: France

Some Introductory Background on France and the French

It is important for Americans, who easily recognize their cultural relationship with the English, to remember that without the help of the French, we might never have won our independence from Britain. The French influence on the United States has been profound, but Americans tend to overlook their deep historical relationship with France, primarily because we share our language with Britain. Both France and the United States had revolutions that defined their future around the same time, and both provided the other with the philosophical fuel to keep their respective revolutionary flames burning. The Americans and the French have a love-hate relationship that goes back centuries, and for Americans to appreciate and understand French behavior, it is important to understand this special relationship. Americans and French are like an old married couple: they have influenced each other, lived with each other, and complained about each other for so long that they mirror each other's similarities and differences in many ways.

Let's start by clearing up some common misperceptions: the French are *not* an unfriendly people. The complaint by many Americans that the French are cold and arrogant is a misperception of a behavior found most often in Paris by certain Americans—and not necessarily in the rest of the country—a behavior not atypical of many people who live in big, harried international cities. These Americans would probably level the same complaint against New Yorkers, and Parisians have certainly heard the same charge leveled against them by French colleagues visiting from Provence. There are, however, specific and important aspects of French culture that make certain interactions with Americans appear as if the French are unfriendly; we'll explore these in the following section. Nor are the French intentionally trying to make things difficult when Americans attempt to work with them. Nor are they intentionally refusing to speak English with you just to make your life miserable. All of these are misperceptions of aspects of French culture that are very different from, and therefore conflict with, certain aspects of American culture. Let's try to sort these through.

Some Historical Context

France is the largest country in western Europe, and this explains certain features of French behavior. For one thing, it straddles the great European north-south divide, meaning that French behavior is an amalgam of both Latin and northern European cultural behavior. Therefore, contradictions are inherent in French behavior, and if you look for consistency in the French, you will be disappointed. While placing a heavy emphasis on the importance of rational thought, for example, the French can also appear to be explosively emotional; while emphasizing the importance of living well, certain aspects of their daily life (such as the average size of Parisian apartments) can be extremely challenging; while supporting individualism, they are dependent on the approval of others (usually seniors); and while capable of making decisions quickly, they are burdened by structure and hierarchy.

Originally a Celtic people (remnants of Gallic Celtic culture can be found in Brittany in the north and elsewhere), the French were conquered by Rome; when Rome fell in the ninth century, they were consolidated into the Frankish empires of Clovis and Charlemagne. After the end of the Holy Roman Empire in the fifteenth century, the development of feudal France culminated in one of the world's greatest monarchies, which was overthrown by one of the world's greatest revolutions in 1789. Since then, France (and in many ways, the rest of the world) has been struggling to deal with the aftershocks of this event, which ended the millennial ancien régime, sounded the death knell of monarchies all over Europe, and laid the groundwork for constitutional and representative government for much of the world. For France, this event led to the Napoleonic empire, several lesser revolutions, the struggle for democracy through several constitutions (*républiques,* in France), two world wars, and the current Fifth Republic, today still struggling with the essentially French question first raised in that great paroxysm of 1789: to what degree must government provide for its people?

An Area Briefing

Politics and Government

France today is a republic (the fifth; the first was established after the French Revolution), based on the parliamentary system. Any politically institutionalized remnants of the ancien régime are illegal. The legislative body is the National Assembly, made up of two houses, and there is a president (elected directly by the people) and a prime minister (the majority legislative leader). There are typically two major parties, representing the left and the right (the respective political persuasions of the left and the right are the result of where such "parties" actually sat in the legislature of the first French republic), with many smaller parties in between. Recently, the French have introduced the concept of "cohabitation," wherein the president and prime minister belong to opposing parties, yet share the responsibilities of the executive.

Schools and Education

The school system in France dramatically determines one's work, and position at work. Schooling is a serious, rigorous, and often challenging experience for most French students. The highest work positions in France are reserved for graduates of *les grandes Écoles,* an elite group of schools that prepares individuals for leadership positions in government, business, finance, and the sciences. Most families encourage their children to acheive academic excellence in the hope that they can make it into a *grande École,* or a university of high standing (the Sorbonne, by the way, is not one of the *grandes Écoles*). After high school, or "lycée," French students take "le Bac"—the baccalaureate exam: they must pass this usually difficult exam in order to graduate from the lycée, and the test they choose to take will determine which, if any, universities they may attend. Of the several *grandes Écoles* (Haute École Commerciale, the business school, and the *Polytechnique,* or engineering school, for example) the *École nationale d'administration* (ENA) is the most prestigious and usually leads to a career in government. Graduates of ENA are known as "Enarques," and graduates with degrees from more than one *grande École* are held in extremely high esteem.

Religion and Demographics

France has an official state religion—Roman Catholicism; however, there are significant populations of Protestants (historically, the Huguenots), Jews, and Muslims. The Muslim population is increasingly significant, as it has dramatically increased in recent years due to the massive immigration from former French colonies in northern and western Africa. There is a disturbing (for some) slightly negative French population growth, as is the case in much of western Europe.

Fundamental Cultural Orientations

1. What's the Best Way for People to Relate to One Another?

OTHER-INDEPENDENT OR OTHER-DEPENDENT? The motto of the French Revolution, "Liberté, Egalité, Fraternité," says a lot about how the French expect individuals to relate with each other in society. Unlike the British or Americans, the French believe that society (the group) serves the individual. Government exists to provide for the people, individuals benefit when society is organized correctly, and individual needs, in many ways, should be the responsibility of a well-ordered society. The British and American perception is more of a world in which society benefits most when individuals are able to pursue their personal goals and are free from the constraints of the government; society for Americans and Britons does its job best by staying out of the individual's way, not when it attempts to provide what the individual can better provide for him- or herself. In France, it is the other way around, but within a context of individual freedom, so that the pendulum never swings so far in France that the individual's freedom or self-identity is threatened. Once that is perceived, the pendulum has gone too far. This is representative, in many ways, of the combination of the Catholic and Latin concept of depending on the group, which was the base upon which France was historically founded, and the influence of the Reformation from the north, wherein salvation was dependent upon an individual's private relationship with God. The result is individual behavior that can be intensely unique, but always fitting into the structures and forms provided from above.

HIERARCHY-ORIENTED OR EGALITY-ORIENTED? For a thousand years, French life was feudal, structured, and class based. Then, in one defining moment, reality changed, and the French have been struggling ever since to create a rational structure in which the goals of the Revolution could be achieved. This results in a powerful emphasis in French daily life on the importance of organization, structure, and hierarchy. One does not change the way things are done easily or quickly, for to make change in the hierarchy means doing something revolutionary. Consequently, the French rigidly oppose change for change's sake, while perhaps acknowledging (or certainly debating) the possible need for it; this has historically meant a slow but steady buildup of volcanic forces that eventually break through in the form of civil unrest and revolutionary change. In France, the rules, the structure, and the organization are more important than efficiency, experimentation, flexibility, or individual circumstance. During the monarchy, French ministers would wrap their official documents in red ribbon for the king's approval—hence the term "red tape." Bureaucracy, administrative detail, and rigid hierarchical organization have defined the French organization (and French society) ever since. Related to this is a tendency toward strong centralization, with decision making located within smaller and smaller groups as one ascends to the top of the hierarchical pyramid. There are many examples of this in all aspects of French life: whom one needs to see (or wait for) in business, the architecture of *les étoiles,* the circles and radiating boulevards in the streets of Paris; the spiral arrondisement (administrative district) system of the city; the fact that all schoolchildren of any particular grade throughout France are following the same curriculum at the same pace, as laid out by the Ministry of Education, centralized in Paris.

RULE-ORIENTED OR RELATIONSHIP-ORIENTED? Class-based, or hierarchically determined, organization inevitably means heavy dependence upon rules and structures. However, this dependency also leads to the peculiarly Latin notion that when the rules don't work (and they often don't), the successful individual is one who can find a way around them; and this means, more often than not, depending upon someone influential with whom one has a particular relationship. This is an important issue in France, and the balance between the creation of rules that serve all, and the need to limit the degree that personal position can preclude one from having to follow those same rules, is always hotly debated. If you are in a privileged position in the French hierarchy (either in society or business), the rules more or less work in your favor, and as you go down the pyramid, it becomes more and more important to be "clever," to know the right person, and to find unique ways to get around the sometimes restraining and often conflicting regulations.

2. What's the Best Way to View Time?

MONOCHRONIC OR POLYCHRONIC? The French exhibit a conflicting mixture of Latin polychronism and northern European monochronism (and it is usually more monochronic in the north of France—Paris included—than in the south). In social situations, therefore, the French are often acceptably late, and in business situations, may think nothing of finishing up work on their desk for a few extra minutes even though a meeting has been called. Nevertheless, things can move briskly in metropolitan areas, and schedules and deadlines, in the absence of any other French priorities, can be surprisingly demanding.

RISK-TAKING OR RISK-AVERSE? Latin cultures, in general, are risk-averse; that is one of the driving reasons for the creation of structure and hierarchies. France is no exception. Decision making can be slow and tedious, as various levels of the hierarchy need to be consulted, and because information must be made available to many, in order for a decision to be made. The French try to do it right the first time; analyze everything carefully, several times, if necessary; and to debate all aspects of a decision until all is clear and agreed upon. Even when individuals are empowered to make the decision, there can be a reticence to take the required final step.

PAST-ORIENTED OR FUTURE-ORIENTED? It should not be surprising, therefore, that in many ways, France is past oriented, at least in the sense that unless there is a compelling reason to change, there probably is no reason to do things differently from the way they have determined to do them in the past. Nevertheless, there is also a very strong French tendency to explore, examine, analyze, and review—and if such activity results in a better way of doing things, a solution to a problem, or even just the revealing of a new problem or new way to look at things, such developments would be welcomed (and if they lead to change, so be it). Here we see that complex French mix of believing that people can control their own destinies through the rigorous application of thought, and the opposing Gallic spirit of *c'est la vie,* and succumbing to the greater forces. This results in an acceptance of the way things are, with the belief that one can do better if only . . . , and the conclusion, therefore, that one must enjoy today and live it to the fullest. It would be difficult to find a Frenchman who would sacrifice the benefits and blessings of today for the uncertainties, even the promises, of tomorrow.

3. What's the Best Way for Society to Work with the World at Large?

LOW-CONTEXT DIRECT OR HIGH-CONTEXT INDIRECT COMMUNICATORS? The French are direct, low-context communicators in that their love for debate, and the truth that may result, makes them less concerned for the amenities of "gentle talk." They usually say what they think—sometimes passionately, at other times carefully—and mincing words is generally not their way. The French will judge you on your ability to demonstrate your intellectual skills, and if this means confrontational ideas, rigorous debate, and heated exchange, all the better. You will be respected for your ability to handle it, even if what you are saying is different from what they believe.

PROCESS-ORIENTED OR RESULT-ORIENTED? One of the most important aspects of French culture, therefore, is the belief in the ability of the rational mind, when correctly applied, to overcome problems and find solutions. The philosophical justifications for the French Revolution were found in a group of French thinkers known as the Philosophes; during the Revolution, that bastion to French Catholic faith, Notre-Dame, was renamed the Temple of Rational Thought. Descartes, the great French philosopher (who, no coincidence here, was also a mathematician) is remembered for his phrase *"Je pense, donc je suis"* ("I think, therefore I am"). Cartesian thought, and the rational application of deductive logic, is a skill that French schoolchildren learn throughout all their studies. Therefore, the process or way in which they think is often more important than the outcomes or conclusion of their thoughts, for they need not worry about the conclusion if the process is correct. The joke in France is that two French managers are discussing the merits of a business plan, and one says to the other, "Well, I think it will work in practice . . . but it will never work in theory." This deductive method results in an enormous emphasis on *why* things are done, sometimes resulting in a masterful work of art, a beautifully executed speech, or an idea with questionable practical application. All are equally admired in France.

FORMAL OR INFORMAL? If there are "correct" and "incorrect" ways to get things done, then this also tends to formalize relationships, both socially and in business. French culture is a formal culture. Children are raised with care, discipline, and structure; society is organized—in the ancien régime into three estates, in the modern world into distinct social classes, each with its own identifying symbols; language is divided into formal and informal forms and phrases; and personal behaviors are ruled by etiquette and protocol. Simple, easy, and casual is not the basic nature of French culture: it is more formal, complicated, and structured.

Greetings and Introductions

Language and Basic Vocabulary

The French love affair with their language is not unwarranted. In the eighteenth century, French was the global language of convenience, certainly of diplomacy, the arts, science, and business. Perhaps no other culture so highly regards its language as a symbol of its culture. It should not be a surprise, therefore, that the French have difficulty with people who do not at least attempt to use French with them, especially when in France. It's logical, *non?* In most cases, the French will very much appreciate any effort you make to use their language, and they will reward your efforts by correcting your pronunciation and grammatical mistakes. It would be wrong to interpret this serious interest in your "getting it right" as demeaning or reprimanding, although it might seem harsh. Think of the French schoolteacher: she or he is demanding, and will work hard to be sure that her or his students learn their lessons properly and well. Doing things correctly, being *bien elevé* (well brought up), requires discipline and serious work, and learning the language requires the same. Rather than being put off by French instruction, look at it as the free tuition it is more usually intended to be: they care enough about you and their language to work with you.

It is strongly advised, therefore, that you learn some of the basic phrases in French, and use them whenever you can. In addition, anyone expecting to work in France over any extended period of time must develop some level of fluency in the language. Sticking with English will only take you so far, and will limit your business success. You should employ the following phrase whenever possible: *"Excusez-moi, s'il vous plaît, de vous deranger, mais je ne parle pas français"* ("Please excuse me for bothering you, but I do not speak French"). After that, you can ask for the moon and the stars and it would be a rare French person who would not try to help you. Be kind, sincere, considerate for their time and their love of their language, and you will be met with delighted and delightful French assistance.

Here are some basic terms to get you started:

bonjour	good day
bonsoir	good evening
au revoir	good-bye
Je m'appelle . . .	My name is . . .
Comment vous appellez-vous?	What is your name?
s'il vous plaît	please
heureux (heureuse) de faire votre connaissance	I am glad to meet you
merci	thank you
de rien	you're welcome
pardon	excuse me
je suis desolé(e)	I'm sorry
a bientôt	see you later
oui	yes
non	no
c'est dommage	that's too bad
hier	yesterday
aujourd'hui	today
demain	tomorrow
monsieur	Mr.
madame	Mrs./Madam
je voudrais	I would like
je comprends	I understand
je ne comprends pas	I don't understand

Honorifics for Men, Women, and Children

Monsieur (Mr.) and *madame* (Mrs.), plus the family name, are an absolute must for you to use when introduced to adults. Unless or until your French colleague specifically invites you to use first names, and despite how he or she might refer to you (after all, the French know that Americans usually prefer informality), you must always use the family name plus the correct French honorific (Mademoiselle—Mlle.—is rarely used these days, unless you are clearly speaking with a child or very young, single female adult). Children in France are expected to be respectful and not overly conversational when speaking with adults, and must always use honorifics when referring to adults. Pets, however, (especially dogs) are still another matter: they are adored, and accompany their masters everywhere, including restaurants (after all, a child is a basically unpredictable being, but a dog can at least be trained). In certain situations, the honorific plus a title may be used (e.g., Monsieur le President). The French can work with the same people in the same office for years, and still greet each other at the start of a business day with *Bonjour, monsieur,* and never use first names. For casual contacts (waiters, store help, etc.), just use *monsieur* or *madame* without the name, but always use the honorific. It is very important to greet people at work or in stores and restaurants with an appropriate *bonjour* or *bonsoir,* plus an *au revoir* upon leaving. If you speak any French at all, it is important to use it, but be sure to begin in the *vous* (formal) form—do *not* switch to the *tu* (informal) form of speech unless and until your French colleague has specifically invited you to or does so him- or herself.

The What, When, and How of Introducing People

Always wait to be introduced to strangers before taking that responsibility upon yourself. The French are most comfortable with a third-party introduction whenever possible. Try to ensure that for yourself ahead of time. Do not presume to seat yourself at a gathering: if possible, wait to be told where to sit. With whom, when, and how you are introduced is a key to understanding how you are perceived and how the French fit you into their hierarchy. Shake hands with everyone individually in a group before departing: the American group wave is not appreciated. Avoid ending the conversation with the American expression "Have a nice day": it sounds controlling and insincere. In addition, avoid personal compliments until you have a close personal relationship. Commenting on how someone is dressed or looks sounds too personal and out of place, and the reaction you get will not be the appreciation you might expect. Once you greet someone you will encounter later that same day in the same circumstances (e.g., at the office), there is no need to greet them again. Kissing is a common greeting once there is a relationship between women and men; usually, there is a kiss on two cheeks (actually an air kiss, first on the left side, and then the right).

Physical Greeting Styles

The handshake is common. The French version is a brisk, firm snap: it is done once, quickly, between men and men, but not as robustly between men and women and women and women. The handshake should be accompanied by the greetings outlined earlier. Smiling and other nonverbal forms of communication need not accompany the handshake when it is between unknowns. Men should wait until a woman extends her hand before reaching for it, and women may take the lead in extending their hand or not. Men must remove their gloves when shaking hands with a woman, but a woman need not remove her gloves when shaking hands with a man. Informal body gestures are not appreciated during the first introduction between strangers, so backslapping or additional touching should always be avoided. Eye contact during the introduction is serious and intense, and should be maintained for as long as the individual is addressing you. The use of business cards is very common; if possible (though not entirely necessary), you should have your business card translated into French on the reverse, and be sure to put any advanced educational degrees and your full title or position on the French side of the card (the French need to know where you fit into the hierarchy of the organization).

Communication Styles

Okay Topics / Not Okay Topics

Okay: politics, scandals, current events, anything interesting (even to the point of being controversial), the arts, sports (very big), music, and philosophy. The important point here is that the French generally love debate, and will seek to involve you in discussions that require that you take a position. They, in turn, might take the opposing position, and a heated dialogue usually ensues. This is not for the faint of heart, but it is done in a spirit of camaraderie, and is an effort to build a relationship based on your intellectual prowess and ability to converse intelligently, wittily, and with élan. Be careful about initiating such discussions yourself, however. *Not okay:* Do not opine about things French unless you absolutely know what you are talking about; equally important, do not allow French opinions to throw you: enjoy the banter and the passion with which it is delivered (the emotion is as fleeting as lightning), and get involved when the conversation touches on subjects on which you do have expertise. Do *not* inquire about a person's occupation in casual conversation. Americans often begin a conversation with "So, what do you do?"; this is too personal in France, and is often not the most interesting topic of conversation. The French would much prefer to learn something interesting (though not too personal at first) about you—your thoughts, opinions, likes and dislikes—delivered in a charming and witty way. Also not okay: personal financial discussions, inquiring about private family matters (the family is sacred), personal background, and the like.

Tone, Volume, and Speed

Discussions between strangers usually start out politely restrained, but can quickly become loud and boisterous, depending upon the nature of the discussion and the setting. At meals, the wine flows, and conversation is an art: it is enjoyed, savored, and commented upon.

Use of Silence

There is rarely a moment of it, except in group discussions when *une ange passe* ("an angel passes"; that slightly awkward moment at the dinner table, for example, when discussion ceases, not for any apparent reason, other than the topic under discussion has been exhausted, and nothing new has yet been introduced).

Physical Gestures and Facial Expressions

There is a unique French gesture: a puff of air exhaled through somewhat pouty lips. The meaning is elusive, but generally it is done as a sign of minor exasperation, a nonverbal way of saying, "Well, what can you do, that's life," "C'est la vie," "I don't know," and so on. The "okay" sign, formed by having the tip of the thumb meet the tip of the forefinger in the shape of a circle, generally means zero in France; if you want to gesture "okay," give the "thumbs up" sign instead.

Waving and Counting

The thumb represents the number 1, the index finger the number 2, and so on. It is insulting to beckon someone with the forefinger (instead, turn your hand so that your palm faces up and motion inward with all four fingers at once). If you need to gesture for a waiter, make a small, subtle motion with your hand as if you were writing (it indicates that you want *l'addition,* or the check).

Physicality and Physical Space

The French might get slightly closer than North Americans are comfortable with, but never extremely so. Never speak with your hands in your pockets: always keep them firmly at your side when standing. If men and women must cross their legs, it should never be ankle over knee; for women, the preferred style is to cross ankle over ankle. Remember, even in public, formal is always better than informal: no gum chewing, *ever;* don't slouch; and don't lean against things.

Eye Contact

Eye contact can be very intense and, at times, disconcerting to many Americans. It is important not to interpret this behavior as a way of intentionally trying to make you uncomfortable. It is how the French show their interest. Conversely, if you look away, your behavior will say to your French colleague that you are either disinterested or rude. Either way, maintain eye contact when it is made with you. Even in public, and between strangers, eye contact can be direct. Men and women look at each other on the street, and making eye contact is a positive way of initiating interest. Therefore, do not interpret stares in public as necessarily threatening: they may or may not be.

Emotive Orientation

While the French delight in the exposition of logic and clear thinking, they can express their logical conclusions, and processes of thought, passionately. This is another example of the combination of northern and Latin European traditions that occurs in France. Conversely, ideas that are not logical, or are badly thought out, can engender equally passionate disbelief, or cool disregard. Expressive gesturing is common as interest and passion are raised. Join in if you like, keep cool if you can. You will always be admired if you can remain unruffled, logical, formal, respectful, and diplomatic.

Protocol in Public

Walking Styles and Waiting in Lines

The French do not easily respect lines or quiet order: relationships may often supersede rules and regulations, especially in situations where the decision maker has control over the outcome; for example, those who have made an effort to even slightly develop a personal relationship with a shopkeeper (a *Bonjour, monsieur* upon entering a shop goes very far) will usually get preferential treatment over those who simply expect to be treated because they happen to be next in line. This is, of course, not always possible (for example, at bus stops); in such situations, a less-than-orderly contest usually results. This is not, however, always the case, and the French can be quite insistent that others obey the rules.

Behavior in Public Places: Airports, Terminals, and the Market

As with many European cultures, mass marketing and customer orientation is a new idea in France, with its tradition of artisanal quality and bourgeois production. Customer service as a concept is growing, but not fully institutionalized. Store hours—department stores excluded—are typically not built around customer convenience (stores are closed on weekends and most evenings—except Thursdays, usually). Waiters can be formal and proud of their important job in a culture that relishes a fine table and meal, and delight in being respected for what they do when serving an interested and knowledgeable patron. In a restaurant, therefore, discuss the menu, comment on the food, and express your satisfaction. As in much of Europe, if you touch the produce in food markets, you buy it; in goods stores, it may be difficult for you to return a product unless there is a flaw in it. Smoking is on the decline, and there may be smokeless areas in public places.

More and more public phones (especially in the major cities) require a *télécarte,* which can be purchased at any nearby *tabac* or newsstand. There are fewer and fewer coin-operated phones, so be prepared to use a *télécarte.*

Bus / Metro / Taxi / Car

Driving is on the right, but people pass very quickly on the left. The metros shut down after midnight or 1 A.M. Your best bet for catching a cab is at designated taxi stands (hotels are good places, but they often charge more for the same ride: a hotel surcharge is added to the meter fare, in some cases). Bring food and water on board commuter trains if your trip is a long one, as there may not be a café car. The French, being private and formal, generally will not bother you on public transportation, nor will they necessarily be receptive to casual chat.

Tipping

Ten percent is usually sufficient in restaurants and taxis; more is considered nouveau and gauche. Porters and hotel help get a franc or two per bag or service event, theater and bathroom attendants usually one franc. Restaurants usually have the 10 percent tip already included on the bill *(service compris),* but if you are unsure, it's okay to ask if service is included or not. Even if it is, it is still appropriate to leave a few francs or some odd change if the service was particularly good.

Punctuality

It is perfectly acceptable to arrive for social events "fashionably late"; that is, about fifteen to twenty minutes or so. The time you are given for a dinner, for example, is when the evening begins: the meal itself will probably be at least one-half hour later than the time you are given to arrive; however, it is always safe to double-check this with the person inviting you. If the time does actually represent the start of the meal, then it is important to be on time, and the twenty minute rule does not apply (though this will probably not be the case). For business meetings, especially in Paris, being late is usually not a problem, but it is safer for the new employee or visitor to be on time (he or she should not be surprised if others are slightly tardy, however). Usually, the meeting will not begin in earnest until all attendees have arrived (or certainly, until all the decision makers have shown up). Resist questioning the late ones for a reason: France is a more polychronic culture, and relationships and other obligations may simply take precedence over a particular meeting or deadline.

Dress

Generally, clothing is formal for both men and women, no matter the occasion—business or social, at work, in a restaurant, or on a street. However, we must carefully define what we mean by formal, for in this case, we are really referring to the "thoughtfulness" with which the French approach clothes and their choice of wardrobe. It need not, in fact, be as "formal" as the American, but it usually is always more conscious and oriented around taste and style. Good taste is everything, and should be reflected in the clothes one wears, as well as all aspects of the way one lives life.

At work, men often wear creative combinations of colors and textures: sport jackets with colored dress shirts and interesting ties, socks, and trousers are more common than the simple, dark, formal suit (except at the highest levels of business, where the dark suit and white shirt are more common); women usually accessorize so that even the simplest of outfits stand out for their interest and style. French women may wear more makeup than American women, and it is fashionable, especially in summer, not to wear stockings. On the street, informal may mean jeans and sneakers, though that is more common as clothing to wear at the gym, the beach, or while jogging (women do *not* wear sneakers to work); for a social gathering, informal more often than not means tastefully coordinated clothes, sometimes including jacket and tie for men (it rarely means jeans, sneakers, or T-shirts). "Formal" usually means formal evening wear, which is very dressy by American standards.

Seasonal Variations

There are four distinct seasons in France, and one needs to dress accordingly. Summers can be hot and humid, and winters can be long, damp, and very cold (but without too much snow, except in the mountain regions to the east). Spring and fall both are typically mild and delightful.

Colors

The French concern for style leads to a creative mixing of colors; at times, even in the workplace, the combinations can be extreme for American tastes, yet in the French context they work well. A colorful tie against a colored shirt, offset with an interestingly colored and textured sport jacket is a common combination for men, and women often accent their outfits with a unique scarf or piece of jewelry. Black is still always very chic for the evening—sometimes, for women, offset with a brightly colored item. Remember, even high fashion in France is a representation of the French preoccupation with proper form, and its logical extension to perfection and quality in dress.

Styles

Around the world, Paris is referred to as a major center for the "newest look," although few people on city's streets can actually afford the latest trends. Nevertheless, even the average person has a heightened sense of fashion, and one should dress with the same thought and élan that one should put into every aspect of his or her life. Essentially, that is the French way of doing things: nothing casual, nothing accidental, and make an intentional (and intelligent) statement, right down to the eyeglasses. The French can combine colors, weaves, textures, and designs in ways not that common to North Americans.

Accessories / Jewelry / Makeup

Makeup, hairstyles, and accessories are very important for women, as all add up to presenting the proper and flattering appearance; men, however, usually do not accessorize with jewelry or cologne to the degree that men in other Latin cultures might.

Personal Hygiene

Despite some old myths, the plumbing in France is for the most part quite modern, and most people do bathe every day. Remember, however, that traditions build up over the centuries (centuries during which central heating did not exist and getting the body unnecessarily wet in the middle of a freezing winter was more dangerous to health than cleaning the skin within a twenty-four-hour period). Nevertheless, there might be less concern for covering up what are, after all, the natural reactions of the human body to the course of the day. Some French see the American concern for neutralizing body odor with deodorants, shampoos, and colognes as an excessive preoccupation. Men, hands out of pockets, always.

Dining and Drinking

Mealtimes and Typical Foods

Unless you're working out on the farm, breakfast (*le petit dejeuner*) is typically a cup or two of strong coffee (black—*noir,* or *un expres*—or café au lait are very common for breakfast) and a croissant or baguette, with butter, cheese, or preserves. The large breakfast is usually not common, and people in the big cities often take their morning meal on the run, sitting or standing at cafés or coffee stands. It is not uncommon in the French home, however, for American favorites to be served; breakfast cereals and yogurt are common.

Lunch (*le dejeuner*) was traditionally the main meal of the day, and even in busy cities today it can still be an elaborate affair, lasting several hours (usually for an important business lunch); or it can be a quick sandwich or salad at *le sandwich* shop on the corner. Lunch is served from 12 or 12:30 P.M. to 1 or 2 P.M. (or later). Sandwiches and salads are often thoughtful affairs, ranging from the common *croque monsieur* (melted cheese on a baguette) to beautifully designed fish, meat, and vegetable combinations. Wine (or occasionally beer, depending upon the food) is typical at all lunches, business and social, in the restaurant, café, or workplace cafeteria, as well as mineral water (*avec gaz*—with carbonation, or *sans gaz*—uncarbonated water) or soft drinks (more and more common, actually). Even the quick business lunch often will include a main course and a dessert and coffee. On Sunday, the family day, the main meal is supper, which is usually served beginning at lunchtime, and can last well into the evening.

Dinner is served from 7:30 to 8:30 P.M., with 8 P.M. the customary time. The evening meal, even in the typical French home, can be an elaborate affair, beginning with a soup or an appetizer, and moving on to a main course (or two), ending with dessert. (Please see the comments in the later section in this chapter regarding formal French meals, either at home or in a restaurant.) Wine is usually served with dinner; no matter how simple or expensive, it is carefully selected to complement the food as perfectly as possible. Dinner parties usually end at around midnight (but can go much later if all are having a good time).

The café is a place for conversation, a snack, some tea or coffee, a drink, an aperitif, a pastry, a quick read, or a smoke. It is open practically at all hours, and customarily has seating both indoors and outdoors (when weather permits). The tables are tiny, and often crammed next to each other, so maintaining privacy between diners is important. Once you are seated (yes, in most you may seat yourself), the waiter will arrive, and you should be prepared to place your order. Once you call for the bill, be prepared to pay it; the waiter will generally wait at your table until you pay. Traditionally, you could sit at the café for as long as you liked; no one would ask you to move on until you were ready. This is still the case in most cafés, in the cities as well as the country. As informal as the cafés can be, though, eating while strolling down the street simply isn't done in France (although there are food stalls in markets or other locations where one can buy crêpes and sandwiches for example; however, it is usually expected that food purchased at a stall will be eaten there or very nearby, whether or not seating is provided).

Regional Differences

French food is as varied as the country, and while Paris is the pinnacle of fine French cuisine, the concern for good eating is a hallmark of French culture everywhere in the country. Lyons (Lyonnaise cuisine) is known for its hearty, family-style food consisting of sausages, cooked vegetables, and hearty meats; some of the world's finest and freshest seafood can be found along the Normandy and Brittany coast (try the oysters: they are unique); in the country north and east of Paris is a cuisine that melds the best of French country and hearty German influences of the Alsace (meats and pâtés); as you move down through the countryside, fine cheeses, meats, breads, and vegetables influence the local cuisines; while Provençale cuisine in the south is known for its Mediterranean and herb-influenced cuisine (bouillabaisse, ratatouille); fresh seafood and fish, grilled outdoors, is a standard along the sparkling Côte d'Azur.

Typical Drinks and Toasting

Mixed drinks before dinner are not common; however, before the meal one might have a champagne or *kir*. Champagne is perhaps the only drink that one can safely have with any dish throughout the meal, although it most often pops up as a preprandial or with the appetizer or fish dish. *Kir* is a blend of currant liqueur and white wine, and *kir royale* substitutes champagne for white wine; finally, a *kir sauvage* might be offered, which is a *kir* made with a variety of different currant liqueurs. Once the meal gets under way, wine will be served in most cases. In France, the wine is carefully chosen to complement the food it is meant to be drunk with; therefore, the wine can change with each course. Mainly, white wines will be served with appetizers or fish, and reds will be served with appetizers and meats. You may be offered several different white or red wines; in this case, the finer red or white is usually served first, so that you may appreciate it best. A sweeter dessert wine may be served with dessert, and after the meal a postprandial liquor or liqueur is common. Preferred after-dinner drinks often are *digestifs* in the form of eau-de-vies (brandies of distilled fruit spirits, not sweet) or liqueurs (blends of fruit or herb essences, usually sweet). Finer brandies, such as cognac, Armagnac, or marc (the different names represent brandies from different regions) are usually reserved as the final drinks of the evening. At formal dinner parties, which may run very late into the evening or morning hours, the very last drink may be . . . orange juice! (This is your cue from the host that it is really time to go.)

Wine is drunk at lunch and dinner and, in the farmlands and vineyard country, can even make its way to the breakfast table. Never add anything to wine, and also be judicious about adding anything (salt, pepper, ketchup, etc.) to food (this implies that the original is not prepared well).

The most common toasts are *salud* or *a votre santé* (to your health).

Table Manners and the Use of Utensils

Do not begin eating until the host says, "*Bon appetit!*"

The French, like all Europeans, do not switch knives and forks, as Americans do. The knife remains in the right hand, and the fork remains in the left. When the meal is finished, the knife and fork are laid parallel to each other across the right side of the plate. If you put both utensils down on the plate for any real amount of time, it is a sign to the waitstaff that you are finished, and your plate may be taken away from you. There are often many additional pieces of cutlery: the knife above your plate is for bread and butter (or it may be a smallish knife laid by the side of the main plate; a bread plate is rare, and bread is usually broken by hand, with a small piece being laid on the left side of the main plate directly on the table). The fork and spoon above your plate are for dessert. If you're unsure of which utensil to use, always start from the outside and work your way in, course by course. When not holding utensils, your hands are expected to be visible above the table: this means that you do not keep them in your lap; instead, rest your wrists on top of the table (never your elbows). At the table, pass all dishes to your left. There will be separate glasses provided at your setting for water, white and red wine, and champagne (after-dinner drink glasses come out after dinner). Never cut your lettuce: deftly fold it with your knife and fork into a little bundle that can be easily picked up with your fork.

Seating Plans

The most honored position is at the head of the table, with the most important guests seated first to the left and then to the right of the head of the table. If there is a hosting couple, one will be seated at each end of the table. In keeping with the practice elsewhere on the Continent, men and women are seated next to one another, and couples are often broken up and seated next to people they may not have previously known. This is done to promote conversation. Men typically rise when women enter the room, and continue to hold doors for women and allow them to enter a room first. Remember, as is the case throughout the Continent, what the French call the first floor is really the second floor, with the first floor usually referred to as the lobby or ground floor (*rez-de-chaussée*—or RC—in France).

Refills and Seconds

If you do not want more food, don't worry—you typically won't be offered any (except in casual, family home environments). You are expected to eat every bit of whatever is on your plate, and that's that: the course offered was the course offered, and you should not ask for seconds. You may always have additional beverages; drink enough to cause your cup or glass to be less than half full, and it will generally be refilled. Portions are generally smaller than in the United States, but there are generally more courses, for both lunch and dinner. It is not about quantity, but quality.

At Home, in a Restaurant, or at Work

There are many varieties of restaurants, beginning with the formal and elegant establishments serving haute cuisine right on down to the crêperie food stand on the street. There are several types in between: the bistro—or, originally, the bar—now usually a family-run establishment offering good, substantial fare that accompanies drinks; the brasserie, offering snacks (not to be confused with fast food) and traditional meals; and less formal restaurants, where reservations may not be necessary. In informal restaurants, you may be required to share a table: if so, do not force conversation; act as if you are seated at a private table. Wait-staff may be summoned by making eye contact; waving or calling their names is very impolite. The power breakfast is not common in France, although you do see it creeping slowly into the business life of the major cities. The business lunch or dinner is a widespread practice, but, depending upon how well developed your relationship is with your French colleagues, it is generally not the time to make business decisions. Take your cue from your French associates: if they bring up business at a meal, then it's okay to discuss it, but wait to take your lead from their conversation. No gum chewing, ever, at the restaurant or on the street. No-smoking sections in restaurants are still a rarity.

When invited to a colleague's home for a formal meal, remember that the meal itself, and the formality surrounding it, is theater, and that you are an actor in this great French play. Play your part well. Once within the home, you will be told where to sit, and there you should remain. Do not wander from room to room: much of the house is really off-limits to guests. Use the toilet before you arrive, as it is considered bad form to have to leave the dinner party, or the table, at any time. Once you (and the group) are invited to another room, most probably the dining room, be sure to allow the more senior members of your party to enter the room ahead of you: men should also move aside to allow women to enter ahead of them.

At the table, be sure to look for place cards, or wait until the host indicates your seat: do not presume to seat yourself, as the seating arrangement is usually predetermined. The meal—after aperitifs and a few appetizers (do not expect much in the way of premeal appetizers; the meal is the important focus)— follows several courses:

- fish (with white wine or champagne)
- meat (with red wine)
- salad (generally, because of the vinegar dressing, wine is not served with salad; the drink is usually mineral water): may not be part of every meal, but if it is served, it comes after the meat course, not alongside or before it
- cheese (usually with a different red wine): usually comprised of several varieties with different shapes, textures, and robustness. Take small portions, along with some bread. When serving yourself, round-shaped cheeses should be cut beginning from the center, in sequential, triangular wedges (never cut round-shaped cheeses from the side); rectangular, conical, or square-shaped cheeses should be sliced in small portions beginning from the cut end. Bread is served throughout the meal, and is the only food, except for sandwiches and asparagus spears, that can properly be eaten at the table with the hand; almost everything in France is eaten with a knife, fork, or spoon. (Asparagus spears are often served on a separate vegetable plate and should be lifted by hand and dipped in the sauce—usually butter—that accompanies it.)
- dessert (with a sweetish dessert wine, usually white): usually not served with coffee
- coffee (usually served after dessert, and often served with an after-dinner drink)
- chocolates (usually served with postprandials)

Being a Good Guest or Host

Paying the Bill

Usually the one who does the inviting pays the bill, although the guest is expected to make an effort to pay. Sometimes other circumstances determine the payee (such as rank). Making payment arrangements ahead of time so that no exchange occurs at the table is a very classy way to host.

Transportation

It's a very nice idea, when acting as the host, to inquire ahead of time as to whether the guests will require transportation. If necessary, you should arrange for taxi service at the end of the meal.

When to Arrive / Chores to Do

If you are invited to dinner at a private home, do not expect to help with the chores, nor should you expect to visit the kitchen. Do not leave the table unless invited to do so. Spouses are often included in business dinners (most commonly both business associates are married). An invitation to a dinner party in France is a special honor, and not often extended to new relationships: if it is offered, accept, enjoy, and play your part well! When it is time to leave, always get up and shake hands with everyone: the group wave is not appreciated.

How to Converse

Be gracious, be witty, and be ready to move from topic to topic without necessarily completing one conversation before another begins. The art is in being able to be entertaining, intelligent, and lively. Prepare yourself to talk about most anything, and follow the guidelines outlined earlier: on things you really do not know much about, be an inquisitive student—ask for information; on things you are expert at, be a kindly teacher. Never be boring!

Gift Giving

In general, gift giving is not common among business associates; it is best not to send a gift at any time, including the holidays, unless you receive one first from your colleagues. Holiday cards are very appropriate, particularly as a thank-you for their business during the previous year, and should be mailed in time to be received the week before Christmas. The French celebrate Christmas Eve as the time for holiday gift giving.

Gifts *are* expected for social events, however, especially as thank-yous for private dinner parties. The best gift in this case is flowers—you should have them sent ahead of time on the day of the dinner. Be sure never to send chrysanthemums (they are used primarily as funeral flowers), or red roses (these usually indicate romantic intent), and always be sure the bouquet is in odd numbers (an old European tradition). If you must bring flowers with you to the dinner party, be sure to unwrap them before presenting them. Another good gift would be fine chocolates (avoid wine, as it may present the hosts with the dilemma of whether it should be brought out to the table, especially when they have no doubt already selected the wine for the meal; the only exceptions would be a French dessert wine or an after-dinner liqueur of good quality). In addition to the gift (and certainly necessary if you did not send or bring one), be sure to send a handwritten thank-you note on a card the next day after the dinner party; it is best if it is messengered and not mailed.

If you are staying with a French family, an appropriate thank-you gift would be a high-quality product that represents your country and is difficult to get in France: gourmet foodstuffs (maple syrup, pralines, lobsters, etc.), coffee-table books about the United States, or anything that reflects your host's personal tastes (a sweatshirt from a famous American college or university for the college-bound child of the family, for example) is appropriate.

Special Holidays and Celebrations

Major Holidays

Most French workers get five to six weeks of paid vacation; August is a leading vacation time. May is a very big month for holidays in France, so doing business during that month can be difficult; when these holidays fall near a weekend, a "bridge" day is often taken, resulting in long three- or four-day weekends. Business slows down again from December 15 to January 6, during the Christmas and New Year's seasons.

January 1	*Le Jour de l'An* (New Year's Day), often celebrated with a meal of oysters
March/April	*Lundi de Pâques* (Easter Monday) marks the end of Holy Week, which begins with Palm Sunday
May 1	*Fête du Travail* (Labor Day) is celebrated on the same day as most European countries
May 8	*Le Huit Mai* (French Armistice Day) follows a week after Labor Day, usually making for two 3-day weekends in a row
May/June	Ascension (on a Monday), five weeks after Easter, and Pentecost (on a Monday), seven weeks after Easter, may also result in a three-day weekend
July 14	*La Fête Nationale* (Bastille Day), commemorating the French Revolution and the establishment of the Republic; a holiday of great celebration (and some mixed emotions, depending upon the politics of the individuals you speak with!)
August 15	Assumption
November 1	*Toussaint* (All Saints' Day)
November 11	World War I Armistice Day
December 25	*Noël* (Christmas)

Business Culture

Daily Office Protocols

In France, office doors are usually closed; knock first (this includes bathrooms) before opening doors, and when leaving rooms, close the doors behind you. Women may be treated with particular respect by French men, both in business and in social situations: this is meant as an honor in most cases, and reflects the French belief that women and men, indeed, are different (and *vive la différence!*). Nevertheless, women do struggle to reach the same levels of achievement as their male counterparts in French business, and it is rare (though not impossible) to see women at the highest levels of business and government in France. Most, but not all, graduates of the elite *grandes Écoles* (which pave the way for a career in business or government) are men. Staying late at the office is common, especially for more senior positions.

Management Styles

Privacy and individual accomplishment of one's tasks are critical; workers provide what their bosses expect of them, and the preparation of plans, methods, and reports can be time-consuming, thorough, and complicated efforts. All of this occurs in a formal and sometimes very rigid hierarchical structure, which means that deadlines and efficiency, while important, are often secondary to attention to detail, rigorous logic, and perfection of form. The *president directeur general* (PDG) is equivalent to the chief executive officer, and most senior level executives are *directeurs;* therefore, the title of director in France is usually reserved for a very senior executive-level position, and should not be used as casually as it is in the United States. Complimenting and rewarding employees publicly is usually not done.

Boss-Subordinate Relations

Rank most definitely has its privileges in France. Hierarchy is something to be respected, and there are definite routes through life that one follows according to one's rank in society and in the workplace. There is a rigid chain of command that must be heeded. No matter what field you are in, there is a proper way for communicating with particular individuals, and an established procedure one is expected to follow. Deviating from the normal channels will generally make more problems for you, even if your intent is to bypass what appear to be obstacles. Bosses are expected to provide guidance, distribute information, and make decisions; subordinates are expected to provide detailed information and follow the decisions made by their superiors.

Conducting a Meeting or Presentation

At meetings of peers, there can be open communication and sharing of ideas; in fact, these sessions often serve as information-sharing and decision-making forums in which all individuals are expected to contribute. Under these circumstances, discussions are usually vibrant, with many people speaking at once; questions are common and interruptions, even of presentations, should be expected. In more formal, conservative organizations, meetings are often gatherings of nonpeers, clearly called together by decision makers in order to gather information from below, clarify goals, and formulate action plans. In these cases, individuals often do not share ideas and are not expected to contribute to mutual problem solving.

Negotiation Styles

The French can be very direct, questioning, and probing; their radar usually zones in on those details of your proposal, for example, that are not clear or require further explanation or logical exposition. A point that is understood is typically not acknowledged, which gives the French a reputation for being detail-conscious and negative. They will respect someone who comes to them with established knowledge and experience. No detail is unimportant, and a carefully planned, logically organized proposal is key.

Each person on the French team really has a very specific, individual task; teamwork is not a concept easily adopted in France. Secretaries are powerful people in the French organization, although they may not represent the person you may be dealing with: therefore, confirmation of appointments, correspondence, and schedules must be made, either with your counterpart or his or her specific secretary.

The first meeting is usually very formal, with the French sizing up you and your organization: it will be conducted in the office. Take copious notes; the French love detail, remember. However, although the contract must be correct down to the dotted i's in order for it to be legal, it really is just a formality in French eyes, and can be overcome, by either party, if such a need arises later on. Because of the French attention to detail, organization, and hierarchy, plan your meeting carefully and well in advance, and prepare a detailed agenda for circulation prior to the scheduled date. Casually changing time and place is not appreciated.

Written Correspondence

Business letters must be very formal and respectful of hierarchy. Last names are usually written in uppercase; dates are given using the day/month/year format (with periods in between, not slashes); an honorific plus a title is as common as an honorific plus the last name; and the opening "Dear . . ." is often left out, with the body of the correspondence beginning immediately after the proper headings. The time of day is written in military style; weights and measures are usually given in metric units. Monetary amounts are written so that periods break up the figure into tens, hundreds, and thousands, and a comma separates the francs from the centimes (e.g., FF10.000,00 = ten thousand French francs). The traditional language used in openings and closings is convoluted and formal; for example:

Sincerely yours *Veuillez agreer, l'expression de mes salutations les plus distinguées*

Please . . . *Nous vous prions de bien vouloir . . .*

The Germanic Cultures:
Germany

Some Introductory Background on Germany and the Germans

If one were to try to identify the precise moment in history when Britain constituted itself into a nation, dates such as 1066 might pop up; certainly, there is a
national entity known as Britain that is many centuries old. If one were to try to
identify the precise moment in history when France constituted itself into a
nation, one could mention Charlemagne, the ninth-century Frankish king, but
also make an argument for 1789, the date of the French Revolution. But when it
comes to Germany, the economic powerhouse and historical political dilemma
of western Europe, fixing a date of national unity is more difficult. Some might
give the establishment of the Holy Roman Empire (962) as the date; some
might say 1871 (the year the Prussian king Wilhelm was crowned kaiser); some
might claim 1989, when the Berlin Wall fell and the two Germanys, east and
west, became one. It is in this dilemma that we see the reasons for much of
what underlies German culture: of the major three western European nations,
Germany has suffered the most with an identity crisis, resulting in a fundamental insecurity that drives many aspects of its cultural, political, economic, and
personal behavior. Is the country Lutheran Protestant or Roman Catholic? (In
fact, Germany is about evenly split between the two, having played a major role
in the Protestant Reformation.) Where do its cultural borders begin and end?
(Historically, German culture is not easily defined by political borders, and significant populations of Germanic people live in many neighboring countries.)
How do its people define what makes them who they are, and therefore different from their neighbors? (German art, literature, music, and philosophy are
filled with a search for the German *Geist,* or "spirit.") Finally, how do the people reveal their essential "Germanness," in their day-to-day lives, their arts, their
sciences, their ways of thinking, and their politics? These are weighty and
important considerations in Germany, as they always have been, and the answers
that Germans have historically come up with to these questions have been alternately enlightening and catastrophic, for them and for the rest of the world.
This issue is at the heart of German cultural behavior.

Some Historical Context

Many historical events conspired to make it difficult for Germany to constitute itself into a unified whole until only very recently, not the least being its location in central Europe and the feudal nature of the fiefdoms and principalities that made up "Germany" from the emergence of the Holy Roman Empire to the coronation of Kaiser Wilhelm in the nineteenth century. After centuries of internecine struggle, it took the application of brute Prussian force to bring the unwieldy confederation of small Germanic states into one political unit. Consequently, Germans admire structure, order, and organization, whether accomplished through rules and regulations or by powerful force applied from above; and it is this desire for order and normalcy, sometimes at all costs, which is at the heart of the German national psyche.

Germany was also the stage for one of the world's great religious conflicts, between the emerging Protestants and the existing Catholics. New reformist Germanic Protestants in the north were creating a culture based not on Catholic hierarchy, the Mass, and the relinquishing of salvation to the authority of others, but one based on empowering individuals to demonstrate and communicate their worthiness through benevolent individual acts, or "good works," directly to the ultimate decision maker. The Reformation would ultimately transform the feudal world, remaking landlords and serfs into burghers, traders, and capitalists, and laying the groundwork for modern capitalism and our culture of commerce.

Finally, Germany has historically been both a bridge and a barrier between East and West, between the Enlightenment and Orientalism, between the Christian West and the Islamic East. These influences also have etched their designs onto German cultural behavior.

An Area Briefing

Politics and Government

Germany today is a democracy, a federal republic of individual states linked by a parliamentary form of government. The chancellor is the chief executive, elected by the Bundestag (the Federal Diet), the lower of the two houses that comprise the German Parliament. The upper house is the Bundesrat, or Federal Council. The members of the Bundestag are elected by the public; the members of the Bundesrat are appointed by the state governments. The chancellor selects his cabinet. There is also a federal judiciary system and state governments whose structures mirror the federal system. The important German political parties are the

Christian Democratic Party/Christian Social Union Party mainly in Bavaria (CDU/CSU): centrist, traditionally Catholic and older voters, social market economy
Free Democratic Party (FDP): centrist, traditionally Protestant

Social Democratic Party (SPD): more state involvement; both intellectuals and
workers

Die Grünen (The Greens): environmentally oriented, very active

Schools and Education

The school system in Germany, as in much of Europe, traditionally determines
one's life career at an early age. After *Grundschule* (or elementary school), one
enters either the *Gymnasium* (high school), the *Realschule* (vocational secondary school), or the *Hauptschule* (basic secondary school). The *Gymnasium*
(pronounced with a hard *g*) usually leads to the *Universität* or *Fachhochschule*
(university or college) only after one has passed the *Abitur,* a difficult exam, at
the end of high school. The *Realschule* and the *Hauptschule* both usually lead
to the unique German institution of *Berufsausbildung* (formerly referred to as the
Lehrling, or apprenticeship, system), wherein students continue their vocational
schooling while working at the same time for a sponsoring German business
organization. During the apprenticeship, they typically learn many skills, and a
job usually awaits them in the sponsoring organization when they graduate.

Religion and Demographics

Northern Germany is primarily Protestant (Lutheran), while southern Germany
is primarily Catholic, although there are large populations of both in both areas.
Eastern Germany experienced a generation of official atheism and, while there
is a strong religious resurgence there now that the communist regime is over,
the people are strongly secular. There is a disturbing (for some) slightly negative German population growth, as is the case in much of western Europe.

Because of reunification, there is no longer an East Germany or a West
Germany; the country is known as the Federal Republic of Germany (FRD).
Demographically, though, western and eastern Germany are still culturally distinct regions. Reunification was, and remains, a surprisingly difficult process (it
was, in fact, a surprise event from the beginning), and the economic costs of
bringing the two Germanys together were far higher than anyone anticipated.
That it has been accomplished as well as it has is a testament to, among other
things, German economic power. The formerly isolated east turned out to be a
heavily polluted and economically ruined region, with a workforce essentially
ignorant of fundamental business concepts and western lifestyles. These differences, coupled with the very real financial support being poured into the East
from the West, has caused many western and eastern Germans to resent one
another.

In addition to the east/west split, the north/south, Protestant/Catholic division is also evident in German cultural life. Northern Germans who live in the
business-oriented cities of the western Ruhr, the north, and the east to Prussia,
are seen as hardworking industrialists, while southern Germans, as represented
by the more conservative Bavaria region, are seen as more rural, traditional, and
agricultural. Complicating these divisions in Germany today is the massive
influx of Turks, along with other Middle Eastern and eastern European peoples,
as "guest workers." The immigrants work at entry-level service jobs, but for
many Germans, they add to the country's already burdened social service sector
by taking jobs away from Germans. This is a particularly sensitive cultural issue

in Germany, where the introduction of new cultures and religions (mainly Islam) is a challenge to the ongoing question of German identity.

Fundamental Cultural Orientations

1. What's the Best Way for People to Relate to One Another?

OTHER-INDEPENDENT OR OTHER-DEPENDENT? Germany, while experiencing the Enlightenment, did not directly contribute to it; rather, Germany's contribution to western European culture was post-Enlightenment objectivism, that philosophically complex search for truth through the application of rigorous and disciplined thought. While the French emphasize the search for a precise conceptual process, the German tradition focuses on the development of an effective method that, having been proven correct through trial, application, and repetition, should not be changed. The individual is subject to established rules and systems that must be respected and followed: when order is maintained, everything is normal; when rules are broken, chaos and anarchy can result. Individuals must, therefore, effectively play their role in the "well-oiled German machine" if the machine is to function well for all. While this concept is understood in many other cultures, including the United States, the particularly rugged individualism of the American is often seen by Germans as contributing to the destabilization of normalcy, the goal so desperately sought for in German society. There is a strong drive toward the "compartmentalization" of life, reflected in the way time is manipulated, agendas are stuck to, doors are closed, roles are clearly defined, work and social life are clearly separated, and rules are followed.

HIERARCHY-ORIENTED OR EGALITY-ORIENTED? There is a strong hierarchy in daily life (and business) in Germany, the result of the feudal experience and the need for strong decision- and rule-making systems. It is a formal culture in which relationships are not made quickly, roles are observed, and rank has its privilege. Nevertheless, the relationships between individuals of different social strata are not necessarily distant (as can be the case in Latin European cultures), and the formality of daily life provides a way for promoting cooperative and smooth interpersonal relationships between all people, socially and at work. The relationship between the local prince and his people in feudal Germany was generally an effective and ecologically balanced system, and it is no coincidence that the modern German business organization mirrors this arrangement. Within the German business unit, there is a definite hierarchy, with the manager on the top, but there is also smooth, harmonious, and curiously open communication within the structure, with everyone performing their role and following the rules.

RULE-ORIENTED OR RELATIONSHIP-ORIENTED? Rules in Germany are made to be obeyed (this is distinctly different south of the Alps, in the Latin cultures, where rules, essentially, are made to be broken). The rules can be explicit (do not cross the street if the light is red) or implicit (never wash your car on a Sunday morning); in either case, you need to know the rules, and if you break them, you will be censured. Disobeying the rules risks disorder, and this cannot be permitted. As a result, flexibility and spontaneity are not as highly valued in Germany as they might be in the United States: thinking "out-of-the-box," brainstorming, challenging rules and authority, and generalized risk taking are not seen as inherently valuable attributes in Germany.

2. What's the Best Way to View Time?

MONOCHRONIC OR POLYCHRONIC? Germany is one of the most mono-chronic cultures in the world (although polychronism increases as one moves south and east within its borders). The trains will generally be on time to the minute; employees must not be late for a meeting (the meeting will start without them if they are, and the doors will be closed); and plans, agendas, and the like are rigorously followed. If your plans must change, if you must be delayed, if the unexpected occurs, it is crucial that you inform key people of the fact as soon as possible. One cannot plan too much, too carefully, or too thoroughly. There is a time and place for everything, and careful planning allows for both work and leisure (Germans have more holidays, for example, than any other major developed nation, and personal life is sacred); it is just that the two usually do not mix.

RISK-TAKING OR RISK-AVERSE? This is generally a risk-averse culture. Before new ideas can be adopted, before changes can be made, before modifications can be accepted, the German needs to know why. After all, they have probably already developed a method or a system for handling the proposed change, and it has probably been effective. Unless the reason for doing something differently is compelling, clear, and proven, the German will not accept it. Information will be analyzed, data gathered, and decisions usually made at the top after careful consideration. The ability to move flexibly and experimentally is not a natural German attribute.

PAST-ORIENTED OR FUTURE-ORIENTED? Germans have a strong sense of control. They believe that with enough careful and methodical compartmentalization, organization, and structure, they can and should exercise as much control over their environment (and their future) as they can. In this sense, Germans can be very forward-looking; however, history has repeatedly shown that events may be beyond human control, and Germans also have a strong sense of how difficult this application of will can be (and that there can always be a point beyond which one does not have influence).

3. What's the Best Way for Society to Work with the World at Large?

LOW-CONTEXT DIRECT OR HIGH-CONTEXT INDIRECT COMMUNICATORS? The German language and methodical, detail-oriented aspects of German culture combine to create a form of speech that is often very direct and low context. Words are used to mean exactly what they are meant to say (it is therefore very important not to interrupt German speakers, and particularly not to end their statements for them). This blunt, precise way of speaking can sound harsh and too controlling to the American ear; it is usually not meant this way, but results from the preoccupation with limiting oneself to statements of fact. This is especially the case in business, while in social situations, Germans can be more subtle and playful in their communication styles.

PROCESS-ORIENTED OR RESULT-ORIENTED? If the French are concerned about "why" things are being done as they are, the Germans are concerned about "how" (leaving the Americans and the British to the "what," "when," and "where"). The objectivist traditions referred to earlier make Germans very linear thinkers, with a desire for facts, figures, details, and evidence. (Just look at the advertising in Germany: products and services are rarely sold solely on their emotional appeal; rather, facts and figures make up the justification for the purchase.)

FORMAL OR INFORMAL? German culture can be quite formal, but that does not mean that Germans cannot be warm, sincere, and friendly; in fact, they often are, but with individuals whom they have grown to know and trust. Although it can take a long time, once relationships have been formed with Germans, they can be informal and casual. However, remember that there is a time and a place for everything in Germany, so one can be warm and friendly at home with friends, while still maintaining the required distance at work. Formalities are a way of maintaining cordial and working relationships with individuals until such time as more personal relationships may develop.

Greetings and Introductions

Language and Basic Vocabulary

German is a complicated and challenging language to master: the syntax can be particularly difficult for English speakers. For one thing, concepts are often created by adding words onto already existing ones, making for especially long words. Nouns, prepositions, adjectives, and verbs must all agree grammatically. Even more confusing to English speakers, verbs are usually at the end of the sentence (another reason why it is important to let German speakers finish their thoughts, or else you won't really know what they mean to say!). Finally, the language is structured so that matter-of-fact statements can sound like commands, which does not easily sit well with independent-minded Americans. Try to avoid reacting negatively, and remember that Germans can be more monochronic and low-context in their speech.

Complicating matters even more are the dialectical differences throughout the country: the Bavarian dialect, for example, is very different from the one that is spoken in Hamburg, and even German speakers may not fully understand one another's terminology and accents. There is a unique dialect in the region just north of Switzerland where the German sounds somewhat singsongy, while the German spoken in the east is more rural and traditional (High German) than the modern (Low) German spoken in the north and the middle west.

Finally, it should be remembered that English is the second language in Germany today, although older people and Germans from the east speak and understand far less of it than younger people and Germans from the west. Business managers in the western part of Germany typically understand enough English to use it in business (this may not be the case with businesspeople in the east, where Russian was the second language spoken and taught during the communist era).

Here are some basic German terms and their meaning in English:

guten Morgen	good morning
guten Tag	good day
guten Abend	good evening
Grüss Gott	a greeting in southern Germany
Hallo	hello (informal)
auf Wiedersehen	good-bye
bitte	please
danke	thank you
auf Wiederhören	good-bye (on telephone)
Entschuldigen Sie bitte	pardon me
Wie geht es Ihnen?	How are you?
sehr gut	very well
Herr	Mr.
Frau	Mrs.

Honorifics for Men, Women, and Children

Herr (Mr.) and *Frau* (Mrs.), plus the family name, are an absolute must for you to use when introduced to adults. Unless or until your German colleague specifically invites you to use first names, and despite how he or she might refer to you (after all, Germans know that Americans usually prefer informality), you must always use the family name plus the correct German honorific (*Fraülein*— Miss—is rarely used these days, unless one is clearly speaking to a child or a very young, single, female adult). Sometimes these honorifics are used with titles in place of names, but never in place of titles; for example, a doctor is referred to as "Herr Doktor" or "Herr Doktor Schmidt," but never just "Doktor Schmidt" or just "Herr Schmidt." If someone has several titles, all must be used in descending order of importance; for example, a doctor who is also a professor (the higher rank) is referred to as "Herr Professor Doktor Schmidt," and his wife, who may or may not be a professor or a doctor herself, is nevertheless correctly referred to as "Frau Doktor Schmidt." Children in Germany are expected to be respectful and not overly conversational when speaking with adults, and must always use honorifics when referring to adults.

If you speak any German at all, by all means use it (your efforts will be appreciated), but be sure to use the formal pronoun *Sie* ("you") at the beginning, and do not switch to the *du* (informal "you") form unless and until your German colleague has specifically invited you to or uses it him- or herself. In the past, this switch from the formal to the informal itself was celebrated with a formal event to mark the occasion (the *Brüderschaftrinken*); it is not done nearly as much today, but it still can be observed, especially in the more rural and conservative south. The ceremony usually involved two men, each of whom would raise a stein of beer and, while linking arms and maintaining direct eye contact, would toast one another and their bonded friendship, and invite the other to refer to him as one would a brother. One of the ensuing privileges was the right to "be familiar" and use informal pronouns and first names. While Germans generally maintain formality with foreigners, especially in the work setting, for an extended period of time, expect them to loosen up a bit sooner than the French in most circumstances; this is especially true when they are with Americans, as Germans understand that Americans are almost immediately informal, and enjoy "trying on" unusual American ways. For casual contacts (e.g., with waiters, store help, etc.), just use *Herr* or *Frau* without the name. It is very important to greet people at work or in stores or restaurants with an appropriate *guten Tag* or *gute Nacht,* as well as an *auf Wiedersehen* upon leaving. A more appropriate form of good-bye in Germany today, especially in quick, casual situations, is *Tschüss,* which sounds like the English word choose, but pronounced with a sibilant *s* (not *z*): it means nothing more than "bye."

The What, When, and How of Introducing People

Always wait to be introduced to strangers before taking that responsibility upon yourself. Germans are most comfortable with a third-party introduction whenever possible. Try to ensure that for yourself ahead of time. Do not presume to seat yourself at a formal gathering: if possible, wait to be told where to sit. With whom, when, and how you are introduced is a key to understanding how you are perceived and how Germans fit you into their hierarchy. If you are not so instructed, assume that men will sit and stand on the outside when with women. Shake hands with everyone individually in a group when being introduced and before departing: the American group wave is not appreciated. Avoid complimenting your colleague until you have a close personal relationship: they are unnecessary in the German context. Once you greet someone you will encounter later that day in the same circumstances (e.g., at the office), there is no need to greet them again. Kissing is a common greeting once women and men have established a relationship; usually, there is one quick kiss on both cheeks (actually an "air kiss," first on the left side, and then the right). In more conservative regions and among older Germans, a man might greet a woman by raising her hand to his lips. The use of business cards is very common; if possible, you should have your business card translated into German on the reverse. Be sure to put any educational degrees, your full title or position, and any advanced professional group affiliation you may have on the German-translated side of the card (the Germans want to know as much about your background and qualifications as possible).

Physical Greeting Styles

The handshake is common. The German version is similar to the American handshake, but usually does not last quite as long. It is done quickly and firmly with a few quick shakes between two men; but not as robustly between men and women or two women. The handshake should be accompanied by the appropriate greeting (see the list of German terms). Smiling and other nonverbal forms of communication need not accompany the handshake when it is between people who have not met previously. Men should wait until a woman extends her hand before reaching for it, and women may take the lead in extending their hand or not. Men must remove their gloves when shaking hands with a woman, but a woman need not remove her gloves when shaking hands with a man. If more than two people are greeting each other, it is not correct to reach across arms to shake hands (making a kind of *X*). Informal body gestures are not appreciated during the first introduction between strangers, so avoid back-slapping, and other forms of touching. Eye contact during the introduction is

serious and direct, and should be maintained as long as the individual is addressing you.

Communication Styles

Okay Topics / Not Okay Topics

Okay: current events, politics (as long as you know what you are talking about),
the arts, sports (very big, especially soccer), music, and philosophy. Germans
tend to shy away from confrontation when carrying on social conversations
with new acquaintances; once relationships are established, however, opinions
can fly. They are usually very inquisitive about aspects of American life in
which they have a particular interest. *Not okay:* Do not give your opinion about
things German unless you absolutely know what you are talking about. Do not
inquire about a person's occupation in casual conversation. Americans often
begin a conversation with "So, what do you do?"; this is too personal in Europe,
and is often not the most interesting topic of conversation. Also not okay: personal financial discussions, questions about private family matters (the family is
sacred), personal background, and the like. Be careful not to raise issues related to the world wars, although such topics do emerge: most Germans carry a
great burden of guilt about the Third Reich (the term *Nazi* is generally not used
in Germany). And remember, Germans have strong feelings and misgivings
about each other (easterners and westerners), which they may or may not share
with you.

Tone, Volume, and Speed

Discussions between strangers usually start out politely restrained; in public or
during your first business meetings, the conversational tone can be slightly subdued and matter of fact. Once people get to know each other, though, the volume can suddenly increase, especially over points of disagreement: do not be
put off by this. Never interrupt others; let each speaker make his or her point
and then respond. At meals, once the beer or wine flows, the conversation
should be easy and conducive to good digestion.

Physical Gestures and Facial Expressions

The okay sign formed by having the tip of the thumb meet the tip of the forefinger should be avoided; if you want to gesture okay, give the "thumbs up"
sign instead. At the end of a meeting, Germans usually signal their approval
or appreciation by gently rapping their knuckles on the tabletop instead of
applause.

Waving and Counting

The thumb represents the number 1, the index finger the number 2, and so on. It
is insulting to beckon someone with the forefinger (instead, turn your hand so
that the palm faces up and motion inward with all four fingers at once). If you
need to gesture for a waiter, make a small, subtle motion with your hand as if
you were writing (it indicates that you want the check).

Physicality and Physical Space

Germans tend to stay slightly farther apart than North Americans. Never speak with your hands in your pockets: always keep them firmly at your side when standing. If women or men must cross their legs, it should never be ankle over knee. Remember, even in public, formal is always better than informal: no gum chewing, ever; don't slouch; and don't lean against things. At meetings, take your cue from the senior participants as to how informal or formal one should act, dress, and sit.

Eye Contact

At times, the eye contact can be very intense and disconcerting to many Americans. It is important not to interpret this behavior as a way of intentionally trying to make you uncomfortable. It is how the Germans (and Europeans generally) show their interest. Conversely, if you look away, your behavior will say to your German colleague that you are either disinterested or rude. Either way, maintain eye contact when it is made with you. Even in public between strangers, eye contact can be direct. Therefore, do not interpret stares in public as necessarily threatening: they may not be meant that way. Standing in someone's line of sight in order to make eye contact is a way of saying "I want to talk with you"; be sure you do this judiciously, and only where and when such an act does not challenge the order of things (i.e., don't do it if it interrupts an ongoing conversation unless you really mean to do that).

Emotive Orientation

While Germans generally appreciate matter-of-fact formality, they can become very emotional if their sense of order, organization, and normalcy is challenged.

Protocol in Public

Walking Styles and Waiting in Lines

The importance of order and organization is apparent even on German streets: men walk on the curbside of women; younger people walk on the curbside of older people; if there are two men and one woman, one man walks on each side of the woman. German men typically open doors and enter rooms ahead of women, and continue to hold the door open once inside: this is particularly true in restaurants (the custom originated during a period in time when the man would have to enter first and clear the space of any troublemakers before inviting a woman to follow him in). Germans are generally quite orderly in public. The one exception is driving behavior, particularly on the notorious autobahns; Germans can be aggressive on their highways, probably due to their incredible cars.

Behavior in Public Places: Airports, Terminals, and the Market

As with many European cultures, mass marketing and customer orientation is a new idea in Germany, with its tradition of artisanal quality and bourgeois production. Customer service as a concept is growing, but not fully institution-alized. Store hours are typically not built around customer convenience (many stores are closed on weekends, and most evenings, by law). As in much of Europe, if you touch the produce in food markets, you buy it; in goods stores, it may be difficult for you to return a product unless there is a flaw in it. Smoking is on the decline, although no-smoking areas in restaurants and other public places are rare (there are no-smoking cars on German trains, however). On the street, do not cross against a red light; wait patiently on the curb instead until the light turns green (on streets where there are no traffic lights, be very careful when crossing: the cars do not necessarily stop for pedestrians). Germans, being private and formal (as are most Europeans) generally will not bother you in public places, but are open to casual chat if they are not preoccupied.

The telecard is appearing more and more frequently at German phones, but most still accept coins (put in 5 DM—deutsche marks—to get a dial tone); pub-lic phones are usually color-coded, with pink receivers indicating that it accepts coins.

Bus / Metro / Taxi / Car

Driving is on the right, but people pass very quickly on the left. The metros generally shut down after midnight or 1 A.M. Your best bet for catching a cab is at designated taxi stands (hotels are good places, but they often charge more for the same ride: a hotel surcharge is added to the meter fare, in some cases). Bring food and water on board a commuter train if your trip is a long one, as there may not be a café car. Consider booking first class on trains, if possible: the fare difference is often not that great, but the comfort is.

Tipping

Tips are generally no more than 10 percent or slightly less, for restaurants and taxis; more is considered nouveau and gauche, and totally inappropriate in the eastern half of Germany. Porters and hotel help get 1 DM per bag or service rendered, theater and bathroom attendants usually 1 DM. Restaurants usually have the 10 percent tip already included on the bill, but if you are unsure, it's okay to ask if service is included or not. Even if it is, it is still appropriate to leave a few pfennigs if the service was particularly good.

Punctuality

Never be late, if you can avoid it, under any circumstance, either social or busi-ness, anywhere in Germany (although as you go south or east, the obsession with timeliness is less severe). This is especially so in the highly organized world of the urban, northwestern German. Trains will leave without you if you are a minute late in Frankfurt; meetings will begin without you in Düsseldorf if you are five minutes late; and dinner parties will begin promptly at 8 P.M., leav-ing you and the other guests slightly embarrassed if you arrive "fashionably late" at 8:20 P.M., in Köln. If you must be late for any reason, it is *absolutely essential* to call and let someone know of your problem—and you should have an appropriate explanation, as well. No kidding.

Dress

Clothing is formal for both men and women, no matter the occasion—business or social, at work, in a restaurant, or on a street. Formal in this case means, at least in the office, a dark suit and tie for men, and a business suit or skirt and blouse for women. Khakis and other informal wear for men are not appropriate in a business setting. On the street, informal may mean jeans and sneakers (they should always be neat and clean), though that is more common as clothing to wear at the gym, the beach, or while jogging (women do not wear sneakers to work); for a social gathering, informal more often than not means tastefully coordinated clothes, although not necessarily a jacket and tie for men (it rarely means jeans, sneakers, and T-shirts). "Formal" usually means formal evening wear, which is very dressy by American standards. Most restaurants do not require a tie for men, although the upscale restaurants expect both men and women to dress well. In the south, you may see some uniquely traditional German clothing worn casually on weekends or on the street, such as lederhosen.

Seasonal Variations

There are four very distinct seasons in Germany, and one needs to dress accordingly. Summers can be hot, and winters can be long, damp, and very cold, with a bone-chilling east wind from the Danubian plain beginning in October and lasting sometimes till the end of April.

Colors

Bright colors and patterns are not suitable for business wear, either for men or for women.

Styles

In the western urban areas, style can be as up-to-date as anywhere else in Europe, although as one moves east and south, styles quickly tend to become much more conservative. In the east, businessmen sometimes wear sport jackets and sweaters in the chilly months.

Accessories / Jewelry / Makeup

Given the German preference for order and symmetry, it shouldn't be surprising that accessories, jewelry, and makeup need to be used judiciously in formal settings. Men and women generally do not use much perfume or cologne.

Personal Hygiene

The preoccupation with cleanliness, sanitation, and health can take on manic proportions in Germany. Even public places are often spotlessly clean. Pharmacies do a bang-up business in herbal and natural remedies and tonics of all types; there are scrubs and cosmetics for every conceivable purpose. Fresh, clean, and natural is the preferred look, always.

Dining and Drinking

Mealtimes and Typical Foods

Even a quick breakfast on the run in a major German city is usually more than a cup of coffee and a roll. Breakfast often also includes cheeses, yogurt, dried cereals, and perhaps some pickled vegetables or fish. It can be substantial.

Lunch was traditionally the main meal of the day, and even in busy cities today it can be a substantial dish of meat or fish, vegetables, and potatoes or noodles. Lunch is usually served from 12 to 1 P.M. Beer or wine typically accompanies all lunches, either business or social, in restaurants, cafés, or workplace cafeterias; mineral water, with or without carbonation, and juice or soft drinks are also available. On Sunday, the family day, the main meal is supper, which is usually served in the middle of the afternoon, and can last well into the evening.

Dinner is usually served from 7 to 8:30 P.M., with 8 P.M. the customary time for dinner parties. The evening meal may be similar to lunch, with meats, fish, vegetables, and dessert. Drinks served with dinner are usually regional beers or wine. Dinner parties usually end at around midnight (but can go much later if all are having a good time).

The *Hofbrau* is a place for conversation, some fine regional beer, and perhaps a snack; it is the German equivalent of the British pub. It is usually open from noon on, and has seating both indoors and outdoors (when weather permits). Just walk right in, sit down or stand, and the waiter will immediately bring a beer over, or ask for your choice. Once you call for the bill, be prepared to pay it; the waiter will generally wait at your table until you pay. You may sit in the hofbrau for as long as you like, and order as much beer or wine as you wish; no one will ask you to move on until you are ready.

Regional Differences

German food does vary, but essentially it is hearty fare designed to get one through a long, cold winter. Sausages and meats of all varieties abound, along with cooked vegetables, potatoes, and noodles (ubiquitous with every meal). Vegetables are well cooked, or preserved in a wonderful variety of tasty pickled dishes. There is a strong French influence in the west, while seafood (eel, trout, herring, etc.) is featured in the north, and heavier noodle-type dishes in the east. A well-prepared wiener schnitzel (a kind of breaded veal cutlet) is an art, and desserts can be large, heavy, and very sweet. Germans freely use dairy cream and butter in most of their cooking.

Typical Drinks and Toasting

Mixed drinks before dinner are not common; however, before the meal one might have an aperitif, consisting of one of many different kinds of herbal liqueurs (these are also drunk after the meal as *digestifs*). They are particularly delightful with a spritz of seltzer water, and are usually served cold. Once the meal gets under way, wine or beer will be served in most cases. Rhine wine, which is usually white and on the slightly sweet side, is usually preferred in Germany, although there are many different kinds that complement many different foods very well. A sweeter wine may be served with dessert, and after the meal a postprandial herbal liquor or liqueur is not unusual.

The most common toasts are *Zum Wohl!* (with wine) and *Prost!* (with beer)—in both cases, generally a wish for good health. It is absolutely essential when making a toast to maintain direct eye contact from the moment the glass is raised to the moment it is placed back down on the table. If many people are being toasted, go around the table and make eye contact with each individual as you make the toast. This becomes even more important as you move west to east through Germany.

Table Manners and the Use of Utensils

Do not begin eating until the host has said, *"Guten Appetit."*

Germans, like all continental Europeans, do not switch knives and forks, as Americans do. The knife remains in the right hand, and the fork remains in the left. When the meal is finished, the knife and fork are laid parallel to each other across the right side of the plate, the tips pointing to the ten o'clock position; the knife should be above the fork, with the blade side pointing in toward the plate. If you put both utensils down on the plate for any real length of time, it is a sign to the waitstaff that you are finished, and your plate may be taken away from you. The fork and spoon above your plate are for dessert. There are often many additional pieces of cutlery; if you're unsure of which utensil to use, always start from the outside and work your way in, course by course. There will be separate glasses provided at your setting for water and white and red wine (after-dinner drink glasses come out after dinner). When not holding utensils, your hands are expected to be visible above the table: this means that you do not keep them in your lap; but instead, rest the wrists on top of the table (never your elbows). At the table, pass all dishes to your left. Salt and pepper shakers or holders should be passed so that the receiving person takes them directly; do not place them down on the table first. In Germany, knives are used only when absolutely necessary. Therefore, do not cut anything with a knife that can be cut easily with the side of a fork: this means, generally, potatoes, usually served in the sliced or *roti* (roasted or sautéed) style. Never cut the lettuce in a salad: deftly fold it with your knife and fork so that it can be picked up in a small bundle with your fork.

Seating Plans

The most honored position is either at the head of the table or in the center, with the most important guests seated first to the left and then to the right of the head of the table. If there is a hosting couple, one partner will be seated at each end of the table. In keeping with the practice elsewhere on the Continent, men and women are seated next to one another, and couples are often broken up and seated next to people they may not have previously known. This is done to promote conversation. Men always rise when women enter the room, and both men and women rise when older people enter or leave a room. Remember, as is the case throughout the Continent, what the Germans call the first floor is really the second floor, with the first floor usually referred to as the lobby or ground floor.

Refills and Seconds

If you do not want more food, leave just a bit on your plate. You may always have additional beverages; drink enough to cause your cup or glass to be less than half full, and it will generally be refilled. Portions are generally about the same size as in the United States.

At Home, in a Restaurant, or at Work

In informal restaurants, you may be required to share a table: if so, do not force conversation; rather, act as if you are seated at a private table. Waitstaff may be summoned by making eye contact; waving or calling their names is very impolite. Breakfast meetings are not common, except perhaps among traveling businesspeople in hotels. The business lunch or dinner is a more widespread practice, but, depending upon how well developed your relationship is with your German colleagues, it is generally not the time to make business decisions. Take your cue from your German associates: if they bring up business, then it's okay to discuss it, but wait to take your lead from their conversation. No gum chewing, ever, at a restaurant or on the street. No-smoking sections in restaurants are still a rarity.

Meals at a German associate's home can be either relaxed or formal; take your cue from the information your host gives you when you are invited. An informal meal will be referred to as the *Abendbrot* (evening bread), while the formal meal is usually referred to as the *Abendessen* (evening meal). It is always best to arrive on time, although here, too, you can get more information at the time of the invitation: if an invitation indicates "c.t." (*cum tempore,* or "with time"), you have a leeway of about fifteen minutes after the stated arrival time; if the invitation indicates "s.t." (*sine tempore,* or "without time"), you are expected to arrive promptly at the hour stated. Once within the home, you will be told where to sit, and there you should remain. Do not wander from room to room: much of the house is really off-limits to guests. At the table, be sure to look for place cards, or wait until the host indicates your seat: do not presume to seat yourself, as the seating arrangement may be predetermined.

Being a Good Guest or Host

Paying the Bill

Usually the one who does the inviting pays the bill, although the guest is expected to make an effort to pay. Sometimes other circumstances determine the payee (such as rank). Making payment arrangements ahead of time so that no exchange occurs at the table is a very classy way to host.

Transportation

It's a very nice idea, when acting as host, to inquire ahead of time as to whether the guests will require transportation. If necessary, you should arrange for taxi service at the end of the meal.

When to Arrive / Chores to Do

If you are invited to dinner at a private home, offer to help with the chores, but you will probably not have to. Do not leave the table until invited to do so. Spouses are often included in business dinners (most commonly if both business associates are married). When it is time to leave, always get up and shake hands with everyone: the group wave is not appreciated. If you are invited to stay overnight at a German home, always leave things tidy and clean up after yourself. By the way, never drop by an associate's home uninvited or unannounced: always phone ahead and ask if it is convenient to stop by.

Gift Giving

In general, gift giving is not common among business associates; it is best not to send a gift at any time, including the holidays, unless you receive one first from your German colleagues. Holiday cards are quite appropriate, particularly as a thank-you for their business during the previous year, and should be mailed in time to be received the week before Christmas.

Gifts are expected for social events, however, especially as thank-yous for private dinner parties. If you choose flowers, bring them with you to the dinner party, and be sure to unwrap them before entering the home or handing them to the hostess. Never send chrysanthemums, heather, or callas (they are used primarily as funeral flowers); also avoid red roses or orchids (these usually indicate romantic intent); and always make sure the bouquet is in odd numbers (an old European tradition). Other good gifts would be fine chocolates, a sweet dessert wine, or an after-dinner liqueur or *digestif* of good quality.

If you are staying with a family, an appropriate thank-you gift would be a high-quality product that represents your country and is difficult to get in Germany: gourmet foodstuffs (maple syrup, pralines, lobsters, etc.), coffee-table books about the United States, or anything that reflects your host's personal tastes (the cap of a famous American team for the football-playing son of the family, for example) is appropriate.

Special Holidays and Celebrations

Major Holidays

Business usually slows down during July, the traditional vacation time, and during the Christmas and New Year's seasons (December 15 to January 5). Holy Week and other Catholic holidays take on greater significance in Catholic areas, especially the south (along with *Faschen,* or the German pre-lenten version of Carnival, usually in February).

January 1	*Neujahr* (New Year's Day)
January 6	*Heilige Drei Könige* (Epiphany)
March/April	*Karfreitag* (Good Friday)
March/April	*Ostersonntag und Ostermontag* (Easter Sunday and Easter Monday)

May 1	*Tag der Arbeit* (Labor Day)
April/May	*Christi Himmelfahrt* (Ascension)
May/June	*Pfingstensonntag und Pfingstenmontag* (Whitsunday and Whitmonday)
May/June	*Fronleichnam* (Corpus Christi)
August 15	*Mariä Himmelfahrt* (Assumption of the Blessed Virgin)
October 3	*Tag der Deutschen Einheit* (German Unity Day)
October 31	*Reformationstag* (Reformation Day)
November 1	*Allerheiligen* (All Saints' Day)
December 25	*Erster Weihnachtstag* (Christmas Day)
December 26	*Zweiter Weihnachtstag* (Boxing Day)
December 31	*Sylvester* (New Year's Eve)

Business Culture

Daily Office Protocols

In Germany, office doors are usually closed (and sometimes locked); knock first (this includes bathrooms) before opening doors, and when leaving rooms, close the doors behind you. Women and men are often treated as equals in Germany today, although this may not be universal across all generations, regions, or industries. Staying late at the office is not necessarily taken as a good sign: it more often will be interpreted as indicating that the individual is incapable of organizing him- or herself well enough to accomplish his or her job in the time permitted. Do not expect people to work over weekends, holidays, or vacations: these times are usually sacred, being reserved for family.

Management Styles

Privacy and individual accomplishment of one's tasks are critical; however, there can be much interaction between senior management and staff, and among team members. Adherence to procedure is believed to be the most effective way of accomplishing a task. Anything out of the ordinary or unusual is usually not appreciated, and must be explained. People and things need to be solid and substantial. The ability to be a smooth-working member of the team is important; sincerity and seriousness, not necessarily friendliness, are preferred attributes. Complimenting and rewarding employees publicly is usually not done.

Boss-Subordinate Relations

Rank most definitely has its privileges in Germany. The hierarchy must be respected, and there are definite routes through life that one follows according to one's rank in society and in the workplace. There can be a rigid chain of command that must be heeded. No matter what field you are in, there is usually a proper way for communicating with particular individuals, and an established procedure one is expected to follow. Deviating from the normal channels will generally make more problems for you, even if your intent is to bypass what appear to be obstacles. Bosses are expected to provide guidance, distribute information, and make decisions; subordinates are expected to provide detailed information and follow the decisions made by their superiors.

The typical large German business organization has essentially three leadership structures:

1. The *Aufsichtsrat*. This is the supervisory board; it approves all major decisions and sets strategy for the organization. It is elected by the shareholders (and/or employees in organizations strongly influenced by unions and worker councils, which in Germany today is most organizations), and it appoints and dismisses the *Vorstand* (the management board) of the company.

2. The *Vorstand*. The management board, appointed by the Aufsichtsrat, conducts the day-to-day business of the organization. The hierarchy is as follows (these titles usually appear on business cards):

Vorsitzender	chairman/president
Stellvertretender Vorsitzender des Vorstandes	deputy chairman
Ordentliches Mitglied des Vorstandes	regular member of the board
Stellvertretendes Mitglied des Vorstandes	deputy member of the board
Generalbevollmachtigter	general manager
Abteilungsleiter	division/department head
Prokurist	corporate secretary (has signing authority)

3. The *Betriebsrat*. The worker's council, represents employees as part of management. The total number of employee representatives on this council depends on the number of employees in the company.

Conducting a Meeting or Presentation

At meetings of peers, there can be open communication and sharing of ideas: in fact, these sessions often serve as information-sharing and decision-making forums in which all individuals are expected to contribute. Under these circumstances, discussions are usually vibrant, with many people speaking; questions are common and interruptions, even of presentations for questions, should be expected. In more formal, conservative organizations, meetings are often gatherings of nonpeers, clearly called together by decision makers in order to gather information from below, clarify goals, and formulate action plans. In these cases, individuals often do not share ideas and are not expected to contribute to mutual problem solving. Facts and figures are essential, and must be clearly outlined and detailed.

Negotiation Styles

Germans respect someone who comes to them with established knowledge and experience. No detail is unimportant, and a carefully planned, logically organized proposal is key. The first meeting may be very matter of fact, with the Germans sizing up you, your organization, and your ideas: it will be conducted in the office. Because time needs to be carefully managed, plan your meeting carefully and well in advance, and prepare a detailed agenda for circulation prior to the scheduled date. Confirm all meetings and the preparations for them well in advance. Casually changing time and place is not appreciated. The best times for meetings are 9 to 10 A.M. and 2 to 3 P.M. (in eastern Germany, Wednesday is not a good day for meetings as it was in the communist days, often the day set aside for organizing the paperwork and reports of the week). Never be late.

Written Correspondence

Your correspondence with German colleagues should be very businesslike, with few references to personal matters. Dates are written using the day/month/year format (with periods in between, not slashes), and an honorific plus a title is as common as an honorific plus the last name. The time of day is written military style; weights and measures are usually given in metric units. Monetary amounts are written so that periods break up the figure into tens, hundreds, and thousands, with a comma separating the marks from the pfennigs (e.g., DM10.000,00 = ten thousand deutsche marks). The traditional language used in openings and closings is:

Dear   *Sehr geehrte Damen und Herren* (plural is used
                     in all cases if you do not know the person)
Very truly yours   *Mit freundlichen Grüssen* or (for bureaucratic or
                     government letters) *Hochachtungsvoll*

**CHAPTER
FIVE**

The Germanic Cultures:
Austria

Note: Please refer to the preceding chapter for information about general Germanic cultural behaviors; the material that follows describes specific Austrian variations on general Germanic customs.

Some Introductory Background and Historical Context on Austria and the Austrians

Never confuse Austrians with Germans. Because of the strong similarities between the two peoples, this is perhaps the most important etiquette rule to be observed in Austria, beyond the statements already made about general Germanic culture in the previous chapter. Yes, Austria is a different nation, with a different history; while Germany was still a loosely organized jumble of princedoms and fiefdoms, Austria had consolidated itself into one of Europe's mightiest political powers, the Austro-Hungarian Empire. Under the powerful rule of the Hapsburgs, in conjunction with the Hungarian monarchs, Austria ruled the central European region for over three hundred years. Austria was always strongly influenced by its German neighbor to the west, its Slavic European neighbors to the north and east, and its Latin neighbors to the south. Austria took its primary language and major western traditions from Germany; from the East, the nation received its color, patience, and flexibility; and from Rome came the nation's religion (the majority of people in Austria are Roman Catholic). Perhaps it is this combination of different cultural traditions that has, in the crucible of history—where no one way stands forever—given Austrians that wise and sublime perspective that they have on the world: that great effort can yield great reward, but that change can be swift and nothing mortal endures; and that in the end, life is to be lived. While consolidating their empire, the Austrians created an aristocracy and a way of life so glittering that it dazzled and defined European manners for three centuries; while keeping the conquering Turks at the gate, Viennese chefs created the croissant, using the symbol of the Islamic faith, the crescent-shaped moon, in celebration of the Austrian victory—to be eaten while drinking the coffee that the Turks brought with them on their way to unconquerable Vienna; and while Europe stumbled from war to war, the Austrians were waltzing to their Strauss, singing along with Mozart, philosophizing with Schopenhauer, and musing with Freud.

An Area Briefing

Politics and Government

The federal government is made up of nine *laender* (provinces), which function fairly independently from each other in the federal system. The executive branch consists of the federal president and the chancellor (the chancellor has a role similar to that of the prime minister in other parliamentary systems), and the legislative branch consists of the parliament and the chancellor's cabinet.

Religion and Demographics

Despite the fact that its culture and traditions have been heavily influenced by Germanic and Protestant ideals, the majority of the people are Catholic. The resulting Latin influence tempers some of the rigid compartmentalization around task and time found in the more Teutonic Germany. There are also small minorities of many other groups. Being surrounded by other eastern European peoples, Austria shares some of the intolerance toward others who are different that is rampant in the region. There is a suspicion of Hungarians in the north, and a fear of Slavs to the east and south. There is, however, a strong comfort level with Germans and Swiss to the west.

Fundamental Cultural Orientations

1. What's the Best Way for People to Relate to One Another?

Much of what has been said about Germany applies to Austria, with the additional consideration that Austria is essentially a more homogeneous culture, and more tradition-bound. This means that there is a strong class system in Austria, and hierarchies are powerful and often hidden. Membership in the right strata of society is a critical determinant of how one lives, and allegiance to one's group and its ways is a powerful force in Austrian behavior. Knowing the right person in the right place is key.

2. What's the Best Way to View Time?

Punctuality and monochronic compartmentalization are important (though perhaps not quite as much as it is in Germany), but the important distinction for Austrians is their orientation to the past. There is little faith in the future, and a resignation to working with the flawed present, but they do find glory in their past achievements. Austrians work to hold on to what they have achieved, not necessarily in the belief of creating a better and sunnier tomorrow.

3. What's the Best Way for Society to Work with the World at Large?

Essentially, Austria has a more formal, structured, and conservative culture than Germany today. In this sense, it is less flexible, more ritualized, and "old-fashioned" (at least, "old-favoring"). Change is not thought to be implicitly good for its own sake, and the reasons for doing things differently from the way they have been done, unless clear and obvious, must be provided—often over and over again.

Greetings and Introductions

In addition to the very formal way of greeting individuals who are not well known, women in particular may be treated with a significantly greater amount of ritualized respect by men. Some older Austrians, in fact, may take the woman's hand (always after she has offered it) and raise it to their lips. It is important that the hand not actually touch the lips, and that the kiss be merely symbolic.

Communication Styles

Okay Topics / Not Okay Topics

Okay: You might want to bone up on anything cultural that is specifically Austrian: Austrian music (mainly classical), Austrian art and architecture, and Austrian history, for example. All of this demonstrates an awareness of the specialness of Austria, which will be appreciated by Austrians, who have a keen nose for people who fail to make a distinction between them and their German cousins. *Not okay:* Be sure not to mention Austria's role during World War II. Don't make idle commitments ("I'll stop up and see you next week"): Austrians will expect you to mean it, and they know you don't. It sounds very shallow to them.

Tone, Volume, and Speed

A major distinction between Austria and Germany is the fact that the Austrians are somewhat more tolerant of fooling around than are the Germans. Austrians have a great sense of humor, and they will accept your joking around as long as you are self-deprecating: if you are teasing others, it can be seen as putting them down, and that is definitely not appreciated.

Waving and Counting

Unlike many other cultures, in Austria you may gesture to someone to come over by raising your hand and sticking your index finger up (just be sure not to wiggle it).

Emotive Orientation

While Austrians generally appreciate matter-of-fact formality, they can become very emotional if their sense of order, organization, and normalcy is challenged.

Tipping

Restaurants usually have a 10 percent tip already included on the bill, but if you are unsure, it's okay to ask if service is included or not. In these cases, it is still appropriate to leave a schilling or two if the service was particularly good.

Dress

In Austria, both men and women may be seen from time to time in more traditional clothing, even for work. For example, they might wear loden (a heavy wool cloth usually in earth colors) and jackets and sweaters with traditional-based designs. Such outfits are acceptable at most work and social situations, and on the street.

Dining and Drinking

Mealtimes and Typical Foods

In Austria, breakfast (*Frühstück*): coffee is typically served with hot milk and referred to as *Melange*. Lunch (*Mittagessen*) and dinner (*Abendessen*) both are usually substantial meals: the noodles and schnitzel you had from lunch might also show up for dinner, and quick luncheon sandwiches are not as common in Austria as they are in Germany. There is also usually a late afternoon break (around four o'clock) for coffee and light refreshments (it's called *Jause*). You might see a variety of different restaurants:

Beise: A place to stop for coffee and snacks or a drink.

Kaffeehaus: Here's where you can linger for hours over one cup of coffee: you will never be thrown out. You can even get newspapers to read (for free!) as long as you return them to the long racks from which they hang (and they are usually available in many different languages).

Keller (cellar): An informal, friendly place that serves native Austrian dishes.

Heuriger and Stube: These restaurants offer wine and beer, plus light refreshments.

Konditorei: Pastries (and sometimes specialty sandwiches) are featured here, and can be washed down with tea or coffee.

Evening dinner parties at a home in Austria will probably not last as long as they might in some of the more cosmopolitan cities in Germany. They will often be over by 11 or 11:30 P.M.—certainly before midnight.

Typical Drinks and Toasting

Because tea was brought by the Turks and other Middle Easterners to Austria, it is sometimes drunk the eastern way: it is served in a glass, and sugar cubes are placed between the teeth in the front, so that as one sips the hot tea, it passes over the sugar cubes, sweetening the tea as it goes down. In addition, there are a staggering number of after-dinner (and before!) aperitifs, *digestifs*, and fruit and herbal eaux-de-vie. The most popular are slivovitz (made from plums), kirsch (made from cherries), and *himbeergeist* (made from herbs and raspberries). The "national liqueur" is *stors* (an herbal concoction).

Gift Giving

The Austrian variation on German customs is that—as a remnant of eastern influences, perhaps—it *is* appropriate for good and trusted business colleagues to give each other gifts, either on the holidays or to celebrate the completion of an important and successful business deal. Good gifts include brandies, liquors, or something that reflects your homeland or the personal tastes and preferences of the recipient (as long as the gift is high quality and is difficult to obtain in Austria). It is worth mentioning that the business dinner is not as common in Austria as it is in Germany: if there is a business meal, it is the long and relaxing, trust-building exercise of the business lunch. In Austria, dinners among business associates are usually reserved to celebrate or seal the deal once it is made (in this case, spouses can be invited).

Special Holidays and Celebrations

Major Holidays

Business usually slows down during July, the traditional vacation time, and during the Christmas and New Year's seasons (December 15 to January 5). Holy Week and other Catholic holidays are very important in Austria.

January 1	*Neujahrstag* (New Year's Day)
January 6	*Heilige Drei Könige* (Epiphany)
March/April	*Karfreitag* (Good Friday)
March/April	*Ostersonntag und Ostermontag* (Easter Sunday and Easter Monday)
May 1	*Staatsfeiertag,* or *Tag der Arbeit* (Labor Day)
April/May	*Christi Himmelfahrt* (Ascension)
May/June	*Pfingstensonntag und Pfingstenmontag* (Whitsunday and Whitmonday)
May/June	*Fronleichnam* (Corpus Christi)
August 15	*Mariä Himmelfahrt* (Assumption of the Blessed Virgin)
October 26	*Nationalfeiertag,* or *Tag der Fahne* (National Holiday, or Flag Day; usually celebrated by climbing in the Alps!)
November 1	*Allerheiligen* (All Saints' Day)
December 8	*Unbeflekte Empfängnis* (Immaculate Conception)
December 25	*Weihnachten* (Christmas Day)
December 26	*Stefanstag* (Saint Stephen's Day)

The Germanic-Latin
Cultures: Switzerland

Some Introductory Background on Switzerland and the Swiss

"Unity, Yes; Uniformity, No!", the Swiss national motto, provides a quick insight into this singular land. Switzerland today is a confederation (the CH sticker you see on the back of those cars in Switzerland stands for Confederation of Helvetia, the formal name for the country) of loosely affiliated, and rather independent-minded, counties or cantons (twenty-six, to be exact). These cantons are divided roughly into German-speaking northern and central Switzerland, French-speaking western Switzerland, and Italian-speaking southern Switzerland. The German culture and language are by far the most influential, and affect the majority of the population; next is the French, and finally the Italian. There is also a small indigenous culture in the central eastern region of Switzerland known as Romansh, which is also the name of the unique language spoken there (only one percent of the Swiss people speak Romansh). Because German language and culture have had the greatest influence on the people's behaviors, much of what we describe as appropriate German behavior not only applies to the German portion of Switzerland, but, in fact, would, with some modification, also be correct in much of the rest of the country as well (with the important exceptions noted in a later section in this chapter). Equally, we can refer to French behavior (with a mixture of German) to describe the French-speaking Swiss, and Italian behavior (with a mixture of German) to describe the Italian-speaking Swiss. Each region speaks a dialect of their mother language that is recognizable to speakers of German, French, and Italian; however, the German that is spoken by most Swiss is a strong variant, known as Schweizerdeutsch (Swiss German), with a different pronunciation and many unique words.

Switzerland has been described as a landlocked island, and the topography and geography of the country explains a lot about Swiss behavior, protocols, and attitudes. The massive Alpine ranges that define the country also define the Swiss character. The Swiss have been described by outsiders as ferociously insular and protective, stubborn, and resistant to any outside influence; and when one looks closely, one begins to see similar attitudes in individual Swiss toward other Swiss from the other side of the mountain. In preindustrial eras (and to some extent, even today), before telephones, trains, and laptops, communicating with one's neighbor just a few miles away was often impossible, due to the imposing mountain standing in between. Those same mountains have protected the Swiss against outsiders, from Hannibal right on through Napoléon (after whose wars Switzerland declared itself nominally neutral), while keeping the Swiss relatively free to develop a way of life, perfected over time, that integrated the different Swiss nationality traits into one well-run and orderly, clocklike machine. It is not coincidental that the product images that come to mind when one thinks of Switzerland are reflections of Swiss German and Latin character: chocolate, finance, and clocks. This is not to say that the clock always runs smoothly; there have been times that this confederation has been held together only with difficulty. Today, the Swiss face one of their greatest challenges: how to maintain the best of what they have created while remaining flexible to the demands of an encroaching world that high mountains cannot keep out. The technological invasion of contemporary Switzerland may be one the people cannot protect themselves against.

Some Historical Context

The political entity known as Switzerland was created out of several provinces of the Holy Roman Empire in the fourteenth century. These provinces loosely cooperated with each other against powerful Teutonic princes in the north, royal French troops in the west and south (northern Italy at the time was ruled by the French), and Austro-Hungarian might from the east. Since the Napoleonic Wars, Switzerland has maintained a formal policy of neutrality—not because it takes no position on European disputes, but rather because it has viewed neutrality as the most effective way to preserve the confederation when more powerful European forces fight. To ensure this neutrality, curiously, requires massive defense: today, Switzerland is, per capita, the most heavily armed nation in the world.

An Area Briefing

Politics and Government

Politically, each of the nation's twenty-six cantons is highly independent and vigorously insular. Nevertheless, the Swiss federal government does function with a bicameral parliament, a president, and a federal judiciary. There is no monarchy, and never has been (although there were feudal lords and princes over various cantons at various times before confederation).

Schools and Education

As with most Germanic cultures, there is an apprenticeship system in Switzerland that links the school system to industry, and makes both responsible to the other. After elementary school (up through age twelve), children can either go to a secondary/apprentice school (*Realschule*) or a secondary school with an emphasis on developing academic skills (*Sekundarschule*). Students in the *Realschule* go directly on to *Lehre,* or the apprenticeship version of high school, while students on the academic track can move on to either the *Lehre* or the *Gymnasium* (middle school), where they can study modern languages, math and science, Latin and Greek, or economics. Students from the *Gymnasium* have the additional option of going on to a university (*Universität*) at age twenty. All men in Switzerland are required to serve in the military for several weeks per year up to age forty.

Religion and Demographics

Despite having been the hotbed of the revolutionary Calvinist or Protestant Reformation in the fifteenth century, curiously, Switzerland today is still predominantly Roman Catholic. There is no doubt, however, that the culture was profoundly influenced by radical Protestant reformist ideals, which conveniently justified the ruggedly strong, individualistic traditions of the rural mountain folk as well as the emerging capitalist burghers.

Fundamental Cultural Orientations

Note: The cultural behavior of the Swiss is roughly similar to that which has been described for Germans, with a strong influence from France for French-speaking Swiss, and some influence from Italy for the smaller Italian-speaking (southern Ticino region) Swiss. Nevertheless, there are some overarching Swiss-specific additions (and, in some cases, exceptions) appropriate to all Swiss that are noted below.

1. What's the Best Way for People to Relate to One Another?

OTHER-INDEPENDENT OR OTHER-DEPENDENT? For the most part, Switzerland would have to be described as an other-dependent culture, because, despite the strong individualist nature of most Swiss, they are dependent on each other as a group for their success against "others" from the outside. This other-dependency, even in the face of individual decision making, is revealed in the way that even superiors in Swiss business organizations, to a degree greater than that in other Germanic cultures, usually do not make decisions until they are confident that all involved in or affected by the decision have "bought into" it. On the street, there is strong pressure to behave in ways that support the greater whole despite the strong tendency toward individualism; therefore, people cannot walk against the red light, wash their cars on Sunday morning, or make too much noise too late on a Saturday night. In terms of decision making, other-dependency increases in Italian- and French-speaking Switzerland, and decreases as one moves into the more individualistic German-speaking regions.

HIERARCHY-ORIENTED OR EGALITY-ORIENTED? Swiss hierarchy can be rigid, and those on top make decisions that are usually unquestioned. Nevertheless, the strong other-dependency noted above dampens the style with which rank and authority are demonstrated, so that those higher up do not flaunt their authority, and make decisions "quietly." In interpersonal relations, those with seniority, rank, and authority have the freedom to act with humility and kindness. If there is one area where status is ostensibly demonstrated, it is with the car that one drives and where one parks in the company lot. This usually makes everything very clear. Hierarchy and rank become even more rigid as one moves from the German-speaking areas to the French- and Italian-speaking areas (very structure- and hierarchy-oriented).

RULE-ORIENTED OR RELATIONSHIP-ORIENTED? Rules in Switzerland are as vital as they are in Germany—even more so in German-speaking Switzerland. There tends to be a more lax interpretation of the predominance of rules over relationships as one moves from German-speaking Switzerland to French-speaking Switzerland: the balance shifts to about fifty-fifty in the Italian-speaking sections.

2. What's the Best Way to View Time?

MONOCHRONIC OR POLYCHRONIC? Switzerland is predominantly a very monochronic culture (remember those Swiss clocks!); nevertheless, there is a variation as one moves from the rigidly monochronic German-speaking areas (avoid being even five minutes late for a meeting or a dinner party in Zurich), to the more flexible French-speaking section (one might arrive five minutes late for that same meeting or dinner party in Geneva), to the even more relaxed Italian-speaking areas in the south (waiting ten or fifteen minutes for your friend to arrive at the ski resort in the southern Alps is not uncommon).

RISK-TAKING OR RISK-AVERSE? Switzerland is generally a risk-averse culture. The Swiss will require substantial information to justify a program or procedure: the German-speaking Swiss will need to see a reliable method; the French-speaking Swiss will require a clearly outlined logical process in which all details are considered; and the Italian-speaking Swiss will need all the facts to be packaged in a presentation that looks as good as it is.

3. What's the Best Way for Society to Work with the World at Large?

LOW-CONTEXT DIRECT OR HIGH-CONTEXT INDIRECT COMMUNICATORS? People are frank and direct in German-speaking areas, more restrained and discursive in the French-speaking area, and emotive and more associative in the Italian-speaking area.

PROCESS-ORIENTED OR RESULT-ORIENTED? The Swiss are a deductive, logical, and detail-conscious people.

FORMAL OR INFORMAL? A formal culture exists in all three regions; the Swiss, in fact, are known for their reserve and their conservative nature. While there is a more relaxed feeling among the rural Swiss, it is still only evident among those with whom one has established a relationship, which can take a long time. Until that all-important relationship (built on dependability and trust) is established, the Swiss can appear standoffish and formal. It is best to follow the formalities until you are invited to become more informal.

Greetings and Introductions

Language and Basic Vocabulary

Please refer to the sections on the German, French, and Italian languages for general notes and specific phrases. In addition, please remember that the Swiss, especially in business, generally speak good English, although they may be hesitant to use it. Any German, French, or Italian you know and use will win you allies among your appropriate Swiss counterparts; it is a sign that you are making a sincere effort to build a personal relationship based on respect and trust, and are trying to put them at ease with what is for some a third or fourth language to master. German (the Swiss Schweitzerdeutsch form) is the major language.

Honorifics for Men, Women, and Children

Please refer to the sections on German, French, and Italian honorifics. In addition, many Swiss names are hyphenated (especially the French names); in such cases, the full name must always be used (for example, Anna-Marie Cartier, once you are invited to use her first name, is always Anna-Marie, never just Anna). In German-speaking Switzerland use *Herr* and *Frau* (avoid *Fraülein:* it is usually reserved for female children and young adolescents); in French-speaking Switzerland use *monsieur* and *madame* (avoid *madamoiselle:* it is usually reserved for female children and young adolescents); and in Italian-speaking Switzerland use *signore* and *signora* (avoid *signorina:* it is usually reserved for female children and young adolescents).

The What, When, and How of Introducing People

In addition to the German, French, and Italian rules regarding greeting styles stated in those chapters, a visitor to Switzerland should say *grüezi* (generally meaning "hello") in the German-speaking areas, *bonjour* in the French-speaking areas, and *buon giorno* in the Italian-speaking areas when meeting someone for the first time.

Physical Greeting Styles

In addition to the appropriate German, French, and Italian introductions (see those sections in this book), here are some Swiss variants: in French-speaking Switzerland, women and men (and women and women) who are close friends will embrace and kiss once on each cheek; women in Italian-speaking Switzerland embrace, but generally do not kiss; men in either of these regions will embrace close friends, but do not kiss; and in the German-speaking areas, kissing, between anyone, usually is done only between very good friends (who also might not have seen each other for a long time), but then might take the form of three kisses (a single kiss on alternating cheeks, done three times). In all cases, to be sure, follow the local lead!

Communication Styles

Okay Topics / Not Okay Topics

Okay: Inquiries about the Romansh culture and "Schwingen" (a unique form of Swiss wrestling, which is a very popular sport), skiing, or other Alpine traditions are very much welcome. *Not okay:* Be sure *not* to discuss the Swiss military or the meaning of Swiss neutrality. The Swiss are extremely sensitive about these topics, as well as their role during the world wars, and any discussion about this, unless brought up and prompted by the Swiss themselves, will not endear you to them.

All aspects of nonverbal behaviors, such as gestures, eye contact, waving and counting, and physical space, follow the rules for German, French, or Italian cultures in their corresponding regions in Switzerland.

Protocol in Public

Customs in the German-speaking, French-speaking, and Italian-speaking regions of Switzerland are, once again, similar to those found in Germany, France, and Italy, respectively.

The telecard is appearing more and more frequently for public telephones; for coin-operated phones, deposit a forty-centime piece (or a larger coin; if the time is unused, you will get a partial refund when you hang up). In the German-speaking region, answer the phone with your last name; in the French-speaking region, answer with "*allo*"; and in the Italian-speaking region, answer with "*pronto.*"

Bus / Metro / Taxi / Car

Driving is on the right, but people pass very quickly on the left. The metros generally shut down after midnight or 1 A.M. Your best bet for catching a cab is at designated taxi stands (hotels are good places, but they often charge more for the same ride: a hotel surcharge is added to the meter fare, in some cases). Consider booking first class on trains, if possible: the fare difference is often not that great, but the comfort is.

Tipping

Tips are usually no more than 10 percent, or slightly less, in restaurants and taxis. Porters and hotel help, as well as theater and bathroom attendants, usually get one Swiss franc. Restaurants usually have the 10 percent tip included already on the bill, but if you are unsure, it's okay to ask if service is included or not. Even if it is, it is still appropriate to leave a few centimes if the service was particularly good.

Punctuality

The safest thing anywhere in Switzerland (even in the more relaxed French- and Italian-speaking regions) is to follow the German monochronic code: you will not be far off if you arrive exactly on time, both for business and social events.

Dress

In Switzerland, all clothes, while more or less subdued, must always be crisp, clean, neat, and in perfect shape. There is no getting around this, no matter how informal you want to be, unless you're fourteen and have just arrived in the country. Another interesting Swiss fashion characteristic is the tendency for men, even in more serious and subdued business suits, to wear white socks. This is an old tradition, harkening back to more physical days spent outdoors, perhaps. And that same executive wearing white socks to the office may change into a jogging outfit on the weekend and wear black dress socks. *Vive la différence!*

Clothing styles for both men and women are more subdued in the German north than in the French- and Italian-speaking sections. In general, one should dress conservatively in Switzerland.

Dining and Drinking

Mealtimes and Typical Foods

Meals in the German, French, and Italian sections of Switzerland are similar in type and follow similar timetables to those in Germany, France, and Italy, respectively. However, the main meal of the day in Switzerland is lunch, which usually lasts from noon until 2 P.M. (or even later, in some cases). The meal generally has three courses, ending with fruit as a dessert. At home, dinner is often a light meal of soup, salad, bread, cold meats, cheeses, and eggs, or perhaps a fondue (see below). The dinner party dinner, however, is quite different, and is the main meal of the day.

In addition to restaurants, there are bars and cafés (in all three languages, the same words are essentially used), where drinks (alcoholic and nonalcoholic) and light refreshments are served. A *Bäckerei* (in German-speaking areas), or *pâtisserie* (in the French-speaking area), or *pasticcerìa* (in the Italian-speaking area) offers sweets and coffee, tea, mineral waters, or sodas. Finally, a *Wursthaus* (in the German-speaking area), or restaurant (in the French-speaking area), or *locanda* (in the Italian-speaking area) features hearty local fare.

Regional Differences

Throughout Switzerland, but especially in the German north, you can find fondue, which is melted cheese (usually Gruyère or Emmentaler—better known as Swiss cheese) mixed with white wine and/or kirsch (a cherry eau-de-vie) and eaten with bits of bread on skewers. You spear a cube of bread and dip the bread cube into the bubbling melted cheese mixture. As you remove the skewer, twist it so the cheese breaks free as you remove the cheese-covered bread (if the bread falls off the skewer into the cheese, the tradition is that you must buy the next bottle of wine for everyone at the table!). Raclette, another cheese dish, is prepared by melting the cheese on little paddles that are usually brought out to the table and placed on a raclette grill. You can add any number of ingredients onto the crispy melted cheese as it grills, such as pearl onions, vegetables, or even bits of thinly sliced meats. A common Swiss breakfast food is *Birchermuesli,* a kind of granola mixture that you will be encouraged to try with milk or yogurt. Most other foods are variants on the French, German, and Italian cuisines.

A special Swiss treat is the Saint Galler bratwurst, a white sausage that is considered to be the Queen of Sausages. You will see these served at separate street stalls, which sell only them. They are eaten alone, or with sautéed onions and a small brown roll (a *Buurli*), but never with mustard.

Typical Drinks and Toasting

Mixed drinks before dinner are not common; however, before the meal one might have an aperitif of wine, vermouth, Campari, or cassis; at the end of the meal, all sorts of after-dinner drinks will be brought out, including grappa (especially in the south), usually made with some sort of herb or plant flavoring; or an eau-de-vie of either cherry (kirschwasser), plum (pflumwasser), or raspberry (framboisie).

The toast in German-speaking Switzerland is *Prost;* in French-speaking Switzerland, *a votre santé* or just *santé;* and in Italian-speaking Switzerland, *salute.* If possible, take the time to clink glasses with everyone at the table (without leaving your seat and moving around the table, if you are already seated at the table).

Table Manners and the Use of Utensils

A particular Swiss variant on the German, French, and Italian rules is that one shows that one is completely finished eating by placing the knife and fork parallel to each other and pointing to the right directly on the middle horizontal of the plate, usually with the fork above the knife. During the meal, if you have finished everything on your plate and would like seconds, merely cross your fork over your knife, making an *X* on your plate (the fork points up toward the left and the knife points up toward the right). And don't worry about asking for seconds—it's considered a compliment to the host and/or hostess—but remember, you have to finish all of your second helping. Please note that the table napkins are usually cloth, and are not necessarily washed between every meal in a house. You may be expected to use an already used napkin if you remain in a home for more than one meal.

Seating Plans

In Switzerland, the place of honor is in the middle of the table (usually down one side) and not at the head or next to the host or hostess (who usually do stay at the head).

Gift Giving

An excellent gift for the Swiss, especially if it's a thank-you for a stay at someone's home, would be some of those really big, fluffy American bath towels (monogrammed would be extra nice). Europeans find them extremely luxurious, and difficult to find.

Special Holidays and Celebrations

Major Holidays

In Switzerland, business slows down during July, the traditional vacation time; during the Christmas and New Year's seasons (from December 15 to January 5); and during the traditional two-week break between school semesters in February (many Swiss take this time off for a ski vacation). Holy Week and other Catholic holidays take on greater significance in Catholic areas, especially the south (along with *Faschen,* or the German pre-Lenten version of Carnival, usually in February). Another major holiday takes place on August 1, which is Independence

(National) Day. Families observe this day by going off and building bonfires into the night: there is much feasting and celebrating.

January 1   *Neujahr/Le Jour de l'An/Anno nuovo* (New Year's Day)
March/April   *Karfreitag/Vendredi Saint/Venerdi Santo* (Good Friday)
March/April   *Ostersonntag und Ostermontag/Lundi de Pâques/*
           Lunedi di Pasqua (Easter Sunday and Easter Monday)
May 1   *Tag der Arbeit/Fête du Travail/Giorno di Lavoro* (Labor Day)
May/June   *Christi Himmelfahrt/Ascension/Ascensione* (Ascension)
May/June   *Pfingstensonntag und Pfingstenmontag/Pentecôte/Pentecoste*
           (Whitsunday and Whitmonday)
August 1   *Nationalfeiertag/Fête Nationale/Giorno Nationale*
           (Independence [National] Day)
September 6   *Erntendankfest/Lundi de jeune federal* (Federal Thanksgiving)
December 25   *Weihnachtstag/Noël/Natale* (Christmas Day)

Business Culture

In addition to the German (and to a lesser extent, the French and Italian) business culture notes found elsewhere in this book, some important customs or practices particular to the Swiss are worth mentioning or emphasizing.

- Be sure to have plenty of business cards on hand. And remember, the Swiss like to put the founding date of the company on the business card; they tend to be impressed if the company is quite old.
- Put your academic degree on your business card. As in Germany and Austria (especially), this carries much clout. If you are a ranking member of an important academic or professional organization, put that on your business card as well, following your title (which should follow your academic degrees, which should follow your name).
- Because of the linguistic complexity of the country, it is acceptable to have business cards in English.
- Envelopes addressed to individuals will generally remain unopened by anyone other than the addressee (even if the addressee has a private secretary). Consider this when addressing time-sensitive documents; you might want to alert the secretary and instruct him or her to forward the information on to the addressee, if necessary.

CHAPTER SEVEN

The Benelux Cultures:
Belgium and Luxembourg

BELGIUM

Some Introductory Background and Historical Context on Belgium and the Belgians

It is not surprising that when looking for a home, the Economic Union (EU) chose Brussels as the "capital of Europe." The history of Belgium makes it the logical seat for that new supranational, pan-European political entity, and this also reveals a singular cultural issue one faces when working with Belgians. The country was formed mainly as a buffer between the two great forces that formed the great north-south European divide: the Protestant, Teutonic north and the Catholic, Latin south. Today, even in this small land, there is a north-south divide that mirrors the greater European division: in the north of Belgium are the Flemish, who are essentially (though not solely) Protestant and speak Flemish (a language very similar to Dutch), and in the south are the Valons, who are essentially (though not solely) Catholic and speak a version of French. The Flemish Belgians refer to their southern cousins as Walloons, and les Valons refer to their northern cousins as les Flamandes. There is little love lost between the two, even though they both are proud of their Belgian nationality. It is not unusual for hostilities to break out from time to time between the two: if you go a few kilometers into Flemish territory and speak French, you will draw uncooperative stares; and if you go a few kilometers south into the Valons and speak Flemish, you will draw the same chilly response. For these reasons, the official Belgian position on all things Flemish and/or Valonaisse, is to recognize both, in all situations. By law, therefore, there is a dual-language policy throughout Belgium, which means, for one thing, that all public signage and official government documents must be in both French and Flemish. The complexity of this issue is revealed most profoundly in Brussels, where French is the unofficial language of choice, yet the city itself is situated in the Flemish part of the country. It is this fact of Belgian life—that the country is a case study in the struggle of Europeans to forge a unified identity out of the European Catholic-Protestant divide—that makes it the natural place to base the EU and the new bureaucracy of western Europe. For better or for worse, the Flemish tend to view their southern Valons cousins as narrow-minded, conservative, family-rooted peasants, while the Valons tend to view their northern Flemish cousins as loutish, nose-to-the-grindstone, insensitive, family-rooted rebels.

As you can see, the family rootedness is perhaps the one single factor that all Belgians can claim in common as a central fact of life, on either side of the divide. Belgians are conservative, home-oriented people. Their first identity, before Valons, Flemish, or Belgian, is as a member of their family. It is no wonder that Belgians have a notorious reputation as difficult people to get to know, very private and insular, and not openly welcoming to outsiders. The Belgian family, Valons or Flemish, is sacred and comes before everything else.

An Area Briefing

Politics and Government

Belgium today is a constitutional monarchy, with the king as the head of state: he and the royal family are generally well respected, so opinions about the Belgian royalty should be kept to a minimum. There is a two-house legislature based on the parliamentary system. The prime minister, as the representative of the majority party in the people's house, is the leader of the government.

Schools and Education

In Belgium, there are primary and secondary schools. A secondary school education puts students on either of three tracks: *l'Enseignement renové* (education ends with the completion of secondary school), *l'École professionelle* (vocational secondary school, leading to a trade), or *l'École secondaire,* leading to university or college. At *l'École secondaire,* students choose either a humanities path (*humanités anciennes*) or a science path (*humanités moderne*). At the college (undergraduate) level, students generally either attend *l'École superieure* for business, nursing, and other specific disciplines, or *l'École normale* for teaching. After college, students may attend *l'université* for law, engineering, medicine, or other advanced disciplines.

Religion and Demographics

Belgium is mainly Catholic in the south (Valons, or Wallonia, when referred to by Flemish-speakers) and Protestant in the north (Flanders, or Flamande when referred to by French-speakers). The divisions reflect the historic struggles for independence of both groups of Belgians from either the Dutch to the north or the Spanish (at the time) to the south.

Fundamental Cultural Orientations

1. What's the Best Way for People to Relate to One Another?

OTHER-INDEPENDENT OR OTHER-DEPENDENT? There is a strong orientation toward the family and intimate or small group allegiances. The individual alone, being on the outside, is an oddity in Belgium; conversely, because of this strong need for affiliation, if you are a foreigner, you have, in a sense, no place to be in Belgium, and it can take time to find a way "in." Groups in Belgium, perhaps because of the size of the country and its population are small, personal, and intimate, however. In this sense, allegiance to a group is merely allegiance to one's own, and does not mean that individuals are subordinate to a team. This uniquely Belgian notion of small-group allegiance is, no doubt, a result of the two major cultures, wherein Catholic mass affiliation is tempered into small group allegiance by Protestant individualism. Building relationships usually takes a long time, trust is built slowly, strangers are held at arm's length, and being invited into a Belgian home is probably one of the world's great achievements.

HIERARCHY-ORIENTED OR EGALITY-ORIENTED? Belgium has a formal culture in which relationships are not made quickly, roles are observed, and rank has its privilege. Nevertheless, there is an easiness about casual relationships when they do occur in Belgium, another example of the combination of the formal and informal, the Catholic and the Protestant, the Flemish and the Valons.

RULE-ORIENTED OR RELATIONSHIP-ORIENTED? The importance of rules, therefore, in Belgium is usually defined in geographic terms: as one moves south, the need for universal systems becomes tempered by particular, specific relationships. This tension is apparent in the way Belgians strive to create a workable bureaucracy (one of the most complex in Europe) that serves all of its people, while the goal of many Belgians is to find a way to live well despite the complexity of social regulations.

2. What's the Best Way to View Time?

MONOCHRONIC OR POLYCHRONIC? Not surprisingly, time relaxes somewhat as one moves south in Belgium. Antwerp, the Flemish center, is punctual and time conscious, even when compared with Brussels, and certainly Bruges. While the clock is always guiding the Belgians, as one moves south, it is simply not the sole reason for what and when things are done.

RISK-TAKING OR RISK-AVERSE? Belgium is a fairly risk-averse culture: perhaps because of the difficulties in managing such a culturally diverse population in such a small area, the need to reduce risk, and build in as many controls and guarantees as possible, in social situations is a constant concern. Without taking many things into consideration, without evaluating all possibilities and all sides to an issue, one runs the risk of not seeing the other point of view, of not building that all-important small-group consensus, and of making decisions that will not fly in the end. One must provide definite proof and evidence, and much detail and data, before a new idea is adopted, and the severe hierarchy requires that any new decision must first be endorsed by the key people at the top. This process of overcoming objections, building consensus, and getting buy-in from the highest of levels can be long and time-consuming.

PAST-ORIENTED OR FUTURE-ORIENTED? Here, again, one finds the mix of two different orientations. Belgium has been described as an extremely conservative culture, and the orientation toward the family and traditional, private ways is strong; nevertheless, in an effort to forge a union between two sometimes opposing forces, there is the equally strong belief that with sincere effort, careful planning, and application Belgians can control their destinies and move forward.

3. What's the Best Way for Society to Work with the World at Large?

LOW-CONTEXT DIRECT OR HIGH-CONTEXT INDIRECT COMMUNICATORS? Here, too, one sees the unique blending of both cultures: at times, Belgians can be very direct and forthright, and in other circumstances (usually when they need to be respectful of rank), they can be very indirect and circumspect in their communication.

PROCESS-ORIENTED OR RESULT-ORIENTED? The strong influence of the French obsession with process, Dutch pragmatism, and German methodology has resulted in an orientation to detail, clear thinking, and deductive causality. How you do things in Belgium is as important as what and why, and all three concerns must be addressed.

FORMAL OR INFORMAL? Informality and spontaneity are reserved for close, intimate relationships of peers; if a hierarchy exists, even in intimate and close relationships (between father and son, for example), following the expected rules is usually more important than casual and breezy relationships.

Greetings and Introductions

Language and Basic Vocabulary

Language, as noted, is an important concern in Belgium. Most businesspeople speak English, and many Belgians, as soon as they hear you speak, will automatically switch into that language for your convenience. Your efforts to speak either French or Flemish will be rewarded only if made in the appropriate areas with the appropriate speakers. Speaking French in a small town outside of Antwerp will generate a less-than-cooperative frisson. And remember, the Dutch-based Flemish language is not Germanic. *Never* make the mistake of confusing the Flemish with the Germans. Flemish Belgians, as most Belgians, have long memories of German occupation, and do not appreciate foreigners incorrectly assuming things Flemish to be German.

Here are some basic terms to use while in Belgium:

For French speakers:

bonjour	good day
bonsoir	good evening
au revoir	good-bye
Je m'appelle . . .	My name is . . .
Comment vous appelez-vous?	What is your name?
heureux (heureuse) de faire votre connaissance	glad to meet you
s'il vous plaît	please
merci	thank you

de rien	you're welcome
pardon	excuse me
je suis desolé(e)	I'm sorry
a bientôt	see you later
oui	yes
non	no
hier	yesterday
aujourd'hui	today
demain	tomorrow
monsieur	Mr.
madame	Mrs./Madam
je comprends	I understand
je voudrais	I would like
je ne comprends pas	I don't understand
c'est dommage	that's too bad

For Flemish speakers:

goedemorgen	good morning
goedemiddag	good afternoon
goedeavond	good evening
goedenacht	good night
dag! or *tot ziens*	good-bye
ja	yes
nee	no
alstublieft	please
dank u	thank you
hartelijk dank	thank you very much
niets te danken	you're welcome
pardon	excuse me
Hoe gaat het?	How are you?
mijnheer	Mr.
mevrouw	Mrs.
juffrouw	Miss
aangenaam kennis te maken	pleased to meet you
Spreekt u Engels?	Do you speak English?

Honorifics for Men, Women, and Children

Use *mijnheer* (Mr.) and *mevrouw* (Mrs.), plus the family name, for Flemish speakers; *monsieur* (Mr.) or *madame* (Mrs.) for French speakers. As in both France and the rest of the Continent, unless or until your Belgian colleague specifically invites you to use first names, and despite how he or she might refer to you, you must always use the family name plus the correct Belgian honorific. Children in Belgium are expected to be respectful and not overly conversational when speaking with adults, and often greet and say good-bye to adults with a kiss. If you speak any French or Flemish at all, by all means use it (your efforts will be appreciated), but be sure to use the formal form of the pronoun "you," and do not switch to the informal form unless or until your Belgian colleague has specifically invited you to or uses it him- or herself. For casual contacts (e.g., with waiters, store help, etc.), just use the appropriate honorific. It is very important to greet people at work, in stores, or in restaurants, with the appropriate greeting according to the time of day.

The What, When, and How of Introducing People

Unlike in other parts of the Continent, if you are with strangers and have not been introduced to anyone by a third party, it is appropriate to introduce yourself to others (with a handshake). However, do not presume to seat yourself at a formal gathering: if possible, wait to be told where to sit. If not otherwise instructed, assume that men will sit and stand on the outside when with women. Shake hands with everyone individually in a group when being introduced and before departing: the American group wave is not appreciated. Once you greet someone you will encounter later that day in the same circumstances (e.g., at the office), there is no need to greet them again. Kissing is a common greeting once women and men have established a relationship; usually, there is one quick kiss on two cheeks (actually an air kiss, first on the left side, and then the right). The use of business cards is very common; if possible, you should have your business card translated into French and/or Flemish on the reverse side.

Physical Greeting Styles

The handshake is common. The Belgian version is similar to the American handshake, but can be a bit softer or lighter. It is done quickly between two men, but not as robustly between men and women, or two women. The handshake should be accompanied by the appropriate greetings (see the list of terms outlined earlier). Smiling and other nonverbal forms of communication need not accompany the handshake when it is between people who have not met previously. Men should wait until a woman extends her hand before reaching for it, and women may take the lead in extending their hand or not. Men must remove their gloves when shaking hands with a woman, but a woman need not remove her gloves when shaking hands with a man. If more than two people are greeting each other, it is not correct to cross over arms to greet someone (making a kind of *X*). Informal body gestures are not appreciated during the first introduction between strangers, so avoid backslapping and other forms of touching. Eye contact should be maintained during the introduction.

Communication Styles

Okay Topics / Not Okay Topics

Okay: current events, politics (as long as you know what you are talking about), the arts, sports (very big, especially soccer), music, philosophy, and Belgian culture. *Not okay:* Do not give your opinion about things Belgian unless you absolutely know what you are talking about. It is especially important to avoid commenting on the French-Flemish problem, or the country's multilingualism. Do not inquire about a person's occupation in casual conversation. Americans often begin a conversation with "So, what do you do?"; this is too personal in Europe, and is often not the most interesting topic of conversation. Also not okay: personal financial discussions, questions about private family matters (the family is sacred), personal background, and the like.

Tone, Volume, and Speed

Discussions between strangers usually start out politely restrained; in public or during your first business meetings, the conversational tone can be slightly subdued and matter of fact, and generally remains so. At meals, once the beer or wine flows, the conversation should be easy and conducive to good digestion.

Physical Gestures and Facial Expressions

The okay sign formed by having the tip of the thumb meet the tip of the forefinger should be avoided; if you want to gesture okay, give the "thumbs up" sign instead. Avoid snapping fingers when conversing: it is considered very rude. Winking at someone usually signals interest or a shared nonverbal understanding: it is not considered in itself a rude gesture. Touching the temples with the forefinger indicates that the other person speaking is "crazy": it does not necessarily mean that what is being said makes sense.

Waving and Counting

The thumb represents the number 1, the index finger the number 2, and so on. It is insulting to beckon someone with the forefinger (instead, turn your hand so that the palm faces up and motion inward with all four fingers at once). If you need to gesture for a waiter, make a small, subtle motion with the hand; if you need the check, make a small, subtle motion with your hand as if you were writing out the bill.

Physicality and Physical Space

Belgians tend to stay slightly farther apart than North Americans are comfortable with in Flemish Belgian, and slightly closer in Valons. Never speak with your hands in your pockets: always keep them firmly at your side when standing. If women must cross their legs, it should not be ankle over knee (this is not an issue for men). Remember, even in public, formal is always better than informal: no gum chewing, ever; don't slouch; and don't lean against things. At meetings, take your cue from the senior participants as to how informal or formal one should act, dress, and sit.

Eye Contact

At times, eye contact can be intense and disconcerting for many Americans, especially in French-speaking Belgium. It is important not to interpret this behavior as a way of intentionally trying to make you uncomfortable; it merely indicates respect and interest. However, direct eye contact between strangers is not appreciated.

Emotive Orientation

Belgians generally appreciate matter-of-fact formality, and even when they are familiar and relaxed with someone, expressing high levels of emotion is generally not appreciated. Keeping things at an even tone is best.

Protocol in Public

Walking Styles and Waiting in Lines

The importance of order and organization is apparent even on Belgian streets: men walk on the curbside of women, younger people walk on the curbside of older people; if there are two men and one woman, one man walks on each side of the woman. In general, Belgians are quite orderly on public lines.

Behavior in Public Places: Airports, Terminals, and the Market

As with many European cultures, mass marketing and customer orientation is a new idea in Belgium, with its tradition of artisanal quality and bourgeois production. Customer service as a concept is growing, but not fully institutionalized. Store hours are typically not built around customer convenience (many stores are closed on weekends and most evenings, by law). As in much of Europe, if you touch the produce in food markets, you buy it; in goods stores, it may be difficult for you to return a product unless there is a flaw in it. Smoking is on the decline, although no-smoking areas in restaurants and other public places are rare. On the street, do not cross against a red light; instead, wait patiently on the curb until the light turns green.

The telecard is appearing more and more frequently at Belgian public phones, but most still accept coins (put in 10 Belgian francs to get a dial tone). People answer the phone by saying, *"Hallo."*

Bus / Metro / Taxi / Car

Driving is on the right, but people pass very quickly on the left. The public transportation system generally shuts down after midnight or 1 A.M. Your best bet for catching a cab is at designated taxi stands (hotels are good places, but often charge more for the same ride: a hotel surcharge is added to the meter fare, in some cases). Consider booking first class on trains, if possible: the fare difference is often not that great, but the comfort is.

Tipping

Tips are generally no more than 10 percent, or slightly less; more is considered nouveau and gauche. No tipping is necessary in taxis. Porters and hotel help get 50 BF per service rendered, theater attendants the same. Restaurants usually have the 10 percent tip already included on the bill, but if you are unsure, it's okay to ask if service is included or not. Even if it is, it is still appropriate to leave a few coins if the service was particularly good.

Punctuality

Try not to be late, if you can avoid it, for social or business occasions anywhere in Belgium, but even more so in the north. If you must be more than fifteen minutes late, it is essential to call ahead and let your business associates or hosts know of your problem—and you should have an appropriate explanation, as well.

Dress

Clothing styles are formal for both men and women, no matter the occasion—business or social, at work, in a restaurant, or on the street. Formal in this case means, at least in the office, a dark suit and tie for men, and a business suit or skirt and blouse for women. Tie-up or lace-up shoes for business wear are best (avoid loafers: they are considered too informal). Khakis and other informal wear are not appropriate for men in business settings. On the street, informal may mean jeans and sneakers (they should always be neat and clean), though that is more common as clothing to wear at the gym, the beach, or while jogging (women do not wear sneakers to work); for a social gathering, informal more often than not means tastefully coordinated clothes, including a jacket (but not necessarily a tie) for men (it rarely means jeans, sneakers, and T-shirts). "Formal" usually means formal evening wear, which is very dressy by American standards. Most restaurants do not require a tie for men, although the upscale restaurants expect both men and women to dress well.

Seasonal Variations

There are four distinct seasons in Belgium, and one needs to dress accordingly. Summers can be hot; while winters, which begin sooner and end later than in North America, can be damp and very cold.

Colors

Bright colors and patterns are generally not suitable for business wear, either for men or for women.

Styles

In the Eurocenter, Brussels, fashion is stylish and very up-to-date. However, more traditional and conservative business attire is preferred in the other major cities.

Accessories / Jewelry / Makeup

These are a matter of personal taste; however, in French-speaking Belgium, there is perhaps more emphasis on the use of accessories as a means of achieving a high-fashion look.

Dining and Drinking

Mealtimes and Typical Foods

Even a quick breakfast on the run in a major Belgian city is usually more than a cup of coffee and a roll. Breakfast (*le petit dejeuner* in French-speaking Belgium; *het ont bijt* in Flemish-speaking Belgium) resembles the French or German breakfasts described in the chapters on those countries. The Belgian breakfast is usually served from 7 to 9 A.M.

Lunch (*le dejeuner* in French-speaking Belgium; *de lunch* in Flemish-speaking Belgium) was traditionally the main meal of the day; in busy cities today, it can be either a quick sandwich or a more substantial dish of meat or fish, vegetables, and potatoes or noodles. Lunch is usually served from around 1 to 2 P.M. Beer or wine typically accompanies all lunches, either business or social, in restaurants, cafés, or workplace cafeterias; mineral water, with or without carbonation, and juice/soft drinks are also available. On Sunday, the family day, the main meal is supper, which is usually served in the middle of the afternoon, and can last well into the evening.

Dinner (*le diner* in French-speaking Belgium; *het avondeten* in Flemish-speaking Belgium) is usually served from 7 to 8:30 P.M., with 8 P.M. the customary time for dinner parties. The evening meal may be similar to lunch, with meats, fish, vegetables, and dessert. A regional beer or wine is usually served with the meal. Dinner parties usually end at around midnight (but can go much later if all are having a good time).

Throughout Belgium, especially in the Valons region, there are cafés and wine bars, bistros and *patisseries,* where drinks and light refreshments are available all day and night, and where one can sit for as long as one cares to.

Typical Belgian foods include waterzooi (a kind of stew), *moules* (mussels), *frites* (French fries, typically served with *moules,* and usually eaten with vinegar or mayonnaise, not ketchup), *carbonnades flamandes* (meat cooked in beer), and eels (*anguilles*).

Regional Differences

Food in the Valons region is similar to French cuisine, while the cuisine in Flanders is rooted in Dutch traditions. Nevertheless, both influence each other, creating a uniquely Belgian cuisine. In Flemish Belgium, bread is not served if potatoes or other starches are part of the meal; and when it is part of the meal, it is often served with butter. In French-speaking Belgium, there will almost always be bread with every meal, but butter is generally not served.

Typical Drinks and Toasting

Mixed drinks before dinner are not common; however, before the meal one might have an aperitif of one of many different kinds of herbal liqueurs, vermouth, and the like; these and other alcoholic beverages are also drunk after the meal as *digestifs*. Once the meal gets under way, wine (in French-speaking Belgium) or beer (in Flemish-speaking Belgium) will be served in most cases.

The most common toasts are *salud,* or *a votre santé* in French-speaking Belgium and *gezondheid* in Flemish-speaking Belgium. It is essential when making a toast to maintain direct eye contact from the moment the glass is raised to the moment it is placed back down on the table. If many people are being toasted, go around the table with your eyes, making contact with each individual as you make the toast. In the north (Flanders), make eye contact as you lift the glass, give the toast, lift the glass again, and then drink.

Table Manners and the Use of Utensils

Belgians, like all Europeans, do not switch knives and forks, as Americans do. The knife remains in the right hand, and the fork remains in the left. When the meal is finished, the knife and fork are laid parallel to each other horizontally across the top half of the plate, with the tines of the fork pointing to the left. If you put both utensils down on the plate for any real length of time, it is a sign to the waitstaff that you are finished, and your plate may be taken away from you. There are often many additional pieces of cutlery; if you're unsure of which utensil to use, always start from the outside and work your way in, course by course. There will be separate glasses provided at your setting for water and white and red wine (after-dinner drink glasses come out after dinner, often in the living room and not at the dining table).

When not holding utensils, your hands are expected to be visible above the table: this means that you do not keep them in your lap; instead, rest your wrists on top of the table (never your elbows). At the table, pass all dishes to your left. Salt and pepper shakers or holders should be passed so that the receiving person takes them directly; do not place them down on the table first. If there is no bread plate, place bread on the left side rim of your main plate.

Seating Plans

The most honored position is either at the head of the table or in the center, with the most important guests seated first to the left and then to the right of the head of the table. If there is a hosting couple, one will be seated at each end of the table. The male guest of honor sits to the right of the hostess, and the female guest of honor sits to the right of the host. In keeping with the practice on the rest of the Continent, men and women are seated next to one another, and couples are often broken up and seated next to people they may not have previously known. This is done to promote conversation. Men always rise when women enter the room, and both men and women rise when older people enter or leave a room. Remember, as is the case throughout the Continent, what the Belgians call the first floor is really the second floor, with the first floor usually referred to as the lobby or ground floor.

Refills and Seconds

If you do not want more food, leave just a bit on your plate. You may always have additional beverages; drink enough to cause your cup or glass to be less than half full, and it will generally be refilled. Portions are generally smaller than in the United States.

At Home, in a Restaurant, or at Work

In informal restaurants, you may be required to share a table: if so, do not force conversation; act as if you are seated at a private table. Waitstaff may be summoned by making eye contact; waving or calling their names is very impolite. Breakfast meetings are not common except perhaps among traveling business-people in hotels. The business lunch or dinner is a more widespread practice, but, depending upon how well developed your relationship is with your Belgian colleagues, it is generally not the time to make business decisions. Take your cue from your Belgian associates: if they bring up business, then it's okay to discuss it, but wait to take your lead from their conversation. No gum chewing, ever, at the restaurant or on the street. No-smoking sections in restaurants are still a rarity.

Meals at a Belgian associate's home can be either relaxed or formal; take your cue from the information your host gives you when you are invited. It is always best to arrive on time. Once within the home, you will be told where to sit, and there you should remain. Do not wander from room to room: much of the house is really off-limits to guests. At the table, be sure to look for place cards, or wait until the host indicates your seat: do not presume to seat yourself, as the seating arrangement may be predetermined.

Being a Good Guest or Host

Paying the Bill

Usually the one who does the inviting pays the bill, although the guest is expected to make an effort to pay. Sometimes other circumstances determine the payee (such as rank). Making payment arrangements ahead of time so that no exchange occurs at the table is a very classy way to host.

Transportation

It's a very nice idea, when acting as the host, to inquire ahead of time as to whether the guests will require transportation. If necessary, you should arrange for taxi service at the end of the meal.

When to Arrive / Chores to Do

If invited to dinner at a private home, it is okay to offer to help with the chores, and expect to be taken up on your offer more often than not. Do not leave the table until invited to do so. Spouses are often included in business dinners (most commonly if both business associates are married). When it is time to leave, always get up and shake hands with everyone: the group wave is not appreciated. If you are invited to stay overnight at a Belgian home, always leave things tidy and clean up after yourself. By the way, never drop by an associate's home uninvited or unannounced: always phone ahead and ask if it is convenient to stop by. Never make phone calls to a home too early in the morning or after 10:30 at night.

Gift Giving

In general, gift giving is not common among business associates; it is best not to send a gift at any time, including the holidays, unless you receive one first from your Belgian colleagues. Holiday cards are very appropriate, particularly as a thank-you for their business during the previous year, and should be mailed in time to be received the week before Christmas.

Gifts *are* expected for social events, however, especially as thank-yous for private dinner parties. If you choose flowers, bring them with you to the dinner party, and be sure to unwrap them before entering the home or handing them to the hostess. Be sure never to send chrysanthemums (they are used primarily as funeral flowers) or red roses (these usually indicate romantic intent), and always be sure the bouquet is in odd numbers (an old European tradition), except for the number 13, which should always be avoided. Other good gifts would be fine chocolates, a sweet dessert wine, or an after-dinner liqueur of good quality.

If you are staying with a family, an appropriate thank-you gift would be a high-quality product that represents your country and is difficult to get in Belgium (a hard thing to do these days!): gourmet foodstuffs (maple syrup, pralines, lobsters, etc.), coffee-table books about the United States, or anything that reflects your host's personal tastes (the cap of a famous American team for the football-playing son of the family, for example) is appropriate. Wine is not a good gift when visiting a Belgian home.

Special Holidays and Celebrations

Major Holidays

Business slows down during August, the traditional vacation time, and again during the Christmas and New Year's seasons (December 15 to January 5).

January 1	New Year's Day
March/April	Easter Sunday and Monday
May 1	Labor Day
April/May	Ascension
May/June	Whitsuntide and Whitmonday (fifty days after Easter)
July 21	Belgian Independence Day
August 15	Assumption
November 1	All Saints' Day
November 2	All Souls' Day
November 11	Veterans Day
December 25	Christmas Day

Business Culture

Daily Office Protocols

In Belgium, doors are sometimes closed, sometimes open; in either case, always knock first (this includes bathrooms) before opening doors, and when leaving rooms, offer to close the doors behind you. Women and men are still not treated as equals in business, especially in Valons. A woman, for example, would rarely be allowed to pick up the bill at a business meal, even if she were the one who made the invitations. Do not expect people to work over weekends, holidays, or vacations: these times are usually sacred, being reserved for family.

Management Styles

Privacy and individual accomplishment of one's tasks are critical; however, there can be much interaction between senior management, staff, and among team members. Adherence to procedure is believed to be the most effective way of accomplishing a task. Anything out of the ordinary or unusual is usually not appreciated, and must be explained. The ability to be a smooth-working member of the team is important; sincerity and seriousness, not necessarily friendliness, are preferred attributes. Complimenting and rewarding employees publicly is usually not done. Business meals usually involve lunch, because a business dinner will interfere with the evening family meal, which is sacred. However, you are more likely to be invited to a business dinner in Flanders than in Valons.

Boss-Subordinate Relations

In Belgium, there is a rigid chain of command that must be respected, and the bureaucracy can be frustrating. Deviating from the normal channels will generally make more problems for you, even if your intent is to bypass what appear to be obstacles. Bosses are expected to provide guidance, distribute information, and make decisions; subordinates are expected to provide detailed information and follow the decisions made by their superiors. Most Belgian business organizations have a structure similar to the French or the German business organization.

Conducting a Meeting or Presentation

At meetings of peers, there can be open communication and sharing of ideas: these sessions often serve as information-sharing and decision-making forums in which all individuals are expected to contribute. Under these circumstances, discussions can be more freewheeling. In more formal, conservative organizations, meetings are often gatherings of nonpeers, clearly called together by decision makers in order to gather information from below, clarify goals, and formulate action plans. In these cases, individuals often do not share ideas and are not expected to contribute to mutual problem solving. Facts and figures are essential, and must be clearly outlined and detailed.

Negotiation Styles

Belgians respect someone who comes to them with established knowledge and experience. No detail is unimportant, and a carefully planned, logically organized proposal is key. The first meeting may be very matter of fact, with the Belgians sizing up you, your organization, and your ideas: it will be conducted in the office. Because time needs to be carefully managed, plan your meeting carefully and well in advance, and prepare a detailed agenda for circulation prior to the scheduled date. Be prepared to answer many questions. Confirm all meetings and the preparations for them well in advance. Casually changing time and place is not appreciated. The best times for meetings are 9 to 10 A.M. and 2 to 3 P.M.

It is wise to have two separate sets of translated business cards: one in French, the other in Flemish, with English on the reverse side for both. Unless you have information to the contrary, it is best to keep your business affairs in Flanders and Valons separate.

Written Correspondence

Your correspondence with Belgian colleagues should be very businesslike, with as few references to personal matters as possible. Dates are written using the day/month/year format (with periods in between, not slashes), and an honorific plus a title is as common as an honorific plus the last name. If you do not speak French or Flemish, use English where appropriate.

LUXEMBOURG

Luxembourgeois (the term means "things Luxembourgish," and is the name of the dialect of French spoken in the country as well) is very similar to the Belgian French patterns of behavior. The country, which is nestled between southern Belgium, Germany, and France, is the modern-day remnant of a feudal principality that has managed to maintain its sovereignty and well-being (and *very* successfully, as well, having one of the highest per capita incomes in the world) by being both very business savvy and very self-protective (do the two go together?). Luxembourgers (the people of this idyllic land) are slightly more conservative than the Belgians, but more flexible in their *outward* acceptance of outsiders (just don't apply for citizenship!). They are very comfortable with English (as well as French and German); all three languages, in addition to the local dialect, are easily spoken and understood in the (mainly) business community. It is a conservative (banking is the biggest business) and traditional country, however, and time is slower, life simpler, the nightlife questionable. Business lunches, for example, can usually last till 2 or 3 P.M.—do not expect to do business in an office before three in the afternoon, and on the street, discreet and well-mannered behavior is the rule. The time orientation is to the past and preserving what has been already accomplished. Holidays are similar to those in Belgium, with the exception of Belgium Independence Day, and these additions:

March/April	Shrove Tuesday
June 23	National Day

CHAPTER EIGHT

The Benelux Cultures:
The Netherlands

Some Introductory Background on the Netherlands and the Dutch

The word *Dutch* is an Anglicized version of the incorrect term the Spanish, who once ruled the Netherlands, used to refer to the people in the Low Countries, mistakenly lumping them together with their neighbors, the Germans, or the *Deutsch*. While the two peoples share many cultural similarities, mistaking the inhabitants of the Netherlands with Germans has always been a serious offense to the Dutch, and may be even more so now (in both twentieth-century world wars, Germany invaded the Netherlands). It is acceptable today, however, to refer to the inhabitants of the Netherlands, as well as their language, as Dutch. Remember also that the country's official name is the Netherlands, although Holland is commonly but incorrectly used (before its independence was recognized in 1648, the region was called Holland). Holland is the name of the largest state in the country, in which the major cities of the country (Amsterdam, Rotterdam, and The Hague) can be found in a broad swath called the Randstad.

If there is one group of people that most Americans find easy to work with, it's the Dutch. No surprise, when you consider that most Dutch today speak almost flawless English. In addition, there is a great similarity in outlook on life and work between the Americans and the Dutch. The Dutch have a reputation for being extremely pragmatic, practical, efficient, nonjudgmental, and organized. The most common American complaints about the Dutch are that they are sometimes stubborn and too closemouthed about things; the most common Dutch complaint about Americans is that Americans are too disorganized, prone to taking risks, and overly concerned about moralizing. But these differences are not severe, and in most cases, the synergy between the two is often enough to see a deal through and establish and maintain close personal relationships. The similarities and differences are, of course, a result of the histories of the two countries. Three important aspects of the Dutch historical experience may explain their cultural behaviors, and why Americans are so comfortable working with them: the Dutch literally created Holland out of the sea; the exposure of the Dutch to other cultures through international trade; and the role that the Netherlands has traditionally played as the sanctuary of Europe.

Some Historical Context

There is a Dutch saying that God made the world, but the Dutch made Holland. In the literal sense, it's true, as the Dutch have physically lifted the land out of the sea to create their country; on a deeper level, the saying expresses the Protestant Dutch notion of success being the result of quiet, determined, industrious work done with humility. The polders, or the system of dams, dikes, and levees that the Dutch have in place to keep the sea from overtaking the land, confirms their belief in the value and rewards of hard work, a modern-day version of the older Protestant (Dutch Reformed, in this case) case for salvation being attained through the demonstration of good works.

Ironically, Holland today is a very secular nation. Over the centuries, the people's formative Protestant ideas took on a practical application, leading to a highly developed sense of business and trade. The lack of natural resources in this essentially reclaimed land propelled the Dutch to seek their fortunes elsewhere, resulting in a tradition of seafaring and exploration that is one of the richest in all of Europe. While the Dutch participated in the European colonization of newly explored lands, their practicality and pragmatism precluded them from developing a moral ethic to justify oppression and some of the more evil aspects of colonization. Instead, the nonproselytizing Dutch way was generally matter of fact, steady, nonjudgmental, and, to a greater degree than most Europeans, tolerant. Their extensive, worldwide trade gave the Dutch an early familiarity with people who were different from themselves, enabling them to deal practically with people and issues, without the need to establish a moral justification for actions.

Finally, the traditional Dutch tolerance for other cultures led the Netherlands to become a sanctuary for the dispossessed, both from within Europe and from outside the Continent: Huguenots from France, Jews from the Middle East, Asians from Dutch territories abroad (Indonesia, most prominently), and—most importantly for Americans—Puritans from Britain. In fact, most Puritans when expelled from Britain went first to Holland, and then continued on to the New World. It is not surprising therefore to find the same reformist traditions in Dutch behavior as we see in American behavior: both share this common Puritan (work ethic) experience.

An Area Briefing

Politics and Government

The Netherlands is a constitutional monarchy, with a representative parliamentary legislative system (and a prime minister). There is a strong belief in government's responsibility to provide a network of social services for all individuals; however, these costly services are a severe burden on the Dutch people, who are among the most heavily taxed in Europe.

Religion and Demographics

Although there is a slight Catholic majority numerically, it is the Protestant tradition of the Dutch Reformed Church that has had the most profound effect on the development of Dutch culture and Dutch ways of life. There is a high degree of literacy, and almost every Dutch citizen speaks at least two (Dutch and English) languages, with many speaking more. The Thirty Years War, which culminated in the liberation of Holland from the Spanish crown in 1648, effectively consolidated Protestantism in Holland. There is, however, in this secular country, a large population of Catholics in the south, and because of the strong intercultural heritage of the Dutch, many religious and ethnic groups from around the world (Indonesians, Malaysians, Indians, Chinese, Turks, Arabs, Jews, etc.), can be found mainly in the urban areas of Amsterdam, Rotterdam, and Utrecht. There is a small indigenous group (the Fries, pronounced "Frees") in the northwest of Holland (the province of Friesland) who speak, along with Dutch and English, their own language, Frisian, which is a combination of Old English, Dutch, and the roots of mysterious pre-Roman languages.

Fundamental Cultural Orientations

Note: Cultural behavior in the Netherlands is roughly similar to what may be found in other Germanic and northern European cultures; the information that follows identifies specific Dutch variations on those customs.

1. What's the Best Way for People to Relate to One Another?

OTHER-INDEPENDENT OR OTHER-DEPENDENT? The Dutch do value the individual, but the most highly regarded individuals are those who work in a cooperative, respectful, and nonconfrontational way with their peers, colleagues, superiors, and subordinates. There is a strong concern in the Netherlands for the welfare of all individuals, the word *individual* being the important distinction between the Dutch sense of social responsibility and that espoused in the collectively oriented social welfare ethos of the Nordic cultures. Privacy is critical, and proximity does not presume friendship or business.

HIERARCHY-ORIENTED OR EGALITY-ORIENTED? It is important to respect hierarchy, but a bureaucracy with low productivity is not valued. Bosses need to earn the respect of their subordinates, and subordinates need to be respectful of superiors. Nevertheless, the strong Protestant work ethic usually dictates that rank is not overtly displayed with signs of status: anything ostentatious is usually discounted. In the family, the parents rule until the children reach independence (usually upon graduation, marriage, or finding work), and then an egalitarian relationship usually rapidly develops.

RULE-ORIENTED OR RELATIONSHIP-ORIENTED? Rules and order are essential; however, extenuating circumstances and personal or social situations may justify a rethinking of the rules and processes. In the Netherlands, there is a determined effort to treat all people fairly and equally, with consideration for the particular needs that individuals and different groups have regarding similar issues.

2. What's the Best Way to View Time?

MONOCHRONIC OR POLYCHRONIC? The culture is mainly monochronic. Do not be late; punctuality is important and the tardy person is regarded as someone who is not worthy of the responsibility he or she has been entrusted with. There is a time and place for everything, and careful planning allows for both family and work: it is just that the two usually do not mix. Respond to requests quickly and sincerely, and take the time to plan thoroughly and carefully. Changing schedules at the last minute is seen as very careless.

RISK-TAKING OR RISK-AVERSE? This is generally a risk-taking culture, but not without careful thought and consideration to all sides, participants, and details. If there is an opportunity that has been identified, analyzed, and evaluated, the Dutch will seize it . . . promptly; once something is assessed as worth trying, the Dutch will go forward full steam. It's just that they do require all the information to be up front first. Taking action without having all the facts is foolhardy; taking bold action after the facts have been examined is heroic. Remember, Dutch explorers were once some of Europe's bravest and most successful.

PAST-ORIENTED OR FUTURE-ORIENTED? The Dutch have a strong belief in their ability to accomplish things, once the correct approach has been identified. Nevertheless, they also have a strong respect for forces beyond one's control, like nature (the sea), and a determined patience that enables them to wait for circumstances to change in order to regain control again (remember the struggles of the Dutch during the two world wars).

3. What's the Best Way for Society to Work with the World at Large?

LOW-CONTEXT DIRECT OR HIGH-CONTEXT INDIRECT COMMUNICATORS? The Dutch are generally low-context communicators, with matter of factness, simplicity, and nonemotionality being hallmarks of their communication style. Based on this, the Dutch have a reputation of being extremely closemouthed: they do not share information unless it is necessary to do so.

PROCESS-ORIENTED OR RESULT-ORIENTED? While the process for decision making is important, and details are critical, the Dutch will also make decisions, as the English, based on precedent and what has been the successful method in the past. This pragmatic approach, mixed with a need for logical fact, makes them similar to Americans in their decision-making and thought-processing systems.

FORMAL OR INFORMAL? Here, too, the Dutch combine both a healthy respect for certain formalities (usually around rank and age, but less so around gender: women and men in Dutch culture share a high level of equality) and a relaxed flexibility toward situations as they develop.

Greetings and Introductions

Language and Basic Vocabulary

The Dutch language has influenced English, and vice versa. Perhaps because of the proximity, similarity of trade orientation, and historical relationship between the Puritans and the Dutch, most Dutch speak English (it is certainly the case in business). Here are some basic Dutch terms and their English meanings:

goedmorgen	good morning
goedeavond	good evening
dag! or *tot ziens*	good-bye
ja	yes
alstublieft	please
hertelijk dank	thanks very much
pardon	excuse me
Hoe gaat het?	How are you?
mijnheer	Mr.
mevrouw	Mrs.
juffrouw	Miss
goedmiddag	good afternoon
goednacht	good night
allo	hello
nee	no
dank u	thank you
niets te danken	you're welcome
aandenaam kennis te maken	pleased to meet you
Spreekt u Engels?	Do you speak English?

Honorifics for Men, Women, and Children

Mijnheer (Mr.) and *mevrouw* (Mrs. or Ms.), plus the family name, are an absolute must to use when you are introduced to adults. Unless or until your Dutch colleague specifically invites you to use first names, and despite how he or she might refer to you, you must always use the family name plus the correct Dutch honorific. Do not be surprised, however, to find the Dutch inviting you to use first names with them quickly, as they are comfortable with a slightly less formal atmosphere in which to conduct both social conversation and business; however, take your cue from them.

Sometimes honorifics are used along with titles, in place of names, but never in place of titles; for example, a doctor is often referred to as "Mijnheer Doktor." Children in the Netherlands are expected to be respectful and not overly conversational when speaking with adults, and must use honorifics when referring to adults; nevertheless, Dutch children are brought up to be independent thinkers, and a free-spirited child is not an uncommon sight. If you speak any Dutch at all, by all means use it (your efforts will be appreciated), but recognize that as soon as you are identified as an English speaker, your Dutch colleagues will probably switch to English. For casual contact (e.g., waiters, store help, etc.), just use *mijnheer* or *mevrouw* without the name. It is very important to greet people at work or in stores or restaurants with a greeting appropriate for the time of day, as well as a *tot ziens* upon leaving.

The What, When, and How of Introducing People

Always wait to be introduced to strangers before taking that responsibility upon yourself. The Dutch are most comfortable with a third-party introduction whenever possible. Try to ensure that for yourself ahead of time. Do not presume to seat yourself at a formal gathering: if possible, wait to be told where to sit. If not instructed, assume that men will sit and stand on the outside when with women. Shake hands with everyone individually in a group when being introduced and before departing: the American group wave is not appreciated. When you are introduced to someone, greeting him or her with a question (e.g, "How are you?" or "How do you do?") is not common: more often than not, it is appropriate simply to repeat your family name, so that you are sure that person knows who you are and that you have the chance to hear his or her name again and learn it. Avoid complimenting your colleague until you have a close personal relationship: they sound unnecessary to the Dutch. Once you greet someone you will encounter later that day in the same circumstances (e.g., at the office), there is no need to greet them again. Kissing is not a common greeting, even between individuals who know each other well. The use of business cards is very common; if possible, you should have your business card translated into Dutch on the reverse, but this is not absolutely necessary, as most every businessperson reads English.

Physical Greeting Styles

The handshake is common. The Dutch version is similar to the American handshake, but usually does not last quite as long. It is done quickly and firmly between two men, but not as robustly between men and women or two women. The handshake should be accompanied by the appropriate greeting (see the list of Dutch terms outlined above). Smiling and other nonverbal forms of communication need not accompany the handshake when it is between two people who have previously not met. Men should wait until a woman extends her hand before reaching for it, and women may take the lead in extending their hand or not. Men must remove their gloves when shaking hands with a woman, but a woman need not remove her gloves when shaking hands with a man. If more than two people are greeting each other, it is not correct to reach across arms to shake hands (making a kind of *X*). Informal body gestures are not appreciated during the first introduction between strangers, so avoid backslapping and other forms of touching. Eye contact during the introduction is serious and intense, and should be maintained as long as the individual is addressing you.

Communication Styles

Okay Topics / Not Okay Topics

Okay: current events, politics (as long as you know what you are talking about), the arts, sports (very big, especially soccer), music, philosophy, and Dutch art and science museums. The Dutch will listen attentively to what everyone has to say, giving all people the opportunity to speak their piece, and rise or fall by their own devices. *Not okay:* The Dutch tend to shy away from direct confrontation. It is important to recognize that small talk and chitchat in general is not the typical Dutch way. Even in social situations, talk may be less animated, and there may simply be less of it; however, the Dutch enjoy the camaraderie of good friends and family. Do not inquire about a person's occupation in casual conversation. Americans often begin a conversation with "So, what do you do?"; this is too personal in Europe, and is often not the most interesting topic of conversation. Also not okay: personal financial discussions, questions about private family matters (family is sacred), personal background, and the like. Anything that smacks of rank, showiness, and status is generally downplayed, and not appreciated.

Tone, Volume, and Speed

Discussions between strangers usually start out politely restrained; in public or during your first business meetings, the conversational tone can be slightly subdued and matter of fact. Once people get to know each other, though, the volume can increase slightly. Never interrupt; let each speaker make his or her point and then respond. Wait your turn. Keep your voice low, especially in public: never make loud, demonstrative calls or shouts, even on the street.

Use of Silence

Short silences, during which people are thinking about what was said and deciding on their response, are not unusual. These need not be awkward: enjoy the brief respite.

Physical Gestures and Facial Expressions

Several gestures are unique to the Netherlands. If the Dutch want to indicate that someone is strange or crazy, they usually tap their temple or forehead; the common American sign (rotating the forefinger near the ear) actually means that you have a telephone call waiting in the Netherlands. Tapping the elbow of an arm bent in a ninety-degree position indicates that the person being spoken with is not dependable or reliable. If a Dutch person puts their thumb in their mouth slightly and sucks on it, it means that they doubt what you are saying; and if they tap their thumbnails together, it indicates that they are extremely displeased. Rubbing the bridge of the nose up and down usually means that the other person is cheap and stingy.

Waving and Counting

The thumb represents the number 1, the index finger the number 2, and so on. It is insulting to beckon someone with the forefinger (instead, turn your hand so that the palm faces up and motion inward with all four fingers at once). Keep your gestures to a minimum. If you need to gesture for a waiter, make a small, subtle motion with your hand as if you were writing (it indicates that you want the check).

Physicality and Physical Space

The Dutch tend to stay slightly farther apart than North Americans. Never speak with your hands in your pockets: always keep them firmly at your side when standing. If women must cross their legs, it should never be ankle over knee (this is not an issue for men). Remember, even in public, formal is always better than informal: no gum chewing, ever; don't slouch; and don't lean against things. At meetings, take your cue from the senior participants as to how informal or formal one should act, dress, and sit.

Eye Contact

At times, the eye contact can be intense and disconcerting to many Americans. It is important not to interpret this behavior as a way of intentionally trying to make you uncomfortable. It is how the Dutch (and most Europeans) show their interest. Conversely, if you look away, your behavior will say to your Dutch colleague that you are either disinterested or rude. Either way, maintain eye contact when it is made with you. Even in public, eye contact can be direct. Standing in someone's line of sight in order to make eye contact is a way of saying "I want to talk with you"; be sure you do this judiciously, and only where and when such an act does not challenge the order of things (i.e., don't do it if it interrupts an ongoing conversation unless it's really important to do so). This is one of the reasons that doors are usually closed in homes and offices, and why privacy is so important.

Protocol in Public

Walking Styles and Waiting in Lines

The importance of order and organization is apparent even on Dutch streets: men walk on the curbside of women; younger people walk on the curbside of older people; if there are two men and one woman, one man walks on each side of the woman. Men precede women up a flight of stairs to avoid walking behind a woman who might be in a skirt or dress. The Dutch are generally orderly in queues, and wait their turns.

Behavior in Public Places: Airports, Terminals, and the Market

As in much of Europe, if you touch the produce in food markets, you buy it; in goods stores, it may be difficult for you to return a product unless there is a flaw in it. Smoking is on the decline, although no-smoking areas in restaurants and other public places are not ubiquitous. On the street, do not cross against a red light; wait patiently on the curb instead until the light turns green (on streets where there are no traffic lights, be very careful when crossing: the cars do not necessarily stop for pedestrians). This is especially important due to the large number of bicycles on the road (most Dutch own and use their bicycles daily, as an effective means of transportation), which follow the same rules as cars.

At Dutch public telephones, the telecard is appearing more and more frequently but most still accept coins (put in five gulden to get a dial tone). The appropriate greeting on the telephone is *met* plus your family name, or, more casually, *hallo* plus your given name.

Bus / Metro / Taxi / Car

Driving is on the right, but people pass very quickly on the left. The public transportation system generally shuts down after midnight or 1 A.M. Your best bet for catching a cab is at designated taxi stands (hotels are good places, but often charge more for the same ride: a hotel surcharge is added to the meter fare, in some cases).

Tipping

Tips are generally no more than 10 percent, or slightly less for restaurants and taxis; more is considered nouveau and gauche. Porters and hotel help get one or two gulden per service rendered. Restaurants usually have the 10 percent tip already included on the bill, but if you are unsure, it's okay to ask if service is included or not. Even if it is, it is still appropriate to leave a few coins if the service was particularly good.

Punctuality

Never be late, if you can avoid it, under any circumstance, either social or business. If you must be late for any reason, it is absolutely essential to call ahead and let someone know of your problem—and you should have an appropriate explanation, as well.

Dress

Clothing styles are formal for both men and women, no matter the occasion— business or social, at work, in a restaurant, or on the street. Formal in this case means, at least in the office, a dark suit and tie for men, and a business suit or skirt and blouse for women. Khakis and other informal wear for men are not appropriate in a business setting. On the street, informal may mean jeans and sneakers (they should always be neat and clean), though that is more common as clothing to wear at the gym, the beach, or while jogging (women do not wear sneakers to work); for a social gathering, informal more often than not means tastefully coordinated clothes, although not necessarily a jacket and tie for men (it rarely means jeans, sneakers, and T-shirts). "Formal" usually means formal evening wear, which is very dressy by American standards. Most restaurants do not require a tie for men, although the upscale restaurants expect both men and women to dress well. The Dutch usually dress up on Sunday. Remember, the need to keep a low profile, and avoid anything showy or status-linked, means that even well-paid senior executives do not necessarily dress any fancier than average employees.

Seasonal Variations

There are four very distinct seasons in the Netherlands, and one needs to dress accordingly. Moreover, it can be rainy a good part of the year, so prepare each day accordingly with raincoats and umbrellas.

Colors

Bright colors and patterns are generally not suitable for business wear, either for men or for women.

Accessories / Jewelry / Makeup

In the Netherlands, understated simplicity and humility are highly valued. As a result, style questions such as accessories and makeup are not considered that important; they are really a matter of personal taste. Men and women generally do not use much perfume or cologne.

Dining and Drinking

Mealtimes and Typical Foods

Even a quick breakfast on the run in a major Dutch city is usually more than a cup of coffee and a roll. Breakfast often also includes cheeses, yogurt, eggs, dried cereals, and perhaps some pickled vegetables or fish. It can be substantial. Fish (especially herring) is an important staple food.

Lunch is usually served from 12 to 1 P.M. Beer or wine typically accompanies all lunches, either business or social, in restaurants, cafés, or workplace cafeterias; mineral water, with or without carbonation, and juice or soft drinks are also available. On Sunday, the family day, the main meal is supper, which is usually served in the middle of the afternoon and can last well into the evening.

At home, dinner is usually served from 6 to 7:30 P.M., with 8 P.M. the customary time for weekend dinner parties. The evening meal may be similar to lunch, with meats, fish, vegetables, and dessert. The drink served with dinner is usually a regional beer or wine.

The Dutch also stop for snacks: once around 10 A.M., and again at 4 P.M. Coffee is regarded as a special treat, and sharing a really good cup of coffee at a café, or at home with friends, is a valued tradition. You may be invited for after-dinner coffee at someone's home; this is usually around 8:30 or 9 P.M., and most often includes snacks and food, so it can be a meal in itself. If you are being invited for coffee after dinner, plan your own dinner accordingly (make it light). If you are invited to dinner with the words (either spoken or written on the invitation) *tenue de ville,* it is okay to come to the meal dressed in the day's business suit (this is usually done more and more anyway, without such a statement having to be made).

Regional Differences

Dutch food does vary, but essentially it is hearty fare of a people near the sea designed to get one through a long cold winter. Sausages, cheeses, breads, and meats of all varieties abound, along with cooked vegetables and potatoes. Dried, fresh, smoked, or pickled fish are dietary staples. Desserts are usually simple cakes and sweets, served with coffee. The Dutch freely use dairy products in most of their cooking. Rijsttafel (from the Dutch words meaning "rice" and "table") is a wonderful treat in the Netherlands: it is an Indonesian meal consisting of rice served with many different small dishes (meat, vegetables, etc.).

Typical Drinks and Toasting

Mixed drinks before dinner are not common; however, before the meal one might have an aperitif (usually *jenever,* a kind of gin with juniper), usually served in the living room. Do not take your aperitif to the table: try to finish it before dinner is announced. Once the meal gets under way, wine or water will be served in most cases; beer is usually drunk in bars or with Asian food.

The most common toast is *proost*. It is absolutely essential when making a toast to maintain direct eye contact from the moment the glass is raised to the moment it is placed back down on the table. If many people are being toasted, go around the table with your eyes, making contact with each individual as you make the toast.

Table Manners and the Use of Utensils

Do not begin eating until the host or hostess has invited you to do so.

The Dutch, like all continental Europeans, do not switch knives and forks, as Americans do. The knife remains in the right hand, and the fork remains in the left. When the meal is finished, the knife and fork are laid parallel to each other across the right side of the plate, the tips pointing to the ten o'clock position; the knife should be above the fork, with the blade side pointing in toward the plate. If you put both utensils down on the plate for any real length of time, it is a sign to the waitstaff that you are finished, and your plate may be taken away from you. The fork and spoon above your plate are usually for dessert. There may be additional pieces of cutlery; if you're unsure of which utensil to use, always start from the outside and work your way in, course by course. There will be separate glasses provided at your setting for water and white and red wine (after-dinner drink glasses come out after dinner). When not holding utensils, your hands are expected to be visible above the table: this means that you do not keep them in your lap; instead, rest your wrists on top of the table (never your elbows). At the table, pass all dishes to your left. Salt and pepper shakers or holders should be passed so that the receiving person takes them directly; do not place them down on the table first. Never cut the lettuce in a salad: deftly fold it with your knife and fork so that it can be picked up in a small bundle with your fork. The only food eaten with the hands is bread or sandwiches.

Seating Plans

The most honored position is either at the head of the table or in the center, with the most important guests seated first to the left and then to the right of the head of the table or the host(s), in descending order of importance; if there is a hosting couple, one will be seated at each end of the table, with the male guest of honor seated to the right of the hostess, and the female guest of honor seated to the right of the host. In keeping with the practice elsewhere on the Continent, men and women are seated next to one another, and couples are often broken up and seated next to people they may not have previously known. This is done to promote conversation. Men always rise when women enter the room, and both men and women rise when older people enter or leave a room. Remember, as is the case throughout the Continent, what the Dutch call the first floor is really the second floor, with the first floor usually referred to as the lobby or ground floor.

Refills and Seconds

If you do not want more food, leave just a bit on your plate. You may always have additional beverages; drink enough to cause your cup or glass to be less than half full, and it will generally be refilled. Portions are generally about the same size as in the United States.

At Home, in a Restaurant, or at Work

In informal restaurants, you may be required to share a table: if so, do not force conversation; rather, act as if you are seated at a private table. Waitstaff may be summoned by making eye contact; waving or calling their names is very impolite. Breakfast meetings are not common, except perhaps among traveling businesspeople in hotels. The business lunch or dinner is a more widespread practice, but, depending upon how well developed your relationship is with your Dutch colleagues, it is generally not the time to make business decisions. Take your cue from your Dutch associates: if they bring up business, then it's okay to discuss it, but wait to take your lead from their conversation. No gum chewing, ever, at a restaurant or on the street. No-smoking sections in restaurants are still a rarity.

Quick snacks are available throughout the day in a variety of Dutch cafés. *Broodjeswinkels* are small shops that sell open-faced sandwiches, which are eaten traditionally with a glass of milk or buttermilk (try it!). *Poffertjes* are informal restaurants that serve fried dough pancakes, usually with powdered sugar. Finally, street stalls sell herring—either raw, salted, smoked, or dried. You buy the herring from a barrel, then hold it by the tail and eat it right there, on the street.

Meals at a Dutch associate's home can be either relaxed or formal; take your cue from the information your host gives you when you are invited. Once within the home, you will be told where to sit, and there you should remain. Do not wander from room to room: much of the house is really off-limits to guests. Use the bathroom if you need to before you arrive, and avoid using the bathroom after sitting down to your meal. At the table, be sure to look for place cards, or wait until the host indicates your seat: do not presume to seat yourself, as the seating arrangement may be predetermined.

Being a Good Guest or Host

Paying the Bill

Usually the one who does the inviting pays the bill, although the guest is expected to make an effort to pay. Sometimes other circumstances determine the payee (such as rank). Making payment arrangements ahead of time so that no exchange occurs at the table is a very classy way to host.

Transportation

It's a very nice idea, when acting as the host, to inquire ahead of time as to whether the guests will require transportation arrangements. If necessary, you should arrange for taxi service at the end of the meal.

When to Arrive / Chores to Do

If invited to dinner at a private home, you may offer to help with the chores, but you will probably not have to. Do not leave the table until invited to do so. Spouses are often included in business dinners (most commonly if both business associates are married). When it is time to leave, always get up and shake hands with everyone: the group wave is not appreciated. If you are invited to stay overnight at a Dutch home, be sure to leave things tidy and clean up after yourself. By the way, never drop by an associate's home uninvited or unannounced: always phone ahead and ask if it is convenient to stop by.

Gift Giving

In general, gift giving is not common among business associates; it is best not to send a business gift at any time, including the holidays, unless you receive one first from your Dutch colleagues. Holiday cards are very appropriate, particularly as a thank-you for their business during the previous year, and should be mailed in time to be received the week before Christmas. Gifts *are* expected for social events, however, especially as thank-yous for private dinner parties. If you choose flowers, bring them with you to the dinner party, and be sure to unwrap them before entering the home or handing them to the hostess. Never send chrysanthemums or white lilies (they are used primarily as funeral flowers); also avoid red roses or orchids (these usually indicate romantic intent); and always make sure the bouquet is in odd numbers (an old European tradition). Other good gifts would be fine chocolates, a sweet dessert wine, or an after-dinner liqueur of good quality.

If you are staying with a family, an appropriate thank-you gift would be a high-quality product that represents your country and is difficult to get in the Netherlands: gourmet foodstuffs (maple syrup, pralines, lobsters, etc.), coffee-table books about the United States, or anything that reflects your host's personal tastes (the cap of a famous American team for the football-playing son of the family, for example) is appropriate.

Special Holidays and Celebrations

Major Holidays

Business usually slows down during the traditional vacation times of July and August, and again during the Christmas and New Year's seasons (December 15 to January 1).

January 1	*Nieuwe Yaar's Dag* (New Year's Day)
January 31	Queen Beatrix's birthday
March/April	*Pasen* (Easter; Friday through Monday)
May	*Hemelvaartsdag* (Ascension; five weeks after Easter)
May/June	Whitmonday (eight weeks after Easter)

May 1	*Dag van de Arbeid* (Labor Day)
May 4	*Herdenkingsdag* (Memorial Day)
May 5	*Bevrijdingsdag* (Liberation Day)
June 29	Prince Bernhard's birthday
September	*Prinsjesdag* (Prince's Day; third Tuesday)
September 6	Prince Claus's birthday
October 3	*Leiden outzet* (celebration of the breaking of the siege of Leiden)
December 5	*Sinterklaas* (St. Nicholas Day; gifts from Sinterklaas are exchanged)
December 25–26	*Kerstmis* (Christmas)
December 31	*Oudejaarsavond* (New Year's Eve)

December 5 is a very special day in Dutch homes. Children put sugar and carrots or hay in shoes placed by the fireplace as food for Sinterklaas's horse. In exchange, Sinterklaas leaves gifts for the children in their shoes, including a chocolate with their first name's initial stamped in it. Later in the day, family members give each other small gifts, often with a humorous poem attached.

Business Culture

Daily Office Protocols

In the Netherlands, office doors are usually closed, and sometimes locked; knock first before opening doors (including those to bathrooms), and when leaving rooms, close the doors behind you. Women and men are often treated as equals in the Netherlands, although this may not be universal in the countryside and across all generations or industries. Staying late at the office is not necessarily taken as a good sign: it more often will be interpreted as an indication that the individual is incapable of organizing him- or herself well enough to accomplish the job in the time permitted. Do not expect people to work over weekends, holidays, or vacations: these are usually reserved for family and are sacred times, although Dutch businesspeople will take work home with them in the evening. It is not improper to call a Dutch colleague at home (if you have been given his or her personal number and permission to do so) on business matters in the evening of a workday, if it is necessary and the matter cannot wait until the next day.

Management Styles

Privacy and individual accomplishment of one's tasks are critical; however, there can be much interaction between senior management and staff, and within and among team members. Quiet, thoughtful, and diligent adherence to procedures is believed to be the most effective way of accomplishing a task. Anything out of the ordinary or unusual is usually not appreciated, and must be explained. People and things need to be credible and substantial. The ability to be a smooth-working member of the team is important; sincerity and seriousness, not necessarily friendliness, are important ingredients. Complimenting and rewarding employees publicly is usually not done.

Boss-Subordinate Relations

The hierarchy must be respected, and there are definite routes through life that one follows according to one's rank in society and in the workplace. However, one must demonstrate one's rank with caution. No matter what field you are in, there is usually a proper way for communicating with particular individuals, and an established procedure one is expected to follow. Deviating from normal channels will generally make more problems for you, even if your intent is to bypass what appear to be obstacles. Bosses are expected to provide guidance, distribute information, and make decisions; subordinates are expected to provide detailed information and follow the decisions made by their superiors. All are expected to work together as equals.

Conducting a Meeting or Presentation

At meetings of peers, there can be open communication and sharing of ideas: in fact, these sessions often serve as information-sharing and decision-making forums in which all individuals are expected to contribute, in their way and in their turn, with no interruptions. In more formal, conservative organizations, meetings are often gatherings of nonpeers, clearly called together by decision makers in order to gather information from below, clarify goals, and formulate action plans; nevertheless, even in these circumstances, there can be mutual problem solving, and superiors and subordinates act and speak more as equals. Every contribution is usually valued. Facts and figures are essential, and must be clearly outlined and detailed.

Negotiation Styles

The Dutch respect someone who comes to them with established knowledge and experience. No detail is unimportant, and a carefully planned, logically organized proposal is key. The first meeting may be very matter of fact, with the Dutch sizing up you, your organization, and your ideas: it will be conducted in the office. The Dutch may begin a business meeting with some casual social discussion, but will move very quickly to the business at hand. Because time needs to be carefully managed, plan your meeting carefully and well in advance, and prepare a detailed agenda for circulation prior to the scheduled date. Several meetings may be necessary before all details are clear and all questions answered. Confirm all meetings and the preparations for them well in advance. Casually changing time and place is not appreciated. The best times for meetings are 9 to 10 A.M. and 2 to 4 P.M. Never be late.

Written Correspondence

Your correspondence with Dutch colleagues should be very businesslike, with few references to personal matters. Dates are written using the day/month/year format (with periods in between, not slashes), and an honorific plus a title is as common as an honorific plus the last name. The time of day is written military style; weights and measures are usually given in metric units. Monetary amounts are written so that periods break up the figure into tens, hundreds, and thousands, and a comma separates the guilder (an "F" sign is used because the currency used to be called a "florin") from the cents.

The Nordic Cultures: Sweden

The three countries of Sweden, Denmark, and Norway are related in language, culture, and ethnic composition, and therefore constitute the core of Scandinavia; greater Scandinavia also includes Iceland, the Faeroe Islands, and Greenland. Finland is not part of Scandinavia (although it is a Nordic culture), as its culture, language, and peoples are essentially different from the Scandinavians. We'll start off our exploration of the Nordic cultures with the largest country, Sweden, using Swedish culture as a base to understand Scandinavian culture in general. A separate chapter is reserved for Norway and Denmark, as variations on the Scandinavian theme, and we'll end our discussion of Nordic cultures with a separate chapter on Finland.

Some Introductory Background on Sweden and the Swedes

Sweden and Denmark have been historic rivals in the region, sometimes resulting in bloody conflicts. It is important, therefore, to recognize that while there is a set of behaviors, values, and protocols that most Scandinavians share in common, foreigners should understand the differences that exist between them. Do not confuse Danes, Swedes, Norwegians, and Finns with one another: there are differences that are felt keenly within the region. Swedes are viewed by other Nordics as aristocratic landowners; Norwegians as rugged, if not uncultured, conservatives; and Danes as aggressive individualists (in a region known for its strong social welfare systems); these are, of course, generalized perceptions by neighbors, but they do provide us with an insight into some of the behavioral differences between Scandinavians.

From the outside looking in, Swedes (and all Scandinavians) have a strong belief in social welfare, and the role of the individual in such a system varies from country to country. In an article written in the *Economist* several years ago, Swedes were referred to as blue-eyed, blond-haired Japanese, thus emphasizing the relationship between the strong group orientation in Japan and the equally powerful belief in Sweden that the individual's first responsibility is to take care of others. It should be noted that Sweden, as is the case with most European countries today, is going through a soul-searching reevaluation of its commitment to the social welfare system, as the costs for such systems place a heavy burden on the country's economic development. In addition, while the benefits of social welfare systems are obvious (most Scandinavians value them, and are willing to pay the cost in high prices and even higher taxation rates), many people, particularly the young, are left demotivated and uninspired in a society where no amount of personal effort seems to make a difference as to what kind of life a person will have. The highly publicized "Swedish Middle Way" between capitalism and socialism has produced a stable middle class, with many of life's necessities well taken care of, but with little opportunity for personal advancement. These are the challenges that Swedes, and other Scandinavians, face in the near future.

Some Historical Context

Swedes, Danes, and Norwegians were, of course, originally from one big Viking family. By the 1500s, Denmark had consolidated its hold on the region, going west as far as England, and east and north into parts of Sweden. Sweden struggled for supremacy, capturing much of the Baltic eastern region, and fighting to hold onto it against Denmark, Russia, and others. Denmark and Sweden continued to be rivals into the 1800s, with Denmark supporting Napoléon, and Sweden opposing him. When Europe was divided up after the Napoleonic Wars, Norway was taken away from Denmark and given to Sweden (as punishment to Denmark for its support of Napoléon). But Norway, with its North Sea fishing culture, could not stay long associated with the landed gentry of Sweden, and struggled for its own independence, finally breaking away from Sweden at the beginning of the twentieth century.

In this part of the world, the land plays a huge role in shaping the broad structure of a society. The Swedish landscape lends itself to large farms and estates, conducive to a landed gentry; the Norwegian landscape is fjordlike, making it more conducive for fishermen and independent businesspeople; the Danish landscape is more like the Dutch, conducive to small family farming. Its flat, littoral features shape a culture that reinforces collective efforts to keep the sea at bay.

An Area Briefing

Politics and Government

It is interesting to note that all Scandinavian governments have only one house in their legislature, representing the people. The absence of a second, upper house representative of the gentry or other groups of conferred status (despite the existence of an aristocracy, at least in Sweden), is an example of the strong egalitarian nature of these societies. In fact, in Viking times, the king was traditionally referred to as "First Among Equals," an interesting notion of authority in a flattened organization. To this day, while the Swedes may be "blue-eyed, blonde-haired Japanese," as the article referred to earlier stated, Scandinavian society differs profoundly from Japanese group orientation in that the Scandinavian concern for others occurs within a flattened hierarchy. The Swedish parliament is called the Riksdag. There is a monarchy, representing the state, which rules side by side with the lawmaking parliament and the prime minister. The monarchy is loved and well-respected, and has, in the past, played a significant role in developing Sweden into a power in the region, a fact which most Swedes are extremely proud of.

Schools and Education

There is compulsory education until the age of fifteen at the *Grundskola,* or preliminary school. The *Grundskola* is comprised of three subschools: the *Låg-stadiet* (primary school, ages seven to nine); the *Mellanstadiet* (middle school, ages ten to twelve); and the Högstadiet (intermediate school, ages thirteen to fifteen). After the *Grundskola,* students can go either to vocational high school or academic high school (*Gymnasieskolan*), which prepares them to go on to the *Universitet* (university).

Religion and Demographics

The Evangelical Lutheran Church is the state church, and the vast majority of the people are members, but Catholics, Jews, and other religious groups are also represented in Sweden. Recently, immigration from eastern Europe, the Middle East, Asia, and Africa has increased the numbers of non-native Swedes; Stockholm today is a surprising mixture of many different peoples, obviously noticeable against the blonde and blue-eyed backdrop of traditional Scandinavia.

Swedes love nature, and most have a small cabin or family home in the country to which they retreat as soon as the weather turns warm; still, many Swedes live in the urban centers of Stockholm and Göteborg. All Swedes have the right to enjoy the land in a unique system of joint private land ownership and public use, and in the precious summer months, the country almost shuts down as people soak up the sun and enjoy the outdoors. Swedes are very quality-of-life driven.

The nomadic people of the Nordic countries, found in northern Sweden, Norway, and Finland, are known as Lapps or Laplanders. When this group is referred to as the Sami people (their name in their indigenous language) by non-Sami Nordics, the term carries a racially negative connotation. It is best to avoid it.

Fundamental Cultural Orientations

1. What's the Best Way for People to Relate to One Another?

OTHER-INDEPENDENT OR OTHER-DEPENDENT? This is an other-dependent culture, but without subordinating individuals and their decision-making abilities to the will of the overarching group. Individuals are encouraged to pursue activities that allow them to define themselves, to make their own decisions; however, the impact of such decisions and activities on others must always be considered. The best personal action is one that provides the most good for all, and does not harm or interfere with the social rights of others. This is another distinction between the group orientation of Sweden and other group-oriented cultures (like former Eastern European communist nations): in Sweden, individual will is honored and protected, yet the people willingly modify their personal decisions so that they are made with consideration for the needs of the greater group. There is a strong allegiance to Sweden as a nation, while, at the same time, personal privacy is ensured. Proximity does not presume friendship or business.

HIERARCHY-ORIENTED OR EGALITY-ORIENTED? Organizational structures are typically flat and not overly burdened with hierarchy; those with authority do not flaunt it. Decisions are made by superiors with input from their subordinates. Status and rank are generally not overtly displayed; anything ostentatious is usually discounted. In the family, children are raised to be independent thinkers at an early age, and men and women share the roles of breadwinners and nurturers equally (housewives and househusbands are both common; each is involved in the tasks of raising children and making a home). At work, women and men can equally share most functions; less distinction is made between the roles of men and women at work (and in society in general) in Sweden (and in the rest of Scandinavia) than in most other parts of the world. The value of each individual is highly respected, as an important part of the larger Swedish organization. The goal in Swedish society (and this is true elsewhere in Scandinavia) is to minimize the differences between groups and individuals. The Swedish concept of *lagom* is critical: it means that nothing should be in excess, nothing should be in the extreme. The best course is always the middle one, and this translates, in organizational terms, to businesses (and societies) being organized and run with the concerns of the majority being preeminent.

RULE-ORIENTED OR RELATIONSHIP-ORIENTED? In Sweden, rules and order are essential, and it is believed that the universal application of rules is the best way to treat all people fairly and equally. There is great consideration for the individual requirements that individuals and differing groups have regarding similar issues.

2. What's the Best Way to View Time?

MONOCHRONIC OR POLYCHRONIC? The Swedish culture is essentially monochronic: punctuality is important in both the business world and personal life. However, life is not as rigidly compartmentalized as, say German monochronism, and here *lagom* also demands moderation in the separation of the personal and the professional, fun and work. Swedes easily mix these elements together, believing that it makes for a better life. This supports the Swedish belief in a kind of utopianism: that a good life is available for most, if moderation and concern for others remain the primary motivation of the individual. Careful planning is important, and the Swede (as is the case again for most Scandinavians) is not automatically open to new and different ideas: time must be taken for careful analysis and to allow opportunities to be evaluated by everyone involved. Changing schedules at the last minute is seen as very careless.

RISK-TAKING OR RISK-AVERSE? The Swedes are generally in the middle in this category (*lagom* again!), but they will see and act on opportunities. However, it will not be without first giving careful thought and consideration to all sides, participants, and details. Everyone involved must be brought into the consultation. New information is not taken at face value: it is usually suspect at first. Taking action without having all the facts is foolhardy, and the Swedes, when they do take action, usually do so carefully and without heroics or fanfare.

PAST-ORIENTED OR FUTURE-ORIENTED? Sweden is really neither past-oriented nor future-oriented, in the sense that the utopian notion of social welfare is focused on the here and now, on making life better for most. There is a certain nostalgia in Sweden for the past glories, and for the more recent past's obvious easy successes with creating the "perfect" middle-class world; the obstacles encountered in attempting to achieve this goal today are seen as troubling and complex. Nevertheless, Swedes do exude a certain confidence over being able to do whatever needs to be done in order to maintain their admittedly high standard of living into the future.

3. What's the Best Way for Society to Work with the World at Large?

LOW-CONTEXT DIRECT OR HIGH-CONTEXT INDIRECT COMMUNICATORS? Sweden is essentially a mixed low-context and high-context culture, with words, being powerful tools for communicating fact and emotion, being chosen carefully and economically. At the same time, Swedes can be indirect in their communication of negative, difficult, or challenging ideas, as direct speech around those issues can disturb cooperation, which is critically important in such an other-dependent culture. Because of the need to maintain cooperation between individuals, it may be difficult for Swedes to say no, and so they have developed many polite ways of indicating negativity. You need to be tuned to this possibility always, especially in situations where differences may be inherent. Swedes may say things like "This may be difficult," or say "*Nja*," combining the Swedish words for "yes" (*ja*) and "no" (*nej*), when they really mean they won't, can't, or don't want to. Sometimes you might hear "*Tja*": this, too, is a way of expressing negativity softly. In context, it really means something like "It doesn't look like I'll be able to do that." In addition, because of the need for consensus, superiors rarely instruct subordinates directly, but rather "invite" them to do certain things. This is a high-context and subtle way of communicating orders, and you should mirror this whenever circumstances require: direct, challenging, and overtly negative speech is not admired or preferred.

PROCESS-ORIENTED OR RESULT-ORIENTED? Swedes need to see the rationale for doing something, and are usually not convinced with merely practical results from the past. Moreover, emotional expression does nothing to reinforce the facts; in fact, emotions are usually avoided in most Swedish scenarios, and remaining cool and under control is always seen as the smarter way to go.

FORMAL OR INFORMAL? Sweden, of all the Scandinavian cultures, is probably the most formal, but formality is selective and appropriate only to specific situations. In general, Scandinavian culture is relaxed and not ritualized. *Lagom,* however, usually leads to disapproval of spontaneity and unbridled creativity, unless it quickly can be harnessed to the service of society. Individual expression must not challenge what is clearly socially acceptable and in the best interests of all.

Greetings and Introductions

Language and Basic Vocabulary

In Swedish, as in all Scandinavian languages, there are several additional vowel sounds, represented by the umlaut over the letters *a* (i.e., *säng*) and *o* (i.e., *böda*). These letters are usually alphabetized after Z at the end of the alphabet. Scandinavian languages are different in many respects from English, although English and Swedish do share, in different ways, an older Germanic root base. Many Swedes speak English, especially in business, but not necessarily on the street, and part of the Swedish reserve you will run into is really hesitation to use English if they do not speak it well. If there is a second language spoken other than English, it will in most cases be German.

Here are some basic Swedish terms and their English translations:

ja	yes
nej	no
var snäll och/tack	please
tack	thank you
ingen orsak	you're welcome
god morgon	good morning
god middag	good afternoon
god afton	good evening
god natt	good night
adjö	good-bye
angenämt	pleased to meet you
Hur mår ni/du?	How are you?
bara bra, tack	very well, thanks
Och ni/du?	And you?
Talar ni Engleska?	Do you speak English?
forlåt/ursäkta	excuse me
jag förstår	I understand
jag förstår inte	I don't understand
Mitt namn ar . . .	My name is . . .

Honorifics for Men, Women, and Children

The terms *herr* (Mr.) and *fru* (Ms.), plus the family name, are an absolute must for you to use when introduced to adults. There is no need to indicate marriage status: in fact, in gender-neutral Sweden, and to a lesser degree in other Nordic countries as well, many couples remain in common-law marriages until the birth of their first child. Unless or until your Swedish colleague specifically invites you to use first names, and despite how he or she might refer to you, you should always use the family name plus the correct honorific. Sometimes these honorifics are used along with titles, in place of names, but never in place of titles; for example, an engineer is referred to as "Engineer Ericsson" or, less likely, "Mister Engineer." Children in Sweden, while not overly conversational, are free-speaking, but in a respectful way.

If you speak any Swedish at all, by all means use it (your efforts will be appreciated, and most Swedes will be amazed that you know some Swedish at all), but recognize that as soon as you are identified as an English speaker, your Swedish colleagues will probably switch to English, if they know it. For casual contacts (e.g., with waiters, store help, etc.), just use *herr* or *fru* without the name. It is very important to greet people at work or in stores or restaurants with a greeting for the appropriate time of day, as well as saying *adjö* (good-bye) upon leaving.

The What, When, and How of Introducing People

Always wait to be introduced to strangers before taking that responsibility upon yourself. Swedes are most comfortable with a third-party introduction whenever possible. Try to ensure that for yourself ahead of time. Do not presume to seat yourself at a formal gathering: if possible, wait to be told where to sit. If not so instructed, assume that men will sit and stand on the outside when with women. Shake hands with everyone individually in a group when being introduced and before departing: the American group wave is not appreciated. When you are introduced to people, it is appropriate simply to repeat your family name, so that you are sure they know who you are, and so that you have the chance to hear their names again and learn them. There is an older tradition in Sweden to refer respectfully to others in the third person; that is, when speaking to Mr. Lindberg, one might say, "Would Mr. Lindberg care to join me for dinner tonight?" Once you greet someone you will encounter later that day in the same circumstances (e.g., at the office), there is no need to greet them again. Kissing is not common as a greeting, even between people who know each other well. The use of business cards is very common; if possible, you should have your business card translated into Swedish on the reverse, but this is not absolutely necessary, as most businesspeople read English.

Physical Greeting Styles

The handshake is common. The Swedish version is similar to the American handshake, but usually does not last as long. It is done quickly and firmly between two men, but not as robustly between men and women or between two women. The handshake should be accompanied by the appropriate greeting (see the list of Swedish terms outlined above). Smiling and other nonverbal forms of communication need not accompany the handshake when it is between people who have not met previously. Men should wait until a woman extends her hand before reaching for it, and women may take the lead in extending their hand or not. Men must remove their gloves when shaking hands with a woman, but a woman need not remove her gloves when shaking hands with a man. If more than two people are greeting each other, it is not correct to reach across arms to shake hands (making a kind of *X*). If a woman is in a group, she is introduced first. Informal body gestures are not appreciated during the first introduction between strangers, so avoid backslapping and other forms of touching. Eye contact during the introduction is direct, and should be maintained as long as the individual is addressing you.

Communication Styles

Okay Topics / Not Okay Topics

Okay: current events, politics (as long as you know what you are talking about and discuss the subject dispassionately; if the conversation becomes confrontational, Swedes will shy away from it), the arts, and vacations and holidays, sports (very big, especially soccer), music, philosophy, the outdoors, and nature. Swedes will listen attentively to what everyone has to say, giving all people the opportunity to speak their piece, and rise or fall by their own devices, but tend to shy away from direct confrontation. *Not okay:* It is important to recognize that small talk and chitchat in general is not the typical Swedish way, and certainly so at the business table. Even in social situations, talk may be less animated, and there may simply be less of it; Swedes do enjoy the camaraderie of good friends and family, but it can take time to establish a close relationship. Do not inquire about a person's occupation in casual conversation. Americans often begin a conversation with "So, what do you do?"; this is too personal in Europe, and is often not the most interesting topic of conversation. Also not okay: personal financial discussions, the Olaf Palme assassination, questions about private family matters (the family is sacred), personal background, and the like. Anything that smacks of rank, showiness, and status is generally downplayed and not appreciated. Do try to show a knowledge (or at least interest) in things Swedish, especially those aspects of the culture that distinguish Swedes from other Scandinavians. Do not compare social welfare systems, or complain about the cost of living in Scandinavia (it is quite high): Swedes, and most Scandinavians, are tired of hearing about it from foreigners.

Tone, Volume, and Speed

Discussions between strangers usually start out politely restrained; in public or during first business meetings, the conversational tone can be slightly subdued and matter of fact, and generally remains so. Do not interrupt others; let each speaker make his or her point and then respond. Keep your voice low, especially in public: never speak loudly or shout, even on the street. Words are carefully thought out and spoken softly. Note that in gender-neutral Sweden, both women and men may start conversations with either gender; one needs to be careful not to assume any sexual intent if approached by someone of the opposite sex until such cues are more clearly expressed. *Lagom* also requires that speech be matter of fact and not filled with the hyperbole Americans are known for. Switch down from "great" to "okay," "fine" to "good," "love" to "like," and so on. There is no need to overemphasize: omit "really" whenever possible. Really.

Use of Silence

Swedes use short periods of silence to think about what was said, and to decide on their response. These need not be awkward moments: enjoy the respite.

Physical Gestures and Facial Expressions

Swedes usually gesture to someone with their chin: for example, a motion of the head means that you should come over and join them. Facial gestures are usually kept to a minimum, and body language is controlled. Do not try to "read" the face for emotional meaning, as Swedes tend not to express overt emotions physically in public. During cold weather, men usually tip their hats in greeting when introduced outdoors to others, and remove hats immediately upon entering a building.

Waving and Counting

The thumb represents the number 1, the index finger the number 2, and so on. It is insulting to beckon someone with the forefinger (instead, turn your hand so that the palm faces up and motion inward with all four fingers at once). Keep your gestures to a minimum. If you need to call for a waiter, just subtly raise your hand.

Physicality and Physical Space

Swedes tend to stay slightly farther apart than North Americans. Never speak with your hands in your pockets: always keep them firmly at your side when standing. If women must cross their legs, it must never be ankle over knee (this is not an issue for men). Remember, even in public, formal is always better than informal: no gum chewing, *ever;* don't slouch; and don't lean against things. At meetings, take your cue from the senior participants as to how informal or formal one should act, dress, and sit.

Eye Contact

Eye contact should be direct. If you look away, your behavior will say to your Swedish colleague that you are either disinterested or rude. Either way, maintain eye contact when it is made with you. Standing in someone's line of sight in order to make eye contact is a way of saying "I want to talk with you"; be sure you do this judiciously, and only where and when such an act does not challenge the order of things (i.e., don't do it if it interrupts an ongoing conversation unless it's really important to do so). This is one of the reasons that doors are usually closed in homes and offices, and why privacy is so important.

Emotive Orientation

Keep emotions at a minimum: cool, calm, and matter of fact is the preferred way in Sweden under all circumstances—whether business and social, under pressure or relaxed, or having fun.

Protocol in Public

Walking Styles and Waiting in Lines

The importance of order and organization is apparent even on the Swedish streets: men walk on the curbside of women; younger people walk on the curbside of older people; if there are two men and one woman, one man walks on each side of the woman. Men precede women up a flight of stairs to avoid walking behind a woman who might be in a skirt or dress. Swedes are generally orderly in queues, and wait their turns. Women might walk arm in arm down the street.

Behavior in Public Places: Airports, Terminals, and the Market

As in much of Europe, if you touch the produce in food markets, you buy it; in goods stores, it may be difficult for you to return a product, unless there is a flaw in it. Smoking is on the decline, although no-smoking areas in restaurants and other public places are not ubiquitous. On the street, do not cross against a red light; wait patiently on the curb instead until the light turns green (on streets where there are no traffic lights, be very careful when crossing: the cars do not necessarily stop for pedestrians). In social welfare–conscious Sweden, street lights in the major cities have sound devices to assist the blind in crossing: a rapid clicking means "green."

The telecard is appearing more and more frequently at Swedish public phones, but most still accept coins (put in five kroner to get a dial tone). The appropriate way to answer the telephone is to say *hallo* plus your family name.

Bus / Metro / Taxi / Car

Driving is on the right, but people pass very quickly on the left. The metro system and buses stop operating after midnight or 1 A.M. Your best bet for catching a cab is at designated taxi stands (hotels are good places, but often charge more for the same ride: a hotel surcharge is added to the meter fare, in some cases).

Drunk driving laws are strictly enforced: do not have even one drink and drive.

Tipping

Tips are generally included in the total price; nevertheless, waiters usually expect an additional 10 percent. Taxi drivers also require about 10 percent, but hotel staff usually gets one or two kroner per service rendered.

Punctuality

Never be late, if you can avoid it, under any circumstance, either social or business. If you must be late for any reason, it is absolutely essential to call ahead and let someone know of your problem—and you should have an appropriate explanation, as well.

Dress

Clothing is formal for both men and women, no matter the occasion—business or social, at work, in a restaurant, or on a street. Formal in this case means, at least in the office, a dark suit and tie for men, and a business suit or skirt and blouse for women. Khakis and other informal wear for men are not appropriate in business settings. On the street, informal may mean jeans and sneakers (they should always be neat and clean), though that is more common as clothing to wear at the gym, the beach, or while jogging (women do not wear sneakers to work); for a social gathering, informal more often than not means tastefully coordinated clothes, although not necessarily a jacket and tie for men (it rarely means jeans, sneakers, and T-shirts). "Formal" usually means formal evening wear, which is very dressy by American standards. Most restaurants do not require a tie for men, although the upscale restaurants expect both men and women to dress well. Swedes usually dress up (somewhat) on Sunday. Remember, the need to keep a low profile, and avoid anything showy or status-linked, means that even well-paid senior executives do not necessarily dress any fancier than average employees. This does not mean that Swedes do not dress well; rather, it means that all Swedes typically dress well, none that much better than others. The only time that American-style casual clothes are really appropriate (including shorts and T-shirts) is during the summer out in the countryside.

Swedes are surprisingly fashion conscious, and well-designed, high-styled clothing is preferred, especially at work and in the evening when going out. This is even the case in the smaller towns.

Seasonal Variations

There are four distinct seasons in Sweden, and one needs to dress appropriately. During the height of summer, the weather can be hot and humid. The long winter (it can last for as much as nine months) demands serious winter clothes: heavy coats, warm gloves, hats, boots, the works. As is the case throughout all the Nordic countries, colder weather allows women (and sometimes men) to wear heavy boots to work, and then to change into more comfortable office shoes.

Colors

Bright colors and patterns are generally not suitable for business wear, either for men or for women, except during the warmer months, when they are appreciated and enjoyed.

Dining and Drinking

Mealtimes and Typical Foods

Breakfast (*frukost*) is served around 7 to 9 A.M. (later in the summer months in the country), and often includes fruit, cheeses, yogurt, dried cereals, rolls, jams, butter, and perhaps some pickled vegetables or fish. Fish (especially herring) is an important staple. Coffee or tea is the typical *frukost* drink.

Lunch (same word, *frukost,* is used in Swedish) is usually served from 12 to 1 P.M. Beer or wine typically accompanies all lunches, either business or social, in restaurants, cafés, or workplace cafeterias; mineral water, with or without carbonation, and juice or soft drinks are also available. Lunch usually consists of an open-faced sandwich containing a wonderful assortment of ingredients (cheeses, vegetables, meats, or fish). On Sunday, the family day, the main meal is supper, which is usually served in the middle of the afternoon, and can last well into the evening.

Dinner (*middag*) is usually served from 6:00 to 7:30 P.M. in Swedish homes, with 8 P.M. the customary time for weekend dinner parties. The evening meal may be similar to lunch, with meats, fish, vegetables, and dessert. Drinks served with dinner are usually regional beers or wine. The traditional Swedish dinner has four courses: fish, meat, salad, and dessert. Coffee is served after the meal (never during) and is usually taken in the living room.

Swedes also stop for snacks: once around 10 A.M., and again at 4 P.M.

Regional Differences

Swedish food does vary, but essentially it is hearty fare designed to get one through a long cold winter. Sausages, cheeses, breads, and meats of all varieties abound, along with cooked vegetables and potatoes. Dried, fresh, smoked, marinated, or pickled fish is a dietary staple. Salmon and the ubiquitous dill appear everywhere. There is a particular fondness for fruit soups, and, when in season, berries of all types (some unique to Scandinavia, such as lingonberries and cloudberries). Desserts are usually simple cakes, crêpes, and sweets, served with coffee. The Swedes freely use dairy products in most of their cooking. Gravlax (cured salmon, usually served with dill), lox (smoked salmon), and marinated salmon are wonderful specialties, along with all sorts of caviars. Try lutfisk (dried cod treated with lye) and, if you can, the delicious reindeer meat. In the winter months, the traditional Thursday meal is pea soup and pancakes served with lingonberry jam (*arter med flask*), and during the holidays there are all sorts of wonderful Christmas treats to try.

The smorgasbord is a famous Swedish tradition. You are expected to make several trips to the smorgasbord table, each time to sample a different kind of food. With each trip, it is important not to fill up your plate; if you do, you will not be able to sample all the foods, and the proper etiquette at the smorgasbord is to do so. Your first plate should be for fish, specifically herring: take some with a boiled potato and a little sour cream. Once finished, change plates, and sample some of the other fish (usually salmon of all varieties, and caviars). Then take a clean plate for the cold meats (put some slices on your plate, along with some salad made from fresh vegetables and pickles). Next, move on to a fourth clean plate for the hot meat course. Finally, there is usually a fifth plate for dessert.

Typical Drinks and Toasting

Mixed drinks before dinner are not common; however, before the meal one might have an aperitif, usually aquavit, served in the living room. Aquavit is a clear liquor, flavored with caraway, and very potent. It is typically served ice cold; men usually drink it in one shot, and women sip it slowly (Danish men usually shoot it, followed by a beer chaser). Do not take your aperitif to the table: try to finish it before dinner is announced. Once the meal gets under way, wine or beer will be served in most cases.

The most common toast is *skoal.* Do not reach for your drink until the host or hostess has said *skoal;* at that moment, you should take your glass and raise it. Wait for the host or hostess to make the first toast; after that, you are free to propose one. It is absolutely essential when making a toast to maintain direct eye contact from the moment the glass is raised to the moment it is placed back down on the table. If many people are being toasted, go around the table with your eyes, making contact with each individual as you make the toast. Do not begin eating until the host has invited you to do so.

At the end of a dinner party, the male guest of honor is usually obligated to thank the host or hostess, acting as a spokesperson for all the guests. The guest of honor usually precedes the thank-you announcement by tapping his knife gently against his water glass, and then saying *Tack for maten* (thank you for the food).

Table Manners and the Use of Utensils

Swedes, like all continental Europeans, do not switch knives and forks, as Americans do. The knife remains in the right hand, and the fork remains in the left. When the meal is finished, the knife and fork are laid parallel to each other across the right side of the plate, the tips pointing to the ten o'clock position; the knife should be above the fork, with the blade side pointing in toward the plate. If you put both utensils down on the plate for any real length of time, it is a sign to the waitstaff that you are finished, and your plate may be taken away from you. The fork and spoon above your plate are usually for dessert. There are often many additional pieces of cutlery; if you're unsure of which utensil to use, always start from the outside and work your way in, course by course. There will be separate glasses provided at your setting for water and white and red wine (after-dinner drink glasses come out after dinner).

When not holding utensils, your hands are expected to be visible above the table: this means that you do not keep them in your lap; instead, rest your wrists on top of the table (never your elbows). At the table, pass all dishes to your left. Salt and pepper shakers or holders should be passed so that the receiving person takes them directly; do not place them down on the table first. Never cut the lettuce in a salad: deftly fold it with your knife and fork so that it can be picked up in a small bundle with your fork. The only food eaten at the table with the hands is bread.

Seating Plans

The most honored position is either at the head of the table or in the center, with the most important guests seated first to the left and then to the right of the head of the table or the host(s) in descending order of importance. If there is a hosting couple, one will be seated at each end of the table, with the male guest of honor seated to the left of the hostess, and the female guest of honor seated to the right of the host. In keeping with the practice elsewhere on the Continent, men and women are seated next to one another, and couples are often broken up and seated next to people they may not have previously known. This is done to promote conversation. Men always rise when women enter the room, and both men and women rise when older people enter or leave a room. Remember, as is the case throughout the Continent, what the Swedes call the first floor is really the second floor, with the first floor usually referred to as the lobby or ground floor.

Refills and Seconds

If you do not want more food, leave just a bit on your plate. You may always have additional beverages; drink enough to cause your cup or glass to be less than half full, and it will generally be refilled. Portions are generally about the same size as in the United States.

At Home, in a Restaurant, or at Work

In informal restaurants, you may be required to share a table: if so, do not force conversation; rather, act as if you are seated at a private table. Waitstaff may be summoned by making eye contact; waving or calling their names is very impolite. Breakfast meetings are not common, except perhaps among traveling businesspeople in hotels. The business lunch or dinner is a more widespread practice, but, depending upon how well developed your relationship is with your Swedish colleagues, it is generally not the time to make business decisions. Take your cue from your Swedish associates: if they bring up business, then it's okay to discuss it, but wait to take your lead from their conversation. No gum chewing, ever, at a restaurant or on the street. No-smoking sections in restaurants are still a rarity.

Meals at a Swedish associate's home can be either relaxed or formal; take your cue from the information your host gives you when you are invited. Unlike other countries, you may be surprised at how quickly you might be invited to a dinner at a Swedish home. Once within the home, you will be told where to sit, and there you should remain. Do not wander from room to room: much of the house is really off-limits to guests. At the table, be sure to look for place cards, or wait until the host indicates your seat: do not presume to seat yourself, as the seating arrangement may be predetermined. At an informal gathering in the Swedish home, you will be expected to remove your shoes, following a Swedish family tradition (you'll know if you need to by looking at the shoes that may or may not be lined up just inside or outside the entrance door); be sure your socks don't have holes in them!

Being a Good Guest or Host

Paying the Bill

Usually the one who does the inviting pays the bill, although the guest is expected to make an effort to pay. Sometimes other circumstances determine the payee (such as rank). Making payment arrangements ahead of time so that no exchange occurs at the table is a very classy way to host.

Transportation

It's a very nice idea, when acting as the host, to inquire ahead of time as to whether the guests will require transportation. If necessary, you should arrange for taxi service at the end of the meal.

When to Arrive / Chores to Do

If invited to dinner at a private home, you may offer to help with the chores, but you will probably not have to. Do not leave the table until invited to do so. Spouses are often included in business dinners (most commonly if both business associates are married). When it is time to leave (usually by 11 P.M. or so), always get up and shake hands with everyone: the group wave is not appreciated. If you are invited to stay overnight at a Swedish home, be sure to leave things tidy and clean up after yourself. By the way, never drop by an associate's home uninvited or unannounced: always phone ahead and ask if it is convenient to stop by.

Gift Giving

In general, gift giving is not common among business associates; it is best not to send a gift at any time, including the holidays, unless you receive one first from your Swedish colleagues. Holiday cards are quite appropriate, particularly as a thank-you for their business during the previous year, and should be mailed in time to be received the week before Christmas.

Gifts are expected for social events, however, especially as thank-yous for private dinner parties. If you choose flowers, bring them with you to the dinner party, and be sure to unwrap them before entering the home or handing them to the hostess. Never send chrysanthemums or white lilies (they are used primarily as funeral flowers); also avoid red roses or orchids (these usually indicate romantic intent); and always make sure the bouquet is in odd numbers (an old European tradition). Other good gifts would be fine chocolates or a quality wine; unlike other European countries, alcohol in Sweden is very expensive, so a bottle of fine wine is very much appreciated as a gift at a dinner party.

If you are staying with a family, an appropriate thank-you gift would be a high-quality product that represents your country and is difficult to get in Sweden: gourmet foodstuffs (maple syrup, pralines, lobsters, etc.), coffee-table books about the United States, or anything that reflects your host's personal tastes (the cap of a famous American team for the football-playing son of the family, for example) is appropriate. Don't give your host something that is easily obtainable in Sweden. If you are given a gift, it might very likely be a small red wooden horse as a home decoration: it is a ubiquitous folk object, and unique to Sweden.

Special Holidays and Celebrations

Major Holidays

Business slows down during July and August, the traditional vacation months, and again during the Christmas and New Year's seasons (December 15 to January 1).

January 1	*Nyarsdagen* (New Year's Day)
January 6	*Trettondagen* (Epiphany)
March/April	*Langfredagen* (Good Friday)
March/April	*Paskdagen* (Easter Sunday) and *Annandag Pask* (Easter Monday)
April 30	The king's birthday
May 1	*Forsta Maj* (May Day)
May 16	*Kristi himmelsfardsdag* (Ascension)
May	*Pingstdagen* (Whitsunday) and *Annandag pingst* (Whitmonday)

June 6   National Flag Day
June   *Midsommerafton* (Midsummer Eve) and *Midsommerdagen*
                (Midsummer Day) (Perhaps the most anticipated and
                celebrated holiday in Sweden: it officially begins the season
                for crayfish, which are highly prized among Swedes)
November 1   *Allhelgonadagen* (All Saints' Day)
November 11   *Mortens dag* (Saint Martin's Day)
December 13   Saint Lucia Day (An important festival in which the girls put
                candles in their hair and parade through city streets)
December 25   *Juldgan* (Christmas)
December 26   *Annandag jul* (Boxing Day)

Business Culture

Daily Office Protocols

In Sweden, doors are usually closed (and sometimes locked); knock first (this includes bathrooms) before opening doors, and when leaving rooms, close the doors behind you. Women and men are often treated as equals in Sweden: be prepared for decision makers to be of either sex, and remember that all members of a team are capable of being involved in the decision-making process. Staying late at the office is not necessarily taken as a good sign: it more often will be interpreted as indicating that the individual is incapable of organizing him- or herself well enough to accomplish the job in the time permitted. Do not expect people to work over weekends, holidays, or vacations: these times are usually sacred, although Swedish businesspeople will take work home with them in the evening. It is not improper to call a Swedish colleague at home (if you have been given his or her personal number and permission to do so) on business matters in the evening of a workday, if it is necessary and the matter cannot wait until the next day.

Management Styles

Privacy and individual accomplishment of one's tasks are critical; however, there can be much interaction between senior management and staff, and within and among team members. Quiet, thoughtful, and diligent adherence to procedures is believed to be the most effective way of accomplishing a task. Anything out of the ordinary or unusual is usually not appreciated, and must be explained. People and things need to be credible and substantial. The ability to be a smooth-working member of the team is important; sincerity and seriousness, not necessarily friendliness, are preferred attributes. Complimenting and rewarding employees publicly is usually not done. Swedes usually get straight down to business with little or no small talk.

Boss-Subordinate Relations

Bosses are expected to provide guidance, distribute information, and make decisions; subordinates are expected to provide detailed information and follow the decisions made by their superiors. All are expected to work together as equals.

The hierarchy is usually extremely accessible and an air of informal respect between workers, staff, and superiors is preferred. Generally, a meeting is held once a year between boss and subordinate to review performance and work-related topics (*utvecklingssamtal,* meaning "development talk," or *planeringssamtal,* meaning "planning talk"). Coworkers of any rank usually do not socialize together after work.

Conducting a Meeting or Presentation

At meetings of peers, there can be open communication and sharing of ideas: in fact, these sessions often serve as information-sharing and decision-making forums in which all individuals are expected to contribute, in their way and in their turn, with no interruptions. In more formal, conservative organizations, meetings are often gatherings of nonpeers, in which decision makers share in mutual problem solving, and superiors and subordinates act and speak more as equals with each other. Everyone is valued. Facts and figures are essential, and must be clearly outlined and detailed. Presentations should include handouts and colorful overheads.

Negotiation Styles

Swedes respect someone who comes to them with established knowledge and experience. No detail is too unimportant, and a carefully proposed, logically organized proposal is the key to getting Swedes to accept a new idea from the outside. The first meeting may be very matter of fact and low key, with the Swedes sizing up you, your organization, and your ideas: it will be conducted in the office. Because time needs to be carefully managed, plan your meeting carefully and well in advance, and prepare a detailed agenda for circulation prior to the scheduled date. Several meetings may be necessary before all details are clear and all questions answered. Confirm all meetings and the preparations for them well in advance. Casually changing time and place is not appreciated. The best times for meetings are 9 to 10 A.M. and 2 to 4 P.M. Never be late. Once decisions are made, they can be confirmed in writing, but you may consider the agreement already active. Avoid open disagreement, confrontation, and conflict at all costs.

Written Correspondence

Your correspondence with Swedish colleagues should be very businesslike, with few references to personal matters. Dates are written using the day/month/year format (with periods in between, not slashes), and an honorific plus a title is as common as an honorific plus the last name.

<blockquote>
CHAPTER TEN
</blockquote>

The Nordic Cultures: Norway and Denmark

NORWAY

Note: Please refer to the previous chapter for information about general Nordic cultural behaviors; the material that follows describes specific Norwegian variations on general Nordic customs.

Some Introductory Background and Historical Context on Norway and the Norwegians

Norwegians appreciate it when you recognize them as being different from their Scandinavian cousins. Do not confuse Danes, Swedes, Norwegians, and Finns with each other: there are differences which are felt keenly within the region. In addition, Norwegians view each other as either urban or rural, and each is seen as possessing its own characteristics. In fact, the ruggedness of the country and the distinctions made between south and north, urban and rural, leads to, among other things, almost a hundred different dialects and very different lifestyles throughout the country. As with other Scandinavians, Norwegians have a strong belief in the social welfare system, but also in individual responsibility to oneself and for others (especially the less fortunate). From time to time the Norwegians, who were perhaps the original Vikings—the tenth-century Norwegian Viking king Harold the Fairhair was the first to consolidate Swedes, Norwegians, and Danes into one Viking empire—ironically have been the pawns in the greater power struggles between Swedes and Danes, and subsequently tend to disassociate themselves from both. Norwegians would prefer to see themselves as the rugged individualists of the region, looking not to the Baltic or Germany or Russia, but rather to the North Sea and England as their sphere.

An Area Briefing

Politics and Government

Norway is a constitutional monarchy, with a one-house parliament (the Storting). An interesting feature of Norwegian government is that executive power rests not in the prime minister, but in the Council of Ministers (the cabinet, in which the prime minister is one among many). There are many political parties with proportional representation.

Schools and Education

Primary school education is similar to Sweden's, but from age sixteen through nineteen students attend upper secondary school, choosing either an academic, vocational, or mixed vocational and academic curriculum. Depending upon the track chosen, they may then move on to college, university, or other vocational, adult education training institutions.

Religion and Demographics

The Evangelical Lutheran Church of Norway is the state church, and the vast majority of the people are members, but Catholics, Jews, and other religious groups are also represented in Norway. Recently, immigration from eastern Europe, the Middle East, Asia, and Africa has increased the numbers of non-native Norwegians; in fact, Oslo (the nation's capital) is a center for foreign workers. Not as much of the population lives along the coast or in the cities as one might expect, no doubt due in part to the Norwegian affinity for traditional rural life.

Fundamental Cultural Orientations

There is perhaps a slightly greater emphasis in Norwegian culture on the role of the individual in the larger social system, relative to Sweden. Although the social welfare system is deeply entrenched in Norway, it is the individual and the fulfillment of his or her personal responsibility to society that makes the social system work. There is also a strong tradition in Norway for helping others and supporting the underdog. Everyone should be equal. The family plays an enormously important role in the daily life of Norwegians: it is the stable, reliable source of dependability in an uncertain world.

Norwegians are essentially monochronic, but perhaps not as much as Swedes, and there is slightly more flexibility around the time issue, especially when it comes to social events. This is no doubt related to the fact that while Swedes tend to be formal, Norwegians are not. They can move fairly quickly onto a first-name basis, and are generally more relaxed, both in business and in social settings. Norwegians have a greater tendency to engage in open discussion, and are not as uncomfortable with confrontation and conflict as might be their Swedish cousins. They are very concerned about environmental, nature, and fairness issues (the Norwegian zest for fairness and egalitarianism is strong).

Greetings and Introductions

Language and Basic Vocabulary

As a Scandinavian language, Norwegian shares similarities with Danish and Swedish; however, as stated, there are numerous dialects. In fact, two basic languages are used in the country: Bøkmål (book language) heard in schools, broadcasting, and government and spoken by the majority of the people; and the more dialectical Nynørsk language, spoken mainly in southwest Norway.

Here are some basic Norwegian terms and their English meanings:

hållø	hello
ådjø	good-bye
gød dåg	good day
gød mørgen	good morning
gød middåg	good afternoon
gød kveld	good evening
gød natt	good night
vennligst	please
tåkk	thank you
månge tåkk	thank you very much
ingen årsak	you're welcome
det gleder meg å treffe Dem	pleased to meet you
jå	yes
nei	no
unnskyld	pardon
beklåger	sorry

Honorifics for Men, Women, and Children

Use *herr* (Mr.), *fru* (Ms.), or *frøken* (Miss) with the last name; there is no need to indicate marriage status. You may be invited by your Norwegian colleague to move on to a first-name basis quite quickly; nevertheless, always begin with last names and honorifics. Men and women sometimes are addressed just by their family name, without the honorific in both formal and informal situations.

The What, When, and How of Introducing People

Norwegian customs are similar to those practiced throughout Scandinavia; however, when a Norwegian says *"mørn,"* it is an informal way of saying hello or good day, not just a way of saying good morning, and may be used at any time of the day or night as a less formal greeting. In addition, Norwegians do not necessarily rise when someone new enters a room (but you should rise always when being introduced to someone new). Lawyers and clergy do not use titles: *herr* plus the family name suffices.

Communication Styles

Okay Topics / Not Okay Topics

Okay: discussing the Norwegian Winter Olympics, and evidencing an interest in and curiosity about things Norwegian. Doors and windows in Norwegian homes (especially older ones) may be covered by draperies and/or wallpaper; don't be embarrassed to ask where a door or window is if you need to. *Not okay:* Avoid controversial topics, such as whaling and the country's dependency on the oil industry; also, you should never ask questions about spouses or raise any issues related to marriage, since many Norwegian couples—as is the case in much of Scandinavia—are, in fact, not married.

Physical Gestures and Facial Expressions

The thumb-to-forefinger circle hand gesture (which signifies "okay" in the United States) is *not okay* in Norway: it is considered rude and obscene, and should be avoided. In some rural areas, spitting toward a person as they turn to leave you brings them good luck, don't be offended if you're "spit good-bye."

Waving and Counting

The "V for Victory" hand gesture, as is the case in all English-speaking countries with the exception of the United States, must always be done with your palms facing out; if done with your palms facing in, it can be construed as a very rude and obscene gesture.

Protocol in Public

Norway currently has few telecard facilities for its public telephone system; you must put in five kroners to get a dial tone. More time means more coins. The appropriate way to answer the telephone is to say *hållø* plus your family name.

Tipping

Tips are generally included in the total price. Unlike the custom in Sweden, there is no need for any additional tip, although some spare change is always appreciated, and you may acknowledge superior service if you wish with an additional 5 to 10 percent.

Dress

Clothing styles are far less formal than in Sweden, although neatness and cleanliness are absolutely essential. For work, men can wear a sports jacket and slacks, with a tie and a dress shirt; suits are not essential. Women often wear dress slacks to work. There are holiday and festival times throughout the year where traditional Norwegian dress is worn as part of the celebrations.

Dining and Drinking

Mealtimes and Typical Foods

Breakfast (*frøkøst*) is usually served around 7 to 9 A.M. (later in the summer months in the country), and often includes cheeses, yogurt, dried cereals, rolls, cold meats, fish, and eggs (hard and soft-boiled). Coffee or tea is the typical *frøkøst* drink.

Lunch (*lunsj*) is usually served from 12 to 1 P.M. The luncheon menu is similar to the fare served at the evening meal in Norwegian homes, or else consists of open-faced sandwiches.

Dinner (*middåg*) is usually served from 5 to 6:30 P.M. in Norwegian homes, with 7 P.M. the customary time for weekend dinner parties. The evening meal may consist of meats, fish, vegetables, and dessert. Drinks served with dinner are usually regional beers or wine. The traditional Norwegian dinner party begins with soup, then moves on to a seafood appetizer, the main meat course with a salad, and ends with dessert. White wine may accompany the soup and appetizer, red wine the meat dish, and a sweet wine the dessert. Coffee follows dinner. Fresh homemade breads and/or thin flatbreads often accompany the evening meal. Dinner parties in the summer can last until 11 or 11:30 P.M.; in the winter, they usually end around 10 P.M. Therefore, if dinner is over sooner, expect to have coffee or a liqueur or perhaps a walk before the party is actually over.

Regional Differences

The smorgasbord is celebrated in Norway as it is throughout all of Scandinavia. The important thing to emphasize here is not to waste any food; take only what you will eat, and you can always return to the smorgasbord for more. Some uniquely Norwegian foods include whale meat, reindeer meat, Norwegian salmon, and *gjetøst,* a sweet Norwegian cheese made from goat's milk.

Typical Drinks and Toasting

The predinner aquavit in Norway is served ice cold; it is downed all at once, followed by a beer chaser. There are three types of beers in Norway: low-alcohol *brigg,* the lager *pilsener,* and high-alcohol *export.* The most common toast is *skøål,* although toasting by making eye contact without speaking is not uncommon (raise the glass, look your contact in the eye, raise the glass to them again, then drink, never breaking eye contact until the glass is back down on the tabletop).

At the end of a dinner party, the male guest of honor is usually obligated to thank the host or hostess, acting as a spokesperson for all the guests. The guest of honor usually precedes the thank-you announcement by tapping his knife gently against his water glass, and then saying, *tåkk før måten* (thank you for the food).

Table Manners and the Use of Utensils

Norwegians cross their knife and fork across the center of the plate when they are finished with their meal: this is a sign that the plate can be removed. Food is usually passed around on platters, so one is free to take as much or as little as one likes. Seconds are allowed, so take a small amount at first, and be sure to finish it all (especially before going on to seconds). At an informal gathering in a Norwegian home, you will generally not be required to remove your shoes. Although bread may be eaten with the hands, the open-faced sandwiches so common at lunch are always eaten with a knife and fork.

Gift Giving

Norwegian gift-giving customs are similar to those in Sweden, with the additional consideration that if you are bringing flowers, avoid any kind of white flower or carnations, as they are used in funerals. Wreaths of any kind are also used in funerals (not at Christmas), so do not send wreaths as a gift, either.

Special Holidays and Celebrations

Major Holidays

Business generally slows down during July and August, the traditional vacation months, and again during the Christmas and New Year's holiday seasons (December 15 to January 1).

January 1	*Første nyttårsdåg* (New Year's Day)
March/April	*Annen paskedåg* (Easter Monday)
March/April	*Långfredåg* (Good Friday)
May 1	*Første mai* (May Day)
May 16	*Kristi himmelsfårtsdåg* (Ascension)
May 17	*Grunnløvsdågen* (Constitution Day)
May	*Annen pinsedåg* (Whitmonday)
December 25	*Første juledåg* (Christmas)
December 26	*Annen juledåg* (Boxing Day)

DENMARK

Note: Please refer to the preceding chapter for information about general Nordic cultural behaviors; the information that follows describes specific Danish variations on general Nordic customs.

Some Introductory Background and Historical Context on Denmark and the Danes

The Danes were perhaps the mightiest force in the Scandinavian region for many centuries, Denmark alternately allying with powerful Hanseatic, German, Balkan, Polish, Russian, and even English governments in its power struggles with Sweden. Therefore, the Danes, while appreciating their Scandinavian roots, tend to see themselves as more continental than their Scandinavian cousins, and there is a certain genteelness and sophistication that lends an air of simplicity and congenial calm to the way Danes live their lives. In addition, there is an affinity in Denmark for the United States and all things American: the Danes, in fact, celebrate the Fourth of July!

The Danes are perhaps the most informal of all the Scandinavians, and have a sense of humor that is very similar to other Europeans. They do not have the same reputation for silent pensiveness and economy of physical, emotional, and verbal expression that is commonly associated with the other Nordic cultures.

An Area Briefing

Politics and Government

Denmark, too, is a constitutional monarchy with a one-house parliament (the Folketing). An interesting Danish variation on this form of government is the fact that the king appoints the prime minister, who is the head of the government (the king is the head of state).

Schools and Education

The education system is similar in structure to that of the rest of Scandinavia.

Religion and Demographics

Evangelical Lutheranism is the state religion and is practiced by the vast majority of the people, but Catholics, Jews, and other religious groups are represented in Denmark. Recently, immigration from eastern Europe, the Middle East, Asia, and Africa has increased the numbers of non-native Danes. Most of the population is located in the Copenhagen area.

Fundamental Cultural Orientations

There is perhaps an even greater emphasis in Danish culture on the role of the individual in the larger social system than is the case in the rest of Scandinavia. Although the social welfare system is entrenched in Denmark, it is the individual and the fulfillment of his or her personal responsibility to society that makes the social system work. There is also a strong tradition in Denmark for helping others and supporting the underdog. Everyone should be equal. The family plays an enormously important role in the daily life of the Danes; it is the stable, reliable source of dependability in an uncertain world.

Danes are rigorously monochronic, perhaps more so than any other Scandinavian people (is this due to their proximity to northern Germany, perhaps?). Nevertheless, they are relatively informal in their social relationships, and even business matters take on a casual, congenial, and unhurried air. They can move fairly quickly to being on a first-name basis, and are generally more informal than other Nordics. Danes, therefore, have a greater tendency to engage in open discussion; and while they are not as uncomfortable with confrontation and conflict as their Swedish cousins, they are gentle in their response to disagreements.

Greetings and Introductions

Language and Basic Vocabulary

Most Danes are fluent in English; certainly the younger generation is, as all children must learn English in school. Almost all Danish businesspeople speak and understand English well.

The traditional Danish greeting, upon meeting and farewell, is *heij,* which is pronounced like the American "hi"; Danes also sometimes say *daus,* which means the same thing. Here are some other basic Danish terms and their English meanings:

jå	yes
nej	no
fårvel	good-bye
gôdmørgen	good morning
gøddåg	good day
gødåften	good evening
våer så venlig åt	please
tåk	thanks

velbekømme	you're welcome
undskyld mig	pardon
måend	men's room
kvinder	ladies' room

Honorifics for Men, Women, and Children

Use *herr* (Mr.), *fru* (Ms.), or *frøken* (Miss) with the last name; there is no need to indicate marriage status. You may be invited by your Danish colleague to move onto a first-name basis quite quickly; nevertheless, always begin with last names and honorifics. Men and women sometimes are addressed just by their family name, without the honorific, which is a form you may also adopt from the beginning of your relationship.

Communication Styles

Okay Topics / Not Okay Topics

Okay: Traditional Danish culture is always a safe topic: showing an interest in anything Danish—from Legos and Hans Christian Andersen to Danish furniture design—is much appreciated. *Not okay:* As mentioned previously regarding other Scandinavian countries, avoid discussing controversial subjects and personal, financial, or family matters.

Physical Gestures and Facial Expressions

The thumb-to-forefinger circle hand gesture (which signifies "okay" in the United States) is not okay in Denmark: it is considered rude and obscene, and should be avoided.

Waving and Counting

The "V for Victory" hand gesture, as is the case in all English-speaking countries with the exception of the United States, must always be done with your palms facing out; if done with your palms facing in, it can be construed as a very rude and obscene gesture.

Protocol in Public

Public phones are mainly coin operated; telecards are only now being introduced in Denmark. Put in a 1-krone piece to get a dial tone. More time means more coins. The appropriate way to answer the telephone is to say *hallo* plus your family name.

Tipping

Tips are generally included in the total price. Unlike the custom in Sweden, there is no need for any additional tip, although some spare change is always appreciated, and you may acknowledge superior service if you wish with an additional 5 to 10 percent.

Dress

Clothing styles are usually far less formal than in Sweden, although neatness and cleanliness are absolutely essential. For work, men can wear a sports jacket and slacks, with a tie and a dress shirt; suits are not essential. Women often wear dress slacks to work. If invited to a Danish home for an informal get-together, clean pressed jeans and an open-neck or sports shirt are fine.

Danes traditionally enjoy public bathing, which is related to the Finnish custom of the sauna. There are many public baths in Denmark: the compartments are usually private, and supply everything that you need—some even have saunas (segregated by sex) and massage facilities. Enjoy!

Dining and Drinking

Mealtimes and Typical Foods

Breakfast (*mørgenmåd*) is served around eight in the morning and often includes cheeses, yogurt (*ymer*), dried cereals, rolls, cold meats, jams, and eggs (hard and soft-boiled). Coffee or tea is the typical drink.

Lunch (*frøkøst*) is usually served from 12 to 2 P.M. Open-faced sandwiches are typical luncheon fare.

Dinner (*middåg*) is served from 6 to 8 P.M. The evening meal may consist of meats, fish, vegetables, and dessert. Drinks served with dinner are usually regional beers or wine. The traditional Danish dinner party begins with soup, then moves on to a seafood appetizer, the main meat course with a salad, and ends with dessert. White wine often accompanies the soup and appetizer, red wine the meat dish, and a sweet wine the dessert. Coffee follows dinner. Fresh homemade breads and/or thin flatbreads often accompany the evening meal. Dinner parties in the summer can last until 11 or 11:30 P.M.; in the winter, they usually end around 10 P.M. Therefore, if dinner is over sooner, expect to have coffee or a liqueur or perhaps a walk before the party is actually over.

Basement cafés are very popular places in which to dine in Denmark: they are cozy, traditional establishments, and moderately priced as well (they are also good places to hold business lunches).

Regional Differences

The smorgasbord is not really a Danish tradition, although there are smorgasbord-type dishes and dining establishments. Danish specialties include beef tartare (usually served with raw egg), meatballs, and herring. There is a kind of special Danish soup called *øllebrød,* which is a mixture of rye bread and beer, sugar, and lemon. *Lågkåge,* a famous Danish dessert, is a trifle-like layer cake made of custard, fruits, and whipped cream.

Typical Drinks and Toasting

In Denmark, predinner drinks are not as common as elsewhere in Scandinavia; if you are invited to dinner, more often than not, you will be ushered directly to the table. However, if drinks are served before dinner, they will usually be set out in the living room, and most probably will consist of the traditional aquavit, possibly followed by a beer chaser. Drinks, in fact, are more common after dinner, and can range from aquavit and liqueurs to scotch and other hard liquors.

More often than not, toasting simply involves lifting your glass, looking at the individual you are toasting, drinking, and lifting the glass again to them in their honor; do not break eye contact during the toast. Even if you are not making a toast, lift your glass before you take your first sip of wine or beer, look around, drink, lift the glass again (to the entire table), and set it down. You may then drink your wine or beer as you would normally from that point on.

Table Manners and the Use of Utensils

Danish custom requires that the fork and knife be placed parallel on the right side of the plate when you are finished, pointing north. If you want seconds, the custom is to turn the tines of the fork downward when you place the fork and knife on your plate. Food is usually passed around on platters, so that you are free to take as much or as little as you like. Take a small amount at first, and be sure to finish it all, especially before going on to a second helping. Although bread may be eaten with the hands, the open-faced sandwiches so common at lunch are always eaten with a knife and fork.

Gift Giving

If you bring flowers to the hostess, they should remain wrapped when you present them. The best flowers to present are bouquets of mixed wildflowers. Red is a good color to wrap gifts in.

Special Holidays and Celebrations

Major Holidays

Business slows down during July and August, the traditional vacation months, and again during the Christmas and New Year's seasons (December 15 to January 1).

On June 23, the Danes celebrate a very special holiday—Saint Hans' Eve. Traditionally, everyone has a fine meal with friends, family, and neighbors on that day, with much drinking and eating. People then gather all the things they want to get rid of that have accumulated over the year and pile it up in front of the house. A rag witch made out of straw and a broom, and sometimes filled with firecrackers, is placed upon the pile, and in the evening the whole thing is set ablaze, while people stand around and sing.

January 1	*Nytår* (New Year's Day)
March/April	*Påskedåg, anden Påskedåg* (Easter Sunday and Monday)
March/April	*Lang fredåg* (Good Friday)
May	*Pinse* (Whitmonday)
June 5	*Grundlòvsdåg* (Constitution Day)
June 23	*Set Hans* (Saint Hans' Eve)
July 4	*Juli* (Fourth of July)
November 10	*Mortenåften* (Saint Martin's Eve; features a traditional meal of goose or duck)
December 24	*Juleåften* (Christmas Eve)
December 25	*Juledåg* (Christmas)
December 26	*Anden Juledåg* (Boxing Day)

The Nordic Cultures: Finland

Note: Please refer to the previous chapters for information about general Nordic cultural behaviors; the information that follows describes specific Finnish variations on general Nordic customs.

Some Introductory Background and Historical Context on Finland and the Finns

Finland is not a part of Scandinavia, as stated in the introduction to the Nordic cultures, but it is a part of the larger Nordic culture. Denmark, Sweden, and Norway share a common Scandinavian root language and a common Viking root culture, based on traditional North Sea and northern European social customs, linked to Germany and England. Finland, however, shares (along with Hungary) a language, Finno-Ugric, which has its roots in central Asia, and which is different from the Scandinavian languages of its neighbors. The people of Scandinavia emerged from northern Europe, while the people of Finland emigrated there from the Baltic region of Estonia; the latter were cousins of the Hungarians, who also initially emigrated west from Russia. Originally all these peoples originated in central Asia, with some tribes headed west to Hungary, Estonia, and Finland, and some headed east (eventually intermingling with the indigenous peoples of the Korean peninsula to create the modern Korea). Like their Hungarian cousins, who are different from their Slavic neighbors ethnically but are similar in culture and traditions, Finns today, while being different from their Scandinavian neighbors ethnically, still share many similar Scandinavian cultural traits. Finland has its roots in the Baltic Sea cultures of Estonia, Latvia, and, by extension, Lithuania, with a historical love-hate relationship with the monolithic Russians (who have historically provided Finland with its freedom from Scandinavian rule, but not without exacting the price of falling under Russian influence). Only recently have the Finns been able to secure a stable independence, politically free from both western (Scandinavian) and eastern (Russian) control.

An Area Briefing

Politics and Government

As is the case with all Nordic cultures, the legislative body is made up of one house, the Eduskunta, and the government is parliamentary with a prime minister and a president. Unlike the rest of Scandinavia, there is no monarchy. There are many political parties, often resulting in a fragmented parliamentary system.

Schools and Education

Educational systems in Finland are similar to those of other Nordic cultures.

Religion and Demographics

The Evangelical Lutheran Church is the state religion, but with a slightly smaller percentage of the population identifying themselves as such than in the rest of the Nordic cultures. Other groups, such as Catholics, are also represented in Finland.

Women represent a significant power base in the country, and women and men almost equally share all societal roles (the nurturing role in the family, as well as in business and government). As with all Nordics, Finns are extremely quality-of-life driven.

Consider also that there is a large Swedish population living in Finland, and some of the people you may come in contact with in Finland may actually be Swedes.

The nomadic people of the Nordic countries, known as Lapps or Laplanders, are also found in Finland. When referred to as the Sami people (their name in their indigenous language) by non-Sami Nordics, the term carries a racially negative connotation. It is best to avoid it. (However, the Finnish name for their country is Suomi—land of the Sami.)

Fundamental Cultural Orientations

1. What's the Best Way for People to Relate to One Another?

Finland is similar in outlook to other Nordic cultures, with an unshakable belief in the social welfare system. What distinguishes the Finnish outlook in this regard, however, is the rugged nature of the landscape and climate and the historical struggles of the Finns against their overbearing neighbors, both east and west: the need to balance compromise with defiance against both Russian aggression and Scandinavian domination has made for an equally powerful belief in the flexible, clever, ingenious individual, one who can find a way through difficult circumstances. In this regard, there is some similarity between the notion of the individual in Finland and the United States, but it stops there. In Finland, the individual must be motivated by an interest in achieving what is good for all and must work within the limits set by the larger group (rugged Nordic winters do not make for easy survival without the help of friends and family). The goal of the Finnish individual is to be recognized by others as dependable, reliable, and trustworthy, so that they become further dependent upon and encumbered by the group, not freed from it. Occasionally this strong individualism runs counter to the social welfare goals of the larger group, but in most cases, group pressures tend to normalize any overtly individualistic behaviors.

2. What's the Best Way to View Time?

As with other Nordic cultures, punctuality and organization are essential in Finland. The climate and historical experiences of Finns in regard to their neighbors make this a risk-averse culture: it may take some time to convince Finns to do something your way, especially if anything about your way runs counter to their own experiences. Rather than being past or future oriented, the Finns, like their Nordic cousins, are oriented to the present, as it represents all that they have achieved and for the most part, need.

3. What's the Best Way for Society to Work with the World at Large?

No other Nordic cultural group has the reputation for reticence, thoughtfulness, and nonemotiveness as the Finns. They are quiet, reflective, somber, and—to some—very stubborn and standoffish. Their unwillingness to speak unless they have something important to say has led others to judge them as slow-witted: this is not any more or less the case than people anywhere, but rather reflects an incorrect judgment on the "Finnish wall" as perceived by others (including other Nordics!). Neither is this aloofness in any way a reflection of authoritarianism or hierarchy (as with their Nordic cousins, Finns believe in very egalitarian, consensus-driven organizations: while the bureaucracies themselves may be complex, they are not hierarchical; they involve many people, but they are not heavily layered); nor is it representative of an overly formal culture. Finnish culture is relatively relaxed, whether in the home, at work or—most certainly—in the sauna!

Greetings and Introductions

Language and Basic Vocabulary

In Finnish, coincidental to the Scandinavian languages, there are a few vowel sounds with diacritical marks that are different from Roman vowel sounds; these letters are usually alphabetized after *Z* at the end of the Finnish alphabet. Many Finns speak English, but the second language of the country is really Swedish; and among older Finns, Russian or Estonian may also be spoken. English is understood by most Finnish businesspeople, who have historically had contact with non-Finns for a long time. As with all non-English speakers, speak slowly and carefully, and avoid English idioms or slang.

Here are some basic Finnish phrases and their English translations:

kylla	yes
ei	no
ole hyva	please
kiitos	thank you
ole hyva	you're welcome
hyvaa huomenta	good morning
hyvaa paivaa	good day
hyvaa iltaa	good evening

nakemiin	good-bye
anteeksi	excuse me
en ymmarra	I don't understand
en puhu suomea	I don't speak Finnish

Honorifics for Men, Women, and Children

For the most part, use *herra* (Mr.) and *rouva* (Ms.); there is no need to indicate marriage status, although some young single women may be referred to as *neiti* (Miss).

The What, When, and How of Introducing People

Always wait to be introduced to strangers before taking that responsibility upon yourself. Finns are most comfortable with a third-party introduction whenever possible. Try to ensure that for yourself ahead of time. Do not presume to seat yourself at a formal gathering: if possible, wait to be told where to sit. If you are not so instructed, assume that men will sit and stand on the outside when with women. Shake hands with everyone individually in a group when being introduced and before departing: the American group wave is not appreciated (although if you see someone at a distance in public, it is permissible to wave at them). When you are introduced to people, it is appropriate simply to repeat your family name, so that you are sure they know who you are, and so that you have the chance to hear their names again and learn them. Avoid personal statements at the beginning of your relationship with Finnish colleagues, and take your cue from them as to when you can start to reveal more personal issues; it may take a surprisingly long time. Once you greet someone, you will encounter later that same day in the same circumstances (e.g., at the office), there is no need to greet them again. Kissing is not a common greeting, even between individuals who know each other well. The use of business cards is very common; if possible, you should have your business card translated into Finnish on the reverse, but this is not necessary, as many businesspeople read English.

Physical Greeting Styles

The handshake is common. The Finnish version is similar to the American handshake, but usually does not last as long. It is done quickly and firmly between two men, but not as robustly between men and women or between two women. The handshake should be accompanied by the appropriate greeting (see the lists of Finnish terms above). Smiling and other nonverbal forms of communication need not accompany the handshake when it is between people who have not met previously. Men should wait until a woman extends her hand before reaching for it, and women may take the lead in extending their hand or not. Men must remove their gloves when shaking hands with a woman, but a woman need not remove her gloves when shaking hands with a man. If a woman is in a group, she is introduced first. Informal body gestures are not appreciated during the first introduction between strangers, so avoid backslapping and other forms of touching. Eye contact during the introduction is direct, and should be maintained as long as the individual is addressing you.

Communication Styles

Okay Topics / Not Okay Topics

Okay: current events, politics (as long as you know what you are talking about and can discuss the subject dispassionately; if the conversation becomes confrontational, Finns will shy away from it), the arts, sports (very big, especially soccer), music, philosophy, the outdoors, and nature. While most Nordics are very nonjudgmental, Finns may be more opinionated: however, they generally will rarely express their opinion openly, especially if it represents a conflict or difference with what was expressed by others. *Not okay:* It is important to recognize that small talk and chitchat in general is not the typical Finnish way, whether in business or socially—even in the sauna. Do not inquire about a person's occupation in casual conversation. Americans often begin a conversation with "So, what do you do?"; this is too personal in Europe, and is often not the most interesting topic of conversation. Also not okay: personal financial discussions, questions about private family matters (the family is sacred), personal background, and the like. Anything that smacks of rank, showiness, and status is generally downplayed and not appreciated. Do try to show a knowledge (or at least interest) in things Finnish, especially those aspects of the culture that distinguish Finns positively from other Nordics. Do not compare social welfare systems, or complain about the cost of living (it is quite high): all Nordics are tired of hearing about this from foreigners. It is especially important, given the high number of Swedes in Finland, not to be critical of Swedes or anything Swedish. You never know when you might be speaking with a Swede or a friend of a Swede.

Tone, Volume, and Speed

Discussions between strangers usually start out politely restrained; in public or during your first business meetings, the conversational tone can be slightly subdued and matter of fact, and generally remains so. Do not interrupt others; let each speaker make his or her point and then respond. Keep your voice low, especially in public: never speak loudly or shout, even on the street. Words are carefully thought out and spoken softly. Note that in gender-equal Finland, women, as well as men, may start conversations with either gender; one needs to be careful not to assume any sexual intent if approached by someone of the opposite sex until such cues are more clearly expressed. Speech should be matter of fact and not filled with the hyperbole Americans are known for. Switch down from "great" to "okay," "fine" to "good," and "love" to "like." There is no need to overemphasize: omit "really" whenever possible. Really.

Use of Silence

Finns use long periods of silence to think about what was said, and to decide on their response. These need not be awkward moments: enjoy the respite. There is a joke (that Finns tell!) about a long-married husband and wife. One night, the wife asks the husband, "Do you love me?" He responds, "Do you remember the day we were married?" "Yes," she says. "And you asked me that question?" he continues. "Yes," she answers. "And what was my answer then?" he inquires. "That you love me," she responds. He summarizes: "There, I told you once. If I ever change my mind, I'll let you know."

Physical Gestures and Facial Expressions

Finnish customs are similar to other Nordic cultures, with a unique variation: folding the arms in front of the body, while not carrying a negative connotation in Scandinavia, is considered rude and standoffish in Finland, much as it is in the United States.

Waving and Counting

The thumb represents the number 1, the index finger the number 2, and so on. It is insulting to beckon someone with the forefinger (instead, turn your hand so that the palm faces up and motion inward with all four fingers at once). Keep your gestures to a minimum. If you need to call for a waiter, just subtly raise your hand.

Physicality and Physical Space

Finns tend to stay slightly farther apart than North Americans. Never speak with your hands in your pockets: always keep them firmly to your side when standing. If women must cross their legs, it should never be ankle over knee (this is not an issue for men). Remember, even in public, formal is always better than informal: no gum chewing, *ever;* don't slouch, and don't lean against things. At meetings, take your cue from the senior participants as to how informal or formal one should act, dress, and sit.

Eye Contact

Eye contact should be direct, but not as direct as in the other Nordic cultures. In fact, during moments of introspection and silent thought, your Finnish colleagues may look away or down, or close their eyes briefly. Nevertheless, maintain eye contact when it is made with you. Standing in someone's line of sight in order to make eye contact is a way of saying "I want to talk with you"; be sure you do this judiciously, and only where and when such an act does not challenge the order of things (i.e., don't do it if it interrupts an ongoing conversation unless it's really important to do so).

Emotive Orientation

Keep emotions at a minimum: cool, calm, and matter of fact is the preferred way. Finnish behavior will seem somber, dry, and uninviting to many Americans. Resist interpreting it this way: it is, in reality, thoughtful, pensive, and meant to be considerate of others. Finns show their spirit for life in other ways: holiday celebrations and winter and summer sports (they love their Finnish version of baseball!), food, and handiwork (whether applied to artistic or scientific endeavors, design can be shockingly colorful, clever, almost whimsical).

Protocol in Public

Finns behave in public in much the same fashion as people do in other Nordic cultures. One important distinction can be found in the sauna, which originated in Finland, and which was originally a Finnish tradition. Whether in celebration of a business deal (and many deals are celebrated this way), as a way of working around a particularly difficult point in a business negotiation (the egalitarian and soothing environment of the sauna makes it an ideal place to sort out problems in an informal and nonconfrontational way), or as a way of hosting guests in a social setting, the sauna (pronounced "sow-nah") has a protocol all its own.

First, recognize that if you are invited into the sauna, it is an honor and a treat. Take it seriously, and do not refuse, unless there is some unusual overriding (and very logical) reason (e.g., a health prohibition). The experience needs to be a peaceful and, in most cases, a quiet—even silent—one. It is the Finnish temple, so to speak. Act accordingly. Most Finns sauna naked, but understand completely if you prefer to wear a towel or bathing suit. Most saunas (except those shared by families or close friends) are separated by gender; if there is only one sauna and people are not covered, the women typically go in first, and when they are finished, the men. You will be offered a towel when you approach the sauna. Be sure to drink several cups of water when you first get in, because the dry heat will dehydrate you rapidly. You may sit or lie down in the sauna, but generally you do not stay inside while standing up. The heat is hotter toward the top, so you may want to take a lower shelf to start with until you adjust to it. You may stay as long or as short a time as you like; you won't be considered soft or a killjoy if you leave soon after you entered, especially if you let your hosts know that you enjoy the sauna, but are not that experienced with it. Once inside, don't be surprised if people splash water on the hot stones that are producing the heat: it generates some steam, which helps make the very dry sauna air more enjoyable. Also, don't be surprised if your host smacks you with birch twigs: it won't hurt, and is designed to increase circulation under the skin while inside the sauna. Once outside, Finns sometimes take a dip in a lake or a shower, or roll in the snow, depending upon your desires (and stamina!). Also, once you leave, a massage may be available to round out the experience. Once everyone has left the sauna, there are usually refreshments to be had, which usually include salty fish, rye bread, and butter (the fish is there to replenish the body's lost salts, which have been sweated away). Drinks are usually vodka, beer, or *kalja* (beer with the alcohol removed).

Most public phones still accept coins (put in a five-mark coin to get a dial tone). The appropriate greeting on the telephone is *hallo* plus your family name if you are the one making the call, to answer, just state your family name.

Tipping

Service is generally included in the total price; sometimes a slightly higher percentage (20 percent) is automatically figured into the bill on holidays and special occasions. If the service is particularly special, you may leave a few extra coins. You will need to tip a few marks to attendants who help you at the hotel or public saunas.

Punctuality

Never be late, if you can avoid it, under any circumstance, either social or business. If you must be late for any reason, it is absolutely essential to call ahead and let someone know of your problem—and you should have an appropriate explanation, as well.

Dress

Finns dress in a manner similar to other Nordic cultures, with the additional note that they can be surprisingly fashion conscious. Do not confuse the country's gray climate and the people's sometimes unexciting personal relationships on the outside with their feelings on the inside; these are often expressed in their concern for fashion (and in Finnish design and art). Men, by the way, usually do not bother to change clothes after work, and will often arrive for an evening's entertainment at restaurants or other homes in that day's work suit. Winter, as is the case throughout all the Nordic countries, allows women (and sometimes men, as well), to wear heavy winter boots to work, and then to change into more comfortable office shoes once inside.

Dining and Drinking

Mealtimes and Typical Foods

Breakfast (*aamiainen*) is served between 7 and 9 A.M., and often includes fruit, cheeses, yogurt, dried cereals, rolls (a Finnish favorite is a yeast-based bread called *pulla*), jams, butter, and perhaps some pickled vegetables or fish. Fish (especially herring) is an important staple. Coffee is the typical drink (Finns are crazy about coffee!).

Lunch (*lounas*) is usually served from 12 to 1 P.M. It often consists of an open-faced sandwich made from a wonderful assortment of ingredients (cheeses, vegetables, meats, or fish), plus soup. The drink with lunch is often milk or buttermilk (there are stands where sandwiches and buttermilk are sold). On Sunday, the family day, the main meal is supper, which is usually served in the middle of the afternoon, and can last well into the evening.

Dinner (*illallinen*) is served from 5 to 6:30 P.M. in Finnish homes, with 7 to 7:30 P.M. the customary time for weekend dinner parties. The evening meal may be similar to lunch, with meats, fish, vegetables, salad, and dessert, which is usually a sweet pudding. The drink served with dinner is usually milk. The traditional Finnish dinner has four courses: fish (usually a herring salad consisting of vegetables, chopped herring, onions, sour cream), meat, salad, and dessert.

Finns also stop for snacks, once around 10 A.M. and again at 4 P.M. Coffee is generally served some time after the meal (never during) and is usually taken in the living room.

Regional Differences

Fish is ubiquitous in Finland, of course, but there is a surprising amount of meat as well—the result of the heavy influence of Russia to the east. Mutton, beef chunks (often served in a stew made with potatoes, beer, and vegetables), or a roast is common. *Rapuja,* or crayfish, is a favorite that all Finns look forward to in the summer (when the crayfish are ready for harvesting). The traditional Finnish dessert pudding is called *kisseli.* The Finns, as do the Swedes, love berries and fresh summer fruits. The Finnish version of the smorgasbord is a cold table called *voileipapoyta:* essentially, the same rules apply for this Finnish smorgasbord as for the Swedish.

Typical Drinks and Toasting

Mixed drinks before dinner are very common in Finland, and usually consist of whiskey, vodka, or other hard liquors. Beer is also widely available, but not aquavit. Do not take your aperitif to the table: try to finish it before dinner is announced. Once the meal gets under way, wine or beer will be served in most cases.

Do not reach for your drink, either at the table or beforehand, until the host or hostess has made a toast; at that moment, you should take your drink and raise it. Wait for the host or hostess to make the first toast; after that, you are free to propose a response. It is absolutely essential when making a toast to maintain direct eye contact from the moment the glass is raised to the moment it is placed back down on the table. If many people are being toasted, look around the table and make eye contact with each individual as you make the toast. A Finnish variation is to never toast the host or hostess; they will open the meal with a toast to the guest(s) of honor or to the entire table, but you do not toast them back. You may, however, toast others at the table.

At the end of the meal, the male guest of honor is usually obligated to thank the host or hostess, acting as a spokesperson for all the guests. This is done quietly, by simply stating a thank-you for the meal to the hostess: it does not require a formal table announcement, nor does other table conversation need to stop. This thank-you should be done as soon as the meal is over (before the coffee, which will be served quite some time later, usually away from the table). Do not wait until the end of the evening to thank the hostess for the meal.

There are some wonderful, special berry liqueurs made from unique Nordic berries that are often served as after-dinner drinks in Finland (they are usually served, as all eau-de-vie should be, ice cold).

Table Manners and the Use of Utensils

Do not begin eating until the host has invited you to do so.

Finns, like all continental Europeans, do not switch knives and forks, as Americans do. The knife remains in the right hand, and the fork remains in the left. When the meal is finished, the knife and fork are laid parallel to each other across the right side of the plate, the tips pointing to the ten o'clock position; the knife should be above the fork, with the blade side pointing in toward the plate. If you put both utensils down on the plate for any real length of time, it is a sign to the waitstaff that you are finished, and your plate may be taken away from you. The fork and spoon above your plate are usually for dessert. There may be additional pieces of cutlery; if you're unsure of which utensil to use, always start from the outside and work your way in, course by course. There will be separate glasses provided at your setting for water and white and red wine (after-dinner drink glasses come out after dinner).

When not holding utensils, your hands are expected to be visible above the table: this means that you do not keep them in your lap; instead, rest your wrists on top of the table (never your elbows). At the table, pass all dishes to your left. Salt and pepper shakers or holders should be passed so that the receiving person takes them directly; do not place them down on the table first. Never cut the lettuce in a salad: deftly fold it with your knife and fork so that it can be picked up in a small bundle with your fork. The only food eaten with the hands is bread; this rule includes the fruit that is often served at the end of the Finnish meal, which is to be skinned and cut with a knife and fork.

Seating Plans

The unique Finnish variation on Nordic customs is that more often than not, men are seated on one side of the table and women on the other, with the host and the hostess at opposite ends of the table. All other general considerations offered for Nordic cultures remain the same.

Refills and Seconds

If you do not want more food, leave just a bit on your plate. The Finns can make quite a point of insisting that you have second helpings, or even more. You are not obligated to have more if you don't want more: if you've eaten most of your first serving, you will not offend your host if you don't take seconds. You may always have additional beverages; drink enough to cause your cup or glass to be less than half full, and it will generally be refilled. Portions are generally about the same size as in the United States.

At Home, in a Restaurant, or at Work

In informal restaurants, you may be required to share a table: if so, do not force conversation; rather, act as if you are seated at a private table. Waitstaff may be summoned by making eye contact; waving or calling their names is very impolite. Breakfast meetings are not common, except perhaps among traveling businesspeople in hotels. The business lunch or dinner is a more widespread practice, but, depending upon how well developed your relationship is with your Finnish colleagues, it is generally not the time to make business decisions. Take your cue from your Finnish associates: if they bring up business, then it's okay to discuss it, but wait to take your lead from their conversation. No gum chewing, ever, at a restaurant or on the street. No-smoking sections in restaurants are still a rarity.

Restaurants (*ravintola*) can range from the informal to the formal, with coffee shops (*kahvili*) and milk bars (that's where you get those open-faced sandwiches and buttermilk, as well as pastries, soups, etc.) being popular places for quick snacks.

You may be invited to a Finnish home soon after you have struck up a relationship; it may be for an evening's meal, or it may be for a "coffee table." This is a very common way for Finns to host in their homes. Guests are invited to arrive in the late afternoon for coffee, pastries, cakes, and cookies. (It may be a lot of one kind of cake, or it may be a mixed variety, so expect either.) In Finnish homes, meals are most often served buffet (get up and get your own) or family style (platters are passed around from guest to guest).

Gift Giving

In contrast to other Nordic cultures, flowers are considered to make wonderful gifts for a dinner party. Be careful not to bring a large bouquet, though—it should be small, perhaps wildflowers. Anything too large might be considered too much, and is really unnecessary. Once again, because alcohol is so expensive in the Nordic countries, and because wine is generally not produced there, a nice bottle of wine is always appreciated. Most of the other Nordic gift-giving rules apply, with the exception of the color red, which in the past was associated with the Russians. It's best to avoid red wrapping.

Major Holidays and Celebrations

Business slows down during July and August, traditional vacation months, and again during the Christmas and New Year's seasons (December 15 to January 1).

Most people still celebrate Labor Day, a tradition long associated with the Communists (the local political party, not the Russians), at parties drinking lemonade (sometimes with added alcohol) and eating pastries.

National Day, observed on December 6, is a very important and moving day for the Finns. People often turn out all the lights in the house, and put candles in the windows, creating a beautiful, peaceful memorial to the struggles for Finnish independence.

January 1	*Uuden/Vuodenpaiva* (New Year's Day)
March/April	Good Friday/Easter/Easter Monday
May 1	*Vappu* (Labor Day)
June	Midsummer Day (actually begins on the evening before Midsummer Day Eve, and is usually celebrated on the weekend closest to the first day of summer)
December 6	*Itsenaisyyspaiva* (National Day)
December 24	*Jouluaatto* (Christmas Eve)
December 25	*Joulupaiva* (Christmas)
December 26	*Tapaninpaiva* (Saint Stephen's Day)

The Baltic Cultures: Estonia, Latvia, and Lithuania

The three Baltic nations of Estonia, Latvia, and Lithuania are related to the Nordic cultures, but most closely with Finland. While being on the "mainland" of the Russian continental shelf, neither the Baltic peoples nor their languages are Slavic. And while these countries have historically been heavily influenced by Russia (more often than not being overrun and ruled by Russia for decades at a time), any Russian or Slavic cultural traditions are by osmosis only, and not native to these cultures. The three Baltic nations looked westward, not eastward, for their trade and essential traditions, and are focused traditionally not on Moscow and the great Russian steppes, but on the Hanseatic traditions of the Baltic region. It is for these reasons that they are included in the section on western Europe, even though they are geographically in the east.

The Baltic nations sit on the eastern edge of the Baltic Sea from north to south in alphabetical order: Estonia, Latvia, and Lithuania. They are similar to each other in that they share common Baltic roots and traditions, and have mutually suffered, endured, and been heavily influenced by their Russian neighbor to the east (and their Swedish, Polish, and German neighbors to the west, but not as significantly as by Russia). Yet they are three different nations, and have three different cultures in a few, but significant, respects. One therefore needs to be sensitive to the feelings that one Balt may have for another, and it is best to take the role of a student when discussing regional issues in any of the Baltic nations: do not compare or judge one group over the other (especially since there are significant populations of any one group to be found in any other Baltic nation, with Russians in all three). In addition, they all three share the common current condition of emerging nations, and all the economic, social, and political difficulties and challenges which that condition imposes, in a difficult natural climate. Economic problems and tensions with ethnic Russians (of which there are many) run high in all three countries. The second language spoken throughout this region is Russian (in Latvia, the majority language is Russian, and Latvian is spoken by a minority of the people); English is little known, understood, or spoken, and business opportunities for foreigners are only now beginning there.

Most Balts are tall and stocky, and with the exception of the Estonians, do not necessarily share the blue eyes and blonde hair of their Nordic cousins (a result of their central Asian roots). It is best not to comment on their size, which is unusually large for Europeans. In all three Baltic states, Midsummer Eve is a very special holiday (usually observed over the course of three days), perhaps more so than Christmas, and is a celebration of the pagan spirit in the region (Lithuania, for example, was the last pagan country in Europe to be Christianized).

Fundamental Cultural Orientations

1. What's the Best Way for People to Relate to One Another?

OTHER-INDEPENDENT OR OTHER-DEPENDENT? Balts are essentially other-dependent—more so than their Nordic cousins, and less so than their Russian neighbors. Nothing will be done without a clear consensus from all involved, although the decisions will usually be made by an identifiable central figure with authority.

HIERARCHY-ORIENTED OR EGALITY-ORIENTED? Balts differ from their Nordic cousins in that the hierarchy is structured vertically: they do not come from the Viking tradition, and there is usually a clear central leader at the top. Authority flows downward, not sideways.

RULE-ORIENTED OR RELATIONSHIP-ORIENTED? Differing again from their Nordic cousins, Balts are more oriented toward relationships being the critical determinants of action, and rules taking a second place. This situation is not without tension, for individuals and for society, as Balts recognize the need for universal established civil systems sometimes at odds with the conflicting claims of family and trusted friends.

2. What's the Best Way to View Time?

MONOCHRONIC OR POLYCHRONIC? The Baltic states are essentially polychronic: time is flexible due to the uncertain and changing requirements of daily life, and this usually means the needs of superiors, unexpected situations over which one has no control, and so on. Be prepared to wait, for delays are common and many things, from luncheon appointments to deadlines and decisions, take longer than one would expect. Compartmentalization of life's activities into progressive tasks does not really occur: many things can happen simultaneously, and all may demand attention at once.

RISK-TAKING OR RISK-AVERSE? Balts are generally risk-averse. There tends to be a high need for consistency and information (perhaps as a way of trying to stabilize a fluid and uncertain environment). It can take a good deal of time to develop the trust Balts must feel in order for business to proceed.

PAST-ORIENTED OR FUTURE-ORIENTED? While there is much hope for the future, there is perhaps greater skepticism that things will change and that anything done on a civil scale can really make a difference in one's private life. There is a certain fatalism that pervades efforts to control one's future, perhaps as insurance in order to make sense of things when they don't work out.

3. What's the Best Way for Society to Work with the World at Large?

LOW-CONTEXT DIRECT OR HIGH-CONTEXT INDIRECT COMMUNICATORS?
Balts are fairly high-context communicators, and rely on the long-term relationship to communicate truth; new contacts are dealt with in a circumspect way, and their speech patterns reveal this hesitancy. There will be a great need to confirm understanding, to restate in order to validate, and to read between the lines in order to determine real meaning. It is important to have a trusted advisor in the country who can assist in ascertaining the meaning of shared information. Music plays a major role in life, and singing, especially chorale singing, communicates feelings and ideas more powerfully than direct speech; music and politics are intertwined.

PROCESS-ORIENTED OR RESULT-ORIENTED? Balts, like Slavs, are practical and yet mystical: in this sense, they are result-oriented, but neither past precedent, causal process, or factual data provide the best or sole path to practical results. Belief, accident, or fate can just as easily provide the answer—although intuition, along with past experience, logic, and scientific fact, may just as easily not.

FORMAL OR INFORMAL? Balts are essentially spontaneous, and highly responsive to the immediate situation. However, deep traditions are taken very seriously, perhaps as a representation of the few dependable markers in the world that one can count on. Therefore, family and religious celebrations, such as marriages, births, deaths, and coming of age, along with annual religious holidays, take on enormous importance in the daily life of individuals and of the country.

Baltic Cultural Variations

1. *Estonia.* The Estonians trace their roots to the peoples of central Asia; it was Estonian tribes who migrated across the Baltic to populate what is now Finland. The people are mainly Lutherans of the Nordic variety, and are perhaps the most similar of all Balts to their Nordic cousins across the shallow Baltic Sea. The Estonians have more of a sea-based culture. They speak a Finno-Ugric dialect that is not intelligible to Latvians or Lithuanians. Estonians are known to be quiet, introspective, reserved, a bit dour, harmony-oriented—in mood, most closely aligned to their Finnish cousins across the sea.

2. *Latvia.* The Latvians look to central Europe for their traditions and roots, and thus have a more Western-oriented culture of work and business. Riga, the capital, is probably the main commercial gateway for all three Baltic nations. Many Latvians claim to have German ancestries; in fact, the German barons of the Medieval Teutonic League ruled Latvia for several centuries. Moreover, the main religion is Lutheran, of the German variety. Latvians and Lithuanians speak a Germanic-Baltic language similar to each other. Latvians also go to great lengths to avoid disharmony, and work well together at common tasks (group orientation).

3. *Lithuania.* The Lithuanians trace their roots and history to eastern Europe—Poland, in fact—and are the proud bearers of an aristocratic tradition that once made Lithuanian princes important members of the emerging Hanseatic League (the powerful post-medieval trading organization that ruled the Baltic region). Lithuanian traditions, for good and bad, are historically linked to the Polish landed gentry, who, beginning in the fifteenth century controlled a major empire spanning what is now most of Ukraine and Belarus. However, the agrarian nature of this society makes Lithuania the poorest of the Baltic nations, and perhaps the most conservative. The main religion is Roman Catholicism, which helps to distinguish Lithuanian life from the Lutheran traditions of its Baltic neighbors. Lithuania is perhaps the most comfortable of the three Baltic states with their Russian guests and Russian ties, although it is the least likely, because of its inherent conservative and Roman Catholic tradition, to modernize economically. Perhaps because of the Catholic influences, Lithuanians are regarded as the most open, communicative, and volatile of the Balts—easily sharing opinions, good and bad, and being more direct, warm, and emotive. Because of the sometimes difficult history between Lithuania and Poland, there is a cool tolerance of each other; be careful not to confuse the two peoples. Lithuanians with Polish-sounding family names are probably descendants of the ruling Polish elite from several centuries ago.

PART TWO

Mediterranean Europe

Conquistadores, Contessas, and Communitas

An Introduction to the Region

Although each nation has its own unique heritage and customs, the European cultures of the Mediterranean can be grouped together because they share the common experience of being south of the Alps (for our purposes, a definition of "southern" Europe) and having been profoundly influenced by the unifying Mediterranean and Latin histories of the region. These factors shaped their world into something distinctly different from cultures north of the Alps, which were influenced by other geographic and historical phenomena. Even though Greece is not a Latin culture, and Portugal, if one used strict geographic criteria, does not front the Mediterranean, both those countries have nevertheless been heavily influenced by the Latin and Mediterranean experience, as distinguished from other countries which might seek entry into this category (such as the Adriatic cultures of the former Yugoslavia that are really more heavily influenced by Slavic and eastern European backgrounds). The Mediterranean world of southern Europe has been at the crossroads of cultures: both a bridge and a barrier between Europe and Africa, Europe and Asia, and a gateway for the Europeanization of the New World. The center of the Roman Catholic and Eastern Orthodox Churches, in a subtropical landscape rich with agricultural potential, this area is markedly different in history, geography, and beliefs, from its northern European cousins. It is as if the Alps formed the dividing line between one European universe and another, bounding this region in on the north just as the Mediterranean does in the south, the Atlantic in the west, and the Slavic world in the east. The region today, while historically cradling many of the great cultures of the Western world, is on the rise, benefiting from the blessings of membership in the Economic Union and participation in the trade and development of Europe as a whole.

Getting Oriented

Mediterranean Europe for our purposes consists of the following macrocultural groups:

The Iberian cultures: Spain and Portugal

The Mediterranean cultures: Italy (including San Marino) and Greece

Iberia reflects its Latin Catholic heritage, but within this Latin peninsula lie three major cultures: Hispanic Spain, Lusitanian Portugal, and the splintered cultures of ancient indigenous groups, which today are evident primarily in the Basques of northern Spain and southern France and the Catalans of northeast Spain. Italy, also with a Latin Catholic tradition, consists of essentially two major cultural divisions: the north and the *Mezzogiorno* (the peninsula south of Rome). Like Spain, one could identify many different groups within Italy beyond these two divisions, but for the purpose of highlighting important cultural behaviors and protocols, this rough division between north and south Italy is sufficient. And finally, there is Greece, essentially a Balkan, Eastern Orthodox culture, despite its classical claims as the birthplace of the Western world.

| CHAPTER THIRTEEN | The Iberian Cultures: Spain |

Some Introductory Background on Spain and the Spaniards

Today, as it once again becomes an important world player in part due to its involvement with the Economic Union (as is the case with most of the countries in the region), Spain presents the visitor and businessperson alike with a country of contrasts and surprising diversity. Contrary to the strong-arm image one may have of fifteenth-century Castilian Spain and its influence on the development of the New World, Spain has always struggled to unify itself into one smooth-working national entity. Only during its historic height in the fifteenth century, under rulers like King Ferdinand and Queen Isabella, did Spain become a powerful, consolidated nation.

Modern Spain, as has been the case throughout much of its history, is a union of diverse and distinct regions, each with its own unique identity. The central Castile region (named after the many castles dotting the landscape) is royal Spain, with its headquarters in Madrid. This is the heart of the conquistador culture, such as it is today, but certainly its roots and remains can be found here. In the northeast is Catalonia, a region so unique that the local language, Catalan, is acknowledged (officially, in fact, by the EU) to be one of Europe's great independent languages. The people are equally fiercely independent. If Madrileños (inhabitants of Madrid) see themselves as the noble bearers of an aristocratic cultural tradition, Catalans see themselves as much more immersed in the here and now, and are known for their strengths in business, the modern arts (recall the great Catalan artist Picasso and the architecture of Gaudi in Barcelona), and trade. There is a sometimes not-too-friendly feud that erupts from time to time between Catalans and Castilians. (The Spanish language, by the way, varies throughout Spain: Castilian is the language most Spanish speakers speak. It exists in its purest form in Madrid, complete with a lisp for many, but not all, words that have sibilant sounds; the reason for this is due to the lisp that King Carlos V suffered from, and the desire of his immediate court, and would-be aristocrats, to curry favor from him. Moreover, the people of Spain are not Spanish: that describes a language which they may or may not speak; the people are Spaniards.) La Mancha, to the south of Madrid, is the wild, formerly abandoned plain, used for grazing and herding; Galicia, in the northwest, was perhaps the poorest region in Spain, but it is known for its spectacular seafood and rough, colorful, agrarian life. The Estremadura, in the border region between Spain and Portugal, is perhaps one of the wildest, least-explored regions in all of Europe. In the north-central region, spanning the Pyrenees in both Spain and southern France, lies the land of the Basques, a fiercely independent people with roots in neither country. Ethnographers trace the Basque culture and language back to pre-Roman, indigenous Europeans. From time to time, there is civil unrest in this region as Basque independence fighters struggle with the Castilian government in Madrid for sovereignty and independence. (The Fiesta de San Fermin, which the tradition of the running of the bulls continues, occurs in the Basque city of Pamplona, and the black beret and red neckerchief, which are hallmarks of the festival, are distinctly Basque.) Then there is Andalusia, that cultural fault line running along the southern coast of Spain, where Spaniards, Moors, and gypsies all vied (and still do, in a new and different way) for dominance. This is the region where Spanish, Arabic, French, and English all come together, and where the resulting Sevillano culture of flamenco and Spanish baroque represents the remarkable fusions of the region. Nevertheless, and despite these unique differences, there is an overriding notion of "Spaniardness" for most Spaniards, of membership, in addition to one's mother region, in a greater (and rising) national Spain.

Some Historical Context

From a peninsula of warring tribes and invading armies (from Rome, France, and North Africa), to one of the world's mightiest empires during the fifteenth century, to an influential player on the royal scene during Europe's religious wars in the two centuries that followed, to a diminished participant in the industrial world, to a collapsed society in the aftermath of its own civil war, Spain has made a remarkable comeback. It would be interesting to see what the future has in store for Spain. For our purposes, though, one of the greatest influences this remarkable culture has had is over the development of the Western Hemisphere. For as North America's cultural fate was determined significantly by its being settled initially by northern Europeans (primarily with reformative, individualistic missions), Spain led the European mission into Central and South America (better known now as Latin America) with a culture that claimed this new land for and in the name of the Spanish king and his Roman Catholic God. While Spain saw its empire fade, and moved from one historical moment on to the next, the powerful influences it exerted on the new lands in Latin America remained as formative absolutes, from which Latin America has struggled to emerge ever since. If you want a taste of fifteenth-century conquistador Spain today, don't go to Madrid: that city—and the rest of Spain, for that matter—has moved on. Go instead to Quito, or Lima, or Bogotá today. There you will see the results of Spain's power, and—for better or worse—the essential elements of Hispanic conquistador culture.

An Area Briefing

Politics and Government

The great Spanish civil war of this century pitted fascism against communism, and stood for many as the embodiment of the struggle of all people to control their own lives, free themselves from tyranny, and create a new society based on equality and opportunity. The utopian notions of communism proved false, and the fascist doctrine led to catastrophe. Spain emerged from this period weakened and shaken. It is no wonder that it held on to its monarchy as strongly as it did. Today, Spain is a constitutional monarchy, the king being a thoroughly modern ruler, and quite beloved in part because of it, and with the prime minister the head of the Cortes (the parliament), a bicameral institution of elected officials representing the people. The memory of Franciso Franco and his fascist reign still hangs heavily over the country, but political freedom currently is strong, and democracy is firmly rooted in Spain. It will take some time, however, for the benefits of this new parliamentary system to provide what the old aristocratic glory of Spain was able to, and no doubt there will be difficulties and challenges along this new representative path.

Schools and Education

The best schools in Spain were originally associated with the Roman Catholic Church, but this has changed dramatically. Remember that while Spain is essentially a Catholic country, there has been a great struggle between the development of a representative civil society and the role of the church, and modern Spanish civil society has often been in conflict with religious authority. The educational system has been a flashpoint for this conflict. Better educated, older Spaniards probably passed through private church-run schools, but younger, highly educated Spaniards are products of the modern Spanish university system (or went to school abroad in France, Germany, the United Kingdom, or the United States). Their ability to speak English is usually a sign of their education (greater competency in English signifies more university and foreign study; lesser competency in English generally signifies more church-sponsored study).

Religion and Demographics

The people are mainly Roman Catholics, with minority populations of Jews, Protestants, and Muslims (in Andalusia mainly). Spain today is demographically a very young country, with over 50 percent of the population under the age of thirty. There is still a rigid separation of the genders in Spain, more so in the less urbanized areas; even in the urban centers of Madrid and Barcelona, women struggle with the glass ceiling at work and the need to perform "two jobs"—that of homemaker and societal nurturer, as well as businesswoman— and to do each twice as good as the Spanish male.

Fundamental Cultural Orientations

1. What's the Best Way for People to Relate to One Another?

OTHER-INDEPENDENT OR OTHER-DEPENDENT? As is the case with all countries in this region—due, no doubt, to the heavy influence of Roman Catholicism—Spanish behavior can be viewed as extremely other-dependent. Most individuals will seek, either formally or informally, the opinions and support of family, friends, and coworkers before venturing off to do or say something on their own. People are most comfortable in the "bosom" of others, and individuals are simply not part of society unless they can claim membership or affiliation with some group, neighborhood, town, or business organization. A consequence of this, of course, is a resistance to the outsider, and a need for all outsiders to become associated with members of the in-group as soon as possible in order to be accepted. There is an old saying in Spain that children live at home until they are old enough to have their parents live in their homes with them. To be alone in Spain is to live a dangerous life. Causing someone to lose face, or experience embarrassment, public ridicule, or criticism of any kind, is a great insult in this other-dependent culture; here, how one is thought of by others is perhaps one of the most important concerns in life. Despite this strong need to look good in the eyes of others, the individual must bear responsibility for him- or herself in the world. In Spain, every individual is unique, and has the right to advance in his or her own way in the world, as long as it is done with consideration for others; the proof of the value of one's individual behavior is whether and the degree to which it positively affects the lives of others.

HIERARCHY-ORIENTED OR EGALITY-ORIENTED? Certainly the younger generation, especially in the cities, feels more empowered as individuals than their elders, but the traditions of the Roman Catholic hierarchy still plays a powerful role in determining who does what and when. Subsequently, the Spanish workplace is rigidly layered, with the individual at the top (*el jefe* or *el padrón*—"the boss") having supreme decision-making authority (but only in a way that honors his role as leader in the group) with the support staff being required to follow step, challenge as little as possible, and solve all problems before they surface at the top.

RULE-ORIENTED OR RELATIONSHIP-ORIENTED? Despite the fact that Spain (and the rest of the region) has tried valiantly to establish civil governments with rules and regulations that would apply to all, the reality mirrors the historical efforts of the Roman Catholic Church, in which authority and its rules could always be circumvented by those clever enough or with connections. One of the lasting legacies of Latin cultures is the rigid social hierarchy and the value people place on finding ingenious ways around rules and regulations in order to live their lives. Most of the time, the way one circumvented the authorities was to rely on the only true sources of dependability in an otherwise cruel and difficult world: one's family, proven friends, and loyal business associates. Therefore, relationships—not rules—rule. Situations, if involving the right people and the right issues, will most always determine the behaviors of individuals, not bland laws or bureaucratic fiats.

2. What's the Best Way to View Time?

MONOCHRONIC OR POLYCHRONIC? Outside of the major cities, time is circular, and very polychronic; it is more monochronic in Madrid and Barcelona, but even there, old agrarian patterns die hard, even if people aren't waking up and heading for the fields in the morning. In rural areas, it is easiest to work in the fields in the cool of the early morning and late afternoon; the midday heat is usually too oppressive, and provides a good opportunity to stoke up on a filling meal and a siesta before heading back out to work until the sun sets.

Working on the Gran Via in Madrid today still means showing up at the office around 9 A.M., but not really getting started until 9:30 or 10 A.M. (coffee, the news, and catching up with the lives of the people working around you usually takes precedence). Lunch will occur around one or two o'clock, and can either be a quick bite at the local sandwich shop on the avenue or last for several hours at an elegant restaurant (those cigars they are smoking at five in the afternoon in the restaurant lounge are not before dinner: they are after lunch). After returning to the office (people would, in an earlier time, retire for a short nap after having gone home for the large main midday meal; this, by the way, is still done in many areas of Spain), workers stay as long as necessary, perhaps up to seven or eight o'clock. At that point, they return home, or meet friends at a local bar for some drinks. Dinner, in either case, is usually not before 10 or 11 P.M. (especially so in the summer), and can last till midnight or later. Many Madrileños often aren't in bed until 1 A.M. and this is an average midweek schedule.

On weekends, Friday and Saturday night revelries more often than not can last until after the sun comes up. When do the Madrileños sleep? An ancient question, and one which begs the wisdom of burning the candle at both ends. Clearly, it is a city only for the young (or young at heart). About the only thing that is said to occur "on time" is the bullfight and theater performances. Don't be late.

RISK-TAKING OR RISK-AVERSE? Latin cultures, in general, are risk-averse, and that is one of the driving reasons for their creation of structure and hierarchies. Spain is no exception. Decision making can be slow and tedious, as various levels of the hierarchy need to be consulted, and as information must be made available to many, in order for it to occur. The belief is to do it right the first time; analyze everything carefully—several times, if necessary—and debate all aspects of a decision until everything is clear and agreed upon. Even when individuals are empowered to make the decision, there can be a reticence to take the required final step. Nevertheless, there is a growing impatience among new entrepreneurs with the tedious risk avoidance, and in Madrid and Barcelona especially, there is a palpable frustration with the traditional risk-averse attitudes.

PAST-ORIENTED OR FUTURE-ORIENTED? Unlike many of their other European cousins, Spaniards are clearly and definitively not looking backward. Maybe because most Spaniards have personal memories of many difficult times, there is a tendency among them not to dwell on the past, but to move forward and beyond the struggles of history. Most of the country is searching to create new ways of handling the challenges of life, and, while none of this means throwing the baby out with the bathwater (after all, the Spanish monarchy is still alive and very well), there is a remarkable ability among Spaniards to be able to get beyond their past and look with energy to the future. Their history defines, but more than is the case with most of their European cousins, it does not control. There is a sense that there are limits to what human beings can control, but no Spaniard would ever admit to being a victim of such control, and most would pridefully seek the opportunity to prove themselves against all odds.

3. What's the Best Way for Society to Work with the World at Large?

LOW-CONTEXT DIRECT OR HIGH-CONTEXT INDIRECT COMMUNICATORS?
Most Spaniards are high-context communicators; depending upon the rank and status of those present, and the situation, Spaniards will be careful about what they say and how they say it to a greater degree than, say, most northern Europeans in the same situation. The importance of hierarchy and other-dependency requires careful speech; in any but the most private moments with trusted family and friends, speaking one's mind openly is done carefully—especially at work. Spaniards, like most Latins, want smooth interpersonal working relationships, notably with outsiders, and will go the distance to reassure you that everything is okay and that all is in order—even when it may not be. This is not based on a desire to deceive, but rather on a need to appear capable, and not to lose face in the eyes of people from cultures with great resources. It is critically important, therefore, to always confirm information, have multiple, independent, and reliable sources to verify or interpret what you are being told, and to be able to read between the lines.

PROCESS-ORIENTED OR RESULT-ORIENTED? As with other Latin cultures, there is a strong reliance on the deductive process: how things are being done is as important as the final result. But Spaniards are also associative in their logic, based on what has worked with others in similar situations (even when the two situations may not be directly related to each other). Because there is great admiration for the process, Spaniards may not understand or, due to external constraints, not be able to follow through with the actions necessary to put the plans in place. It is therefore that much more important for non-Spaniards to stay involved with them, helping them to implement what has been agreed to. This must be done, however, with sensitivity toward the pride that Spaniards feel in being able to handle things on their own: therefore, never be intrusive, but always be available; always be open to learning about their ways, while providing them with the resources and information they need, whenever possible, to assist them in making things happen.

FORMAL OR INFORMAL? In Spain, there are definitely "correct" and "incorrect" ways to get things done, which tends to formalize human relationships, both socially and in business. Spain has a formal culture. Family members relate to one another according to formal rules that respect traditional family roles. *El jefe, el padrón, la madre, el niño, la niña, mi amigo:* no matter the role, there is a formal way of relating between the actors. This does not have to be artificial or contrived; in fact, it is often loving and spontaneous. But it is respectful and formal. Even the language is divided into formal and informal forms and phrases, and personal behaviors are ruled by etiquette and protocol. Honor and personal pride are critical, and this means a bit more formality. Never insult the honor or personal pride of a Spaniard.

Greetings and Introductions

Language and Basic Vocabulary

Unless you are in Catalonia, basic Spanish will see you through almost anywhere in Spain (even in Barcelona, they will accept Spanish from non-Spaniards, but not necessarily from Spaniards). And be sure to use the Spanish you know, even if you learned it in the Americas or in school: Spaniards love it when you try.

Here are some basic Spanish terms and their English meanings:

buenos días	good morning
buenas tardes	good afternoon
buenas noches	good evening
Hola! ¿Como estas?	Hello, how are you? (informal)
¿Como esta Usted?	How are you? (formal)
adiós	good-bye
por favor	please
gracias	thank you
de nada	you're welcome
con permiso	pardon me
muy bien	very well
con mucho gusto	pleased to meet you
un placer	a pleasure
señor (don = very senior)	Mr.
señora (doña = very senior)	Mrs.
señorita	Miss
ingeniero(a)	engineer
abogado(a)	lawyer
doctor	doctor
gerente	manager

Honorifics for Men, Women, and Children

You must use *señor* (Mr.) and *señora* (Mrs.) plus the family name when introduced to strangers. Unless and until your Spanish colleague specifically invites you to use first names, and despite how he or she might refer to you, you must always use the family name plus the correct Spanish honorific (*señorita*—Miss—is rarely used these days in Spain, unless you are clearly speaking with a child or a very young, single female adult). If you do not know whether a woman is married or not, use *señora* (please note: this is different in Latin America, where *señorita* is used; there, if you do not know whether a woman is married or not, and she is clearly not an old woman, it is safer to use *señorita*). Children in Spain are expected to be respectful and not overly conversational when speaking with adults, and must always use honorifics when referring to adults. In situations where a title is known or used, the honorific plus the title is usually employed, either with or without the name (e.g., Señor Ingeniero, or Señor Ingeniero Cortez). For casual contacts (e.g., with waiters, store help, etc.), just use *señor* or *señora* without the name. It is very important to greet people at work or in stores or restaurants with an appropriate greeting for the time of day—*buenos días, buenas tardes,* or *buenas noches*—and *adiós* upon leaving. If you speak any Spanish at all, it is important to use it, but be sure to use the formal pronoun *usted* at the beginning, and do not switch to the *tu* (informal "you") form unless and until your Spanish colleague has specifically invited you to or uses it him- or herself. However, in the office, you might see the *tu* form used between superiors and staff (certainly more so than in Latin America, where it would not be appreciated); this is more a sign of a good working relationship than a disregard for the difference in rank (it is always keenly known).

Spanish family names are often hyphenated, with the mother's family name added after the father's family name. In formal speech and in written correspondence, the fully hyphenated name is used; in face-to-face introductions, usually only the father's family name is used. For example, José Ramón Mendez-Rodriguez is Señor Mendez in face-to-face introductions, with Mendez being Jose's father's family name, and Rodriquez being Jose's mother's family name. Women often keep their family name when they marry, but add their husband's father's family name after with the conjunction *de* (for example, Señora Maria Isabel Sanchez de Rodriguez is married to Señor Rodriguez, and her maiden name is Sanchez; in face-to-face communication, she would more often be referred to as Señora de Rodriguez, or more informally as Señora Rodriguez).

The What, When, and How of Introducing People

Always wait to be introduced to strangers before taking that responsibility upon yourself. Spaniards are most comfortable with a third-party introduction whenever possible. Try to ensure that for yourself ahead of time. Do not presume to seat yourself at a gathering: if possible, wait to be told where to sit. Shake hands with everyone individually in a group before departing: the American group wave is not appreciated. Avoid ending a conversation with the American expression "Have a nice day": it sounds controlling and insincere. Once you greet someone you will encounter later that day in the same circumstances (e.g., at the office), there is no need to greet them again. Kissing is a common greeting once you have established a strong relationship, whether between women or men and women; it usually consists of a kiss on two cheeks (actually an "air kiss," first on the left side, and then on the right).

Physical Greeting Styles

The handshake is common. The Spanish version is a brisk, firm snap: it is done once, quickly, between two men, but not as robustly between men and women or two women. The handshake should be accompanied by the appropriate greeting (see the list of Spanish terms above). Smiling and other nonverbal forms of communication need not accompany the handshake when it is between people who have not met previously. Men should wait until a woman extends her hand before reaching for it, and women may take the lead in extending their hand or not. Men must remove their gloves when shaking hands with a woman, but a woman need not remove her gloves when shaking hands with a man. Between family members, friends, or trusted business colleagues, an extra touch on the elbow, a hug, or other forms of touching may be expected. Eye contact during the introduction is important, and should be maintained as long as the individual is addressing you.

The use of business cards is common; if possible, you should have yours translated into Spanish on the reverse side. Be sure to put any advanced educational degrees and your full title or position on both sides of your business card. Such emblems of your status are very important to Spaniards; they want to know they are doing business with an important person.

Communication Styles

Okay Topics / Not Okay Topics

Okay: politics, current events, the arts, sports (soccer and bullfighting are both very big), music, and philosophy. Be careful about initiating such discussions yourself, however: Spaniards love it when foreigners are knowledgeable and interested in Spain, but you need to know what you are talking about if you give your opinion about things Spanish (it seems arrogant and insulting, otherwise). *Not okay:* Do not inquire about a person's occupation or income in casual conversation. Americans often begin a conversation with "So, what do you do?"; this is too personal in Spain, and is often not the most interesting topic of conversation. Also not okay: questions about private family matters (the family is sacred) or a person's background, the Spanish civil war, your opinions about Franco, Gibraltar (Spain wants it back), or negative thoughts about bull-fights (positive reactions to the bullfight, however, will get you endless hours of instruction and indoctrination into the personalities, history, and major events of the sport). *Tertulias,* or gatherings of friends (mainly male), most often done regularly at a certain day and time and at a certain café, are an institution in Spain; at them, all sorts of topics are discussed, usually after dinner and well into the night.

Tone, Volume, and Speed

Discussions between strangers usually start out politely restrained, but can quickly become animated and very lively, depending upon the nature of the topic. At meals, the wine flows, and conversation is an art: it is enjoyed, savored, and commented upon, but it never gets out of hand, and is always carried on respectfully. In business settings, speak softly and with restraint. It garners respect.

Use of Silence

There is rarely a moment of it, except in group discussions where something has been said which can cause someone a public loss of face. Enjoy the simultaneous conversations and frequent interruptions: it shows interest. Hang in there.

Physical Gestures and Facial Expressions

The U.S. "okay" sign, given with the thumb and the forefinger, is considered vulgar and obscene: avoid it. In addition, winking and whistling—usually by men and often accompanied with a positive comment—is meant to be a friendly introduction between men and women; it is known as the *piripo,* and is not an insult. If a woman is not interested, she merely need not acknowledge it. But, if a woman's eyes meet a man's eyes under these circumstances, it is an indication of interest.

Waving and Counting

The thumb represents the number 1, the index finger the number 2, and so on. It is insulting to beckon someone with the forefinger (instead, turn your hand so that the palm faces down and motion inward with all four fingers at once). If you need to gesture for a waiter, subtly raise your hand. Waving or beckoning is done with the palm down and the fingers moving forward and back in a kind of scratching motion.

Physicality and Physical Space

Spaniards tend to get closer than North Americans are generally comfortable with, but never extremely so. Do not step back when your Spanish associate steps forward. Never speak with your hands in your pockets: always keep them firmly at your side when standing. If men and women must cross their legs, it must never be ankle over knee (the preferred style for women is to cross ankle over ankle). Remember, even in public, formal is always better than informal: no gum chewing, *ever;* don't slouch; and don't lean against things.

Eye Contact

Eye contact can be direct, and at times may be disconcerting for many Americans. It is important not to interpret this behavior as a way of intentionally trying to make you uncomfortable. It is the way Spaniards show their interest. Conversely, if you look away, your behavior will say to your Spanish colleague that you are either disinterested or rude. Either way, maintain eye contact when it is made with you. If strangers' eyes meet and linger, it can imply romantic interest. Act accordingly.

Emotive Orientation

Spaniards are animated and physically expressive. Nevertheless, while expressive gesturing is common, until you know people well, you want to indicate restraint, while not seeming lifeless. Join in if you like, but keep cool if you can. Spaniards will always admire you if you can remain logical, formal, respectful, and diplomatic.

Protocol in Public

Walking Styles and Waiting in Lines

It is more important in Spain to maintain one's face by being first in line (and never last) than it is to maintain a queue. Don't be too distressed if someone walks right up to the front of the line at a bank, a restaurant, or a store and gets served first because of the relationship he or she has with the clerk, while you have been waiting patiently on line for forty minutes.

Behavior in Public Places: Airports, Terminals, and the Market

Customer service, as a concept, is catching on, but is not fully institutionalized. Store hours are typically not built around customer convenience (many stores are closed on weekends and most evenings—except Thursdays, usually). Personally thanking store owners, waiters, chefs, and hotel managers for their services is very much appreciated. As in much of Europe, if you touch the produce in food markets, you buy it; in goods stores, it may be difficult for you to return a product unless there is a flaw in it. Smoking is on the decline, and there may be smokeless areas in public places. When answering a phone, use the phrase *digame* (speak to me), *por favor*.

Bus / Metro / Taxi / Car

Driving is on the right, but people pass very quickly on the left. The metro systems shut down after midnight or 1 A.M. Your best bet for catching a cab is at designated taxi stands (hotels are good places, but often charge more for the same ride: a hotel surcharge is added to the meter fare, in some cases). Bring food and water on board a commuter train if your trip is a long one, as there may not be a café car.

Tipping

A 10 percent tip is usually sufficient in restaurants and taxis; more is considered nouveau and gauche. Porters and hotel help get a peseta or two per service rendered, theater and bathroom attendants usually one peseta. Restaurants sometimes have the 10 percent tip already included on the bill, but if you are unsure, it's okay to ask if service is included or not. Even if it is, it is still appropriate to leave a few pesetas or odd change if the service was particularly good.

Punctuality

It is perfectly acceptable—in fact, essential—to arrive at social events about one-half hour late. If you arrive sooner, you will be running the risk of interrupting the host or hostess as they get ready. In Madrid or Barcelona, being late for business meetings by five to fifteen minutes is usually not a problem, but it is safer for the new employee or a visitor to be on time (but he or she should not be surprised if others are tardy). The meeting will not begin in earnest until all attendees have arrived (or at least until all the decision makers have shown up). Resist questioning the late ones for a reason; they always have one, usually involving an obligation with more important people, like superiors, old friends, or family.

Dress

Clothing is carefully selected and formal for both men and women, no matter the occasion—business or social, at work, in a restaurant, or on the street. Good taste is everything, and should be reflected in the clothes one wears. At work, men wear very stylish suits (dark is best), white shirts, and interesting and sophisticated ties; polished shoes are the order of the day, and accessories such as stylish watches, cuff links, and tie clips are common. Women usually accessorize so that even the simplest of outfits stands out for its interest and style. Spanish women may wear more makeup and jewelry than American women, and it is fashionable, especially in summer, not to wear stockings.

On the street, informal may mean jeans and sneakers, though that is more common as clothing to wear at the gym, the beach, or while jogging (women do not wear sneakers to work); for a social gathering, informal more often than not means tastefully coordinated clothes, sometimes including a jacket and tie for men (it rarely means jeans, sneakers, and T-shirts). "Formal" usually means formal evening wear, which is very dressy by American standards.

Seasonal Variations

There are two basic seasons in Spain, and one needs to dress accordingly. Summers can be hot and dry, and winters can be damp and cool (there is little snow, however, except in the mountain regions).

Colors

Bright colors are best reserved for accessories, as offsets to the more sophisticated dark or soft hues and beiges of the outfits themselves.

Styles

Around the world, Madrid is referred to as a major fashion center for both men and women, although few people on the city's streets can actually afford the latest trends. Nevertheless, even the average person has a heightened sense of fashion, and one should dress with the same thought and care that one should put into every aspect of his or her life. Spaniards can combine colors, weaves, textures, and designs in ways not common to North Americans. Both men's and women's shoes can be remarkably stylish.

Accessories / Jewelry / Makeup

The right makeup, hairstyle, and accessories are very important for women. Men also accessorize.

Personal Hygiene

Spaniards are very concerned about cleanliness and smelling good; perfumes and colognes are often used.

Dining and Drinking

Mealtimes and Typical Foods

Breakfast (*el desayuno*) is served from about 7:30 to 9 A.M., and usually consists of the coffee, rolls, butter, and marmalade typical of the quick continental breakfast. Coffee in the morning will automatically be assumed to be *café con leche*, with lots of hot milk. *Churros*, which are sugar-coated fried sticks of dough, are a wonderful breakfast treat. Don't miss them.

Lunch (*el almuerzo*) was traditionally the main meal of the day; even today, in busy cities, it can be an elaborate affair lasting several hours (usually an important business lunch)—or it can be a quick sandwich or a salad at a shop on the corner. Lunch is served from 1 or 1:30 to 2:30 P.M. (and sometimes even later). It usually consists of at least one course, or maybe two or more, usually one hot and one cold, one fish and/or meat, and salad. Even the quick business lunch often will include a main course and a dessert and coffee. On Sunday, the family day, the main meal is supper, which is usually served at lunchtime and can last well into the evening.

Dinner (*la cena*) is usually served about 8:30 P.M. In major cities, dinner may not start until ten o'clock or later, even during the week, and can last past midnight. You might find all but tourist restaurants closed prior to 8:30 or 9 P.M. If the main meal of the day was lunch, then the family dinner at home is light. If it is a more formal dinner out, it will most usually be preceded by drinks and snacks at a tapas bar prior to going on to the restaurant. If you are invited to what sounds like a restaurant at around, say, eight o'clock, you can assume it is really a tapas bar, and you are only going there for drinks for an hour or so prior to the meal somewhere else; if you are unsure, ask. Some people start and complete their meals at tapas bars, but if you are entertaining for the night, a tapas is usually just the first stop. There are often tapas bars known for specific snacks, such as seafood, squid, mushrooms, and so on, but at the very least, there are always olives and bread. The drinks served at tapas bars are most often sherries (*jerez*) or vermouth. Sherries are the unique nutlike wines of Spain, and must be sampled. Most of the sherries drunk at tapas or before a meal are dry (*fino* or *manzanilla,* which have a slightly salty aftertaste that may take some getting used to); after dinner, the sweet and creme sherries are served. Spaniards like mixed drinks as well at tapas bars, often sweet ones made of alcohol and Sprite, 7-Up, or cola. Wine is usually served with dinner; no matter how simple or expensive, it is carefully selected to complement the food as perfectly as possible. Dinner parties usually end at around midnight, but can go much later if all are having a good time.

In addition to the tapas bars, of course, cafés can be found everywhere. They are the place to go for conversation, a snack, some tea or coffee, a drink, an aperitif, or a pastry. They are open practically at all hours, and customarily have seating both indoors and outdoors (when the weather permits). The tables are usually tiny, and often crammed next to each other, so maintaining privacy between diners is important. Once you are seated (yes, in most you may seat yourself), the waiter will arrive, and you should be prepared to place your order. Once you call for the bill, be prepared to pay it; the waiter will generally wait at your table until you pay. Traditionally, you could sit at a café for as long as you liked; no one would ask you to move on until you were ready. This is still the case in most cafés, in the cities as well as the country. As informal as cafés can be, though, eating while strolling down the street simply isn't done in Spain (although there are food stalls in markets or other locations where one can buy ice cream and sandwiches, for example; however, it is usually expected that food purchased at a stall will be eaten there or very nearby, whether or not seating is provided). Sometimes tapas and regular bars are called *mesóns:* they are usually a notch fancier, and a bit more comfortable.

Regional Differences

The seafood is spectacular in Spain, even in inland Madrid: somehow Madrileños seem to get the freshest seafood available all the time. Paella is a mixture of seafood, vegetables, and meat (usually in the form of spicy chorizo sausages); *mariscada* is similar to paella, except that it usually only contains seafood.

There are essentially two sauces that accompany either, a *verde* or green sauce (mainly garlic, parsley, and oil) or a *roja* or red sauce (mainly garlic, pimentos, and oil). *Zarzuela,* a stewlike *mariscada,* is distinctly from Catalonia. Try calamari (squid, usually served in its own ink), eel, lobster, and shrimp whenever possible, along with any of the wonderful soups (they are usually meals in themselves): *sopa de ajo* (garlic soup), *cocido madrileño* (soup plus vegetables and meat), and the Andalusian cold soup specialty, gazpacho (best when rich with garlic and tomatoes). Flan, of course, is the quintessential Spanish dessert, and a favorite after-dinner confection, instead of chocolate, is marzipan or *turron* (a hard almond-and-vanilla, meringue-type candy). There can be wonderful Spanish cheeses also served right after the main course of the meal, before or as a substitute for dessert.

Typical Drinks and Toasting

Mixed drinks before dinner are common; before the meal, one usually has sherry or vermouth. Once the meal gets under way, wine will be served in most cases. In Spain, the wine is carefully chosen to complement the food it is meant to be drunk with; therefore, the wine can change with each course. White wine (*blanco*) will be served with appetizers or fish, and reds (*tinto*) will be served with appetizers and meats. (A common appetizer or first course is ham—*jamón*—and melon.) You may be offered several different white or red wines; in this case, the finer red or white is usually served first, so that you may appreciate it best. A sweeter sherry may be served with dessert, and after the meal a postprandial liquor or liqueur is common. The wines of Spain are world renowned, and the better ones compete with the best French wines. There are fine Spanish sparkling wines, known as *cavas*, which can be drunk, like champagne, at the beginning, throughout, and at the end of the meal. Fine Spanish brandies are also wonderful after-dinner drinks.

Wine is drunk at lunch and dinner and, in the farmlands and vineyard country, can even make its way to the breakfast table. Never add anything to wine, and you should also be judicious about adding anything (salt, pepper, ketchup, etc.) to food (this implies that the original is not prepared well). The most common toast is *salud* (to your health).

Table Manners and the Use of Utensils

Do not begin eating until the host says, *"Buen apetito!"*

Like all continental Europeans, Spaniards do not switch knives and forks, as Americans do. The knife remains in the right hand, and the fork remains in the left. When the meal is finished, the knife and fork are laid parallel to each other across the right side of the plate. If you put both utensils down on the plate for any real length of time, it is a sign to the waitstaff that you are finished, and your plate may be taken away from you. Alternately, if you lay your cutlery down on either side of the plate, it means that you haven't finished; but if you really are, the host might interpret this as a sign that you were not happy with the meal.

The fork and spoon above your plate are for dessert. There are often many additional pieces of cutlery; if you're unsure of which utensil to use, always start from the outside and work your way in, course by course. Bread is usually served without butter (therefore, there usually will not be a butter knife, nor will there be a bread dish: bread is placed on the rim of your main plate or on the table by your plate). There will be separate glasses provided at your setting for water and white and red wine (after-dinner drink glasses come out after dinner).

When not holding utensils, your hands are expected to be visible above the table: this means that you do not keep them in your lap; instead, rest your wrists on top of the table (never your elbows). At the table, pass all dishes to your left. Never cut the lettuce in a salad: deftly fold it with your knife and fork into a little bundle that can be easily picked up with your fork.

Seating Plans

The most honored position is at the head of the table, with the most important guest seated immediately to the right of the host (women to the right of the host, and men to the right of the hostess). If there is a hosting couple, one will be seated at each end of the table. In keeping with the practice elsewhere on the continent, men and women are seated next to one another, and couples are often broken up and seated next to people they may not have previously known. This is done to promote conversation. Men typically rise when women enter the room, and continue to hold doors for women and allow them to enter a room first. Remember, as is the case throughout the Continent, what the Spaniards call the first floor is really the second floor, with the first floor usually referred to as the lobby or ground floor.

Refills and Seconds

If you do not want more food, don't worry, you typically won't be offered any (except in casual home environments where food is served on platters, family style)—you are expected to eat every bit of whatever is on your plate. You may always have additional beverages; drink enough to cause your cup or glass to be less than half full, and it will generally be refilled. Portions may be slightly smaller than in the United States, but there are usually more courses, for both lunch and dinner. In Spain, food is not about quantity, but quality.

At Home, in a Restaurant, or at Work

There are many varieties of restaurants, beginning with the formal and elegant establishment serving haute cuisine right on down to the food stand on the street. *Tabernas* are family-run restaurants that have been around for a while; they are usually fun, reliable, with a shorter menu (whatever the family cook is preparing for the day is best). *Marisquerias* serve only seafood, *asadors* usually serve cooked meats of all sorts, and there are many other wonderful, informal outdoor restaurants that make dining in Spain a real treat.

In informal restaurants, you may be required to share a table: if so, do not force conversation; act as if you are seated at a private table and if conversation naturally develops, then join in. Waitstaff may be summoned by making eye contact; waving or calling their names is very impolite. The business breakfast is not common in Spain. The business lunch (more common than dinner) is more widespread, but, depending upon how well developed your relationship is with your Spanish colleagues, it is generally not the time to make business decisions. Take your cue from your Spanish associates: if they bring up business, then it's okay to discuss it, but wait to take your lead from their conversation. No gum chewing, *ever,* at a restaurant or on the street. No-smoking sections in restaurants are still a rarity.

When you arrive at a Spanish associate's home for a formal meal, you will be told where to sit, and there you should remain. Do not wander from room to room: much of the house is really off-limits to guests. Use the toilet before you arrive, as it is considered bad form to have to leave the dinner party, or the table, at any time. Once you (and the group) are invited to another room, most probably the dining room, be sure to allow the more senior members of your party to enter the room ahead of you: men should also move aside to allow women to enter the room ahead of them. At the table, be sure to look for place cards, or wait until the host indicates your seat: do not presume to seat yourself, as the seating arrangement is usually predetermined.

Being a Good Guest or Host

Paying the Bill

Usually the one who does the inviting pays the bill, although the guest is expected to make an effort to pay. Sometimes other circumstances determine the payee (such as rank). Making payment arrangements ahead of time so that no exchange occurs at the table is a very classy way to host. Women, if out with men, will not really be able to pay the bill at a restaurant: if you want to, make arrangements ahead of time, and don't wait for the check to arrive at the table. The only time it is considered appropriate for a woman to pay the bill is if she is a businesswoman from abroad.

Transportation

It's a very nice idea, when acting as the host, to inquire ahead of time as to whether your guests will require transportation. If necessary, you should arrange for taxi service at the end of the meal.

When to Arrive / Chores to Do

If invited to dinner at a private home, you may offer to help with the chores, but you often will likely be turned down; nor should you expect to visit the kitchen. Do not leave the table unless invited to do so. Spouses do not attend business dinners without a special invitation to do so. Being invited to a private dinner party in Spain is a special honor, one not often extended to new acquaintances. If such an invitation is offered, accept it as an opportunity to build a new and close relationship: that is what your Spanish associate is looking for. When it is time to leave, always get up and shake hands with everyone: the group wave is not appreciated.

Gift Giving

In general, gift giving is common among business associates, and you can certainly expect to give and receive gifts from them over the holidays. Holiday cards are also very appropriate, particularly as a thank-you for your Spanish colleagues' business during the previous year, and should be mailed in time to be received the week before Christmas. Spaniards celebrate Three Kings Day (as all Latin American cultures do), January 6, as the time for holiday gift giving.

Gifts are expected for social events, especially as thank-yous for private dinner parties. The best gift in this case is expensive flowers—and be sure to have them sent ahead of time on the day of the dinner (simple floral arrangements are not appreciated). Never send chrysanthemums (they are used primarily as funeral flowers) or red roses (these usually indicate romantic intent), and always be sure the bouquet is in odd numbers (an old European tradition). If you must bring flowers with you to the dinner party, unwrap them before presenting them to your hostess. Another good gift would be chocolates (avoid wine, as it may present the hosts with the dilemma of whether it should be brought out to the table, especially when they have no doubt already selected the wine for the meal; the only exceptions would be a dessert wine, a brandy, or an after-dinner liqueur of good quality). In addition to the gift (and certainly necessary if you did not send or bring one), be sure to send a handwritten thank-you note on a card the next day after the dinner party; it is best if it is messengered and not mailed.

If you are staying with a Spanish family, an appropriate thank-you gift would be a high-quality product that represents your country and is difficult to get in Spain: coffee-table books about the United States, small American-made electronic gadgets, a set of American bath towels (always a good gift most everywhere, since they are usually more luxurious), or anything that reflects your host's personal tastes (the cap of a famous American team for the football-playing son of the family, for example) is appropriate.

For both social and business gifts, it is best to avoid food items, even imported gourmet foodstuffs—since the Spanish really love their remarkable cuisine. As with other European cultures, gifts are generally opened at the time they are given and received.

Special Holidays and Celebrations

Major Holidays

Most Spanish workers get five weeks of paid vacation; August is a leading vacation time. Business slows down from December 15 to January 6, and Holy Week is sometimes a more difficult time in which to accomplish work than Christmas. In addition, there are many regional fiestas and saints' days throughout the year that usually close down businesses for a day or two; check with your local contacts. There are also three bank holidays (the Monday after Easter; at the end of May; and at the end of August).

As you establish personal relationships with your Spanish colleagues, you may be invited to special family events, such as a wedding, a baptism, or a *Quinceañera* (the celebration of a girl's fifteenth birthday, equivalent to the American "sweet sixteen" party or a debutante coming-out ball); be sure to go, and bring a gift (money is *not* appropriate).

January 1   *Año Nuevo* (New Year's Day)
January 6   *El Dia de los Reyes* (Three Kings Day; this is the gift-giving day, when children put their shoes out the evening before, and small gifts are found in them in the morning: this is a nice opportunity to give a gift to your Spanish associate, if you know they have children, and if you are present around this time of year)

March 19	*Fiesta de San José* (Feast of San José)
March/April	*Samana Santa/Pasqua* (Holy Week and Easter)
May 1	*Dia del Trabajo* (Labor Day)
June	Corpus Christi
May/June	Ascension (on a Monday), five weeks after Easter, and Pentecost (on a Monday), seven weeks after Easter
June 24	*Cumpleaños del Rey* (The king's birthday)
July 25	*Dia de San Jaime* (Saint James's Day)
August 15	*Asunción* (Assumption)
October 12	*Dia de Cristobal Colon* (Columbus Day)
November 1	*Dia de los Santos* (All Saints' Day)
December 8	*Imaculada Concepción* (Immaculate Conception)
December 25	*Navidad* (Christmas)

Business Culture

Daily Office Protocols

In Spain, doors are usually closed; knock first (this includes bathrooms) before opening doors, and when leaving rooms, close the doors behind you. Women may be treated with particular respect by Spanish men, in both business and in social situations: this is meant as an honor in most cases, and reflects the Spanish recognition that women and men are indeed different. However, it is not common for women to attain positions of authority in Spain; in the traditional Spanish workplace, women are usually relegated to lower-level management and administrative support positions. Women do struggle to reach the same levels of achievement as their male counterparts in Spanish business, and it is rare (though not impossible) to see women at the highest levels of business and government in Spain.

Management Styles

Privacy and individual accomplishment of one's tasks are critical; workers provide what their bosses expect of them, and the preparation of plans, methods, and reports can be time-consuming and complicated efforts. Gathering the information required in order to do what your boss expects from you, or creating consensus among your colleagues in order to accomplish a particular goal, can take a long time. All of this occurs in a formal and sometimes very rigid hierarchical structure, which means that deadlines and efficiency are secondary to attention to detail, rigorous logic, and perfection of form. Because of this rigid rank and hierarchy orientation, titles in Spain are very important; the highest ones (e.g., vice president) are usually reserved for very senior, executive-level positions, and should not be used as casually as they are in the United States. Complimenting and rewarding employees publicly is usually not done.

Boss-Subordinate Relations

Rank most definitely has its privileges in Spain. Pride and self-importance require that Spaniards always do business with the most important people in any organization (and this should be the same for the non-Spaniard working with them). There is a rigid chain of command that must be heeded. No matter what field you are in, there is a proper way for communicating with particular individuals, and an established procedure one is expected to follow. Deviating from the normal channels will generally make more problems for you, even if your intent is to bypass what appear to be obstacles. Bosses are expected to provide guidance, distribute information, and make decisions; subordinates are expected to provide detailed information and follow the decisions made by their superiors.

Conducting a Meeting or Presentation

At meetings of peers, there can be open communication and sharing of ideas: in fact, these sessions often serve as information-sharing and decision-making forums in which all individuals are expected to contribute. Under these circumstances, discussions are usually vibrant, with many people speaking at once; questions are common and interruptions, even of presentations, should be expected. In more formal, conservative organizations, meetings are often gatherings of nonpeers, clearly called together by decision makers in order to gather information from below, clarify goals, and formulate action plans. In these cases, individuals often do not share ideas and are not expected to contribute to mutual problem solving. Remember, because a close personal relationship is often demonstrated through physicality in Latin cultures, the nearer your Spanish colleagues are to you, the better they are responding to your proposal.

Negotiation Styles

Spaniards generally play their cards close to the vest: they do not divulge information easily (it is seen as the source of power). They are usually circumspect in their communication styles, and will indicate their thoughts in indirect ways. They will respect someone who comes to them with established knowledge and experience, and will build relationships based on your level in society and the organization. Whether you are worth knowing and doing business with may be more important than the details of your proposal. Nevertheless, details are important, and a carefully planned, logically organized, and beautifully presented proposal is key.

The first meeting is usually very formal, with the Spaniards sizing up you and your organization: it will be conducted in the office. Take copious notes afterward, but put on a warm, dignified demeanor during the meeting. Never be condescending. Although the contract must be legal down to the dotted i's, it really is just a legal formality to the Spaniards, and can be overcome, by either party, if such a need arises later on. Plan your meetings as carefully and as well in advance as you can, but expect changes. The goal, at least for the first meeting, is the development of a good feeling of respect and positive trust between yourself and your Spanish colleagues (simpatico). Remember also that the meeting might start and end much later than you anticipated; nevertheless, as with most polychronic cultures, you should always arrive on time.

Written Correspondence

Business letters must be very formal and respectful of hierarchy. Last names are usually written in uppercase; dates are given using the day/month/year format (with periods in between, not slashes); and an honorific plus a title is as common as an honorific plus the last name. The time of day is written in military style; weights and measures are usually given in metric units. Monetary amounts are written so that periods break up the figure into tens, hundreds, and thousands, and a comma separates pesetas from centavos (e.g., $P10.000,00 = ten thousand pesetas).

The traditional language used in openings and closings is convoluted and formal, and you should write your e-mails, letters, and faxes using a precise formula. Be sure to inquire first, in all communications, about your colleague's health and progress, then move on to the substance of your communication, and close with a salutation and your personal wish for their success and well-being (the Latin communication "sandwich").

The Iberian Cultures:
Portugal

Note: Please refer to the preceding chapter on Spain for information about general Iberian-Latin cultural behaviors; the material that follows describes specific Portuguese variations on general Iberian-Latin customs.

Some Introductory Background and Historical Context on Portugal and the Portuguese

Once the first and greatest of the western European colonial powers, Portugal attained the height of its influence in the sixteenth century. But the nation lost its position when the Age of Exploration ended, and by the twentieth century it had become the sleepy backdoor of Europe. A small agricultural and fishing nation, Portugal struggled for its independence from both Spain and France in the eighteenth century, and developed into a democratic republic in the twentieth. During this effort to move from autocratic monarchism to republican democracy, Portugal experienced conquest and military dictatorship, while experiencing a diminished role and a limited influence on the world stage.

Today, however, due in part to its membership in the Economic Union (EU), Portugal is reviving. The Algarve (the Portuguese riviera along the country's southern Atlantic coast) is a major European tourist destination; the nation is a modern democracy; business development, investment, and industry are growing. Nevertheless, there is in Portugal today still much evidence of a slower, more traditional and conservative approach to life; here, things take longer to accomplish than anywhere else in western Europe, outsiders are respectfully but warmly held at arm's length, and new ideas are entertained cautiously and at first with reservation. Portugal is not an Hispanic culture; rather, the original people of the region were the Lusitanes, whose origins seem to be indigenous European. Portugal is therefore referred to as a "Luso-" or "Lusitanian" culture, although it is similar in many behavioral ways to its larger Hispanic cousin, Spain. One of the greatest differences between the two is language: Portuguese is different from Spanish. It is very important therefore not to assume that Spanish will be understood, spoken, or even appreciated if used in Portugal, and to not confuse things Portuguese with things Spanish. Spain annexed Portugal more than once, and Portugal historically has had to struggle for its independence from the Spanish crown: the Portuguese people remember.

An Area Briefing

Politics and Government

Today, Portugal is a representative republic, with a unicameral legislature and a popularly elected president. The monarchy was overthrown earlier in the century and replaced by a military dictatorship, and then by a Marxist-oriented regime, which finally, through a silent revolution in the mid 1970s, gave way to the democracy of today. This is a new development in the previously rigid and monarchical/authoritarian civil tradition of Portugal, and whether it will last is open to speculation. While workers might still long for the entitlements of the Marxist era, most Portuguese today see more benefit in the current open-market economy and popular government, and Portugal will probably stay on this path for the immediate future.

Schools and Education

The Portuguese educational system is similar in structure and history to the Spainish experience; however, British and French education has historically been available for those Portuguese who could afford it. This was due in part to the on-again-off-again relations between Portugal and France, depending upon France's relationship with its rival neighbor Spain, and Portugal's steady trade relationship with Britain (the entire port wine industry, for example, has traditionally been run by on-site British firms in Oporto and Lisbon) and its support for Britain in its wars with Spain.

Religion and Demographics

The people are mainly Roman Catholics, with surprisingly large minority populations of Jews and Protestants. Portugal is not as young a country demographically as Spain, perhaps because a significant number of young people have emigrated from Portugal, leaving behind an older population. There is a strong history of emigration from Portugal, beginning with the Age of Exploration, and there are significant populations of Portuguese around the world, many of whom maintain close ties with Portugal (in fact, the Portuguese government still works on behalf of many of its citizens abroad in remaining Portuguese-controlled colonies). Macao was the last remaining Portuguese colony in Asia until 1999, when it was returned to the Chinese, and in the last few centuries Portugal had outposts throughout Asia and Africa. The largest country in Latin America, Brazil, was founded by Portugal, and Portuguese is still the fifth most spoken language in the world (it is spoken by more people outside of Portugal than within).

There is still a very rigid separation of the genders in Portugal, more so in the less urbanized areas; even in the urban centers, women struggle with the glass ceiling at work and the need to work "two jobs"—that of homemaker and societal nurturer, as well as businesswoman—and to do each twice as good as the Portuguese male. Portuguese women must struggle even harder than Spanish women struggle for the preferred positions in business.

Fundamental Cultural Orientations

1. What's the Best Way for People to Relate to One Another?

OTHER-INDEPENDENT OR OTHER-DEPENDENT? As is the case with all countries in this region—due, no doubt, to the heavy influence of Roman Catholicism—Portuguese behavior can be viewed as extremely other-dependent. Most individuals will seek, either formally or informally, the opinions and support of family, friends, and coworkers before venturing off to do or say something on their own. People are most comfortable in the "bosom" of others, and individuals are simply not part of society unless they can claim membership or affiliation with some group, neighborhood, town, or business organization. A consequence of this, of course, is a strong resistance to the outsider, and a need for all outsiders to become associated with members of the in-group as soon as possible. Causing someone to lose face, or experience embarrassment, public ridicule, or criticism of any kind, is a great insult in this other-dependent culture; here, how one is thought of by others is perhaps one of the most important concerns in life. In Portugal, the role of the individual is significantly more subordinate to the larger group than it is in Spain.

HIERARCHY-ORIENTED OR EGALITY-ORIENTED? Certainly the younger generation, especially in the cities, feels more empowered as individuals than their elders, but the Roman Catholic hierarchy still plays a powerful role in determining who does what and when. Subsequently, the Portuguese workplace is rigidly hierarchical, with individuals at the top having supreme decision-making authority and the support staff being required to follow step, challenge as little as possible, and solve all problems before they surface at the top. Respect for age is a significant concern in Portugal, demonstrated in daily life by the deference paid to older people, whether family or strangers, by younger people. Gender roles are usually severely defined; it is rare for a Portuguese woman to be able to develop professional authority of any real measure in society.

RULE-ORIENTED OR RELATIONSHIP-ORIENTED? Portugal is clearly a relation-based culture, and while respect for the law is important, what really makes things happen in Portugal is the connection one has with particular individuals. One of the lasting legacies of Latin cultures is the rigid social hierarchy and the value people place on finding ingenious ways around rules and regulations in order to live. Most of the time, the way one circumvented the authorities was to rely on the only true sources of dependability in an otherwise cruel and difficult world: one's family, proven friends, and loyal business associates. Therefore, relationships—not rules—rule. Situations, if involving the right people and the right issues, will most always determine the behaviors of individuals, not bland laws or bureaucratic fiats. It is perhaps this strong reliance on interpersonal ties that has historically made the imposition of rules so authoritarian from time to time.

2. What's the Best Way to View Time?

MONOCHRONIC OR POLYCHRONIC? In Portugal, time is secondary to almost everything else. This is an extremely polychronic culture, especially noteworthy against the backdrop of a relatively time-conscious modern Europe. Nothing will be rushed. Things will take much longer in Portugal, whether in the Algarve or Lisbon, whether business or social. Dinners will start half an hour to an hour later than scheduled, and linger throughout the evening; meetings will begin and end when the decision makers (not the agenda) say so; and business ventures will be negotiated and decided upon at an organic pace.

RISK-TAKING OR RISK-AVERSE? Latin cultures, in general, are risk-averse, and that is one of the driving reasons for their reliance on structure and hierarchies. Portugal is no exception. Decision making can be slow and tedious, as various levels of the hierarchy need to be consulted, and as information must be made available to many, in order for it to occur. However, this is due more to the need for hierarchy, consensus, and the avoidance of change than it is because of a deductive concern for detail and precision. Even when individuals are empowered to make the decision, there can be a reticence to take the required final step. Repetition, and the need to review with new (and more senior or more technically proficient) individuals, coupled with the need to digest carefully all concerns while building personal trust with the individuals involved, will mean that much information will need to be shared before even the smallest decision can be made. There is a great need for security and risk minimization.

PAST-ORIENTED OR FUTURE-ORIENTED? There is not so much a longing for the past as a fear of the future: the past may not have been so great, but the uncertain future is filled with insecurity. It is best to live in the here and now in Portugal.

3. What's the Best Way for Society to Work with the World at Large?

LOW-CONTEXT DIRECT OR HIGH-CONTEXT INDIRECT COMMUNICATORS? The Portuguese are more often than not high-context communicators; depending upon the rank and status of those present, and the situation, the Portuguese will be careful about what they say and how they say it to a greater degree than, say, northern Europeans in the same situation. The importance of hierarchy and other-dependency requires careful speech; in any but the most private moments with trusted family and friends, speaking one's mind openly is done carefully—especially at work. The Portuguese, like most Latins, absolutely require smooth interpersonal working relationships, notably with outsiders, but will not go to extremes to paint rosy pictures just to avoid conflict. The inherent assumption common to other Latin cultures that with time things will work out is not a Portuguese view: generally, their outlook is more pessimistic. Things in Portugal might not work out; in fact, when they don't, there is almost satisfaction when result justifies the expectation. The need for saving or keeping face is strong, but when things don't happen as they should, individuals feel less responsible, and therefore may not be compelled to speak indirectly or evasively about negative events.

PROCESS-ORIENTED OR RESULT-ORIENTED? As with other Latin cultures, there is a strong reliance on the deductive process: how things are being done is as important as the final result. But the Portuguese are also associative in their logic, based on what has worked with others in similar situations (even when the two situations may not be directly related to each other). Again, because the Portuguese expect to encounter difficulties in implementing plans, it is therefore all the more important for non-Portuguese to stay involved with them, helping them to ensure fulfillment of the agreed-to program.

FORMAL OR INFORMAL? There are "correct" and "incorrect" ways to get things done, which tends to formalize human relationships, both socially and in business in Portugal. Portugal has a formal culture, despite the ease and warmth with which outsiders are received. Family members relate to one another according to formal rules that respect traditional family roles and age. This does not have to be artificial or contrived; in fact, it is often loving and spontaneous. But it is respectful and formal. Even the language is divided into formal and informal forms and phrases, and personal behaviors are ruled by etiquette and protocol.

Greetings and Introductions

Language and Basic Vocabulary

Portuguese is not a form of or the same as Spanish: confusing the two is not appreciated. If you speak a little Portuguese, use it; you will surprise your hosts, and your effort will be rewarded. If you speak Spanish, apologize first for not speaking Portuguese, then try English or French (many Portuguese understand French); rely on Spanish last (or only after invited to use it by your Portuguese hosts). Portuguese pronunciation may be difficult at first (the relationship between Portuguese and Spanish is not as evident when spoken as when read).

Here are some basic Portuguese terms and their English meanings:

bom dia	good morning
boa tarde	good afternoon
boa noite	good evening
adeus	good-bye
por favor	please
obrigado/a	thank you
muito obrigado/a	thank you very much
con licença	you're welcome
nao compreendo	pardon me
¿Como esta?	How are you?
muito bem, obrigado/a	very well
sim	yes
nao	no
senhor	Mr.
senhora	Mrs.
menina	Miss
engenero	engineer
gerente	manager

Honorifics for Men, Women, and Children

You must use *senhor* (Mr.) and *senhora* (Mrs.), plus the family name, when introduced to strangers. Unless and until your Portuguese colleague specifically invites you to use first names, and despite how he or she might refer to you, you must always use the family name plus the correct Portuguese honorific (*menina* is not out of fashion as its equivalent can be in other Latin European cultures, and is used frequently). If you do not know whether a woman is married or not, use *senhora* (this is also true in Brazil). Children in Portugal are expected to be respectful and not overly conversational when speaking with adults, and must always use honorifics when referring to adults. In situations where a title is known or used, the honorific plus the title is usually employed, either with or without the name (e.g., Senor Ingeniero, or Senor Ingeniero Cortes). For casual contacts (e.g., with waiters, store help, etc.), just use *senhor* or *senhora* without the name. It is very important to greet people at work or in stores or restaurants with an appropriate greeting for the time of day—*bom dia, boa tarde,* or *boa noite*—and *adeus* upon leaving. If you speak any Portuguese at all, it is important to use it, but be sure to use the formal form in the beginning, and do not switch to the informal form unless and until your Portuguese colleague has specifically invited you to or uses it him- or herself.

Unlike the Spanish practice, Portuguese family names may or may not include the mother's family name; if this occurs, it is usually only in formal situations and with powerful families or individuals.

The What, When, and How of Introducing People

Always wait to be introduced to strangers before taking that responsibility upon yourself. The Portuguese are most comfortable with a third-party introduction whenever possible. Try to ensure that for yourself ahead of time. Do not presume to seat yourself at a gathering: if possible, wait to be told where to sit. Shake hands with everyone individually in a group before departing: the American group wave is not appreciated. Avoid ending the conversation with the American expression "Have a nice day": it sounds controlling and insincere. Once you greet someone you will encounter later that day in the same circumstances (e.g., at the office), there is no need to greet them again. Kissing in public is not a common greeting, even between close friends, as the Portuguese are more reserved around others. However, in private, and certainly among family members, the Latin "air kiss" is expected.

Physical Greeting Styles

The handshake is common. The Portuguese version is a firm one between two men, but is softer between men and women or two women. The handshake should be accompanied by the appropriate greetings (see the list of Portuguese terms as stated earlier). Smiling and other nonverbal forms of communication need not accompany the handshake when it is between people who have not met previously. Men should wait until a woman extends her hand before reaching for it, and women may take the lead in extending their hand or not. Men must remove their gloves when shaking hands with a woman, but a woman need not remove her gloves when shaking hands with a man. Between family, friends, or trusted business colleagues, an extra touch on the elbow, a hug, and generally more physicality may be expected. Eye contact during the introduction is important, and should be maintained as long as the individual is addressing you.

The use of business cards is common, but it's not necessary to translate your card into Portuguese on the back (do not use a card if there is a Spanish translation on the back). Be sure to put any advanced educational degrees and your full title or position on your card. Such emblems of your status are very important to the Portuguese; they want to know they are doing business with an important person.

Communication Styles

Okay Topics / Not Okay Topics

Okay: politics, current events, the arts, sports (soccer is very big), music (especially fado, the uniquely plaintive Portuguese ballad form), and philosophy—just as long as the topic is not immediately controversial. *Not okay:* Do not inquire about a person's occupation, family situation, or income in casual conversation. Americans often begin a conversation with "So, what do you do?"; this is too personal in Portugal, and is often not the most interesting topic of conversation. Also not okay: questions about private family matters (the family is sacred), or a person's background, the "revolution" of the 1970s, the former monarchy, your opinions about Spain, and negative thoughts about bullfights (the Portuguese bullfight is not the same as the Spanish one—for one thing, the bull in Portugal is generally not killed—and is not nearly the national passion it is across the border).

Tone, Volume, and Speed

Discussions between strangers usually start out politely restrained and remain that way. Even at meals, while the wine flows, conversation is a peaceful art: it is enjoyed, savored, and commented upon, but it never gets out of hand, and is always carried on respectfully. In business settings, speak softly and with restraint. It garners respect.

Use of Silence

There is rarely a moment of it, except in group discussions where something has been said that could cause someone a public loss of face. Enjoy the simultaneous conversations and frequent interruptions: it shows interest. Hang in there.

Physical Gestures and Facial Expressions

The U.S. "okay" sign, given with the thumb and the forefinger, is considered vulgar and obscene: avoid it. In addition, winking and whistling (often accompanied by a comment) is interpreted as a nonverbal introduction between men and women but is considered rude. Nevertheless, if a woman's eyes meet a man's eyes under these circumstances, it is taken as an indication of interest.

Waving and Counting

The thumb represents the number 1, the index finger the number 2, and so on. It is insulting to beckon someone with the forefinger (instead, turn your hand so that the palm faces down and motion inward with all four fingers at once). If you need to gesture for a waiter, subtly raise your hand. Waving or beckoning is done with the palm down and the fingers forward moving and back in a kind of scratching motion.

Physicality and Physical Space

The Portuguese tend to get closer than North Americans are generally comfortable with, but never extremely so. Do not step back when your Portuguese associate steps forward. Never speak with your hands in your pockets: always keep them firmly at your side when standing. If men and women must cross their legs, it must never be ankle over knee (for women, the preferred style is to cross ankle over ankle). Remember, even in public, formal is always better than informal: no gum chewing, *ever;* don't slouch; and don't lean against things.

Eye Contact

Eye contact in Portugal can be direct at times. It is important not to interpret this behavior as a way of intentionally trying to make you uncomfortable. It is the way the Portuguese show their interest. Conversely, if you look away, your behavior will say to your Portuguese colleague that you are either disinterested or rude. Either way, maintain eye contact when it is made with you. If strangers' eyes meet and linger, it may imply romantic interest. Act accordingly.

Emotive Orientation

Unlike people from other Latin cultures, the Portuguese are usually restrained in their demonstration of emotion and feeling; some have referred to them as "dour" Latins. Keep cool and respectful, and minimize your body language and emotional expression.

Protocol in Public

Walking Styles and Waiting in Lines

It is more important in Portugal to maintain one's face by being first in line (and never last) than it is to maintain a queue. This never results, however, in the apparent chaos or jostling that one might see in other Latin cultures: it is most always restrained.

Behavior in Public Places: Airports, Terminals, and the Market

Customer service, as a concept, is catching on, but is not fully institutionalized. Store hours are typically not built around customer convenience (many stores are closed on weekends and most evenings—except Thursdays, usually). Personally thanking store owners, waiters, chefs, and hotel managers for their services is very much appreciated. As in much of Europe, if you touch the produce in food markets, you buy it; in goods stores, it may be difficult for you to return a product unless there is a flaw in it. Smoking is on the decline, and there may be smokeless areas in public places.

When answering a phone, use the word *ishtay* (who is it).

Bus / Metro / Taxi / Car

Driving is on the right, but people pass very quickly on the left. Public transportation systems shut down after midnight or 1 A.M. Your best bet for catching a cab is at designated taxi stands (hotels are good places, but often charge more for the same ride: a hotel surcharge is added to the meter fare, in some cases).

Tipping

A 15 percent tip is usually sufficient in restaurants and taxis; more is considered nouveau and gauche. Porters and hotel help get approximately twenty-five escudos per service rendered, theater and bathroom attendants usually the same. Restaurants sometimes have the 15 percent tip already included on the bill, but if you are unsure, it's okay to ask if service is included or not. Even if it is, it is still appropriate to leave a few escudos in change.

Punctuality

It is perfectly acceptable—in fact, essential—to arrive at social events about one-half hour late. If you arrive sooner, you will be running the risk of interrupting the host or hostess as they get ready. Being late for business meetings by fifteen minutes or more is usually not a problem, but it is safer for the new employee or the visitor to be on time (however, he or she should not be surprised if others are tardy). The meeting will not begin in earnest until all attendees have arrived (or at least until all the decision makers have shown up). Resist questioning the late ones for a reason; they always have one, usually involving an obliga-tion with more important people, like superiors, old friends, or family. It's not important to know the details.

Dress

Clothing is generally formal for both men and women, no matter the occasion—business or social, at work, in a restaurant, or on the street. Good taste is important, and should be reflected in the clothes one wears. At work, men wear very stylish suits (dark is best), white shirts, and interesting and sophisticated ties; polished shoes are the order of the day, and accessories such as stylish watches, cuff links, and tie clips are common. Women usually accessorize so that even the simplest of outfits stands out for its interest and style. Portuguese women may not wear as much makeup or use as many accessories as their Spanish counterparts; it is fashionable, especially in summer, not to wear stockings.

On the street, informal may mean jeans and sneakers, though that is more common as clothing to wear at the gym, the beach, or while jogging (women do not wear sneakers to work); for a social gathering, informal more often than not means tastefully coordinated clothes, sometimes including a jacket and tie for men (it rarely means jeans, sneakers, and T-shirts). "Formal" usually means formal evening wear, which is very dressy by American standards.

Seasonal Variations

There are two basic seasons in Portugal, and one needs to dress accordingly. Summers are hot, and winters can be damp and cool (there is little snow, however, except in the mountain regions).

Colors

Bright colors are best reserved for accessories, as offsets to the more sophisticated dark or soft hues and beiges of the outfits themselves.

Personal Hygiene

The Portuguese are very concerned about cleanliness, although colognes and perfumes are not as common as in Spain.

Dining and Drinking

Mealtimes and Typical Foods

Breakfast (*o pequeno almoço*) is served from about 7:30 to 9 A.M., and usually consists of coffee, rolls, butter, and marmalade, typical of the quick continental breakfast. Coffee in the morning will automatically be assumed to be café au lait style, with lots of hot milk.

Lunch (*o almoço*) was traditionally the main meal of the day; even today, in busy cities it can be an elaborate affair lasting several hours (usually an important business lunch)—or it can be a quick sandwich or a salad at a shop on the corner. Lunch is served from 1 or 1:30 to 2:30 P.M. (or even later). It usually consists of at least one course, or maybe two or more, hot and cold, fish and/or meat, and salad. Even the quick business lunch often will include a main course and a dessert and coffee. Bread is served with the meal (in northern Portugal, a type of bread made with corn is interesting to try). On Sunday, the family day, the main meal is supper, which is usually served at lunchtime and can last well into the evening.

Dinner (*o jantar*) is served from 7 P.M. on, with 8 to 9 P.M. the customary time. In major cities, dinner may not start until 10 P.M. or later, even during the week, and can last well past midnight. You might find all but tourist restaurants closed prior to 8:30 or 9 P.M. If the main meal of the day was lunch, then the family dinner at home is light. A formal meal usually ends with some port wine and cheese or *aguardente* (a kind of Portuguese eau-de-vie). Wine is usually served with dinner; no matter how simple or expensive, it is carefully selected to complement the food as perfectly as possible. Dinner parties usually end at around midnight, but can go much later if all are having a good time.

In Portugal, as in all of Mediterranean Europe, cafés are found everywhere. They are the place to go for conversation, a snack, some tea or coffee, a drink, an aperitif, or a pastry. They are open practically at all hours, and customarily have seating both indoors and outdoors (when weather permits). The tables are tiny, and often crammed next to each other, so maintaining privacy between diners is important. Once you are seated (yes, in most you may seat yourself), the waiter will arrive, and you should be prepared to place your order. Once you call for the bill, be prepared to pay it; the waiter will generally wait at your table until you pay. Traditionally, you could sit at the café for as long as you liked; no one would ask you to move on until you were ready. This is still the case in most cafés, in the cities as well as the country. As informal as the cafés can be, though, eating while strolling down the street simply isn't done in Portugal unless you are eating an ice cream cone (although there are food stalls in markets or other locations where one can buy crêpes and sandwiches, for example; however, it is usually expected that food purchased at a stall will be eaten there or very nearby, whether or not seating is provided).

Regional Differences

The seafood is spectacular in Portugal. The favorite fish is the cod (*bacalhao*): you can have it salted, or in stews, or as a fishcake (*bolinhos de bacalhao*). There is a special cooking pan, called a *cataplana,* in which the Portuguese cook their versions of seafood stews and paellas. Try anything *na cataplana* for a real seafood treat. The meats are usually ham and pork of all varieties—dried, air cured, etc.—served as main courses and as appetizers. Flan, or a white cheese and sweet fruit, is usually served for dessert. A favorite after-dinner confection is figs stuffed with almonds or chocolate.

Typical Drinks and Toasting

Mixed drinks before dinner are not common; sherry or vermouth are usually preferred. Once the meal gets under way, wine will be served in most cases. In Portugal, the wine is carefully chosen to complement the food it is meant to be drunk with; therefore, the wine can change with each course. White wine (*blanco*) will be served with appetizers or fish, and reds (*tinto*) will be served with appetizers and meats; try the ubiquitous Portuguese "green wine" (*vinho verde*), which is young and fruity. *Aguardentes* and brandies are wonderful after-dinner treats.

The most famous of all Portuguese wines, of course, is port, produced in the Oporto region. Port (like its Spanish cousin, Madeira) is a fortified wine (this means brandy has been added during the wine-making process; the result is a very strong and sweet wine). There are drier (and even white) ports that are sometimes drunk prior to the meal, but most ports are drunk after the meal, with cheese, figs, chocolate, or on their own. Ruby port is the most common; vintage port is finer; but tawny port is usually the best.

Wine is drunk at lunch and dinner and, in the farmlands and vineyard country, can even make its way to the breakfast table. Never add anything to wine, and you should also be judicious about adding anything (salt, pepper, ketchup, etc.) to food (this implies that the original is not well prepared). The most common toast is *salud* (to your health).

Table Manners and the Use of Utensils

Do not begin eating until the host says, *"Bom appetito!"*

Like all continental Europeans, Portuguese do not switch knives and forks, as Americans do. The knife remains in the right hand, and the fork remains in the left. When the meal is finished, the knife and fork are laid parallel to each other across the right side of the plate. If you put both utensils down on the plate for any real length of time, it is a sign to the waitstaff that you are finished, and your plate may be taken away from you. Alternately, if you lay your cutlery down on either side of the plate, it means that you haven't finished; but if you really are, the host might interpret this as a sign that you were not happy with the meal.

The fork and spoon above your plate are for dessert. There may be several additional pieces of cutlery; if you're unsure of which utensil to use, always start from the outside and work your way in, course by course. Bread is usually served without butter (therefore, there usually will not be a butter knife, nor will there be a bread dish: bread is placed on the rim of your main plate or on the table by your plate). There will be separate glasses provided at your setting for water and white and red wine (after-dinner drink glasses come out after dinner).

When not holding utensils, your hands are expected to be visible above the table: this means that you do not keep them in your lap; instead, rest your wrists on top of the table (never your elbows). Keep your napkin visible, and when you are finished with the meal, fold it first before putting it down on the table. Pass all dishes to your left at the table. Never cut the lettuce in a salad: deftly fold it with your knife and fork into a little bundle that can be easily picked up with your fork.

Seating Plans

The most honored position is at the head of the table, with the primary guest seated immediately to the right of the host (women to the right of the host, and men to the right of the hostess). If there is a hosting couple, one will be seated at each end of the table. In keeping with the practice elsewhere on the Continent, men and women are seated next to one another, and couples are often broken up and seated next to people they may not have previously known. This is done to promote conversation. Men typically rise when women enter the room, and continue to hold doors for women and allow them to enter a room first. Remember, as is the case throughout the Continent, what the Portuguese call the first floor is really the second floor, with the first floor usually referred to as the lobby or ground floor.

Refills and Seconds

At a dinner party, if you do not want more food, leave a little on your plate: you will be offered seconds anyway, and if you eat everything on your plate, you will be expected to take more. You may always have additional beverages; drink enough to cause your cup or glass to be less than half full, and it will generally be refilled. Portions are generous, and there are generally several courses, for both lunch and dinner.

At Home, in a Restaurant, or at Work

There are many varieties of restaurants, beginning with the formal and elegant establishment serving haute cuisine right on down to the food stand on the street (try the *cervejaria:* an informal, sometimes cafeteria-style restaurant with very traditional, honest meals and snacks at a good price). There are many other wonderful, informal outdoor restaurants that make dining in Portugal a real treat.

In informal restaurants, you may be required to share a table: if so, do not force conversation; act as if you are seated at a private table. Waitstaff may be summoned by making eye contact; waving or calling their names is very impolite. The business breakfast is not common in Portugal. The business lunch (more common than dinner) is more widespread, but, depending upon how well developed your relationship is with your Portuguese colleagues, it is generally not the time to make business decisions. Take your cue from your Portuguese associates: if they bring up business, then it's okay to discuss it, but wait to take your lead from their conversation. No gum chewing, ever, at the restaurant or on the street. No-smoking sections in restaurants are still a rarity.

When you arrive at a Portuguese associate's home for a formal meal, you will be told where to sit, and there you should remain. Do not wander from room to room: much of the house is really off-limits to guests. Once you (and the group) are invited to another room, most probably the dining room, be sure to allow the more senior members of your party to enter the room ahead of you: men should also move aside to allow women to enter the room ahead of them. At the table, wait until the host indicates your seat: do not presume to seat yourself, as the seating arrangement is usually predetermined.

Being a Good Guest or Host

Paying the Bill

Usually the one who does the inviting pays the bill, although the guest is expected to make an effort to pay. Sometimes other circumstances determine the payee (such as rank). Making payment arrangements ahead of time so that no exchange occurs at the table is a very classy way to host. Women, if at a restaurant with men, will not really be able to pay the bill at a restaurant: if you want to, make arrangements ahead of time, and don't wait for the check to arrive at the table. The only time it is considered appropriate for a woman to pay the bill is if she is a businesswoman from abroad.

Transportation

It's a very nice idea, when acting as the host, to inquire ahead of time as to whether the guests will require transportation. If necessary, you should arrange for taxi service at the end of the meal.

When to Arrive / Chores to Do

If invited to dinner at a private home, do offer to help with the chores; but if you are only going to be in that home for that one evening, you should expect to be told no, and you should not visit the kitchen unless invited to do so. Outside of private homes, spouses may attend business dinners, but don't assume this is the case: wait for an invitation, or diplomatically inquire further (e.g., "Will your wife be joining us?"). Being invited to a dinner party in Portugal is a special honor, one not often extended to new relationships. If such an invitation is offered, accept it as an opportunity to build a new and close relationship: that is what your Portuguese associate is looking for. When it is time to leave, always get up and shake hands with everyone: the group wave is not appreciated. You may stay quite late (past midnight in both homes and restaurants).

Gift Giving

In general, gift giving is not common among business associates, although your Portuguese colleagues might appreciate high-quality, business-related items (agendas, electronic gadgets, etc.) as gifts. However, holiday cards are very appropriate, particularly as a thank-you for their business during the previous year, and should be mailed in time to be received the week before Christmas.

Gifts are appropriate for social events, especially as thank-yous for private dinner parties, but are not essential. If you do want to bring a gift, of course, it will be appreciated. The best gift in this case is flowers (not too elaborate, but not simple wildflowers, either). Never send chrysanthemums (they are used primarily as funeral flowers) or red roses (these usually indicate romantic intent), and always be sure the bouquet is in odd numbers (an old European tradition) except thirteen, which is considered unlucky. Another good gift would be chocolates (avoid wine, as it may present the hosts with the dilemma of whether it should be brought out to the table, especially when they have no doubt already selected the wine for the meal; dessert wine, brandy, and after-dinner liqueurs should also be avoided, as this is the land of port and *aguardente*). It is not necessary to write a thank-you note the next day.

If you are staying with a Portuguese family, an appropriate thank-you gift would be a high-quality product that represents your country and is difficult to get in Portugal: coffee-table books about the United States, small American-made electronic gadgets, a set of American bath towels (always a good gift most everywhere, since they are usually more luxurious), or anything that reflects your host's personal tastes (the cap of a famous American team for the football-playing son of the family, for example) is appropriate. For both social and business gifts, it is best to avoid food items—even imported gourmet foodstuffs—since the Portuguese really love their cuisine. As with other European cultures, gifts are generally opened at the time they are given and received.

Special Holidays and Celebrations

Major Holidays

Most Portuguese workers get four weeks of paid vacation; August is a leading vacation time. Business slows down from December 15 to January 5, and Holy Week is sometimes a more difficult time in which to accomplish work than Christmas. In addition, there are many regional fiestas and saints' days throughout the year that usually close down business for a day or two; among the most important of these are the Feast of Saint Anthony, Lisbon's patron saint, celebrated in that city on June 13, and the Feast of Saint John (June), Oporto's patron saint, celebrated in that city on June 24. Each town has its own saint's day, so be sure to check ahead of time when visiting.

As you establish personal relationships with your Portuguese colleagues, you may be invited to special family events, such as a wedding or a baptism: be sure to go, and bring a gift (money is *not* appropriate).

January 1	*Ano Novo* (New Year's Day)
February	*Carnaval* (Shrove Tuesday/Mardi Gras)
April 25	*Dia da Liberdade* (Liberty Day)
March/April	*Sexta-feira Santa* (Good Friday)
May 1	*Dia do Trabalhao* (Labor Day)
May/June	*Corpo de Deus* (Corpus Christi)
June 10	*Die de Camoes* (Camoes Day)
August 15	*Assuncao* (Assumption)
October 5	*Dia de Republica* (Republic Day)
November 1	*Todos-os-Santos* (All Saints' Day)
December 1	*Restauracao* (Restoration of Independence Day)
December 8	*Imaculada Caonceicao* (Immaculate Conception)
December 25	*Natal* (Christmas)

Business Culture

Daily Office Protocols

In Portugal, doors are usually closed; knock first (this includes bathrooms) before opening doors, and when leaving rooms, close the doors behind you. Women may be treated with particular respect by Portuguese men, but will be regarded as a curiosity in business settings. Age and hierarchy must be respected. See "What's the Best Way to View Time?" and "Punctuality" (as stated earlier) for more about Portuguese attitudes toward schedules and timeliness.

Management Styles

Privacy is important, but building consensus with others and avoiding risk before taking action on almost every aspect of work is critical. Workers provide what their bosses expect of them, and the preparation of plans, methods, and reports can be time-consuming and complicated efforts. Gathering the information required in order to do what your boss expects from you, or creating consensus among your colleagues in order to accomplish a particular goal, can take a long time. All of this occurs in a formal and sometimes very rigid hierarchical structure, which means that deadlines and efficiency are secondary to attention to detail, rigorous logic, and perfection of form. Because of this rigid rank and hierarchy orientation, titles in Portugal are important; the highest ones (e.g., vice president) are usually reserved for very senior, executive-level positions, and should not be used as casually as they are in the United States. Complimenting and rewarding employees publicly is usually not done.

Boss-Subordinate Relations

Rank most definitely has its privileges in Portugal. The Portuguese like to do business with the most important people in any organization (and this should be the same for the non-Portuguese working with them). There is often a rigid chain of command that must be heeded. No matter what field you are in, there is an established procedure one is expected to follow. Deviating from the normal channels will generally make more problems for you, even if your intent is to bypass what appear to be obstacles. Bosses are expected to provide guidance, distribute information, and make decisions; subordinates are expected to provide detailed information and follow the decisions made by their superiors.

Conducting a Meeting or Presentation

At meetings of peers, there can be open communication and sharing of ideas: in fact, these sessions often serve as information-sharing and decision-making forums in which all individuals are expected to contribute. Under these circumstances, discussions are usually vibrant, with many people speaking at once; questions are common and interruptions, even of presentations, should be expected. In more formal, conservative organizations, meetings are often gatherings of nonpeers, clearly called together by decision makers in order to gather information from below, clarify goals, and formulate action plans. In these cases, individuals often do not share ideas and are not expected to contribute to mutual problem solving. Remember, because a close personal relationship is often demonstrated through physicality in Latin cultures, the nearer your Portuguese colleagues are to you, the better they are responding to your proposal.

Negotiation Styles

The Portuguese will most always play their cards close to the vest: they do not divulge information easily (it is seen as the source of power). They are usually circumspect in their communication styles, and will indicate their thoughts in indirect ways. They will respect someone who comes to them with established knowledge and experience, and will build relationships based on your level in society and the organization. Whether you are worth knowing and doing business with may be more important than the details of your proposal. Nevertheless, details are important, and a carefully planned, logically organized, and beautifully presented proposal is key.

The first meeting is usually very formal, with the Portuguese sizing up you and your organization: it will be conducted in the office. Take copious notes afterward, but put on a warm, dignified demeanor during the meeting. Never be condescending. Although the contract must be legal down to the dotted i's, it really is just a legal formality to the Portuguese, and can be overcome, by either party, if such a need arises later on. Plan your meetings as carefully and as well in advance as you can, but expect changes. The goal, at least for the first meeting, is the development of a good feeling of respect and positive trust between yourself and your Portuguese colleagues. Remember also that the meeting might start and end much later than you anticipated; nevertheless, as with most polychronic cultures, you should always arrive on time.

Written Correspondence

Business letters should be very formal and respectful of hierarchy. Last names are usually written in uppercase; dates are given using the day/month/year format (with periods in between, not slashes); and an honorific plus a title is as common as an honorific plus the last name. The time of day is written in military style; weights and measures are usually given in metric units. Monetary amounts are written so that periods break up the figure into tens, hundreds, and thousands, and a comma separates the escudos from the centavos.

The traditional language used in openings and closings is more convoluted and formal than the American style, and you should write your e-mails, letters, and faxes using a precise formula. Be sure to inquire first, in all communications, about your colleague's health and progress, then move on to the substance of your communication, and close with a salutation and your personal wish for their success and well-being (the Latin communication "sandwich").

CHAPTER
FIFTEEN

The Mediterranean Cultures: Italy

Some Introductory Background on Italy and the Italians

Most Americans have images of Italy derived either from a travel tour or as a result of the Italian-American immigrant experience. Both present just a very small slice of the Italian culture, and making judgments about Italy from these limited perspectives is a great mistake. The travel tour shows Italy only as a country of food and monuments, and the Italian-American experience is really the southern Italian culture further altered by the immigrant mind-set, which is quite different from the northern Italian culture of today.

In many ways, Italy is a country in name only. Historically, its many regions remained—due in part to its geography, to its rivers, mountains, and climate, to its politics, and to the many different groups who at any one time were ruling sections of the invasion-vulnerable peninsula—independent from one another, with one's town, neighborhood, and family claiming one's loyalty first. If Americans see themselves first as Americans, and then as citizens of a particular state, city, and neighborhood, Italians (and many continental Europeans follow similar patterns) see themselves first as coming from a particular neighborhood, then as citizens of a certain city, then as residents of a particular region, and lastly as Italians. In fact, Italy was first unified into a nation-state in the nineteenth century (the unification struggle known as the Risorgimento, led by Guiseppe Garibaldi), and today can still be segmented into large, culturally distinct regions that must each be considered when discussing protocol and etiquette.

Rome roughly constitutes the dividing line between north and south, representing in many ways a combination of, and sometimes a compromise between, both cultures, with strong influences from both north and south determining Roman behaviors. The region south of Rome is known as the Mezzogiorno (middle of the day), perhaps in reference to the fact that it is more highly agricultural than the north, and the climate is significantly more subtropical: farmers in the Mezzogiorno work in the fields in the cool of the early morning and late afternoon, reserving the middle of the day for food and rest (the main lunch meal and the accompanying siesta). In the Mezzogiorno, they view the north as a foreign land populated by "Germans and French," who work all day and don't know how to enjoy life. If Milan is the business center of Italy in the north, and Naples is the heart of the Mezzogiorno in the south, then Rome is the administrative capital that tries constantly to balance the two and keep the country together. It is not always successful at this. There is a constant, more-or-less vocal movement in the north seeking independence, based in part on the feeling that they make the money, which Rome takes through unfair taxation and spends on the less-productive south; and there is an equally vocal movement in the south that believes that the north is trying to destroy Italy to advance its own selfish interests. Neapolitans and Milanese are in many ways as different as two people from two different countries.

In a sense, this conflict, like all conflicts in Italian culture, is subordinate to the "great Italian solution" to all of the country's problems—which, according to Luigi Barzini, the well-known Italian social critic, is to ignore the problem as much as possible, since it is viewed as insoluble anyway. Italy may be a wonderful place to visit precisely because so much day-to-day cultural energy is put into decorating life as it is, and making it as wondrous, beautiful, and enjoyable as possible—thus covering up, as it were, the difficulties, rather than solving them. The final flaw in this gorgeous Italian tapestry, according to Barzini and other observers, is the refusal to deal with what really requires fundamental attention, based significantly on the fact that historically, solutions more often than not did not work. In this self-fulfilling prophecy, politicians and business-people act only in their self-interest, nothing really changes, and one mustn't get too upset with problems, since they will never be fixed anyway. The Italian alternative, therefore, is to live each day as best as one can, with family, friends, food, and art becoming the focal points of life. The roots of this denying fatalism, and the remarkably beautiful and equally frustrating state of day-to-day existence in modern Italy that results, can be found in the country's history.

Some Historical Context

Rome, the center of the great classical civilization and the subsequent center of western Christianity, is also the heart of the Italian state. From the pre-Roman indigenous Etruscans, through the great Roman Empire to the rise of Vatican power in the Holy Roman Empire, the Renaissance, and the conquest of Italy by various royal houses of Europe, right on through the Risorgimento and Italy's role in the world wars of the twentieth century, the great sweep of Italian history lays the basis for understanding the roots of Italian multiple personalities today. The unchangeable Roman Catholic Church and the rigid hierarchies of the European monarchies that ruled Italy at various times in the past (the French in the north and south, the Germans in the east) provided sources for the group- and status-orientation of Italian life today. The endless wheel of history has never really altered the day-to-day existence of the average Italian; in fact, it seems to have ensured that the Italians' only true faith is to their family and trusted friends, creating a kind of cynicism toward civic life, and justifying individual self-interest that only coincidentally benefits others. Even the uncertainty of the early Etruscan agricultural life (which is still mirrored in many of the pagan and superstitious aspects of Italian rural life today) was underscored by the seismically unstable earth itself. The fascist dictator Benito Mussolini was quoted as having said, "It is not difficult to govern the Italians . . . merely useless." It is not just that life goes on, but that since the people are deeply skeptical that no effort will really change things, they behave accordingly, as actors in a drama that has no conclusion, living day to day on a gorgeously decorated stage.

An Area Briefing

Politics and Government

Today Italy is a parliamentary democracy, with a prime minister and a president, and a bicameral legislature. The monarchy was only officially dismantled in the middle of the twentieth century, having already been displaced by the twenty-year fascist interlude of Mussolini. The only historical experience Italians had with democratic government prior to the twentieth century was classical preimperial Rome, and they knew how that turned out. Because Italians require much information to minimize risk, but have loyalties to subjective interests and make decisions based on association and intuitive processes, there is little room for compromise, resulting at best in a government rarely unified enough to govern effectively, and at worst in a government corrupted by self-interest.

Schools and Education

Schooling for Italian children begins with the primary school (*scuòla elementare*) and the intermediate school (*scuòla mèdia*). At the age of fourteen, students graduate into one of three "high schools": the *licei* (classical studies for five years), *istituti tècnici* (technical studies for four to five years), or *scuòli professionali* (vocational studies for three to five years). At the end of the *licei* studies, if you pass the *maturità,* you can move on to the *università* (university), while graduates from the other two high schools can also move on to a university by taking supplementary courses and passing the *maturità*. There are many universities in Italy, most of them specializing in certain fields; few of them, however, offer the credentials of a complete modern university education. It is for this reason that students attending an Italian university usually do so for a specific field of study (graphic arts, Renaissance painting, medieval religious studies, etc.); the University of Bologna, by the way, is the oldest European university, founded in the twelfth century.

Religion and Demographics

Roman Catholics comprise over 90 percent of the population, and the Vatican, officially an independent sovereign state, claims spiritual authority over the people. While the church and the state have often historically been at odds (Roman Catholicism is not the official religion of Italy: the state is nominally secular), Italians are predominantly churchgoing. There are significant minority populations of Jews, Protestants, and Greek Orthodox Church members, as well. Italy demographically is an older country, with a declining population. Women, despite some gains especially in the northern urban centers, primarily fulfill the role of homemaker, and rarely achieve levels of authority in Italian businesses. If Italian women are successful at work, they are nevertheless expected to fulfill the role of homemaker and wife, as well.

Fundamental Cultural Orientations

1. What's the Best Way for People to Relate to One Another?

OTHER-INDEPENDENT OR OTHER-DEPENDENT? Italians are other-dependent, primarily, but with a significant sense of individual or personal responsibility, and a desire to look good in the eyes of others. This Italian variety of saving face is known as *bella figura,* meaning "beautiful face," a concept that requires one to always present oneself as "correct," formal, important—in a sense, beautiful. Taken further, the idea also suggests that if one presents oneself this way, it adds to the correctness or beauty of society as a whole. Loyalty to family, friends, and close neighbors means that there is a concern for always conducting oneself correctly, to presenting *bella figura,* or the right figure, in all circumstances. One can, and must, be clever enough to take care of oneself and one's own, but ultimately, it must always appear correct in the eyes of others. This concept is stronger the further south in Italy one goes. Ultimately, the group orientation in Sicily, for example, is the key ingredient of all interpersonal relationships; whom one knows is critical, and how one is seen determines how one will be treated.

HIERARCHY-ORIENTED OR EGALITY-ORIENTED? In larger traditional Italian businesses, the *cordata,* or chain of command, strictly determines how the organization is run: it is a rigidly organized pyramid, and represents the belief in hierarchy and levels of status that imposes itself on all aspects of Italian society (and that makes daily life through the resulting bureaucracy so frustrating; one response, of course, by individuals is to be clever enough to find ways around it, and one's ability to do this, for themselves and their family, is a source of pride and *bella figura*). There is great respect for age and for power, and men automatically have authority in business over women. This concern for structure and hierarchical organization is equally evident in both the north and south.

RULE-ORIENTED OR RELATIONSHIP-ORIENTED? The explicit bureaucratic rules, of course, can sometimes be baffling (and contradictory!) in their byzantine complexity, and the implicit social rules must be, if not mastered, at least respected. In either case, the ultimate determinant of human action is the flesh-and-blood relationships within and between families, friends, and neighbors; therefore, family histories, marriages, and associations are critically important. In the north, this condition is less severe; in the south, it is everything—effectively leading to the existence and the power of the Mafia in Sicily. As civil government vainly attempts to keep order through the application of universal law, organized groups based on subjective relationships rise to fill the vacuum.

2. What's the Best Way to View Time?

MONOCHRONIC OR POLYCHRONIC? Outside of the major northern cities, time is circular, and very polychronic; it is most monochronic in Milan, but as one moves south, old agrarian patterns die hard, even if people aren't waking up and heading for the fields in the morning today. In rural areas, it is easiest to work in the fields in the cool of the early morning and late afternoon; the mid-day heat is usually too oppressive, and provides a good opportunity to stoke up on a filling meal and a siesta before heading back out until the sun sets.

Working in Milan means arriving in the office at 9 A.M., and pretty much setting to one's work; meetings start when scheduled, and the average lunch (not the high-powered business lunch) usually doesn't last more than an hour; even dinner parties begin within a half hour of their stated time. In Rome, one might arrive at the office at 9 A.M., but the real work doesn't begin until 9:30 A.M. or so; lunch can be a more leisurely affair, beginning at 1 P.M. and lasting until 2:30; meetings and appointments start within a half hour of the stated time; one doesn't leave the office to return home until 7 or 7:30 P.M., or even later; and dinner parties start one hour after the stated arrival time. In Naples, one arrives at the office between 8:30 and 9:30 A.M., but work doesn't start earnestly until 10 A.M. or so; lunch is at 1 or 2 P.M. and can last until 4 P.M.; one stays in the office until 7 or 8 P.M.; meetings and appointments begin and end pretty much when the decision makers arrive and leave; and dinner parties do not begin until one or two hours after the stated time. Throughout Italy, Friday and Saturday night revelries more often than not last until after the sun comes up. And as one moves south through Italy, the clock slows down.

RISK-TAKING OR RISK-AVERSE? Latin cultures, in general, are risk-averse, and that is one of the driving reasons for their creation of structure and hierarchies. In Italy this tendency is more extreme as one moves south through the country. Decision making can be slow and tedious in Naples, but quicker in Milan; in both cases, more or less, various levels of the hierarchy need to be consulted, and information must be made available to many, eventually moving through the *cordata* to the final individual decision maker, who listens to the advice from below, and then makes the final decision. While debate is common, evidence supporting alternate views must fit with subjective expectations, or else it is ultimately unconvincing. Even when individuals are empowered to make the decision, there can be a reticence to take the required final step.

PAST-ORIENTED OR FUTURE-ORIENTED? Italians are essentially fatalistic; however, the past, while glorious in those aspects that celebrate Italy's enormous cultural contributions (art, food, music, engineering, literature, etc.), is not necessarily mourned for. Nevertheless, the future is not longed for, either, and because of a general pessimism about being able to control future events, the pervasive attitude is to live for the here and now, as best as one can.

3. What's the Best Way for Society to Work with the World at Large?

LOW-CONTEXT DIRECT OR HIGH-CONTEXT INDIRECT COMMUNICATORS? This is a very high-context culture, with the circumstances (and individuals) of the moment determining the style of communication with which information is exchanged. However, the reason for this is not the need to avoid confrontation or maintain harmony, but the need to maintain *bella figura* and personal pride; Italians will eagerly join in a raucous debate, and can press a point very vigorously. The emotional level can be quite high; speech is often direct, but action is the result of the context and circumstance.

PROCESS-ORIENTED OR RESULT-ORIENTED? As with other Latin cultures, there is a strong reliance on the deductive process: how things are being done may be more important than the final result. Therefore, in Italy, things must appear as good as they essentially need to be; however, because there is an inherent disbelief in the effectiveness of human action, there is sometimes a greater emphasis placed on the appearance of things than on how they actually are. (Mussolini was said to have arranged for the same troops to march around the square over and over again to give the appearance he had more soldiers than he really did.) Presentations must be beautifully and artfully packaged. Individuals must look good: the package may be more important than what's inside. But Italians are also associative in their logic, based on what has worked with others in similar situations (even when the two situations may not be directly related to each other). Therefore, despite the obvious merits of an idea, if it doesn't fit with an individual's subjective experience or opinion, it is often rejected. In addition, the risk-averse nature of Italian culture means much information and detail must be analyzed. For these reasons, Italians may not understand or be able to follow through with the actions necessary to put the plans in place. It is therefore all the more important for non-Italians to stay involved with them, helping them to implement what has been agreed to.

FORMAL OR INFORMAL? In Italy, there are "correct" and "incorrect" ways to get things done, which tends to formalize human relationships, both socially and in business. Family members relate to one another according to formal rules that respect traditional family roles. This does not have to be artificial or contrived; in fact, it is often loving and spontaneous. But it is respectful and formal. Even the language is divided into formal and informal forms and phrases, and personal behaviors are ruled by etiquette and protocol. Honor and personal pride are critical, and this means a bit more formality. Never insult the honor or personal pride of the Italians, their families, their towns, or their friends.

Greetings and Introductions

Language and Basic Vocabulary

Most Italians in Italy do not speak English well; you will probably need a translator in business situations. In the north, there may be more opportunity to do business with English speakers, but one should consider that this will probably be more the exception than the rule. The second language for Italians is usually determined by their area: French in the Piedmont near France and Switzerland; German in the Tyrol and Dolomites in the north and east; English, perhaps, in the center, depending upon individual experience.

Here are some basic Italian phrases and their English translations:

buòn giorno	good morning/afternoon
buòna sera	good evening
buòna nòtte	good night
ciao!	hello/good-bye (informal)
arrivederci/arrivedella	good-bye
per favore	please
gràzie	thank you

prego	you're welcome/can I help?
scusi	excuse me/sorry
Parla inglese?	Do you speak English?
Non parlo d'italiano	I don't speak Italian
sì	yes
nò	no
Come sta?	How are you?
Bènè, gràzie, e lei?	Very well, thanks, and you?
piacere	pleased to meet you
signore	Mr.
signora	Mrs.
signorina	Miss
dottore/dottoressa	doctor (applicable to anyone with a university degree, not just a doctorate)
ingegnère	engineer
professore	professor
avvocato	lawyer

Here are some pronunciation tips:

c is pronounced like the *ch* in *church* when followed by *e* or *i*
ch is pronounced like the *c* in *cat*
g is pronounced like the *j* in *jet* when followed by *e* or *i*
gh is pronounced like the *g* in *girl*
gl is pronounced like the *lli* in *million*
gn is pronounced like the *ni* in *onion*

Honorifics for Men, Women, and Children

You must use *signore* (Mr.) and *signora* (Mrs.), plus the family name, when introduced to strangers. Unless and until your Italian colleague specifically invites you to use first names, and despite how he or she might refer to you, you must always use the family name plus the correct Italian honorific (*signorina*— abbreviated Srna.—is rarely used these days in Italy—more so in the south, though—unless you are clearly speaking with a child or a very young, single female adult, or if you do not know whether a woman is married or not and she is clearly not an older woman). Children in Italy are expected to be respectful and not overly conversational when speaking with adults, and must always use honorifics when referring to adults.

In situations where a title is known or used, the honorific plus the title is usually employed, either with or without the name (e.g., Signore Ingègnere, or Signore Ingègnere Milani). For casual contacts (e.g., with waiters, store help, etc.), just use *signorina* or *camerière* (for a male waiter) without the name; sometimes the word *senta* is used (it means, roughly, "please come here to me"). It is very important to greet people at work or in stores or restaurants with an appropriate greeting for the time of day—*buòn giorno* or *buòna sera*— and *arrivederci* upon leaving. If you speak any Italian at all, it is important to use it, but be sure to use the formal pronoun *lei* at the beginning, and do not switch to the *tu* (informal) form unless and until your Italian colleague has specifically invited you to or uses it him- or herself.

The What, When, and How of Introducing People

Always wait to be introduced to strangers before taking that responsibility upon yourself. You will always be introduced to older people and women first (when introducing yourself, you must also follow this protocol). Italians are most comfortable with a third-party introduction whenever possible. Try to ensure that for yourself ahead of time. Do not presume to seat yourself at a gathering: if possible, wait to be told where to sit. Shake hands with everyone individually in a group before departing: the American group wave is not appreciated. Once you greet someone you will encounter later that day in the same circumstances (e.g., at the office), there is no need to greet them again. Kissing is a common greeting once you have established a relationship, whether between women or men and women; it usually consists of a kiss on two cheeks (actually an "air kiss," first on the left side, and then the right). You might progress to this stage with your Italian colleagues as quickly as the second or third meeting.

Physical Greeting Styles

The handshake is common. The Italian version is done firmly between two men, but not as robustly between men and women or two women. The handshake should be accompanied by the appropriate greetings (as outlined above), and is usually accompanied by a touch on the elbow or shoulder, especially if this is the second or a later meeting. Smiling and other nonverbal forms of communication may accompany the handshake, especially between people who have met once before. Men should wait until a woman extends her hand before reaching for it, and women may take the lead in extending their hand or not. Men must remove their gloves when shaking hands with a woman, but a woman need not remove her gloves when shaking hands with a man. Between family members, friends, or trusted business colleagues, a hug or other forms of touching may be expected. Eye contact during the introduction is important, and should be maintained as long as the individual is addressing you.

The use of business cards is common; if possible, you should have yours translated into Italian on the reverse. Be sure to put any advanced educational degrees and your full title or position on both sides of your business card. Such emblems of your status are very important to Italians: they want to know they are doing business with an important person. However, very senior businesspeople usually have less information on their business cards: in this case, they almost function as a calling card, and nothing more.

Communication Styles

Okay Topics / Not Okay Topics

Okay: food and wine, politics—only if you know what you are talking about—current events, movies, the arts, sports (soccer is a national mania), music, Italian architecture, opera, and philosophy. Go ahead and enthuse about Italian cultural life; Italians love it. *Not okay:* Do not inquire about a person's occupation or income in casual conversation. Americans often begin a conversation with "So, what do you do?" This is too personal in Italy; it sounds like prying, and is often not the most interesting topic of conversation. Also not okay: questions about private family matters (the family is sacred) or personal background, Mussolini and World War II, the Vatican and its policies, Italian-American stereotypes, or negative comments about the local soccer team (a soccer team commands the devotion of its fans like nothing else: weekend afternoons are spent gathered around the television watching its match).

Tone, Volume, and Speed

In business settings, the one with authority rarely has to raise his or her voice; nevertheless, in general, Italians speak loudly and animatedly, and in a polychronic, simultaneous way. Go ahead and jump in: interruptions are to be expected, but always remain respectful and never get angry.

Use of Silence

There is rarely a moment of it. Enjoy the simultaneous conversations and frequent interruptions: it shows interest. Hang in there.

Physical Gestures and Facial Expressions

Italians are extremely expressive communicators. The U.S. "okay" sign, given with the thumb and the forefinger making a circle, may be considered vulgar and obscene: avoid it. In addition, winking and whistling (often accompanied with a positive comment) is meant to be a friendly introduction between men and women; it is not an insult. If a woman is not interested, she merely need not acknowledge it. But if a woman's eyes meet a man's eyes under these circumstances, it is an indication of interest.

Stroking the cheek with your thumb indicates that the person who is speaking is crafty (*furbo,* or clever like a fox); stroking the fingers underneath the chin means disinterest or defiance; tapping the elbow of one arm with the hand of the other indicates that a person or their offer is cheap; sharply raising the forearm while karate-chopping the inside of the elbow of that arm with the hand of the other is an obscene and insulting gesture; so is grabbing the upper front two teeth with the underside of the thumbnail and sharply removing the thumb from the mouth; pulling the bottom eyelid of one eye downward with the index finger is an indication to be careful about what one is saying, or an expression of doubt and disbelief. Finally, the *còrno,* or making the sign of goat horns by raising the pinky and index finger up while the middle two fingers remain curled, is the ultimate insult to a man's *bella figura:* it implies that he is unable to keep his wife satisfied and is being cuckolded. Two men often walk down the street arm in arm, usually after a social event, as do two women: it is a sign of friendship and closeness, nothing more.

Waving and Counting

The thumb represents the number 1, the index finger the number 2, and so on. It is insulting to beckon someone with the forefinger (instead, turn your hand so that the palm faces down and motion inward with all four fingers at once). If you need to gesture for a waiter, subtly raise your hand. Waving or beckoning is done with the palm down and the fingers moving forward and back in a kind of scratching motion.

Physicality and Physical Space

Italians tend to get much closer than people of North America or northern Europe do. Do not step back when your Italian associate steps forward. Never speak with your hands in your pockets: always keep them firmly at your side when standing. If men and women must cross their legs, it must never be ankle over knee (for women, the preferred style is to cross ankle over ankle). Remember, even in public, formal is always better than informal: no gum chewing, *ever;* don't slouch; and don't lean against things. Italians often gesture with their hands, and their facial expressiveness is strong.

Eye Contact

Eye contact is direct most of the time in Italy. It is important not to interpret this behavior as a way of intentionally trying to make you uncomfortable. It is the way Italians show their interest. Conversely, if you look away, your behavior will say to your Italian colleague that you are either disinterested or rude. Either way, maintain eye contact when it is made with you. If strangers' eyes meet and linger, it implies romantic interest. Act accordingly.

Emotive Orientation

Italians, as we've said, are animated and physically expressive. Nevertheless, while passionate gestures are common, until you know people well, you want to indicate restraint, while not seeming lifeless. Join in if you like, but keep cool if you can. Italians will always admire you if you can remain logical, formal, respectful, and diplomatic, especially at first; later they will admire you if you can passionately defend and promote your ideas while always being respectful of others and not taking yourself too seriously.

Protocol in Public

Walking Styles and Waiting in Lines

It is more important in Italy to maintain one's face by being first in line (and never last) than it is to maintain a queue. Don't be too distressed if someone walks right up to the front of the line at a bank, a restaurant, or a store and gets served first because of the relationship he or she has with the clerk, while you have been waiting patiently in line for forty minutes. Never be last, ever, anywhere, and do whatever it takes to make sure of that.

Behavior in Public Places: Airports, Terminals, and the Market

Customer service, as a concept, is catching on, but is not fully institutionalized. Store hours are typically not built around customer convenience (many stores are closed on weekends and most evenings—except Thursdays, usually). Personally thanking store owners, waiters, chefs, and hotel managers for their services is very much appreciated. As in much of Europe when you buy goods in stores, it may be difficult for you to return the item unless there is a flaw in it. Smoking is on the decline, and there may be smokeless areas in public places.

The *passeggiata* is a common custom throughout Italy; it can occur either before dinner (usually in smaller towns), around dusk, or after dinner (usually in the major cities), and involves strolling the streets, having an aperitif or coffee, seeing who you bump into, talking with neighbors and friends. You must stop and speak with everyone you know, or with people who show an interest in you. While Italians don an air of formality to preserve position and *bella figura,* they are an open and warm people, genuinely interested in new faces and in getting to know you.

When answering a phone, say *pronto.* Most newer public phones accept telecards; some older phones still require that you first purchase a *gettone* (token), which you use in place of coins, at the local tobacconist or newsstand.

Bus / Metro / Taxi / Car

Driving is on the right, but people pass very quickly on the left. The metro system shuts down after midnight or 1 A.M. Your best bet for catching a cab is at designated taxi stands (hotels are good places, but often charge more for the same ride: a hotel surcharge is added to the meter fare, in some cases). Bring food and water on board a commuter train if your trip is a long one, as there may not be a café car.

On public transportation, younger people should give up their seats to older people, and men should still give up their seats to women. Intercity trains are either *locale* (these are slow, and stop at every possible town, and have one class of service: second), *dirètto* (which are semi-express, but still make many stops, and may have first- and second-class service), and *espresso* (these are express trains between major cities only, some with international service, and most have all service classes).

Tipping

A 10 percent tip is usually sufficient for restaurants and taxis; more is considered nouveau and gauche. Porters and hotel help get 1,000 to 1,500 lire per service rendered; theater and bathroom attendants usually get the same, but on the lower side. Restaurants usually have the 10 percent tip already included on the bill; if you are unsure, it's okay to ask if service is included or not. Even if it is, it is still appropriate to leave odd change equal to about another 5 percent if the service was particularly good.

Punctuality

As we move south in Italy, timeliness becomes less and less of a concern. It is perfectly acceptable—in fact, essential—to arrive at social events about one-half hour late in the north, and one hour late in the extreme south. If you arrive sooner, you will be running the risk of interrupting the host or hostess as they get ready. In Milan, being late for business meetings by five to fifteen minutes is usually not a problem, but it is safer for the new employee or a visitor to be on time (but he or she should not be surprised if others are tardy—in Rome, one-half hour is normal; in Naples, one hour). The meeting will not begin in earnest until all attendees have arrived (or at least until all the decision makers have shown up). Resist questioning the late ones for a reason; they always have one, usually involving obligations with more important people, like superiors, old friends, or family. It's not important to know the details.

Dress

It is difficult to outstyle the Italians, especially the Milanese (for many, Milan is the very center of the fashion and design world). Clothing is very formal for both men and women, no matter the occasion—business or social, at work, in a restaurant, or on the street. Good taste is everything, and should be reflected in the clothes one wears. At work, men wear very stylish suits (dark is best), white shirts, and interesting and sophisticated ties; polished shoes are the order of the day, and accessories such as stylish watches, cuff links, and tie clips are common. Women usually accessorize so that even the simplest of outfits stands out for its interest and style. Italian businesswomen may wear more makeup and jewelry than American women, and it is fashionable, especially in summer, not to wear stockings. On the street, informal may mean jeans and sneakers, though that is more common as clothing to wear at the gym, the beach, or while jogging (women do not wear sneakers to work); for a social gathering, informal more often than not means tastefully coordinated clothes, sometimes including a jacket and tie for men (it rarely means jeans, sneakers, and T-shirts). "Formal" usually means formal evening wear, which is very dressy by American standards.

Seasonal Variations

There are two basic seasons in Italy, with summer being more severe in the south, and winter more severe in the north; one needs to dress accordingly. Summers can be hot and humid, and winters can be damp and cool (there is little snow, however, except in the mountain regions).

Colors

Bright colors are best reserved for accessories, as offsets to the more sophisticated dark or soft hues and tones of the outfits themselves.

Styles

Fashionable men and women in Italy usually look to Milan for "the newest look," although few people can actually afford the latest trends. Nevertheless, even the average person has a heightened sense of fashion, and one should dress with the same thought and care that one should put into every aspect of his or her life. Italians also can combine colors, weaves, textures, and designs in ways not common to North Americans. Both men's and women's shoes can be remarkably stylish.

Accessories / Jewelry / Makeup

The right makeup, hairstyle, and accessories are very important for women. Men also accessorize, and cologne is commonly used.

Personal Hygiene

Italians are very concerned about cleanliness and smelling good; perfumes and colognes are often used.

Dining and Drinking

Mealtimes and Typical Foods

Breakfast (*la prima colazione*) is served from about 8 to 8:30 A.M., and usually consists of the coffee, rolls, butter, and marmalade typical of the quick continental breakfast. Coffee in the morning is usually cappuccino; the other hot drink can be hot chocolate; espresso is usually reserved for after dinner. Breakfast can be more substantial, and start earlier, in the south.

Lunch (*la colazione*) is still the main meal of the day in both rural and urban settings. It can be an elaborate affair lasting several hours—sometimes less—but it usually always involves several courses, whether at home or in a restaurant. Lunch is usually served after 1 P.M., and typically includes soup, a main course or pasta, salad, and dessert (usually cheese with fruit). It ends with a cup of strong, black espresso. (Espresso is always drunk in quick sips: it is not lingered over, as it gets cold and unpleasant quickly. Espresso in the south is served with a twist of lemon, but this is not the case for north of Rome, and is a giveaway as to one's origins in Italy.) Cappuccino is reserved mainly for the morning coffee, and espresso (or its cousins, such as *macchiato*—with a spot of milk—and *streto*—an even denser version of espresso) for every other meal or snack. If you want decaffeinated coffee, look for the term *hag:* it means without caffeine. Wine and water are served throughout lunch, along with bread (in Italy, except in some places in the north, olive oil generally replaces butter, and is served in a small plate for dipping bread into, or you may be offered a small bottle of olive oil to pour onto your bread plate: use carefully and sparingly, and dip your bread into it from time to time). On Sunday, the family day, the main meal is supper, which is usually served at lunchtime and can last well into the evening.

Dinner (*il pranzo*) is served from 8:30 P.M. on, with 8 to 9 P.M. the customary starting time in the north, 9 P.M. in Rome, and 10 P.M. in Naples. In major cities, if dinner is substituted for lunch as the main meal of the day, it can last well past midnight. You might find all but tourist restaurants closed prior to 8:30 or 9 P.M. If the main meal of the day was lunch, then the family dinner at home is light. In this case, *il pranzo* is usually some cold cuts, salad, soup, and dessert. If it is a more formal dinner out, it will more closely resemble the full lunch.

Italian regional wines are usually served with dinner; no matter how simple or expensive, they are carefully selected to complement the food as perfectly as possible. Wine is considered to be a food in Italy (there is an old saying, "Eating teaches drinking"), and it should be savored, enjoyed, and never used to get drunk. Italians are not as ethnocentric about their wines as other Europeans: they will enjoy a wine from the United States, for example, as long as it is good, and such wines, in fact, make good gifts (bring along more than one bottle, so that one can be drunk at the meal, and another can serve as the gift).

Dinner parties or large lunches often start with an aperitif (cinzano, vermouth, campari, etc.), and end with after-dinner drinks, such as grappa (a brandy made from grape skins and stems) or sambuca (an anise-flavored drink often served with a coffee bean) after coffee. Dinner parties usually end at around midnight, but can go much later if all are having a good time.

Formal Italian meals usually follow this order:

- antipasto (appetizers, such as prosciutto or pâtes and fruit)
- soup
- pasta (usually a small portion)
- main dish (usually meat or fish, or sometimes beginning with fish and moving on to meat), often served with vegetables
- salad
- cheese
- dessert
- fruit
- espresso and after-dinner drinks

Note that in the Italian dinner, fruit and cheese are often taken separately, with the dessert in between (the fruit is used more as a palate cleanser, and is often pears, oranges, or something that can cut through the flavors of the meal). Moreover, espresso is often served with the after-dinner drink. Portions are usually smaller than in the United States (although as one moves south, portions usually get larger, which is typical in more agrarian environments). In Rome, there is a custom of having a bowl of pasta after, not during, dinner, around midnight (*dopa cena*—literally, "after supper").

Cafés are found everywhere in Italy, usually at the center of town and neighborhood life. They are the places to go for conversation, a snack, some tea or coffee, a drink, an aperitif, or a pastry. They are open practically at all hours, and customarily have seating both indoors and outdoors (when the weather permits). The tables are tiny, and often crammed next to each other, so maintaining privacy between diners is important. Once you are seated (yes, in most you may seat yourself), the waiter will arrive, and you should be prepared to place your order. Once you call for the bill, be prepared to pay it; the waiter will generally wait at your table until you pay. Traditionally, you could sit in a café for as long as you liked; no one would ask you to move on until you were ready. This is still the case in most cafés, in the cities as well as the country. As informal as cafés can be, though, eating while strolling down the street simply isn't done in Italy, with the exception of the ice cream cone (gelato comes in an unbelievable selection of flavors), although there are food stalls in markets or other places where one can buy crêpes and sandwiches, for example; however, it is usually expected that food purchased at a stall will be eaten there or very nearby, whether or not seating is provided. In bars, it is common to go to the cashier first, pay, obtain a receipt, take your place at the bar, and give your order with your receipt (and a small tip) to the barman, who will then serve you your drink.

In addition to Italy's wonderful formal restaurants, try the *trattorias,* which are family-run, less-expensive establishments that feature limited family-style menus, and *tàvola caldas* (literally, "warm tables"), which are the places to go for a quick, hot meal (they are usually best at lunchtime).

Regional Differences

Italian food is considered by some to be the finest cuisine in the world, rivaling French in its consistent requirement for fresh and inventive ways to use the incredible varieties of food in the country. As one moves from north to south through Italy, the food shifts from rice-based dishes (risottos) to wheat-based dishes (noodles and pastas, pizzas and gnocchis), from carefully prepared complex dishes to more simple and hearty fare (stews, soups, etc.). Seafood and fish are abundant throughout the country due to its enormous coastline, and the vegetables and the fruits are extraordinary, especially as one moves south. Some say that the finest food in Italy can be found in the Bologna region, the home of tortellini and prosciutto. Bolognese food is rich, heavy, and complex. Florentine and Tuscan dishes rely on boar, meats, beans, lots of olive oil, herbs, and garlic. Genoa is the home of gnocchi and pestos and wonderful fresh fish stews. The Lombard region (Milan is the capital) is famous for its osso buco, lamb dishes, and polenta, and Rome for the fabulous varieties of pastas, meats, and vegetables. In the Veneto area to the east you can find wonderful fried fish from the Adriatic, and lots of fresh vegetables prepared in countless ways. Finally, into the south and beyond to Sicily, you find the home of the pizza, fresh farm vegetables, figs, olive oil, and herbs.

Typical Drinks and Toasting

Coffee is drunk throughout the day in Italy, and provides the perfect social requirement for exchanging information and news, or building those all-important business relationships. If you are invited to a coffee bar for a cup of espresso, do not hesitate. It will take very little time, as coffee is usually drunk quickly, and not lingered over.

Mixed drinks before dinner are not common; before the meal, one usually has an aperitif of vermouth or campari. Once the meal gets under way, wine will be served in most cases. White wine (*bianco*) will be served with appetizers or fish, and reds (*rosa*) will be served with appetizers and meats. You may be offered several different white or red wines; and in this case, the finer red or white is usually served first, so that you may appreciate it best. A sweeter wine may be served with dessert. Wine is drunk at lunch and dinner and, in the farmlands and vineyard country, can even make its way to the breakfast table. Never add anything to wine, and you should also be judicious about adding anything (salt, pepper, ketchup, etc.) to food (this implies that the original is not well prepared). The most common toast is *salute* (to your health), or, more informally, *cin-cin*.

Table Manners and the Use of Utensils

Do not begin eating until the host says, "*Buòn appetito!*"

Like all continental Europeans, Italians do not switch knives and forks, as Americans do. The knife remains in the right hand, and the fork remains in the left. When the meal is finished, the knife and fork are laid parallel to each other across the right side of the plate, with the tines of the fork facing downward. If you put both utensils down on the plate for any real length of time, it is a sign to the waitstaff that you are finished, and your plate may be taken away from you. Alternately, if you lay your cutlery down on either side of the plate, it means you haven't finished; but if you really are, the host might interpret this as a sign that you were not happy with the meal.

The fork and spoon above your plate are for dessert. There are often many additional pieces of cutlery; if you're unsure of which utensil to use, always start from the outside and work your way in, course by course. Bread is usually served without butter (therefore, there will usually not be a butter knife, but there may be a bread dish: if so, this usually means that olive oil will be served to dip the bread into; if not, you can place your bread on the side of your main plate or on the table throughout the meal). There will be separate glasses provided at your setting for water and white and red wine (after-dinner drink glasses come out after dinner).

When not holding utensils, your hands are expected to be visible above the table: this means that you do not keep them in your lap; instead, rest your wrists on top of the table (never your elbows). At the table, pass all dishes to your left. Never cut the lettuce in your salad: deftly fold it with your knife and fork into a little bundle that can be easily picked up with your fork.

If you have a small plate as well as a larger one, plus a bowl, most likely the small plate will be for antipasto (salad plates will come out later), and the large plate for the main course; the bowl will be for soup if a soup spoon is present, or for pasta if a soup spoon is not present. If you are served pasta, do not use a spoon to assist yourself while eating it: use a fork and the sides of the bowl or plate against which to inconspicuously twirl the pasta onto the fork. Do not slurp the pasta strands into your mouth: place the entire forkful into your mouth at once. If there is gravy or sauce, you can generally use your bread to soak some of it up, but do so carefully, and don't mop the bread around the plate. By the way, the hostess or the waiter might use a special pair of cutlery scissors to cut up meat or other items right in front of you: don't worry, it's quite normal.

Seating Plans

The most honored position is in the middle at each side of the table, with the most important guest seated immediately to the right of the host (women to the right of the host, and men to the right of the hostess). If there is a hosting couple, one will be seated on each side of the table. In keeping with the practice on the rest of the Continent, men and women are seated next to one another, and couples are often broken up and seated next to people they may not have previously known. This is done to promote conversation. Men typically rise when women enter the room, and continue to hold doors for women and allow them to enter a room first. Remember, as is the case throughout the Continent, what the Italians call the first floor is really the second floor, with the first floor usually referred to as the lobby or ground floor.

Refills and Seconds

At a private dinner party, if you do not want more food, you will really have to insist several times before the hostess will believe you. Take a little extra anyway. You won't be expected to eat everything on your plate, but eat as much as you can. Pace yourself! You may always have additional beverages; drink enough to cause your cup or glass to be less than half full, and it will generally be refilled. Portions are generally smaller than in the United States, but there are usually more courses, for both lunch and dinner. In Italy, food is not about quantity, but quality.

At Home, in a Restaurant, or at Work

In informal restaurants, you may be required to share a table: if so, do not force conversation; act as if you are seated at a private table. Waitstaff may be summoned by making eye contact; waving or calling their names is very impolite. The working breakfast is not common in Italy, although you do see it creeping into the business life of the major cities very slowly. The business lunch (more common than dinner) is quite widespread, but, depending upon how well developed your relationship is with your Italian colleagues, it is generally not the time to make business decisions. Take your cue from your Italian associates: if they bring up business, then it's okay to discuss it, but wait to take your lead from their conversation. No gum chewing, ever, at a restaurant or on the street. No-smoking sections in restaurants are still a rarity.

When you arrive at an Italian associate's home for a formal meal, you will be told where to sit, and there you should remain. Do not wander from room to room: much of the house is really off-limits to guests. Use the toilet before you arrive, as it is considered bad form to have to leave the dinner party, or the table, at any time. Once you (and the group) are invited to another room, most probably the dining room, be sure to allow the more senior members of your party to enter the room ahead of you: men should also move aside to allow women to enter the room ahead of them. At the table, be sure to look for place cards or wait until the host indicates your seat: do not presume to seat yourself, as the seating arrangement is usually predetermined. Spouses who accompany their partners on business trips to Italy may be invited to attend dinners (but usually not lunches).

Being a Good Guest or Host

Paying the Bill

Usually the one who does the inviting pays the bill, although the guest is expected to make an effort to pay. Sometimes other circumstances determine the payee (such as rank). Making payment arrangements ahead of time so that no exchange occurs at the table is a very classy way to host. Women will not really be able to pay the bill at a restaurant when at the table with men: if you want to, make arrangements ahead of time, and don't wait for the check to arrive at the table.

Transportation

It's a very nice idea, when acting as the host, to inquire ahead of time as to whether your guests will require transportation. If necessary, you should arrange for taxi service at the end of the meal.

When to Arrive / Chores to Do

If invited to dinner at a private home, you may offer to help with the chores, but you should not expect to visit the kitchen at first (your invitation may be taken up later in the evening, or certainly on the second visit). Do not leave the table unless invited to do so. Being invited to a private dinner party in Italy is a special honor, one not often extended to new acquaintances. If such an invitation is offered, accept it as an opportunity to build a new and close relationship: that is what your Italian associate is looking for. When it is time to leave, always get up and shake hands with everyone: the group wave is not appreciated.

Gift Giving

In general, gift giving is common among business associates, although it is best not to send a gift at any time, including the holidays, unless you receive one first from your Italian colleague, thus "kick-starting" the process. However, holiday cards are also very appropriate, particularly as a thank-you for your colleague's business during the previous year, and should be mailed in time to be received the week before Christmas. Good business gifts include office-related items of fine quality that are also representative of your country.

Gifts are expected for social events, especially as thank-yous for private dinner parties. The best gift in this case is a formal bouquet of flowers—and it is best to have them sent ahead of time on the day of the dinner (simple floral arrangements are not appreciated). Never send chrysanthemums (they are used primarily as funeral flowers) or red roses (these usually indicate romantic intent), and always be sure the bouquet is in odd numbers (an old European tradition). If you must bring flowers with you to the dinner party, unwrap them before presenting them to the hostess. Other good gifts would be a box of fine pastries or chocolates; American wines (bring several bottles, so that one may be used with the meal, and the others by the hosts later), if you can find some good-quality choices; or a dessert wine. It is not necessary to send a thank-you note the next day for all but the most formal of dinner parties, especially if you brought a gift the night before. Bringing or sending gifts to someone's home is a more common practice in the north than in the south.

If you are staying with an Italian family, an appropriate thank-you gift would be a high-quality product that represents your country and is difficult to get in Italy: coffee-table books about the United States, or anything that reflects your host's personal tastes (the cap of a famous American team for the football-playing son of the family, for example), are appropriate. Gifts to avoid would be cutlery, handkerchiefs, embroidered linens, or a brooch: they all indicate the parting of ways and the ending of relationships.

For both social and business gifts, quality American foodstuffs are appreciated, such as fresh lobsters or maple syrup (no beef jerky or citrus fruits, though; there's plenty of the latter and no desire for the former). As with other European cultures, gifts are generally opened at the time they are given and received.

Special Holidays and Celebrations

Major Holidays

Most Italian workers get several weeks of paid vacation; August is a leading vacation time. Business slows down from December 15 to January 5, and Holy

Week is sometimes a more difficult time in which to accomplish work than Christmas. In addition, there are regional fiestas and saints' days throughout the year that usually close down businesses for a day or two; check with your local contacts. As you establish personal relationships with your Italian colleagues, you may be invited to special family events, such as a wedding or a baptism; be sure to go, and bring a gift (money is not appropriate).

January 1	New Year's Day
January 6	Epiphany
March/April	Holy Week and Easter Sunday and Monday (usually celebrated as the first day of spring, as well, with trips to the country or family homes)
April 25	Liberation Day
May 1	Labor Day
June 2	Republic Day
August 15	*Ferragosto* (Assumption of Mary; usually celebrated with trips to the country)
November 1	All Saints' Day
December 8	Immaculate Conception
December 25	Christmas
December 26	Saint Stephen's Day

Business Culture

Daily Office Protocols

In Italy, doors are often closed; knock first (this includes bathrooms) before opening doors, and when leaving rooms, close the doors behind you. Women may be treated with particular respect by Italian men, but never to the point of attaining equal recognition or authority in business settings. It is more common for women to be relegated to lower-level management and administrative support positions. It is rare (though not impossible) to see women at the highest levels of business and government in Italy.

Management Styles

Privacy and individual accomplishment of one's tasks are critical. Workers provide what their bosses expect of them, and the preparation of plans, methods, and reports can be time-consuming and complicated efforts. Gathering the information required in order to do what your boss expects from you, or creating consensus among your colleagues in order to accomplish a particular goal, can take a long time. All of this occurs in a formal and sometimes very rigid hierarchical structure, which means that deadlines and efficiency are usually secondary to attention to detail, rigorous logic, and perfection of form. Because of this rigid rank and hierarchy orientation, titles in Italy are very important; the highest ones (e.g., vice president) are usually reserved for very senior, executive-level positions, and should not be used as casually as they are in the United States. Complimenting and rewarding employees publicly is usually not done.

Boss-Subordinate Relations

Rank most definitely has its privileges in Italy. Pride and self-importance require that Italians always do business with the most important people in any organization (and this should be the same for the non-Italian working with them). No matter what field you are in, there is a proper way for communicating with particular individuals, and an established procedure one is expected to follow. Deviating from the normal channels will generally make more problems for you, even if your intent is to bypass what appear to be obstacles. Bosses are expected to provide guidance, distribute information, and make decisions; subordinates are expected to provide detailed information and follow the decisions made by their superiors.

Conducting a Meeting or Presentation

At meetings of peers, there can be open communication and sharing of ideas: in fact, these sessions often serve as information-sharing and decision-making forums in which all individuals are expected to contribute. Under these circumstances, discussions are usually vibrant, with many people speaking at once; questions are common and interruptions, even of presentations, should be expected. In more formal, conservative organizations, meetings are often gatherings of nonpeers, clearly called together by decision makers in order to gather information from below, clarify goals, and formulate action plans. In these cases, individuals often do not share ideas and are not expected to contribute to mutual problem solving. Remember, because a close personal relationship is often demonstrated through physicality in Latin cultures, the nearer your Italian colleagues are to you, the better they are responding to your proposal.

Negotiation Styles

Italians generally play their cards close to the vest at first, but will open up as trust develops: they do not divulge information easily at the beginning (it is seen as the source of power). Initially, they may be circumspect in their communication styles, and will indicate their thoughts in indirect, associative ways; they can, however, quickly become pointedly direct as negotiations move forward. They will respect someone who comes to them with established knowledge and experience, and will build relationships based on your level in society and the organization. Whether you are worth knowing and doing business with may be more important than the details of your proposal. Nevertheless, details are important, and a carefully planned, logically organized, and beautifully presented proposal (translated into Italian, even if your presentation is delivered in English) is key. A presentation that does not look as good as it needs to reflects a lack of concern and disrespect to those attending, and will often be rejected out of hand at the start.

The first meeting is usually very formal, with the Italians sizing up you and your organization: it will be conducted in the office. Put on a warm, dignified demeanor during the meeting. Never be condescending. Although the contract must be legal down to the dotted i's, it really is just a legal formality to Italians, and can be overcome, by either party, if such a need arises later on. Plan your meetings as carefully and as well in advance as you can, but expect changes.

The goal, at least for the first meeting, is the development of a good feeling of respect and positive trust between yourself and your Italian colleagues. Never do anything to cause them to lose face in front of their counterparts, and do everything you can to show how your proposal enhances their *bella figura;* this is especially important as you move south in Italy. Remember also that the meeting might start and end much later than you anticipated; nevertheless, as with most polychronic cultures, you should always arrive on time.

Written Correspondence

Business letters must be very formal and respectful of hierarchy. Last names are usually written in uppercase; dates are given using the day/month/year format (with periods in between, not slashes); and an honorific plus a title is as common as an honorific plus the last name. The time of day is written in military style; weights and measures are usually given in metric units. Monetary amounts are written so that periods break up the figure into tens, hundreds, and thousands (e.g., L10.000.000 = ten million lire).

The traditional language used in openings and closings is more convoluted and formal than the American style, and you should write your e-mails, letters, and faxes using a precise formula. Be sure to inquire first, in all communications, about your colleagues' health and progress, then move on to the substance of your communication, and close with a salutation and your personal wish for their success and well-being (the Latin communication "sandwich").

The Mediterranean Cultures: Greece

Some Introductory Background on Greece and the Greeks

The shield that is used on most official government documents in Greece is a two-headed eagle, with the two heads looking in opposite directions, east and west. This is a metaphor for Greek customs, culture, and history: contradictory, unpredictable, looking both to the east and the west, going one way and then the other. If there is one constant about Greek culture, it is this dichotomy; for every statement we make about Greek behavior, there is an equally true statement describing the opposite behavior. Nevertheless, there are important protocols and etiquette to follow that emerge out of this culture of contradictions.

The dual nature of modern Greece is not surprising when one considers its geography, topography, and history. Located at the crossroads between the East and the West, Greece is essentially a Balkan country, straddling one of the world's great cultural fault lines, yet deeply rooted in antiquity and the unique, pre-Roman Greek classical culture. Physically, Greece is a tortured peninsula of islands, archipelagoes, bays, isthmuses, rugged mountains, and challenging seas, which has historically kept its peoples separated from both the rest of the world and themselves, reinforcing insularity and powerful notions of the difference between insiders and outsiders. Finally, Greece has, above all else, endured the rise and fall of civilizations, resulting in an approach to the world that is all-encompassing and oxymoronic: cynical, hopeful, rejecting, welcoming, warm, distant, controlling, fatalistic. Modern Greece is a world within a world, always intense, challenging, and vibrant.

Some Historical Context

Greeks know their Aristotle . . . and Plato, Homer, Euripides, and so on. They look to their past the way Americans look to the future, and they are extremely proud of the cultural contributions of classical Greece. The gifts they gave the world include democracy, free speech, and philosophical notions of the nature of life, individuals, and society that still guide us today, and they will remind you of it. But the subsequent centuries provided Greece with Orthodox Christianity, conflicts with its Muslim neighbors that are still unresolved, and a Greek diaspora that both spread Greek culture around the world but drained much talent from the homeland.

After the decline of ancient Greece, which remained the standard by which learning and culture was measured in the West, the nation adopted the Eastern Orthodox faith (the Greek Orthodox Church), until falling under Ottoman Turkish control for much of the Middle Ages. After playing an important part in removing the Turks from the Balkans, Greece fell into disputes with many of its Balkan neighbors, as well as Muslim Turkey, several times in the last two centuries. Needless to say, these Balkan Wars, not to mention the two world wars, left Greece occupied, invaded, and ultimately devastated. Only recently has Greece emerged as a democracy once again, though it is no longer a major country on the world stage.

An Area Briefing

Politics and Government

Today Greece is a parliamentary democracy, with a president, a prime minister (the real executive power, representing the majority party), and a unicameral legislature (the Chamber of Deputies). Despite the presence of a Greek royalty, the monarchy holds no office in Greece and does not represent the country in any way. This system is new; after occupation by the Nazis during World War II, the subsequent fierce civil war between communists and noncommunists, military dictatorships, and scandal-ridden governments, the democracy in Greece today is shaky. Politics is a way of life in Greece: everybody is involved with it, from the cabdriver on the street to the professional politician in Athens. You will not escape it in Greece.

Schools and Education

Despite the classical traditions of schooling that were once part of ancient Greece, the educational system in Greece today is similar to current standard European practices: there is the equivalent of elementary, middle, and high school (*gymnasium*) levels, with students, after passing a final exam, having the option to go on to university or technical (vocational) training academies. While the literacy rate is very high in Greece, higher education is not as common as in other western European countries, and a significant number of students leave school after gymnasium. Those who continue on to university often do so abroad. Girls do not attend university in nearly the same numbers as boys, and even at the gymnasium level, girls do not take the academic track as frequently as boys.

Religion and Demographics

Over 95 percent of the population is Eastern Orthodox, and the Greek Orthodox Church is the official state religion. There is little practical separation of religion and daily life; Greek Orthodox doctrines are woven through all state, public, civic, and day-to-day events, including schooling and politics. The Eastern Orthodox religious calendar differs from the western church, which means that holiday dates are different in Greece (be sure you double-check before you plan schedules). The pervasiveness of the Church's influence affects daily business and personal activities (for example, most homes have icons, and church activity is strong).

If you go to a Greek Orthodox church, you will notice how communal the atmosphere is. It is not formal (although the rites certainly are, in many ways): people wander about, there are few pews, and there is much discussion and socializing during the service. By the way, you might see icons resembling people, animals, objects, even body parts, resting on altars, shrines, and by candles: these are left by the faithful as tokens to their patron saint for a cause (to heal the sick, or protect the traveler, or end some suffering). In Greece, there is a very good chance that once you get to know someone well, you will be invited to a wedding, a baptism, or some other Orthodox family event. By all means, go; it will be informal, fun, and a wonderful way to get to know your Greek associates better. In the Eastern Orthodox religion, one's name day is celebrated more than one's birthday: the name day is usually the birthday of the saint after whom one was either named or who is taken as one's own protector.

Women and men in Greece still play very different roles in society. While women do work, they hold little authority in the business organization, and are still required to fulfill the role of mother and wife, often subordinate to the man. The scenario of the hardworking Greek woman slaving in the office and at home while her husband is at the café with his business associates and buddies is still not uncommon.

Demographically, Greece is an old country, due in part to the departure of many young people looking for work opportunities abroad, which in turn contributes to a negative population growth.

Fundamental Cultural Orientations

1. What's the Best Way for People to Relate to One Another?

OTHER-INDEPENDENT OR OTHER-DEPENDENT? Family and friends are everything: the in-group with which you are associated determines your field of vision and requires absolute loyalty, while out-groups are to be avoided, ignored, or, when necessary, destroyed. In this sense, Greeks are extremely other-dependent. They are socially needy: no Greek can exist alone (in fact, there is no word in Greek for the English word *privacy:* the closest it comes is the state of individual exile that was used in classical Greece as a punishment worse than death and applied to the worst offenders in society), and nothing can be accomplished without the concern of others. Nevertheless, what happens in one's life is the responsibility of the individual; and it is the individual, through his or her character, personality, and being, who determines what happens. In this sense, the individual has primacy in Greek culture. This is one of the many Greek dichotomies: the individual personality (one's *philotimo,* or self-pride) must be honored, preserved, and respected, and is the sole source of action and seat of all responsibility; nevertheless, the action one takes and the decisions one makes are never in a vacuum, and must always be for the benefit of others (family, friends, business associates, etc.). Individuals will be judged, rewarded, or punished by others according to how their actions are viewed by the group. This results in the need to depend on others in order for anything to happen, and yet, because of the importance of personal pride, Greeks are generally notoriously bad team players. In social life, nothing is more important than preserving the honor of one's family . . . except perhaps one's own honor. The Greek dance is a wonderful illustration of this dichotomy: the dancer dances alone, usually with a handkerchief as a partner, in a deep personal reverie (the *kefi,* or personal mood or feeling), but is often surrounded by others doing the same, each relying on the other to spread the *kefi* that inspires each to dance to their own internal music. No one applauds the individual Greek dancer when they are finished.

HIERARCHY-ORIENTED OR EGALITY-ORIENTED? The Greek culture observes very rigid hierarchies: older people are respected by younger ones, the wife respects the husband, the subordinate listens to the boss, children follow their parents and respect their teachers, and so on. But the other side to this is the fact that Greeks will not hesitate to question authority, challenge a rule, or say whatever they feel to whomever they like whenever the opportunity arises. Children need to obey their parents, but are equally tolerated (even secretly admired and encouraged) when they demonstrate stubbornness (*pisma*). Bosses' orders will be ignored if their subordinates disagree with them, and students will ritually ignore common classroom proceedings, such as not cheating on an exam, if it benefits them or if a friend needs their help. Such behaviors are, if not sanctioned, at least understood and therefore often overlooked. Hierarchies are powerful and understood as a necessary way to structure groups, organizations, and society; however, individuals are encouraged, admired, and rewarded for standing up to them, acting as equals, and demanding access.

RULE-ORIENTED OR RELATIONSHIP-ORIENTED? In Greece, as in other Mediterranean cultures, the explicit bureaucratic rules are, of course, sometimes baffling (and contradictory) in their byzantine complexity (there will be many documents to be stamped and regulations to be followed when doing business there: try not to get too frustrated and cultivate patience; it will serve you well over time); however, the implicit basic social rules are rather informal, and while equally powerful, are few and easy to master. The family is all, social contact is everything, and *philotimo* must always be maintained and respected. The ultimate determinant of human action is the flesh-and-blood relationships between families, friends, and neighbors; therefore, family histories, marriages, and associations are critically important. Nothing happens without others, and everything is possible between friends; rules sometimes can be helpful, but, when in the way, can surely be overcome with the right relationships and the application of cleverness and tenacity. There are rules for everything, but few seem to be enforced: driving is an exercise in machismo, and even walking down a crowded street is a challenge, since the implicit rule of walking to the right or left does not exist. Streets are remarkably noisy at night in the cities, despite the obvious need to be quiet.

2. What's the Best Way to View Time?

MONOCHRONIC OR POLYCHRONIC? It is perfectly all right to come to a meeting a half-hour late, as long as you can explain yourself, or as long as you are in charge! For newcomers to Greece, it is important to arrive on time, but be prepared to wait. This is an extremely polychronic country, and the clock is merely a guide. If your business colleague runs into an old friend on the way to the office, there is a very good chance that they will stop in a café for a coffee or a drink, even if it means you are kept waiting at the office for a while. Social events usually do not begin until at least one hour later than their stated time (arrive no earlier than 9 P.M. for a dinner party scheduled for 8 P.M.) and have no end time (for example, although many nightclubs close in Athens at 2 A.M., the party usually continues throughout the night at cafés and on street corners). Things usually take a long time to happen, conclusions are reached with excruciating slowness (if ever at all), and planning is often difficult. This is all due, in no small part, to intervening difficulties, such as poor infrastructure, bad traffic, or convoluted bureaucracies. Nevertheless, your Greek associate will then surprise you by showing up at your home to finish the project begun in the office, work round-the-clock as the deadline actually approaches, and make quick decisions in order to seize an apparent business opportunity. Be prepared for a roller-coaster ride when it comes to the clock.

RISK-TAKING OR RISK-AVERSE? Decision making can be slow and tedious for a number of reasons: you may not be speaking with someone who is high enough up in the organization to make a decision, or your Greek colleague may require more information before taking the risk and making a decision. The culture is notoriously risk-averse, and it will take many glasses of ouzo at the café and several more visits to the country than you perhaps expected to make before your deal is finalized. This is partly because a Greek needs to get to know you and your company personally, and be able to trust you. Historically, Greeks have learned that trust is perhaps the most elusive of all values between people, and so it is the one most needed. While debate is common, evidence supporting alternate views must fit with subjective expectations, or else it is ultimately unconvincing. Even when individuals are empowered to make the decision (and these are usually at the top of the family, business, or political pyramid), there can be a reticence to take the required final step.

PAST-ORIENTED OR FUTURE-ORIENTED? Greeks are mainly fatalistic; the past is mourned for, revisited, reveled in. As a culture, Greece looks back; and as individuals, Greeks remember their ancestors, their lineage, their family's enemies and friends. Once you are inside the Greeks' world (and this takes time, trust, perseverance, and passing important explicit and implicit tests), everything is possible. Insiders must consider insider needs whenever taking individual action; if you are on the outside, however, you will not achieve your goals with Greeks, and may be the victim, at worst, of their revenge, anger, or hostility, or, at best, of benign neglect. There is a general skepticism about society's being able to control events or the future; the pervasive attitude is to live for the here and now, as best as one can, with friends, family, good food, and a lust for the daily pleasures of life.

3. What's the Best Way for Society to Work with the World at Large?

LOW-CONTEXT DIRECT OR HIGH-CONTEXT INDIRECT COMMUNICATORS? Essentially, Greeks are very direct communicators: they say what they feel in most cases. Debate, logic, argument, rhetoric: all these are rooted in ancient

Greek education and philosophy. They can be passionate, challenging, and direct. The other side, of course, is that they can be equally evasive, nonverbal, and silent, if it is useful for them to be, or if they simply choose not to involve you or be involved with you. The context will determine the communication style used: if they are comfortable with insiders, or don't care about their future relationship with an outsider, all will be clearly known to both. *Kouvenda,* or conversation, is a way of life: it is an expression of the total tension that envelops the Greek's existence. There are always at least two sides to everything, more angles from which to view things, more new ways of interpreting something—and these are usually all dependent on the individual personalities involved. *Kouvenda* is the way one reveals oneself to others and to the world. It is an in-your-face challenge to others and to life: here I am, this is what I think. Greeks live and express the complexities of their world of dualities through *kouvenda.*

PROCESS-ORIENTED OR RESULT-ORIENTED? While logic, and the ability to argue or debate, is critical, the final conclusion, and certainly any resulting action, will usually be made based on intuitive feeling and subjective experience. Greeks are perhaps, in the long run, more associative in the way they process information, based on what has worked with others in the past in similar situations (even when, logically, the two situations may not be directly related to each other). Therefore, despite the obvious merits of an idea, if it doesn't fit with an individual's subjective experience or opinion, it is often rejected. In addition, the risk-averse nature of Greek culture means that much information and detail must be analyzed. For these reasons, Greeks may not understand or be able to follow through with the actions necessary to put the plans in place. It is therefore all the more important for non-Greeks to stay involved with them, helping them to implement what has been agreed to.

FORMAL OR INFORMAL? Greeks are informal, spontaneous, almost unpredictable. Formality, certainly stuffiness, is rejected out of hand. The other side of this, again, is that respect for the accomplishments of the individual must be demonstrated, even while perhaps being challenged.

Greetings and Introductions

Language and Basic Vocabulary

Most Greeks speak the common, or demotic, form of the language (formal Greek—not classical, which is now only a historic language—is known as Katharevusa, and while having been used in the past in official papers, is rarely used today). It would be very useful to pull out the old fraternity or sorority Greek alphabet if you don't speak the language, so that you can at least identify the letters you will see when you visit. It will make your life much easier; once you can phonetically read the letters, many of the words (at least the ones used on public signage) have cognate structures that will enable you to guess their meaning.

Most Greek businesspeople speak some English, and possibly German or French (if they are more highly educated). Most Greeks on the street do not.

Here are some basic Greek phrases sounded out phonetically. Please note that there are no question marks in Greek: instead, when writing, use the semicolon; when speaking, merely change the tone of your voice. Also note that the Greek words for *yes* and *no* sound opposite to their meaning to English speakers.

kahleemehrah	good morning
kahleesperah	good afternoon/evening
kahleeneetkah	good night
ahndeeo	good-bye
parakhalo	please
ehffkhareesto	thank you
ehffkareestos	you're welcome
seenghnomee	excuse me
Meelahteh ahngleekah;	Do you speak English?
Dhehn meelo ehleneekah	I don't speak Greek
neh	yes
okhee	no
Poss eestah;	How are you?
Pollee kahlah ehfkhareesto;	Very well, thanks, and you?
Dhehn kahtahlahvehno	I do not understand
keereeoss	Mr.
keereeah	Mrs.
dheespeneedhah	Miss
eeahtross	doctor

Honorifics for Men, Women, and Children

You must use *keereeoss* (Mr.) and *keereeah* (Mrs.), plus the family name, when introduced to strangers. Sometimes, among close friends and associates, the honorific will be used with the first name. Unless and until your Greek colleague specifically invites you to use first names, and despite how he or she might refer to you, you must always use the family name plus the correct Greek honorific (*dheespeneedha*—Miss—is very common and still widely used in Greece). Children in Greece are expected to be respectful when speaking with adults, but do not always use honorifics, and can be quite playful and sometimes rude, but never in a bad way. In situations where a title is known or used, the honorific plus the title is usually employed either with or without the name. For casual contacts (e.g., with waiters, store help, etc.), just use *parakahlo* (waiter) without the name; you may see some people tap a fork or a knife against a glass to get a waiter's attention, but don't do this; it is generally considered rude. It is very important to greet people at work or in stores or restaurants in an appropriate way, and to say good-bye upon leaving. If you speak any Greek at all, it is important to use it; it will absolutely delight your Greek associates, and help build that all-important relationship.

The What, When, and How of Introducing People

Always wait to be introduced to strangers before taking that responsibility upon yourself. You will always be introduced to older people and men first, women second (you must, when introducing yourself, also follow this protocol). Greeks are most comfortable with a third-party introduction whenever possible, so wait a moment before introducing yourself to a new group; if, after a few moments, no introduction is forthcoming, go ahead and do the job yourself. Language may be the issue to overcome. Do not presume to seat yourself at a gathering: if possible, wait to be told where to sit. Shake hands with everyone individually in a group before departing: the American group wave is not appreciated. Kissing is a common greeting with and between all genders (women/women or men/men or women/men) once you have established a relationship; it usually consists of a kiss on two cheeks (actually an "air kiss," first on the left side, and then the right). You may progress to this stage with your Greek colleagues as quickly as the second or third meeting.

Physical Greeting Styles

The handshake is common. The Greek version is done firmly between two men, but not as robustly between men and women or two women. The handshake should be accompanied by the appropriate greetings (outlined earlier), and may be accompanied by a kiss or an embrace. Smiling and other nonverbal forms of communication may also accompany the handshake, especially between people who have met once before. Men should wait until a woman extends her hand before reaching for it, and women may take the lead in extending their hand or not; this may or may not occur, especially among older women. Between family members, friends, or trusted business colleagues, a hug or other forms of touching may be expected. Eye contact during the introduction is very important, and must be maintained as long as the individual is addressing you.

The use of business cards is common; if possible, you should have yours translated into Greek on the reverse side. Be sure to put any advanced educational degrees and your full title or position on both sides of your business card. Such emblems of your status are very important to Greeks; they want to know they are doing business with an important person. Nevertheless, while respecting your titles, Greeks will not be intimidated by them.

Communication Styles

Okay Topics / Not Okay Topics

Okay: food and wine, politics (it is inevitable; learn what you can, and bear with the rest), current events, movies, the arts, philosophy, Greek classical culture (a must), music, and Greek architecture. Go ahead and enthuse about Greek cultural life and history; Greeks love it. *Not okay:* Do not inquire about a person's occupation or income in casual conversation, although this will probably be asked of you. Greeks are extremely curious, and will probe you with personal questions about your family, job, and lifestyle. This is meant to get to know you, and to learn more about the United States: answer in general and in full for the greatest comfort and maximum effect (e.g., "Well, in the United States, the average salary for my position is ———, but you know, the average mortgage on a house is ———, and it costs about ——— to live a middle-class life"). Greeks will not be satisfied with vague answers, and will distrust you if you avoid their questions. Do not, however, ask such questions in return, since they will embarrass many Greeks.

Always show an eagerness to learn more about Greece and its culture. Display your knowledge of Greece: it will pay off geometrically. But do not give your opinion about Turks, Muslims, World War II, the Cyprus problem, and so on. The Greeks will ask you your feelings about these issues; deflect the questions, then ask them to help you understand these issues better.

If you compliment something, it may be given to you as a gift. You will then be required to acknowledge the kindness with something of equal value—not necessarily immediately; that would cheapen their gift—but soon thereafter.

Greeks tend to minimize, criticize, and deny in their style of communication. Do not take it personally; it is a way of preserving some control in a world that is generally uncontrollable. This is especially true if you compliment someone: they will deny it, for fear of bringing bad luck upon themselves.

Tone, Volume, and Speed

Between strangers who might have a future business relationship, the tone is usually lower; once a relationship has been established, the tone, volume, and speed of conversation is often rapid, loud, and boisterous.

Use of Silence

There is rarely a moment of it. Enjoy the simultaneous conversations and frequent interruptions: it shows interest. Hang in there.

Physical Gestures and Facial Expressions

Greeks are extremely expressive communicators when they want to be, but can be stone-faced as well, if necessary. Compliment someone, and the Greek will usually blow a little puff of air out through pursed lips: this is to ward off the evil eye or bad spirits that no doubt will come now that you've said something nice about them. The U.S. "okay" sign, made with the thumb and the forefinger, may be considered vulgar and obscene: avoid it. As is the case with certain other eastern Mediterranean cultures, nodding the head upward means "no" (be careful, it looks somewhat like the Western nod for "yes"), and tilting the head from side to side generally indicates satisfaction or receptivity (here too, it looks more like the Western shaking of the head from left to right for "no"). The smile is tricky: if Greeks are earnestly having a good time, then laughter and smiling are genuine; however, Greeks will often smile (with no other accompanying indication of mirth) when they are angry and displeased; it is more, really, a showing of the teeth, and is often accompanied with the upward tilt of the head (and sometimes a small clicking sound with the tongue). In addition, winking, whistling (often accompanied with a small positive comment) is meant to be a friendly introduction between men and women; it is not an insult. If a woman is not interested, she need not acknowledge it. (Conversely, if a woman's eyes meet a man's eyes under these circumstances, it is an indication of interest.) Two men often walk down the street arm in arm, usually after a social event, as do two women: it is a sign of friendship and closeness, nothing more.

Waving and Counting

The thumb represents the number 1, the index finger the number 2, and so on. It is insulting to beckon someone with the forefinger (instead, turn your hand so that the palm faces down and motion inward with all four fingers at once). Be very careful never to raise an open palm to anyone; to raise your hand with an open palm at face level is an insult (this is especially important for Americans, who often wave with an open palm facing their intended recipient). If you need to gesture for a waiter, subtly raise your hand with your index finger slightly outstretched.

Physicality and Physical Space

Greeks tend to get much closer than North Americans or northern Europeans. Do not step back when your Greek associate steps forward. Never speak with your hands in your pockets: always keep them firmly to your side when standing. If men and women must cross their legs, it must never be ankle over knee (for women, the preferred style is to cross ankle over ankle). Remember, even in public, formal is always better than informal: no gum chewing, *ever;* don't slouch; and don't lean against things. Greeks often gesture with their hands, and their facial expressiveness is strong.

Eye Contact

Eye contact can be fiercely direct most of the time. It is important not to interpret this behavior as a way of intentionally trying to make you uncomfortable. It is the way the Greeks show their interest. Conversely, if you look away, your behavior will say to your Greek colleague that you are either disinterested or rude. Either way, maintain eye contact when it is made with you. If strangers' eyes meet and linger, it implies romantic interest. Act accordingly. Sometimes the upward nod of the head, which means "no" or disinterest in Greece, is accompanied by raised eyebrows; sometimes just raising the eyebrows is enough!

Emotive Orientation

Greeks are animated and physically expressive. Nevertheless, until you know people well, you want to indicate restraint, while not seeming lifeless. Join in if you like, but keep cool if you can. Greeks will always admire you if you passionately defend and promote your ideas while always being respectful of others and not taking yourself too seriously.

Dancing is an important way of expressing oneself in Greece. The traditional Greek dance is either performed alone or with members of the same sex in a line or circle.

Protocol in Public

Walking Styles and Waiting in Lines

It is more important in Greece to maintain one's face by being first in line (and never last) than it is to maintain a queue. Don't be too distressed if someone walks right up to the front of the line at a bank, a restaurant, or a store and gets served first because of the relationship he or she has with the clerk, while you have been waiting patiently in line for forty minutes. Never be last, anywhere, and do whatever it takes to make sure of that. There can be much jostling and bumping on the street because of this. Don't get angry; keep your sense of humor, and join in. If you don't, you'll be left out in the cold.

Behavior in Public Places: Airports, Terminals, and the Market

Customer service, as a concept, is catching on, but is not fully institutionalized. Store hours are typically not built around customer convenience (many stores are closed on weekends and most evenings—except Thursdays, usually). Personally chatting with and thanking store owners, waiters, chefs, and hotel managers is very much appreciated: it's the best way to ensure good service for yourself. As in much of Europe, once you buy an item in a store it may be difficult for you to return a product unless there is a flaw in it. Expect to bargain everywhere, except in the most well-established chain shops and restaurants; Greeks are suspicious of people who do not bargain. Smoking is definitely not on the decline; people light up anywhere and everywhere (in restaurants, on the public transportation systems, the works).

Social life in Greece occurs more often than not, and whenever possible, on the street, in cafés, and at the market—any place and any time where people can get together and talk. Be ready to meet people, have a coffee, take time out at a café. Embrace every opportunity to get to know the Greek people personally and their culture a little better.

Bus / Metro / Taxi / Car

Driving is on the right, but people pass very quickly on the left; in fact, the way people drive in Greece is described more often than not as chaotic. Do not rely on cars staying in their lanes (or even on the road, for that matter: in the streets, cars often pull up directly on the sidewalk).

The metros shut down after midnight. Your best bet for catching a cab is at designated taxi stands (hotels are good places, but often charge more for the same ride: a hotel surcharge is added to the meter fare, in some cases).

On public transportation, younger people should give up their seats to older people, and men should still give up their seats to women, especially if they are pregnant or have babies or small children with them.

Tipping

A 10 percent tip is usually sufficient for restaurants and taxis; more is considered nouveau and gauche. Porters and hotel help get about thirty drachma per service rendered; theater and bathroom attendants usually get the same. Restaurants usually have the 10 percent tip already included on the bill, but if you are unsure, it's okay to ask if service is included or not. Even if it is, it is still appropriate to leave odd change equal to about another 5 percent if the service was particularly good.

Punctuality

In Greece, punctuality is a nonissue in the sense that things can start on time, but also may not. It is important for visitors to be on time, but expect to wait.

Dress

Err on the formal side, until you know to dress otherwise; this is a good rule both in social situations and at the office. You may be surprised at how informal dress is at work and how formal it is in social situations. At work, men may wear stylish suits (dark is best), white shirts, and interesting and sophisticated ties, but they also may wear slacks and a sport jacket, sometimes with a pull-over sweater vest underneath the jacket (how one dresses at work is really a reflection of rank and job title, so observe carefully, and always start out dressing as if you were higher up). Men often wear accessories, such as watches (not so much to keep track of the time, but to match the outfit!), cuff links, and tie clips. Women usually accessorize so that even the simplest of outfits stands out for its interest and style. Greek women usually do not wear more makeup and jewelry than American women (sometimes wear even less, or none at all); and it is fashionable, especially in summer, not to wear stockings. Some women still retain the custom of wearing only black for a period of time once their husbands die (very orthodox, usually older women choose to wear black for the rest of their lives).

On the street, informal may mean jeans and sneakers, though that is more common as clothing to wear at the gym, the beach, or while jogging (women do not wear sneakers to work); for a social gathering, informal more often than not means tastefully coordinated clothes, sometimes including a jacket and tie for men (it rarely means jeans, sneakers, and T-shirts). "Formal" usually means formal evening wear, which is very dressy by American standards.

Seasonal Variations

There are two basic seasons in Greece, with dry, warm to hot weather from March through October, and wet, cool to mildly cold weather from November through February. The mountain climate can be very different from the shore, and northern Greece can be surprisingly cold in the winter. Men usually dress more casually in the hot months, but take your cue from your associates—do not remove your jacket or tie unless and until your Greek colleague has done so first.

Colors

Bright colors are best reserved for accessories, as offsets to the more sophisticated dark or soft hues and tones of the outfits themselves.

Styles

"High" style is not as critical in Greece as in other western Mediterranean cultures, but a good appearance is always important. Cologne and perfume are not as commonly used as in the western Mediterranean. Men may sometimes be seen playing with strands of "worry beads" (the beads are distantly related to Catholic rosary beads) as they talk and go about their daily routines: this is stress-reducing behavior, and requires no action or comment from you.

Personal Hygiene

As can sometimes be the case in some of the neighboring countries, hygiene standards may not, in some cases, be as important to Greeks as they are to Americans. Recognize that hot running water may be a precious commodity in some parts of Greece, so your daily bath may have to be forsaken from time to time.

Dining and Drinking

Mealtimes and Typical Foods

Breakfast (*to proeeno*) is served from about 7 to 8:30 A.M., and usually consists of coffee, rolls, butter, honey, and sometimes jams (especially rose-petal jam, a real treat!); this is the Greek version of the quick continental breakfast. Coffee in Greece is called Greek coffee, but it is better known in the United States as "Turkish coffee": it is served in little cups, and even at breakfast it is thick and black, and sometimes very presweetened (test it first before adding sweetener). Never drink Greek coffee in big gulps, or else, as you get to the bottom of the cup (which will be very quickly), you will get a mouthful of coffee grinds. This is very unpleasant. Tea is also a common beverage, although mainly for later in the day, and is sometimes drunk out of glasses. Many Greeks hold a cube of sugar between their front teeth and let the tea wash over it as they drink.

Lunch (*toh gevma*) is still the main meal of the day in both rural and urban areas. Whether at home or at a restaurant, it can be an elaborate affair lasting several hours with several courses, or it can be a quick sandwich and a salad or yogurt. Lunch is usually served about 1:30 P.M. It is usually taken with water, coffee, beer, or wine. If lunch is the main meal of the day, the various courses can include appetizers, hot plates of meat and/or fish, and fruit for dessert. (When the main meal is dinner, the fruit is also followed by dessert, usually baklava—a pastry dripping in honey and nuts). On Sunday, the family day, the main meal is supper, which is usually served at lunchtime and can last well into the evening.

Dinner (*toh theepno*) is served from 8:30 P.M. on. In major cities, if it is substituted for lunch as the main meal of the day, dinner can last well past midnight. You might find all but tourist restaurants closed prior to 8:30 or 9 P.M. If the main meal of the day was lunch, then the family dinner at home is light, and is often similar to the fast lunch described above. If it is a more formal dinner, the meal will begin with appetizers (*mezedes*), usually meatballs (*keftedes*), stuffed grape leaves (*dolmades*), small, savory pies of cheese and spinach and nuts (*spanakopita*), and *taramousalata* (a mix or dip of caviar). Ouzo is usually drunk with *mezedes:* it is a clear, anise-flavored liquor that is prepared by pouring small amounts of water into a glass already containing the ouzo, until the liquid in the glass turns milky or cloudy—then it is ready to be drunk. The main course can be grilled fish, grilled meats (usually lamb, or souvlaki), meat casseroles (moussaka) made with vegetables and potatoes, or gyros (meats wrapped sandwich style in pita bread). Good Greek wines or beers are usually served with dinner. Greek wine is commonly made with resin added for additional bite; most table wines are resinated (retsina). If you do not want a resinated wine, ask for wine *aretsina* (without resin). It may be more expensive.

Formal Greek meals usually follow this order:

* *mezedes*
* main course: meat or fish (sometimes both), in casserole or with vegetables, usually served with rice
* salad
* fruit
* dessert
* Greek coffee
* Greek brandy

An enormous amount of food is usually offered at a private party, and even in restaurants, typical Greek portions are large. If you don't want seconds at someone's home, you need to leave a little food on your plate; and if you don't like one particular food, you'll need to ask for some seconds of the kind you do like to compliment the hostess. It is polite to refuse once or twice when asked if you will have more, but more often than not you will be pressured into having more of something ("It is so delicious, but I couldn't eat another thing, no thanks"; "Please, but really, I can't, no thanks"; "Okay, it is so delicious, I will have just a small bit more, thank you").

Cafés (kafenion) are found everywhere in Greece, usually at the center of town and neighborhood life. They are the place to go for conversation, a snack, some tea or coffee, a drink, an aperitif, or a pastry. They are open practically all the time, and customarily have seating both indoors and outdoors (when the weather permits). The tables are tiny, and often crammed next to each other, so maintaining privacy between diners is important. Once you are seated (yes, in most you may seat yourself), the waiter will arrive, and you should be prepared to place your order. Once you call for the bill, be prepared to pay it; the waiter will generally wait at your table until you pay. Traditionally, you could sit in a café for as long as you liked; no one would ask you to move on until you were ready. This is still the case in most cafés, in the cities as well as the country. As informal as cafés can be, though, eating while strolling down the street simply isn't done in Greece (although there are food stalls in markets or other places where one can buy gyros, for example; however, it is usually expected that food purchased at a stall will be eaten there or very nearby, whether or not seating is provided).

In addition to Greece's wonderful formal restaurants and cafés, try the *zakharoplastios,* which serve warm pastries, drinks, and sandwiches, and the *galaktoplia* (milk restaurants), which serve dairy products and desserts.

Typical Drinks and Toasting

Wine is drunk at lunch and dinner, but if you are drinking ouzo, be sure to take small sips (although Greek men will be measured by their ability to drain a glass in one shot, you don't have to). The more you drink, the more you will be offered to drink: know when to stop, and if you don't want to drink anymore, leave your glass more than half full. If you really cannot drink, you'll need a very good excuse, like doctor's orders. The most common toast is *kalymata* (to your health).

Table Manners and the Use of Utensils

Do not begin eating until your host invites you to.

Greeks really do not waste their dinnerware by throwing them against the wall, or destroy the glasses by dashing them into the fireplace. However, the vibrancy of Greek life has earned them this reputation: no doubt, there have been late-night gatherings where the dishes, the glasses, and probably several cooked chickens as well all went flying against the wall. Unless it's already being done, and in obvious good-natured fun, don't do this.

Like all continental Europeans, Greeks do not switch knives and forks, as Americans do. The knife remains in the right hand, and the fork remains in the left. When you're finished with your meal, cross your knife and fork on your plate, with the knife underneath the fork and the tines of the fork facing down. If you place your napkin up on the table or on the plate, most Greeks will also take this to mean that you are finished.

The fork and spoon above your plate are usually for dessert. If you're unsure of which utensil to use, always start from the outside and work your way in, course by course. Bread is usually served without butter (therefore, there usually will not be a butter knife), and there usually is no bread plate (place your bread on the side of your main plate or on the table throughout the meal). Sometimes wine is served in water glasses (after-dinner drink glasses come out after dinner).

When not holding utensils, your hands are expected to be visible above the table: this means that you do not keep them in your lap; instead, rest your wrists on top of the table, and sometimes your elbows (take your cue from how informal things are getting at the table, and they can get that way pretty quickly). At the table, pass all dishes to your left. If there is gravy or sauce, you can generally use your bread to soak some of it up. The very informal atmosphere typical of the Greek table also means that guests can sometimes feel free to eat from or taste the food on each other's plates, and eat many more different kinds of food with their hands: take your cue from those around you.

Seating Plans

The most honored positions are in the middle of the table at each side, with the most important guest seated immediately to the right of the host (women to the right of the host, and men to the right of the hostess). If there is a hosting couple, one will be seated at each side of the table. In keeping with the practice elsewhere on the Continent, men and women may be seated next to one another, and couples may be broken up and seated next to people they may not have previously known. This is done to promote conversation, which, after all, is the main pleasure at the table. More traditional hosts might seat men next to men, and women next to women, or segregate them completely. Men typically do not rise when women enter the room, and may or may not enter a room first when women are present. At the table, the oldest or most honored guest is served first, and women do most of the serving: men remain with the guests. Remember, as is the case throughout the Continent, what the Greeks call the first floor is really the second floor, with the first floor usually referred to as the lobby or ground floor.

Refills and Seconds

At a private dinner party, if you do not want more food, you will really have to insist several times before the hostess will believe you. Take a little extra if you can of something you like. You won't be expected to eat everything on your plate, but eat as much as you can. Pace yourself! You may always have additional beverages; drink enough to cause your cup or glass to be less than half full, and it will generally be refilled. Portions may or may not be smaller than in the United States, but there are usually more courses, for both lunch and dinner.

At Home, in a Restaurant, or at Work

In informal restaurants, you may be required to share a table: if so, do not force conversation but be open to its possibility; act as if you are seated at a private table. Waitstaff may be summoned by making eye contact; waving or calling their names is very impolite. The business breakfast is not common in Greece. The business lunch or dinner is more widespread, but, depending upon how well developed your relationship is with your Greek colleagues, it is generally not the time to make business decisions. Take your cue from your Greek associates: if they bring up business, then it's okay to discuss it, but wait to take your lead from their conversation. No gum chewing, ever, at a restaurant or on the street. No-smoking sections in restaurants are still a rarity. In all but the fanciest restaurants, you will be invited to go into the kitchen and check out the food before it is prepared; this is especially the case when ordering seafood or fish.

When you arrive at a Greek colleague's home for a formal meal, you will be told where to sit, and there you should remain. Do not wander from room to room: much of the house is really off-limits to guests. Once you (and the group) are invited to another room, most probably the dining room, be sure to allow the more senior members of your party to enter the room ahead of you. At the table, do not presume to seat yourself, as the seating arrangement may be predetermined. Spouses who accompany their partners on business trips may be invited to attend dinners (but usually not lunches). In Greece, women can expect men to approach them whenever they are in public, including restaurants.

You may be invited to visit someone socially before dinner: this is a more casual visit, and can occur in the home or at work. It will usually start at around 5:30 P.M. and last until about 7 or 7:30 P.M. The purpose of this informal call is just to say hello or get to know one better (the next invitation is usually for dinner). If you're visiting someone's home, be sure to leave before 7:30 P.M., because your hosts will want to get ready for their own dinner: don't stay unless they absolutely, positively insist several times. You'll be offered fruits, iced water, coffee, maybe some ouzo, and pastries.

Being a Good Guest or Host

Paying the Bill

Usually the one who does the inviting pays the bill, although the guest is expected to make an effort to pay. Sometimes other circumstances determine the payee (such as rank). Making payment arrangements ahead of time so that no exchange occurs at the table is a very classy way to host. If men are at the table, women will not really be able to pay the bill at a restaurant: if you want to, make arrangements ahead of time, and don't wait for the check to arrive at the table. The only time it is considered appropriate for a woman to pay the bill is if she is a businesswoman from abroad.

Transportation

It's a very nice idea, when acting as the host, to inquire ahead of time as to whether your guests will require transportation. If necessary, you should arrange for taxi service at the end of the meal.

In Greece, you might be picked up from and taken back to your hotel by your host. Greeks are extremely gracious.

When to Arrive / Chores to Do

If invited to dinner at a private home, offer to help with the chores, but be prepared to be turned down at first. Ask again, and your offer will probably be accepted. Otherwise, do not leave the table unless invited to do so. When it is time to leave, always get up and shake hands with everyone: the group wave is not appreciated. Greeks will invite you into their homes more quickly than any other people in Europe; it is an invitation that should not be rejected, as it represents a desire to build a long-term trusting relationship. By the way, if you are staying in a Greek home, your hosts will expect to be involved in all your daily activities. You are now part of the family, so don't leave them out of your plans.

Gift Giving

In general, gift giving is common among business associates, although it is best not to send a gift at any time, including the holidays, unless you receive one first from your Greek colleague. However, holiday cards are also very appropriate, particularly as a thank-you for your colleagues' business during the previous year, and should be mailed in time to be received the week before Christmas. Good business gifts include office-related items of fine quality that are also representative of your country.

Gifts are expected for social events, especially as thank-yous for private dinner parties. The best gift in this case is a growing potted plant—not a cut floral arrangement—and you should bring it along with you when you arrive. It should always be wrapped, and you should unwrap it only in the presence of the hostess. Other good gifts would be cakes and pastries; a box of fine chocolates; American wines (bring several bottles, so that one may be used with the meal, and the others by the hosts later), if you can find some good-quality choices; or a dessert wine. If there are children in the family, it is important to bring a little something for them, such as a toy or candy, in addition to the gift for the hostess. It is not necessary to send a thank-you note the next day for all but the most formal of dinner parties, especially if you brought a gift the night before.

If you are staying with a Greek family, an appropriate thank-you gift would be a high-quality, practical product that represents your country and is difficult to get in Greece: small, American-made electronic gadgets or a set of American bath towels (always a good gift most everywhere, since they are usually more luxurious). As with other European cultures, gifts are generally opened at the time they are given and received.

Special Holidays and Celebrations

Major Holidays

Most Greek workers get several weeks of paid vacation; August is a leading vacation time. Business slows down from December 20 to January 5, and Holy Week is sometimes a more difficult time in which to accomplish work than Christmas. (On the Greek Orthodox calendar, Easter is a far more important holiday than Christmas; remember that the Greek Orthodox calendar is different from other Christian calendars). In addition, there are myriad regional saints' days throughout the year that usually close down businesses for a day or two; check with your local contacts.

As you establish personal relationships with your Greek colleagues, you may be invited to special family events, such as a wedding, a name day celebration, or a baptism; be sure to go, and bring a gift (money is not appropriate).

January 1	*Protochronia* (Saint Basil's Day/New Year's Day)
January 6	*ton Thephanion* (Epiphany)
January 7	*Christougenna* (Orthodox Christmas Day)
February 26	*Kathari Defteri* (First Day of Lent)
March 25	*Ikosti Pemti Martiou* (Greek Independence Day)
April 12	*Megali Paraskevi* (Holy Friday)
April 14	*Pascha* (Easter Sunday)
April 15	*Deftera tou Pascha* (Easter Monday)
May 1	*Protomagia* (May Day)
May 21	Saint Constantine and Saint Helen Celebration
May 23	Ascension Day
June 2	Pentecost
August 15	*tis Panagias* (Assumption)
October 3	Feast of Saint Dionysus the Areopagite (the patron saint of Athens; celebrated only in that city)
October 28	*Ikosti Ogdoi Oktovriou* ("No" Day: commemorates the Greek defiance of the Italian invasion during World War II)
December 26	*Defteri imera ton Christougennon* (Saint Stephen's Day)

Business Culture

Daily Office Protocols

In Greece, doors are mostly left open. However, you must knock first before opening closed doors (this includes bathrooms), and when leaving rooms, it's proper to always close the doors behind you.

Women do not hold equal authority as men in business organizations. It is more common for women to be relegated to lower-level management and administrative support positions. It is rare (though not impossible) to see women at the highest levels of business and government in Greece.

At business meetings, you may be introduced (or not) to many more people than you expected; these people, in turn, may (or may not) remain silent throughout most of the meeting. They are probably trusted advisers, family members, or friends of your Greek associate. Do not fret too much about them (and don't ask to be introduced to them, if the introduction wasn't originally made): they certainly are not representatives of the competition.

The workday can start late, and end late, and may consist of two distinct periods, separated by lunch and a short nap (especially when outside of the cities). When making appointments, be sure to schedule them way in advance, and confirm them several times as the date and time approach. Expect a lot of chitchat at the beginning of the meeting about nonbusiness issues, and take your cue from your colleagues as to when to get down to substantive issues.

Management Styles

Privacy and individual accomplishment of one's tasks are critical. Workers provide what their bosses expect of them, and the preparation of plans, methods, and reports can be time-consuming and complicated efforts. Gathering the information required in order to do what your boss expects from you, or creating agreement among your colleagues in order to accomplish a particular goal, can take a long time. Unless the boss is patriarchal, committed, involved, supportive, sharp, definitive, willing to learn, and open to staff suggestions, he will not succeed as a leader. The rigid hierarchical structure relegates deadlines and efficiency as secondary to attention to detail, rigorous logic, and perfection of form. Because of this rigid rank and hierarchy orientation, titles in Greece are very important; the highest ones (e.g., vice president) are usually reserved for very senior, executive-level positions, and should not be used as casually as they are in the United States. Complimenting and rewarding employees publicly is successful only when the manager is absolutely sure that such action meets with the approval of all in attendance.

Boss-Subordinate Relations

Rank most definitely has its privileges in Greece, but it does not protect one from the individual opinions, actions, or inaction from those one needs to work with, whether they are above, equal to, or below one's level. Pride and self-importance require that Greeks always do business with the most important people in any organization (and this should be the same for the non-Greek working with them). Deviating from established procedures is appropriate if it is successful and is the way the entire team wants to go. The difficulty is in getting consensus among powerful egos whose strong primary inclination is to prove themselves at the expense of others.

Conducting a Meeting or Presentation

Meetings can be information-sharing and decision-making forums in which all individuals are expected to contribute. Under these circumstances, discussions are usually vibrant, with many people speaking at once; questions are common and interruptions, even of presentations, should be expected. The leader is expected to provide a way of rallying the divergent opinions to one cause, and it is best to use outside dangers as a way to do this: nothing unites the Greeks into a team faster than the outside(r) threat. Remember, because a close personal relationship is often demonstrated through physicality, the nearer your Greek colleagues are to you, the better they are responding to your proposal.

Negotiation Styles

Greeks generally play their cards close to the vest at first, but will open up as trust develops: they do not divulge information easily at the beginning (it is seen as the source of power). Initially, they may be circumspect in their communication styles, and will indicate their thoughts in indirect, associative ways; they can, however, quickly become pointedly direct as negotiations move forward. They will respect someone who comes to them with established knowledge and experience, although they will never take it at face value, and will always test it and demand proof. Whether you are worth knowing and doing business with may be more important than the details of your proposal. Nevertheless, details are important, and a carefully organized proposal is key.

The first meeting is usually just a formality, with the Greeks sizing up you and your organization: it will be conducted in the office. Put on a warm, dignified demeanor during the meeting. Never be condescending or offer an ultimatum: always give your Greek colleagues a backdoor from which they can escape, if needed. You will be expected to bargain, and bargain hard. Play the game: you will be respected for it. Although the contract must be legal down to the dotted i's, it really is just a legal formality to the Greek, and can be overcome, by either party, if such a need arises later on. Plan your meetings as carefully and as well in advance as you can, but expect changes. The goal, at least for the first meeting, is the development of a good feeling of respect and positive trust between yourself and your Greek colleagues. Never do anything to cause them to lose face in front of their counterparts; do everything you can to show how your proposal enhances their *philotimo*.

Written Correspondence

Your business letters must be clear, precise, and respectful. Don't be flowery: it will be seen as very insincere. Last names are usually written in uppercase; dates are given using the day/month/year format (with periods in between, not slashes); and an honorific plus a title is as common as an honorific plus the last name. The time of day is written in military style; weights and measures are usually given in metric measurements. Monetary amounts are written so that periods break up the figures into tens, hundreds, and thousands (10.000 = ten thousand drachmas).

Be sure to inquire first, in all communications, about your colleagues' health and other nonbusiness issues, then move on to the substance of your communication, and close with a salutation and your personal wish for their success and well-being (the polychronic communication "sandwich").

PART THREE

Central and Eastern Europe

Chivalry, Slivovitz, and Slavs

An Introduction to the Region

Before the breakup of the Soviet Union, there was West and there was East. Life was, if not easier, at least simpler. However, with the end of the Soviet clamp on central and eastern Europe, the complexities of the region, along with ancient differences and rivalries, have reemerged. Today we know that while the region differentiates itself from the rest of Europe in that most of its peoples (but not all) are Slavs, what was once only "eastern Europe" must more clearly be separated into "central Europe" and "eastern Europe." Central Europe includes Poland, the Czech Republic, Slovakia, Hungary, Romania, Croatia, and Slovenia. What is now more accurately described as eastern Europe includes Russia, Belarus, Ukraine, Moldova, Bulgaria, Macedonia, Serbia, Albania, and Bosnia.

As we saw previously, this region straddles one of the world's great cultural divides, sitting as it does at the center of the great north-south, east-west cross between the Latin, northern, and Slavic sections of Europe. The influence of these varied cultural entities are represented in the different ethnographies, languages, and religions of the people. Most of the countries in central Europe, for example, are mainly Roman Catholic (or a mixture of Roman Catholic and Protestant), and look to Rome and the West in general for their roots; their languages, mostly Slavic, are written in Latin script. Most of the countries in eastern Europe are mainly Eastern Orthodox (or a mixture of versions of Eastern Orthodox and Islam), and look to ancient Constantinople and the East for their roots; their languages are also mostly Slavic, too, yet are written in the "Russian" Cyrillic text. This chart might help:

Central Europe (Latin text)	**Eastern Europe** (Cyrillic text)
Western Slavs:	*Eastern Slavs:*
Poland (Roman Catholic)	Russia (Orthodox)
Slovakia (Roman Catholic/ Orthodox)	Belarus (Orthodox)
	Ukraine (Orthodox/Uniate)
Czech Republic (Protestant/ Roman Catholic)	Moldova (Orthodox)

Central Europe (Latin text)	**Eastern Europe** (Cyrillic text)
Southern Slavs:	*Southern Slavs:*
Slovenia (Roman Catholic/ Protestant)	Bulgaria (Orthodox)
Croatia (Roman Catholic)	Serbia (Orthodox)
	Macedonia (Orthodox)
Non-Slavs:	*Non-Slavs:*
Romania (Latin, Orthodox)	Bosnia (Muslim/Orthodox/ Roman Catholic)
Hungary (Central Asian, Roman Catholic)	Albania (Muslim)

Getting Oriented

There is no doubt that the complexities of the region will make for as many exceptions as there are rules regarding cultural behaviors. But when compared to countries outside of the region, there are some very clear rules regarding general protocol and etiquette for most Slavic cultures that can be useful. One important start is to recognize the similarities between Slavic behavior, in general, and Latin behavior. No surprise here, for whether Roman Catholic or Orthodox, both are rooted in hierarchically organized Christian traditions—as opposed to Protestant northern European cultures. There is a clear relationship between the two, with the very important exception that Latin behavior is usually risk-averse, while Slavic culture generally results in risk-taking behavior. While Latins require much detail, information, and group consensus before making a decision or taking action, Slavs may move quickly, without considering these factors, if presented with an opportunity that needs to be taken quickly. Perhaps because life for many in this region has been so difficult, there is a sense that there is nothing to lose, and everything to gain, by doing something, risking a little, for possible gain. Another major distinction between Latin and Slavic behavior is that while Latins have a strong orientation to process and deductive thought, Slavs are more oriented toward associative thinking. We'll elaborate these points as we begin by looking first at central Europe, and then eastern Europe.

The Central European Cultures: Poland

Some Introductory Background on Poland and the Poles

The Poles are a Slavic people, which makes them different from their German neighbors to the west. Do not confuse the two. In fact, it is important not to confuse the Poles with any of their neighbors, as they have often struggled against them in the past. Germans, Lithuanians (with whom Poles have a cool relationship), Russians, and Czechs (historically the least threatening of all the neighbors, perhaps) all present Poles with the opportunity to distinguish themselves, and they welcome the chance. Poles are extremely interested in Americans, since their information about the United States had been extremely limited and skewed during the Cold War, and many have relatives in the States. If you are a Polish American, you will receive a very warm welcome there, and will probably not be left alone. As a culture, the Poles began over one thousand years ago, and have survived, more or less, intact up to today.

Some Historical Context

Poland stands as a buffer between Germany and Russia, two of the mightiest enemies in European history, and as such, its geography has played a significant role in the formation of the Polish psyche. A people who have been overrun by Germans as they moved east against Russia, and by Russians as they moved west against Germany, Poles have had to fight for their sovereignty time and time again. As part of their struggle, they have hitched their fortunes to the rising stars of such neighbors as Lithuania, Ukraine, and Sweden—sometimes being protected by them, other times being absorbed by them. Twice in the last century, Poland completely disappeared as a nation. Yet the culture is unique and different from its neighbors. Alternately defensive and suspicious, risk-avoiding and risk-taking, formal yet warm, the Polish character is the result of living between the bear on one side and the wolf on the other.

An Area Briefing

Politics and Government

Most recently, Poland has emerged out of the bear's control. From the end of World War II until 1989, Poland was ruled by Moscow, an "honor" bestowed upon the Polish people by the Soviet Russians who came to their rescue after the Germans overran Poland during the war. Most modern Poles have tasted freedom for the first time only recently, and their knowledge of the West and Western ways is limited. The government today, however, after the struggles of the Solidarity labor movement in the late 1980s freed Poland from the decaying grip of the Soviets, is a parliamentary democracy, with a president and a prime minister, and a bicameral legislature. There is a vigorous multiparty system in place.

Schools and Education

The educational system in Poland today is similar to standard current European practices: there is the equivalent of elementary, middle, and high school levels, with students, after passing a final exam, having the option to go on to a university or technical (vocational) training academies. While the literacy rate is very high in Poland, higher education is not as common as in other western European countries, and a significant number of students leave school after high school. Those who continue on to a university often do so abroad. Education under the Communists was extremely ideological and, despite efforts to promote the trades, the arts, and the sciences, extremely lacking in comparison to Western education. The school system in Poland, like all government-run operations under the Communists, suffered from a lack of skilled labor, resources, money, and commitment, and endured as a corrupt bureaucracy, like the rest of the government, dedicated to the personal entitlement of those who ran it. It is changing today.

Religion and Demographics

About 95 percent of the population is Roman Catholic, and Poland is one of the most devout Roman Catholic nations in Europe (Poles are extremely proud of the fact that the pope is Polish, the first ever to come from their country). The Roman Catholic Church played a revolutionary role in moving Poland away from Communism and toward democracy, in some ways an irony considering the conservative nature of the Roman Catholic faith. Today, the church provides a sense of stability and structure for individuals and families struggling with the uncertainties that modern capitalism and democracy bring, especially in relation to the ordered and controlled lives they previously lived under the Communists.

Women and men traditionally had different roles in Polish society; even today, women do not hold equal positions of authority at work (despite the theoretical egalitarianism of women and men under the Communists). Non-Polish businesswomen need to have their credibility established prior to their visit, and must behave in a strictly professional fashion in order to be taken seriously.

Young people today are very eager to live a different life from that of their parents, and struggle to find opportunities in Poland today.

Fundamental Cultural Orientations

1. What's the Best Way for People to Relate to One Another?

OTHER-INDEPENDENT OR OTHER-DEPENDENT? Family and friends are everything: the in-group with which you are associated determines your field of vision and requires your loyalty, while out-groups tend to be avoided and are met, at first, with caution at best, and suspicion at worst. This means that non-Poles will be received warmly, especially if from the west (the Poles' curiosity will overcome their caution), but will need time to prove themselves in order to be treated as an insider. Poles will make every effort to host you well, in order that you, as a guest, will not experience the difficulties of daily life, and will often do this at their own sacrifice. Nevertheless, this concern for others, for membership in a greater family (your own, the neighborhood, the church, etc.), does not preclude taking personal responsibility for what happens in one's life. Within Poland today, there is a growing desire for individuals to assume greater control over their lives. The struggle for the Pole is in finding a way to gain greater individual responsibility in a world where decisions that control one's life are often still made by greater powers; this results in a rejection of personal responsibility when events are bad, and a drive for personal power (sometimes at the expense of others, rules, morality, etc.) when the opportunity appears.

HIERARCHY-ORIENTED OR EGALITY-ORIENTED? There is a strong need for structure and organization, with power and authority coming from above. At the same time, because of the Communist experience (only the most recent in a long historical line of imposed authority), there is curiosity and a keen interest (especially among the young) in more egalitarian structures and relationships. Working in a traditional Polish organization means working within a definite hierarchy, and having access to decision makers means having the ear of the top team (group orientation usually means that there may be more than one individual identified as a decision maker). Although there was a revolution against the Polish Communist system, the church and family life fill this need for structure today: while citizens may no longer be subordinate to the state, within the family, younger is subordinate to older, women are subordinate to men, students are subordinate to teachers, and staff is subordinate to the boss.

RULE-ORIENTED OR RELATIONSHIP-ORIENTED? Rules can be complex (especially when working with government agencies) and bothersome, but are always subordinate to the individual relationships one has with authorities who may be able to overcome the rules. Clever Poles either know someone who can get them out of a jam, or help them take advantage of a favorable opportunity, or are themselves ingenious enough to make a situation work in their favor, despite the existence of rules that are supposed to be for the welfare and benefit of all. The Polish experience has been that official rules were never designed for the benefit of all, and that systems and processes, while perhaps a theoretically good idea, mainly benefited only those who instituted them, leaving most others to fend for themselves. The Western belief that processes and systems, rules and regulations, can be created for the universal benefit of society was the result of western European events, such as the Enlightenment, which never occurred in or had a minimal impact on most of eastern Europe. Therefore, while there may be a great interest in, and almost admiration for, Western thought and philosophy in Poland, there is little experience to justify its benefits; for example, the German methodological tradition more than once became a political threat to Poland. Poles will as easily rely on their subjective intuitive notions of right and wrong, beliefs, and their personal relationships to make decisions, as they will on processes, rules, and systems.

2. What's the Best Way to View Time?

MONOCHRONIC OR POLYCHRONIC? Poles are generally monochronic, being northern European. They will generally arrive on time for meetings and appointments, and even their social events, such as dinners, usually start within five minutes or so of the stated time. In fact, Poles usually start their day rather early. Nevertheless, perhaps because of Roman Catholic and Latin influences, as well as the challenges of day-to-day life in a developing nation, Poles are flexible to polychronic influences: anything can happen to derail a schedule or slow down a plan. Therefore, agendas can be changed quickly, last-minute adjustments are common, and group functions may not end on time. In fact, business meetings and social events both seem to be open-ended affairs (this means that Poles get up early for work, but may also stay up very late into the evening!). Get your sleep when you can when you visit Poland.

RISK-TAKING OR RISK-AVERSE? Here is that Slavic duality: seize an opportunity when you see it or make it, for it may not come again, and there is often little to lose; at the same time, one must be careful not to take any action that may jeopardize one's situation, or the situation of others (especially one's family), any further. The former approach therefore usually lends to quick and sudden risk taking, while the latter usually causes slow and plodding movement toward a specific goal. You will see both mind-sets in Poland (and in most Slavic countries). As market economies, and perhaps democracies, develop in the region, there will be an increase in risk taking, and as long as it succeeds without corrupting the general society, this former tendency will be reinforced; if such action is seen as advancing individual power at the expense of society, the latter tendency will be reinforced. You will feel both attitudes at different times, while working in Poland, and to prepare yourself to respond to either—to both the eager Pole who has an opportunity that is too good to be true, and to the Pole who demands more and more information without making a decision—requires some substantial pre-trip homework.

PAST-ORIENTED OR FUTURE-ORIENTED? The past plays a significant role in Polish society: it is both a weight and a source of identity. It controls and limits possibilities, but it also defines who the Poles are. Poles believe that individuals do have some control over what happens to them, and must struggle, in all ways possible, to exercise control over the future. Nevertheless, there is great acceptance of the fact that much of what will happen is beyond the control of mere individuals, even powerful ones, and that ultimately God is the source of all events.

3. What's the Best Way for Society to Work with the World at Large?

LOW-CONTEXT DIRECT OR HIGH-CONTEXT INDIRECT COMMUNICATORS?
Poles generally say what is on their minds, and can be direct and clear in their thoughts with others; nevertheless, communication is never done in a completely direct way, and Poles are very sensitive to the feelings of others. They allow these feelings to determine how and what they say, so there is a softness even to the most difficult or controversial topics under discussion. The context (whom one is with, the impact of what is being discussed, and other factors) will determine how and what is communicated.

PROCESS-ORIENTED OR RESULT-ORIENTED? Subjective experience, belief, and judgment are as important as proof, evidence, and logic. While Poles admired the intellectual developments of the west, their own experience (the Polish "renaissance" of the sixteenth century, exemplified by such figures as the astronomer Nicolaus Copernicus, and increased freedom for certain minority groups—i.e., the Jews) had limited impact on the ultimate fate of their country in the face of greater European events. Therefore, while facts and figures, proof and logic count, they rarely tip the scale against feeling, intuition, belief, and associative experience.

FORMAL OR INFORMAL? Poles are warm and generous, but not informal. Individuals are not admired for their ability to be spontaneous; they are admired for their ability to know and do the right thing in the right circumstance, through their adherence to established protocol and etiquette.

Greetings and Introductions

Language and Basic Vocabulary

Most Poles do not speak English, although many businesspeople do know enough of that language to be understood. Depending on the people you are talking to, they may also speak German (certainly in the western parts of Poland), and Russian (a related Slavic language) is also understood and spoken by many. Slavic languages are pronounced just as they are written, often with the elimination of unpronounced vowels. When written, however, there are some differences between Slavic languages and English pronunciations, as follows:

- *t* is pronounced like the *ty* in *not yet*
- *n* is pronounced like the *n* in *onion*
- *s* is pronounced like the *sh* in *ship*
- *z* is pronounced like the *s* in *pleasure*
- *c* is pronounced like the *ts* in *tsetse*
- *č* is pronounced like the *ch* in *cheese*
- *ch* is pronounced like the *h* in *hello* (sometimes just slightly more guttural)
- *j* is pronounced like the *y* in *young*
- *r* is pronounced like the *rs* in *Persian*
- *w* is pronounced like the *v* in *victory*

If you know Polish, or are learning it and are faced with the option, it is important always to use the *formal* form of the language with people you do not know well (this requirement extends to structure and words, beyond just the appropriate pronouns, as in Latin languages); only children may be addressed in the informal linguistic form upon first meeting.

Here are some basic Polish phrases and their English meanings:

dzień dobry	good day/morning/afternoon
dobry wieczór	good evening
dobra noc	good night
czesc	hello
do widzenia	good-bye
proszę	please
dziękuję	thank you
proszę bardzo	you're welcome
(or, *nie ma za co*)	
milo mi (cie, pan, pana,	pleased to meet you
pania) poznac	
pan	Mr.
pani	Mrs.
panna	Miss
doktor	doctor

Honorifics for Men, Women, and Children

You must use *pan* (Mr.) and *pani* (Mrs.), plus the family name, when introduced to strangers. Sometimes, among close friends and associates, the honorific may be used with the first name. Unless and until your Polish colleague specifically invites you to use first names, and despite how he or she might refer to you, you must always use the family name plus the correct Polish honorific (*panna*—Miss—is seldom used, unless you are clearly speaking with a child; otherwise, all women should be referred to as *pani*). Married women take their husband's last name, but indicate their gender by changing the last letter when it is a vowel (which it almost always is) into an *a,* or adding an *a* to the last name; for example, Pan Brszynski's wife is referred to as Pani Brszynska. Children in Poland are absolutely required to be respectful when speaking with adults, and must always use honorifics.

In situations where a title is known, the honorific plus the title is usually employed, either with or without the name. For casual contacts (e.g., with waiters, store help, etc.), just use *pan* without the name. In Poland, one does not move from the formal to the informal form of the language without performing a Polish version of the traditional German *Brüderschaftrinken* ceremony (in fact, the ceremony is more common there today than in Germany). While maintaining strong eye contact with your associate, link your right arms, hold your drinks above the table, and toast each other, then down the drink at once. Once done, this ritual allows you to move to the informal language form. (You may be invited to do so without this ceremony: that's okay, too.) It is very important to greet people at work or in stores or restaurants with an appropriate greeting for the time of day (see list of Polish terms as stated earlier) and to say hello and good-bye upon leaving. If you speak any Polish at all, it is important to use it; it will absolutely delight your Polish associates, and help build that all-important relationship.

The What, When, and How of Introducing People

Always wait to be introduced to strangers before taking that responsibility upon yourself. You will always be introduced to women first, then men, in descending order of age. Poles are most comfortable with a third-party introduction whenever possible, so wait a moment before introducing yourself to a new group; if, after a few minutes, no introduction is forthcoming, go ahead and do the job yourself. Women do not necessarily rise when someone enters a room, but men always do, for both women and men. Do not presume to seat yourself at a gathering: if possible, wait to be told where to sit. Shake hands with everyone individually in a group before departing: the American group wave is not appreciated. Once you greet someone you will encounter later that day in the same circumstances (e.g., at the office), there is no need to greet them again. Kissing is a common greeting with and between all genders (women/women or men/men or women/men) once you have established a relationship; it usually involves three "air kisses," first on the left side, and then the right, and then on the left again. This is usually done only between very close friends, family members, and highly regarded business associates.

Physical Greeting Styles

The handshake is common. The Polish version is similar to the German one, a firm grip but with several quick shakes between two men. It is not done as robustly between men and women or two women. The handshake should be accompanied by the appropriate greetings (as outlined earlier), and may be accompanied by a kiss or an embrace. Older Polish men may lift the hand of the woman and bring it to their lips for an "air kiss" (the lips never really touch the top of the woman's hand). Men must remove their gloves when shaking hands with women, but women do not need to remove their gloves when shaking hands. Smiling and other nonverbal forms of communication may not always accompany the handshake, especially between people who have not met before. Men should wait until a woman extends her hand before reaching for it, and women may take the lead in extending their hand or not; this may or may not occur, especially among older women. Eye contact during the introduction is very important, and must be maintained as long as the individual is addressing you.

The use of business cards is common; if possible, you should have yours translated into Polish on the reverse side. Be sure to put any advanced educational degrees and your full title or position on both sides of your business card. Such emblems of your status are very important to Poles: they want to know who you are. But keep in mind that you may not necessarily receive a business card from your Polish associate: they are not as easily printed in the East, and are not as readily available. Using an English-language business card, as well as speaking English and obviously being from the United States, is a real advantage in Poland today, for you will often be given preferential treatment. Don't hide your American identity under a bushel; at the same time, be yourself, and try to display your knowledge and awareness of Polish customs and protocols.

Communication Styles

Okay Topics / Not Okay Topics

Okay: anything positive (as long as they bring it up first) about your home country, especially if it is in the West, such as your work routines or family life. Your knowledge of and interest in Polish culture and history will be appreciated, although it may be dismissed at first (in fact, if you display too much knowledge, it will seem a bit strange); persist respectfully in wanting to know more, though, and you will be treated with great admiration and respect. *Not okay:* While you should not inquire about a person's occupation or income in casual conversation, this and many other aspects of your life (though not necessarily your personal life) will probably be asked of you. This is meant to get to know you, and to learn more about the United States: answer in general and in full for the greatest comfort and maximum effect (e.g., "Well, in the United States, the average salary for my position is ———, but you know, the average mortgage on a house is ———, and it costs about ——— to live a middle-class life"). Until you've established your relationship, do not discuss World War II, the Holocaust, or Roman Catholicism (or religion in general).

Tone, Volume, and Speed

Poles tend to speak softly, slowly, and calmly. It is disrespectful and immature to raise one's voice. It is especially important for women that they not appear loud or assertive: the traditional role of women as nurturers and homemakers in Poland is strong, and even in business settings, the woman who is perceived as aggressive loses authority. On the street, all individuals are expected to maintain decorum: loud, disruptive behavior and boisterous laughter are seen as very bad behavior, especially coming from women.

Use of Silence

There may be some, depending upon the circumstances, the topics being discussed, the roles of the individuals involved, and the degree to which personal relationships have been established.

Physical Gestures and Facial Expressions

Until Poles get to know you, they may appear to be reserved and formal. This will change as trust and familiarity grow. Hand gestures, in general, are limited. Flicking a few fingers against the neck is an invitation (usually between men) to join the person for a drink of vodka.

Waving and Counting

The thumb represents the number 1, the index finger the number 2, and so on. It is insulting to beckon someone with the forefinger (instead, turn your hand so that the palm faces down and motion inward with all four fingers at once). If you need to gesture for a waiter, subtly raise your hand with your index finger outstretched slightly.

Physicality and Physical Space

Poles tend to stay slightly farther apart than North Americans, as is the case with other northern Europeans. When two people do not know each other, they stand even slightly farther apart, lending an air of formality to the greeting. However, when people know each other, there might be less space between them.

Never speak with your hands in your pockets: keep them always firmly to your side when standing. If men and women must cross their legs, it must never be ankle over knee (for women, the preferred style is to cross ankle over ankle). Remember, even in public, formal is always better than informal: no gum chewing, *ever;* don't slouch; and don't lean against things.

Eye Contact

Eye contact can be direct most of the time. It is important not to interpret this behavior as a way of intentionally trying to make you uncomfortable. It is a Polish sign of respect. If you look away, your behavior will say to your Polish colleague that you are either disinterested or rude. Either way, maintain eye contact when it is made with you, especially when making a toast. If strangers' eyes meet and linger, it implies romantic interest. Women should be especially careful about making casual eye contact with men.

Emotive Orientation

At first, Poles generally limit their emotiveness with "outsiders"; once you are "inside," however, they can be more openly emotional, especially when not in public. Even among individuals who know each other well, public displays of emotion are rare.

Protocol in Public

Walking Styles and Waiting in Lines

Lines are usually respected. There may be certain situations, however, where lines are ignored, such as at public bus stops. This will not generally present a challenge, however.

People stay to the right when walking on the street.

Behavior in Public Places: Airports, Terminals, and the Market

Customer service as a concept simply did not exist in eastern and central Europe during the Communist era, and even today it is less and less evident the farther east across the region you go. As employees of the state, with guaranteed jobs, store clerks simply had no motivation to be nice, let alone serve, during the Communist days. Today, as a concept, it is catching on, but slowly. Store hours are typically not built around customer convenience (many stores are closed on weekends and most evenings—except Thursdays, usually). Personally thanking store owners, waiters, chefs, and hotel managers for their services will appear strange to them, as such a custom did not exist under Communism.

In goods stores, it may be difficult for you to return a product unless there is a flaw in it. Bargaining does not occur, in general. Smoking in public places is still a common occurrence, although the Poles are slowly becoming aware of the need to control it. In Poland, unescorted women can expect men to approach them whenever they are in public, but rarely in restaurants.

Bus / Metro / Taxi / Car

Driving is on the right, but people pass very quickly on the left; in fact, the way people drive in Poland is described more often than not as chaotic. Do not drive if you've been drinking: DWI laws are strictly enforced (Poles use designated drivers when they socialize for an evening).

The metros shut down after midnight. Your best bet for catching a cab is at designated taxi stands (hotels are good places, but often charge more for the same ride: a hotel surcharge is added to the meter fare, in some cases).

On public transportation, younger people should give up their seats to older people, and men should still give up their seats to women, especially if they are pregnant or have babies or small children with them.

Tipping

A 10 percent tip is usually sufficient for restaurants and taxis; more is considered nouveau and gauche. Porters and hotel help get about 300 zlotys per service rendered; theater and bathroom attendants usually get the same. Restaurants usually have the 10 percent tip already included on the bill, but if you are unsure, it's okay to ask if service is included or not. Even if it is, it is still appropriate to leave some odd change if the service was particularly good.

Punctuality

Be punctual for starting times; Poles generally are. Expect open-ended situations, however (meetings can go on longer than expected, and dinners usually go on into the early morning hours). The Polish workday usually starts early (many businesses open at 8 A.M.), but it can end early as well (workers usually go home around 3 P.M., office staff usually no later than 4 P.M.). Even managers and executives are rarely in their offices after 4 or 5 P.M. Consider, however, that the Polish workweek includes Saturday morning. This also means that most Poles usually do not take lunch during the day; instead, they will often have a sandwich at midmorning as a snack, and wait till they get home around 3 P.M. for a full lunch (dinner, in this case, is usually light, and is served around 8 P.M. or slightly later). Business lunches, therefore, are really more like late afternoon meals, taken after work around 4 or 5 P.M.

Dress

Err on the formal side, until you know to dress otherwise; this is a good rule both in social situations and at the office. You may be surprised at how informal dress is at work and how formal it is in social situations. At work, men may wear stylish suits (dark is best), white shirts, and interesting and sophisticated ties, but they also may wear slacks and a sport jacket, sometimes with a pullover sweater vest underneath the jacket (how one dresses at work is really a reflection of rank and job title, so observe carefully, and always start out dressing as if you were higher up). The long, cold winters in Poland require layers of clothing, and sweaters and vests help keep people warm throughout the workday. Polish women often dress up for work, especially in the cities; it is fashionable, especially in summer, not to wear stockings.

On the street, informal may mean jeans and sneakers, though that is more common as clothing to wear at the gym, the beach, or while jogging (women do not wear sneakers to work). For a social gathering, informal more often than not means tastefully coordinated clothes, sometimes including a jacket and tie for men; it can also mean clean, pressed jeans and a nice dress shirt, but no sneakers or T-shirts. "Formal" usually means formal evening wear, which is very dressy by American standards.

Seasonal Variations

The extremely cold and damp winter requires layers of clothes and protective boots and rain gear. However, do not be surprised to see Poles stripping down quickly whenever the rare warm day does break through. Sunbathing is a pleasure in all Slavic cultures, and done whenever possible (no nudity, though). Summers, though short, can be warm and sunny. Never remove your jacket or tie unless and until your Polish colleague has done so first.

Colors

Most colors are simple, natural, and not ostentatious. Be conservative in the use of color, even with accessories: they need to blend with, not stand out from, the outfit.

Styles

Style is not critical, but a good appearance is always important. Cologne and perfume are not commonly used.

Personal Hygiene

Recognize that hot running water may be expensive in Poland, so depending on where in Poland you are, your daily bath may have to be forsaken from time to time. However, cleanliness and neatness is highly valued.

Dining and Drinking

Mealtimes and Typical Foods

Breakfast (*sniadanie*) is served from about 7 to 8 A.M., and usually consists of coffee, rolls, butter, jams, and tea. Tea is the drink of preference in Poland (coffee, in fact, though appreciated, is sometimes difficult to obtain), and is often drunk out of glasses. Some Poles hold a cube of sugar between their front teeth and let the tea wash over it as they drink.

Lunch (*obiad*) is still the main meal of the day in both rural and urban areas; it is served around 3 to 4 P.M. during the week, and around 1 to 2 P.M. on Sundays. It usually consists of several courses, beginning with a soup, then a meat course with vegetables (potatoes and cabbage are common), bread (of all kinds), a salad (sometimes with pickled vegetables), and ending with a dessert of preserved fruit or pastries (sometimes both) and tea. Beer or vodka is served with lunch. Meat courses may include veal or beef, served in cabbage rolls (*golabki*) or boiled or roasted. Special foods, often showing up as appetizers in restaurants or at Sunday dinners, include fruit and vegetable soups (try the beet soup, known as *barsczc,* or borscht), pierogi (dumplings stuffed with meat, cheese, or vegetables), steak tartare, smoked eel (*wegorz*), and smoked sausages (kielbasas). Preserved, marinated, or pickled fish is often served.

Dinner (*kolacja*) is served from 8:30 to 9 P.M. or later. It is usually just a light meal of sandwiches, pastries, and/or salad. Tea, beer, or vodka is served.

Cafés are not that common (remember, there is a long winter season!), but the indoor *kawiarnia* are as close as one comes to them in Poland. They serve drinks, pastries, light snacks, and the like. *Mleczny,* or milk bars, serve snacks and sandwiches with soft drinks, but no alcoholic beverages. *Karczma* are fun old-fashioned taverns, usually family-run, where traditional Polish food is served, in quantity.

Typical Drinks and Toasting

The Polish national drink is vodka; it will be served with all meals, as well as in between meals, and at all social events. Vodka will usually come out onto the table, along with assorted snacks, during business meetings, at virtually any time of day, including first thing in the morning. Do not drink all the vodka that is offered to you, for every time you drink a glass, it will be refilled. The more you drink, the more you will be offered to drink: know when to stop. It can be served room temperature or it may be iced ahead of time (the most formal way to serve it); it will rarely be poured over ice. If you really cannot drink, you'll need a very good excuse, like doctor's orders. Vodka is usually drunk in one shot.

The most common toast is *na zdrowie* (to your health). Another popular toast is *stolat,* meaning "one hundred years," implying that you should live to be one hundred years old. Never break eye contact while making a toast, from the moment the glass leaves the table until you place it back down (blinking is allowed, however!). There can be many different toasts throughout a meal; you will be expected to make a toast in a small group at some point during the meal, especially if you have been toasted personally or are the guest of honor.

Table Manners and the Use of Utensils

Do not begin eating until everyone has received food on their plates and the host invites you to start; this is usually done by saying *smacznego.*

Like all continental Europeans, Poles do not switch knives and forks, as Americans do. The knife remains in the right hand, and the fork remains in the left. When the meal is finished, place your fork and knife horizontally across the plate, facing left; this indicates that you are finished.

If you're unsure of which utensil to use, always start from the outside and work your way in, course by course. The fork and spoon above your plate are usually for dessert. Occasionally, soup is served without spoons: this means you are expected to lift the soup bowl up to your lips and sip it like a drink (the soup will usually be served in smaller bowls resembling cups, if this is the case). Bread is usually served without butter (therefore, there will usually not be a butter knife), and there usually is no bread plate (place your bread on the side of your main plate or on the table throughout the meal).

Your hands are expected to be visible above the table: this means that you do not keep them in your lap; instead, rest your wrists on top of the table. At the table, pass all dishes to your left. Wine is sometimes served in water glasses (after-dinner drink glasses come out after dinner). If there is gravy or sauce, you can generally use your bread to soak some of it up.

Seating Plans

The most honored position is at the head of the table, with the most important guest seated immediately to the right of the host (women to the right of the host, and men to the right of the hostess). If there is a hosting couple, one will be seated at each side of the table. In keeping with the practice elsewhere on the Continent, men and women are seated next to one another, and couples are often broken up and seated next to people they may not have previously known. This is done to promote conversation, which, after all, is the main pleasure at the table. Men typically rise when women enter the room, and may or may not enter a room first when a woman is present. At the table, the oldest or most honored guest is served first. Remember, as is the case throughout the Continent, what the Poles call the first floor is really the second floor, with the first floor usually referred to as the lobby or ground floor.

Refills and Seconds

At a private dinner party, if you do not want more food, you will really have to insist several times before the hostess will believe you. Take a little extra if you can of something you like. If you do not want more, you must leave a little food on your plate to be believed. You may always have additional beverages; drink enough to cause your cup or glass to be less than half full, and it will generally be refilled. Portions are generally slightly smaller than in the United States, but there are usually more courses, for both lunch and dinner.

At Home, in a Restaurant, or at Work

In informal restaurants, you may be required to share a table: if so, do not force conversation; act as if you are seated at a private table. Waitstaff may be summoned by making eye contact; waving or calling their names is very impolite. The business breakfast is not done here. The business lunch or dinner, depending upon how well developed your relationship is with your Polish colleagues, is generally not the time to make business decisions. Take your cue from your Polish associates: if they bring up business, then it's okay to discuss it, but wait to take your lead from their conversation. No gum chewing, ever, at the restaurant or on the street. No-smoking sections in restaurants are still a rarity.

When you arrive at a Polish colleague's home for a formal meal, you will be told where to sit, and there you should remain. Do not wander from room to room: much of the house is really off-limits to guests. Once you (and the group) are invited to another room, most probably the dining room, be sure to allow the more senior members of your party to enter the room ahead of you. At the table, do not presume to seat yourself, as the seating arrangement is usually predetermined. Spouses who accompany their partners on business trips are rarely invited to attend business meals.

Be prepared to arrive at about 8 or 8:30 P.M., and be prepared to stay late: you will insult your hosts if you end the evening too early (this means staying at least past midnight, even during the midweek). As is the case throughout much of the region (and more so, the farther east you go), you might have to remove your shoes before entering a Polish home (check to see if there are pairs of shoes lined up at the entrance to the home: if there are, it means that you should remove yours as well); be sure your socks are in good shape. You might be offered slippers to wear.

Being a Good Guest or Host

Paying the Bill

Usually the one who does the inviting pays the bill, although the guest is expected to make an effort to pay. Sometimes other circumstances determine the payee (such as rank). Making payment arrangements ahead of time so that no exchange occurs at the table is a very classy way to host. If men are also at the table, women will not really be able to pay the bill at a restaurant: if you want to, make arrangements ahead of time, and don't wait for the check to arrive at the table. The only time it is considered appropriate for a woman to pay the bill is if she is a businesswoman from abroad.

Transportation

It's a very nice idea, when acting as the host, to inquire ahead of time as to whether your guests will require transportation. If necessary, you should arrange for taxi service at the end of the meal.

In Poland, you may be picked up from and taken back to your hotel by the host. Poles are extremely warm and gracious.

When to Arrive / Chores to Do

If invited to dinner at a private home, offer to help with the chores, but be prepared to be turned down at first. Ask again, and your offer will probably be accepted. Otherwise, do not leave the table unless invited to do so. When it is time to leave, always get up and shake hands with everyone: the group wave is not appreciated.

An invitation to visit a Polish home may not occur, however, mainly because Poles view their homes as smaller and less comfortable than the ones to which Westerners are accustomed. If you are invited into a home, your desires become your hosts' most important concerns, so be sensitive to imposing yourself on their daily routine.

Gift Giving

In general, gift giving is common among business associates. The best gifts are useful office items, such as pen and pencil sets, nicely bound agendas, and the like. Mementos of life in the United States are very well received (towels, coffee-table books on the United States, and well-packaged gourmet foodstuffs are always appreciated). Holiday cards are very appropriate, particularly as a thank-you for your Polish colleagues' business during the previous year, and should be mailed in time to be received the week before Christmas.

Gifts are expected for social events, especially as thank-yous for private dinner parties. The best gift in this case is a cut floral bouquet—and you should bring it along with you when you arrive. It should always be wrapped, and you should unwrap it only in the presence of the hostess. Other good gifts would be cakes and pastries, a box of fine chocolates, or wine (bring several bottles, so that one may be used with the meal, and the others by the hosts later). Do not bring vodka: there is already plenty. If there are children in the family, it is thoughtful to bring a little something for them, such as a toy or candy, in addition to the gift for the hostess. As with other European cultures, gifts are generally opened at the time they are given and received.

Special Holidays and Celebrations

Major Holidays

Most Polish workers get several weeks of paid vacation; August is the top vacation month. Business slows down from December 15 to January 2, and Holy Week is sometimes a more difficult time in which to accomplish work than Christmas. Curiously, as is the case in Greek Orthodox cultures, name days (the birthdays of the saints after whom people were named) are often more important celebrations than birthdays.

January 1	*Nowy Rok* (New Year's Day; also Grandparent's Day; not an official national holiday)
March/April	*Dobry Piatek* (Good Friday)
March/April	*Wielkanok* (Easter)
March 8	Women's Day (not an official national holiday)
May 1	*Praca* (Labor Day)
May 3	*Konstytucia* (Constitution Day)
May 26	Mother's Day (not an official national holiday)
May/June	Corpus Christi
November 1	All Saints' Day
November 11	*Niezaleznosc* (Independence Day)
December 25	*Boze Narodzenie* (Christmas)

Business Culture

Daily Office Protocols

In Poland, office doors are mostly closed; you must knock first (this includes bathrooms) before opening doors, and when leaving rooms, close the doors behind you.

Women do not hold equal authority as men in business organizations. It is more common for women to be relegated to lower-level management and administrative support positions. It is rare (though not impossible) to see women at the highest levels of business and government in Poland.

The workday starts very early, but ends around midafternoon. When making appointments, be sure to schedule them way in advance, and confirm them several times as the date and time approaches. Expect some chitchat at the beginning of the meeting about nonbusiness issues, but don't fret: Poles usually move fairly quickly to substantive issues.

Management Styles

Privacy and individual accomplishment of one's tasks are critical. Workers provide what their bosses expect of them, and the preparation of plans, methods, and reports can be time-consuming and complicated efforts toward perfection. Gathering the information required in order to do what your boss expects from you, or creating consensus among your colleagues in order to accomplish a particular goal, can take a long time. All of this occurs in a formal and sometimes very rigid hierarchical structure. Titles in Poland are very important; the highest ones (e.g., vice president) are usually reserved for very senior, executive-level positions, and should not be used as casually as they are in the United States. Complimenting and rewarding employees publicly is viewed suspiciously.

Boss-Subordinate Relations

In Poland, rank most definitely has its privileges, in the form of decision-making authority. Deviating from established procedures typically does not get things done any faster. You must get close to the decision makers, who are most often at the top; if this is your first meeting in Poland, you may not be speaking with the decision makers, but merely gatekeepers who are there to size up you and your organization, and report back to their supervisors.

Conducting a Meeting or Presentation

Meetings can, if decision makers are present, be information-sharing and decision-making forums in which all individuals are expected to contribute; if not, they are merely opportunities for information exchange and trust building. Data, facts, and figures are all important, but not more important than the good feeling your Polish associates finally have about you when you leave. Because Poles have learned to deal with limited resources for so long, presentations need not be fancy, just as long as they are clear and easily understood. Make your copies before you arrive, as the necessary technology may not be readily available. Presentations in English are fine, but backup documentation should also be in Polish.

Negotiation Styles

Poles can display two opposing behaviors: they can play their cards close to the vest at first, not divulging information easily, and then open up as trust develops; or they can almost be effusive in their eagerness to work with you (this is because they indeed are: Western business generally means good new opportunities!). If they are in the former mode, they may appear circumspect in their communication styles, and will indicate their thoughts in indirect, associative ways; they can, however, quickly become pointedly direct as negotiations move forward. If they are in their latter mode, they will most definitely be more eager to speak openly and move the negotiations along. If you are from the West, they will assume you have the ability to do everything you say and more, and will also assume you already have the knowledge and experience required for the work; they will also try to persuade you of the same about them, which may or may not in fact be true (you need to confirm this independently). The first meeting is usually just a formality, with the Poles sizing up you and your organization: it will be conducted in the office. Put on a warm, dignified demeanor during the meeting. Never be condescending or offer an ultimatum; bargaining is not their style. Contracts are serious matters here: they should be clear, concise, and translated into both Polish and English.

Written Correspondence

Be clear, precise, and respectful in your business correspondence; don't be too flowery. Last names are usually written in uppercase; dates are given using the day/month/year format (with periods in between, not slashes); and an honorific plus a title is as common as an honorific plus the last name. The time of day is written in military style; weights and measurements are given in metric units. Monetary amounts are written so that periods break up the figures into tens, hundreds, and thousands (10.000 = ten thousand zlotys). You can get straight to the point in written business communications.

The Central European Cultures: The Czech Republic and Slovakia

Some Introductory Background on the Czech Republic and Slovakia and the Czechs and Slovaks

If you look at a map of Europe, you will see that Prague is farther west than Vienna, and almost as far west as Berlin: this says something about the Czech people. They are the most heavily Western-influenced of all the Slavs. This means that they share similar traditions with Western cultures, have many of the same fundamental views of life, and have experienced, in greater or lesser degrees, the events that shaped much of Western thought. Nevertheless, they also have had their own Slavic experiences, and bring these to the cultural table, as well.

The Czech Republic, formerly part of the extinct nation known as Czechoslovakia, is divided into two sections: in the west, Moravia, and in the center and east, Bohemia. Most recently, the country has experienced two major events: the "Velvet Revolution" of 1989, which freed it from the Soviet yoke; and the creation of two separate nations, the Czech Republic and Slovakia, out of the former state of Czechoslovakia. Prior to the separation, Slovakia was the land of the Slovenes, a different people from the Czechs, and this historic difference eventually culminated in the peaceful separation of the two countries in the twentieth century. The nature of these two recent dramatic events, and the proximity of the country to western Europe, is evidence of and the result of the Czech sensibility of humanitarianism and tolerance, unique among nations in the region. The revolt against the Communists was peaceful; the separation of the nation into its two halves was accomplished without violence; the first president of the new Czech Republic, Vaclav Havel, was a poet, novelist, and pacifist. Humanism and humanitarian ideals keep the Slavic and western elements of Czech society hanging together, and this is one of the main contributions of Czech culture to the region.

Some Historical Context

Czechoslovakia played a major role in the Protestant reformation of the fifteenth century, and Jan Hus, the great Protestant Czech leader, is still revered as a martyr today. The famous defenestration of Prague in the sixteenth century, during which the Catholic hierarchy was literally thrown out the window, was one of the highlights of a major struggle for the spiritual soul of central Europe. Reeling as it did from these religious wars, and being one of Europe's major centers of medieval scholarly thought, the country, particularly the western Czech section, developed a level of scholarship equal to the best of Europe. The Czech cultural renaissance of the sixteenth century established the Czech people as important contributors to European philosophy, art, and science. Nevertheless, European politics overran this renaissance, as the struggles within the Austro-Hungarian Empire ripped the Czechoslovak peoples apart in the eighteenth century, leaving the northern Protestant Czechs under the rule of the Austrians, and the southern Catholic Slovenes (currently Slovaks) under Hungarian domination. Over time, this division resulted in, among other things, the western Czechs becoming more urbanized, secular, and Western-oriented, with the southern Slovenes remaining more conservative, rural, and insular. It can be said the Czechs are central European Slavs facing west, while Slovaks are central European Slavs facing east. During World War II, the Czechs resisted the German invasion, while the Slovaks made a deal for a puppet regime whose rule and ruler (Msgr. Tiso) many Slovaks still admire today and who is equally detested by most Czechs. Today, the Czechs pride themselves on being a tolerant and urbane people, and Slovaks pride themselves on being a people on the ramparts of defending the nation and its native Slavic soul against untrustworthy neighbors (i.e., Hungary and Russia).

An Area Briefing

Politics and Government

The Czech Republic today is a parliamentary democracy, with a prime minister (the leader of the majority party) and a bicameral legislature. There are many different parties in Czech politics, and the Czech people are glorying in the new freedoms they have after having evicted the Soviets in the early 1990s. As is the case in much of the region, the Communist Party still plays some role in local politics, but not as much as in other countries in the region where there is a greater yearning among the people for more stable and predictable days, when at least their basic needs were taken care of by the government. The Slovak political system is similar in structure, but less flexible in practice, with fewer parties, less vigorous activity, and apparently greater corruption.

Schools and Education

The educational systems in both countries today are similar to those found elsewhere in Europe. There is the equivalent of elementary, middle, and high school levels, with students, after passing a final exam, having the option to go on to a university or technical (vocational) training academies. The literacy rate in both countries is high, and some of Europe's finest universities were in the Czech Republic. Education under the Communists was extremely ideological and, despite efforts to promote the trades, the arts, and the sciences, extremely lacking in comparison to Western education. However, the older, more rigorous scholastic traditions have rebounded, and the educational system is improving.

Religion and Demographics

In the Czech Republic, the population is divided among Protestants, Roman Catholics, and many other groups; the fact is, however, that the country is extremely secularized, and is perhaps the least devout nation within the region. While the fall of Communism allowed for the rise of the church elsewhere, the very strong Western influences in the Czech Republic, coupled with the equally powerful humanitarian tradition that developed in Czechoslovakia in response to the religious intolerances of its earlier history, has served to keep interest in religious practice low in the Czech Republic. This is not the case in Slovakia, where the Catholic Church has been re-embraced and plays a major role in daily life for the majority of the population.

Prague today has reclaimed its role as the Paris of the region, with a business and social climate of almost frenetic activity; Bratislava (the Slovakian capital) is a center for manufacturing and heavy industry, which form that country's economic base. There are more Americans in Prague than there are in Paris at the moment of this writing; despite its cosmopolitan air, Prague still manages to be one of the world's most beautifully preserved medieval cities.

The role of women in the Czech Republic also is considerably different from that of women elsewhere in the region. Women were once seen as subordinate to men, but in the Czech Republic today, they are seen as the equals of men in both business and in social affairs. However, women are still expected to fulfill the role of wife and mother, which is a considerably greater burden, since fathers and husbands are still not as encumbered with domestic responsibilities in their roles as women are in theirs. Non-Czech businesswomen who visit the country must behave in a strictly professional fashion in order to be taken seriously. In Slovakia, the role of women is more restricted and more traditional. This differing perspective on women's role in society illustrates a fundamental distinction between the two countries. There is a greater eagerness to adopt western reforms in the Czech Republic, and an ambivalence about leaving the demand economy of the past in Slovakia.

Fundamental Cultural Orientations

1. What's the Best Way for People to Relate to One Another?

OTHER-INDEPENDENT OR OTHER-DEPENDENT? Czechs are fairly individualistic; while family members and trusted friends form the social nucleus, individuals are responsible for their own affairs, often act independently, and are rewarded for independent action when it succeeds, and accept responsibility for it when it fails. The greater your status, the more you are expected to act independently; but actions must reflect well on others. There is great tolerance of out-groups, although this does not mean that Czechs will automatically accept you: this will still take time, and is based on a cultivated relationship of trust. Slovaks are considerably more group-oriented; individuals striking out on their own are often viewed with suspicion, and usually face a difficult time.

HIERARCHY-ORIENTED OR EGALITY-ORIENTED? In both countries, there is a strong need for structure and organization, with power and authority coming from above. At the same time, in the Czech Republic, there is resistance to any authority or imposed structure that is without clearly expressed humanitarian benefits. Working in a traditional Czech or Slovak organization means working within a definite hierarchy, and having access to decision makers means having the ear of the top team. Things must "fit right" within a just scheme of nature, or else no structure or hierarchy is worth it. In the social life of the Czech Republic, egalitarianism means that every individual should have an equal opportunity to succeed, but the rules of etiquette still require men to defer to women in public, and younger people to defer to their elders. In Slovakia, any resistance to the established structure and hierarchy usually takes the form of an outside effort to seize power and authority.

RULE-ORIENTED OR RELATIONSHIP-ORIENTED? The strong western influence of secular rationality and applied method provides Czechs with a strong intellectual tradition of respecting the universality of rules and systems; this is less the case in Slovakia, where there is more reliance on one's relationships with others. For both Czechs and Slovaks, such systems have not always worked in their favor, and relationships between individuals and the manipulation of rules and systems for one's benefit still play equal roles in society. Clever Czechs or Slovaks either know someone who can get them out of a jam, or help them take advantage of a favorable situation, or are themselves ingenious enough to make a situation work in their favor, despite the existence of rules that are supposed to be for the welfare and benefit of all. Again, the one qualification that, for the Czechs, tips the scales toward a preference for universal rules is that even when things are interpreted subjectively, the results should not harm others; this is not necessarily the same consideration in Slovakia.

2. What's the Best Way to View Time?

MONOCHRONIC OR POLYCHRONIC? Czechs are generally monochronic, but there is a strong polychronic tone to this; they often arrive late for business and social events, and often do not keep their own agendas. However, this is due less to an inherent orientation to polychronism as it is to a reaction to the frenzied pace of the new life that has literally overtaken the resources and former infrastructure of the country. People are simply having to learn new ways in a fairly chaotic environment. Expect to be kept waiting, and for schedules to change at a moment's notice, but not without an apology, reflecting an awareness that this is not the preferred way to do things. Just the reverse is true in Slovakia: Slovaks are generally polychronic, but with a strong monochronic tone. The result is often the same, but the starting point is different.

RISK-TAKING OR RISK-AVERSE? Here is that Slavic duality again: seize an opportunity when you see it or make it, for it may not come again, and there is often little to lose; at the same time, one must be careful not to take any action that may jeopardize one's own situation, or the situation of others (especially one's family) any further. The former approach therefore usually leads to quick and sudden risk taking, while the latter usually causes a slow and plodding movement toward a specific goal. You will see both mind-sets in the Czech Republic and Slovakia (and in most Slavic countries), especially in work situations. You will feel both approaches at different times, and to prepare yourself to respond to either—to both the eager Czech or Slovak who has an opportunity that is too good to be true, and to the Czech or Slovak who demands more and more information without making a decision—requires some substantial pre-trip homework. There may be more initial risk taking by the Czech, and more initial risk avoidance by the Slovak; in the end, both are capable of both behaviors.

PAST-ORIENTED OR FUTURE-ORIENTED? The past plays a significant role in both Czech and Slovak society: it is both a weight and a source of identity. It controls and limits possibilities, but it also defines who the Czechs and Slovaks are. Czechs believe that individuals do have some control over what happens to them, and must struggle, in all ways possible, to exercise control over the future, while Slovaks perhaps are more fate-oriented. While the individual does play a significant role in the Czech Republic, the individual's ability to control events and to plan for the future is less of a consideration in Slovakia.

3. What's the Best Way for Society to Work with the World at Large?

LOW-CONTEXT DIRECT OR HIGH-CONTEXT INDIRECT COMMUNICATORS? Czechs generally say what is on their minds, and can be direct and clear in their thoughts with others; nevertheless, communication is never done in a direct way, and Czechs are also very sensitive to the feelings of others. They allow these feelings to determine how and what they say, so there is a softness even to the most difficult or controversial topic under discussion. The context (who one is with, the impact of what is being discussed, and other factors) will determine how and what is communicated. This is perhaps even more the case in Slovakia.

PROCESS-ORIENTED OR RESULT-ORIENTED? Subjective experience, belief, and judgment play a powerful role in decision making in both countries, but in the Czech Republic, a greater role is played by facts, numbers, logic, and rationalism.

FORMAL OR INFORMAL? Both Czech and Slovak cultures are formal cultures: they are central European, and the heir, along with Austria and Hungary, to the eighteenth-century charm of respectful, interpersonal human relationships. While there is apparently a significant generational gap in this area in the Czech Republic, formality and the proper ways of doing things are still regarded as important. Individuals are not admired for their ability to be casual; they are admired for their ability to know and do the right thing in the right circumstance, through adherence to established protocol and etiquette.

Greetings and Introductions

Language and Basic Vocabulary

Many Czechs speak some English today; most Slovaks do not. The Czech and Slovak languages are similar and mutually intelligible to speakers of either. The second language for most Czechs and Slovaks is German, not English, and many older Czechs and Slovaks also speak Russian (but will usually hesitate to use it).

All Slavic languages are pronounced just as they are written, Czech and Slovak included, often with the elimination of unpronounced vowels. Most Czechs and Slovaks will prefer to use their own language and will only use the other, if they know it, if it is the only practical alternative. When written, however, there are some differences between the Czech and the Slovak languages and English pronunciations, as follows:

- *ť* is pronounced like the *ty* in *not yet*
- *ň* is pronounced like the *n* in *onion*
- *š* is pronounced like the *sh* in *ship*
- *ž* is pronounced like the *s* in *pleasure*
- *c* is pronounced like the *ts* in *tsetse*
- *č* is pronounced like the *ch* in *cheese*
- *ch* is pronounced like the *h* in *hello* (sometimes just slightly more guttural)
- *j* is pronounced like the *y* in *young*
- *ǒ* is pronounced like the *aw* in *awe*

Here are some basic Czech and Slovak phrases, with their English translations:

Czech	Slovak	English
dobrý den	*dobrý deň*	hello
na zhledanou	*do videnia*	good-bye
ahoj	*ahoj*	hi and 'bye (informal)
ano/ne	*áno/nie*	yes/no
dobré ráno	*dobré rano*	good morning
dobré odpoledne	*dobré popoludne*	good afternoon
dobré noc	*dobru noc*	good night
Jak se matte?	*Ako sa mate?*	How are you?
prosím	*prosím*	please/you're welcome
tesi mne	*ze vas spoznavam*	pleased to meet you
děkuji	*jakuyen/ďakujem*	thank you
vitejte	*viiajte*	welcome
Jak se ymenujete?	*Ako sa volate?*	What is your name?
pane	*pán*	Mr.
paní	*pani*	Mrs.
slečna	*slečna*	Miss
doktor	*doktor*	doctor

Honorifics for Men, Women, and Children

You must use *pan* (Mr.) and *pani* (Mrs.), plus the family name, when introduced to strangers. Sometimes, among close friends and associates, the honorific may be used with the first name. Unless and until your Czech or Slovak colleague specifically invites you to use first names, and despite how he or she might refer to you, you must always use the family name plus the correct Czech/Slovak honorific (*slečna*—Miss—is not used as much as it used to be, but is still used from time to time for younger women and for female children). Married women take their husband's last name, but in Slovakia may also indicate their gender by changing the last letter when it is a vowel (which it almost always is) into an *a* (or adding *ova* to the last name); for example, Pan Schmidt's wife is referred to as Pani Schmidtova. Children in both countries are absolutely required to be respectful when speaking with adults, and must always use honorifics.

In situations where a title is known, the honorific plus the title is usually used, either with or without the name. For casual contacts (i.e., with waiters, store help, etc.), just use *pan* or *slečna* without the name. It is important to greet people at work or in stores or restaurants with an appropriate greeting (see the list of Czech and Slovak terms, earlier in this chapter) and to say good-bye upon leaving. If you speak any Czech or Slovak at all, it is important to use it; it will absolutely delight your Czech or Slovak associates, and help build that all-important relationship.

The What, When, and How of Introducing People

Always wait to be introduced to strangers before taking that responsibility upon yourself. You will always be introduced to women first, then men, in descending order of age. Czechs and Slovaks are most comfortable with a third-party introduction whenever possible, so wait a moment before introducing yourself to a new group; if, after a few minutes, no introduction is forthcoming, go ahead and do the honors yourself. Women do not necessarily rise when someone enters a room, but men always do, for both women and men. Do not presume to seat yourself at a gathering: if possible, wait to be told where to sit. Shake hands with everyone individually in a group before departing: the American group wave is not appreciated. Once you greet someone you will encounter later that day in the same circumstances (e.g., at the office), there is no need to greet them again. Kissing is a common greeting with and between all genders (women/women or men/men or women/men) once you have established a familiar relationship; it usually involves three "air kisses," first on the left side, and then on the right, and then on the left again. This is usually done only between very close friends, family members, and highly regarded business associates.

Physical Greeting Styles

The handshake is common. The Czech/Slovak handshake is similar to the German one, a firm grip but with several quick shakes, between two men. It is not done as robustly between men and women or two women. The handshake should be accompanied by the appropriate greetings (as outlined earlier), and may be accompanied by a kiss or an embrace. Never shake hands across another pair of shaking hands (resulting in an *X,* which is considered bad luck). Older men may lift the hand of the woman and bring it to their lips for an "air kiss" (the lips never really touch the top of the woman's hand). Men must remove their gloves when shaking hands with women, but women do not need to remove their gloves. Smiling and other nonverbal forms of communication may not always accompany the handshake, especially between people who have not met before. Men should wait until a woman extends her hand before reaching for it, and women may take the lead in extending their hand or not; this may or may not occur, especially among older women. Eye contact during the introduction is very important, and must be maintained as long as the individual is addressing you.

The use of business cards is common; if possible, you should have yours translated into either Czech or Slovak (but never both, as it indicates you are working both sides of the fence) on the reverse side. Be sure to put any advanced educational degrees and your full title or position on both sides of your translated business card. Such evidence of your status is very important: the Czechs and the Slovaks both want to know who you are. Also, if your company has been around more than fifty years or so, put its founding date on the card after the company name: this indicates stability, and is impressive. Be aware, though, that you may not necessarily receive a business card in return: they are not as easily printed in the East, and are not as readily available. Using an English-language business card, as well as speaking English and obviously being from the United States, is a real advantage in the Czech Republic or Slovakia today, for you will often be given preferential treatment. Don't hide your American identity under a bushel; at the same time, be yourself, and try to display your knowledge and awareness of Czech and Slovak customs and protocols.

Communication Styles

Okay Topics / Not Okay Topics

Okay: anything positive (as long as they bring it up first) about your home country, especially if it is in the West, such as your work routines or family life. Your knowledge of and interest in Czech or Slovak culture and history will be appreciated, although it may be dismissed at first (in fact, if you display too much knowledge, it will seem a bit strange); persist in wanting to know more, though, and you will be treated with great admiration and respect. *Not okay:* While you should not inquire about a person's occupation or income in casual conversation, this and many other aspects of your life (though not necessarily your personal life) will probably be asked of you. This is meant to get to know you, and to learn more about the United States: answer in general and in full for the greatest comfort and maximum effect (e.g., "Well, in America, the average salary for my position is ———, but you know, the average mortgage on a house is ———, and it costs about ——— to live a middle-class life"). Most Slovaks and Czechs will ask a great many questions about the West, and probably offer a few opinions, as well (which may or may not be correct: remember, under the Communists, only a limited amount of very skewed information was passed along about the rest of the world to the population). Do not discuss World War II or the Holocaust, or give your opinion about Czechs or Slovaks or any other ethnic group in the region (e.g., Germans, Hungarians, Russians, Gypsies, etc.). As should be the case everywhere in the world, be a teacher when the topic of your country comes up, and be a student when the topic of their country comes up. Generally, it is best to avoid complimenting people, as it usually strikes both Czechs and Slovaks as insincere and unnecessary.

Tone, Volume, and Speed

Both Czechs and Slovaks tend to speak softly, slowly, and calmly. It is disrespectful and immature to raise one's voice. It is especially important for women that they not appear loud or assertive: the traditional nurturing role of women is still strong in both countries (despite the fact that in both countries both men and women work), and even in business settings, the woman who is perceived as aggressive loses authority. On the street, all individuals are expected to maintain decorum: loud, disruptive behavior and boisterous laughter are seen as very bad behavior, especially coming from women.

Use of Silence

There may be some (perhaps more likely in Slovakia), depending upon the circumstances, individuals involved, their rank, topics being discussed, and degree of personal relationship established.

Physical Gestures and Facial Expressions

Until both Czechs and Slovaks get to know you, they may appear to be reserved and formal. This will change as trust and familiarity grow. Hand gestures, in general, are limited. Flicking a few fingers against the neck is an invitation (usually between men) to join the person for a drink of vodka. The "okay" sign, made with the forefinger and the thumb, is generally not understood; the "thumbs up" sign is a more accepted practice. Smiling is generally not done casually: in public, with strangers, smiling is seen as odd; even greeting someone with a smile is unusual.

Waving and Counting

The thumb represents the number 1, the index finger the number 2, and so on. In the Czech Republic, you may beckon someone by merely extending the index finger and raising your hand (but do not wiggle the index finger). In Slovakia, it is insulting to beckon someone with the forefinger (instead, turn your hand so that the palm faces down and motion inward with all four fingers at once). If you need to gesture for a waiter, subtly raise your hand with your index finger slightly outstretched.

Physicality and Physical Space

Czechs and Slovaks tend to get slightly closer than northern Europeans; however, when two people do not know each other, they stand just slightly farther apart at first, lending an air of formality to the greeting. Never speak with your hands in your pockets: always keep them firmly to your side when standing. If men and women must cross their legs, it should never be ankle over knee (for women, the most preferred style is to cross ankle over ankle). Remember, in public, formal is always better than informal: no gum chewing, *ever;* don't slouch; and don't lean against things.

Eye Contact

Eye contact will be direct most of the time. It is important not to interpret this behavior as a way of intentionally trying to make you uncomfortable; rather, it is a sign of respect. If you look away, your behavior will say to your Czech or Slovak colleague that you are either disinterested or rude. Either way, maintain eye contact when it is made with you, especially when making a toast. If two strangers' eyes meet and linger, it implies (romantic) interest. Women should be especially careful about making casual eye contact with men.

Emotive Orientation

At first, both Czechs and Slovaks are generally limited in their emotiveness with "outsiders"; once you are "inside," however, they can be more openly emotional, especially when not in public. However, being in public reduces emotiveness considerably. Even among individuals who know each other well, public displays of emotion are rare.

Protocol in Public

Walking Styles and Waiting in Lines

Lines are usually respected. There may be certain situations, however, where lines are ignored, such as at public bus stops. This will not generally present a challenge, however. People stay to the right when walking on the street. Men accompanied by women, as well as the younger of two people, walk on the curbside; if more than two people are walking together, the "odd" gender is flanked by the pair from the opposite gender. When a close relationship has been established, individuals often walk arm in arm on the street, no matter their genders.

Behavior in Public Places: Airports, Terminals, and the Market

Customer service as a concept simply did not exist in eastern and central Europe during the Communist era, and even today it is less and less evident the farther east across the region you go. As employees of the state, with guaranteed jobs, store clerks simply had no motivation to be nice, let alone serve, during the Communist days. Today, as a concept, it is catching on, but slowly. Store hours are typically not built around customer convenience (most stores are closed on weekends and most evenings—except Thursdays, usually). Personally thanking store owners, waiters, chefs, and hotel managers for their services seems strange to them, as it was not a custom under the Communists. As in much of Europe, if you touch the produce in food markets, you buy it; in goods stores, it may be difficult for you to return a product unless there is a flaw in it. Bargaining does not occur, in general. In most stores, you pay for the item you want first; the cashier will then give you a receipt; you then pick up the item with your receipt and leave. When you pay for something, put your money on the counter, and not in the hand of the clerk: in return, the clerk will put any change down on the counter, and not directly into your hand. Smoking in public places is still a common occurrence, although the Czechs and Slovaks are slowly becoming aware of the need to control it. Never applaud in a church (you might go to one for a concert; it is a common form of entertainment) unless others do first. Unescorted women can expect men to approach them whenever they are in public, but rarely in restaurants.

Bus / Metro / Taxi / Car

Driving is on the right, but people pass very quickly on the left. Do not drive if you've been drinking: DWI laws are strictly enforced. The metros shut down after midnight. Your best bet for catching a cab is at designated taxi stands (hotels are good places, but often charge more for the same ride: a hotel surcharge is added to the meter fare, in some cases).

On public transportation, younger people should give up their seats to older people, and men should give up their seats to women, especially if they are pregnant or have babies or small children with them.

Tipping

A 10 percent tip is usually sufficient for restaurants and taxis; more is considered nouveau and gauche. (Remember, under the Communists, tipping was not permitted.) Porters and hotel help get about five koruna per service rendered, theater and bathroom attendants usually slightly less. Restaurants may not have the 10 percent tip already included on the bill, so be sure to ask. Even if it is included, it is still appropriate to leave some odd change, bringing the total tip to about 15 percent. Include the tip when you pay the bill at the cashier: do not leave either the bill payment or the tip on the table (the bill is usually made out and left on the table when you order).

Answer your telephone by saying *"prosim."* If you are using a public phone, you will hear the phrase *mint se,* notifying you that it is time to insert another coin for the call to continue.

Punctuality

Be punctual for starting times in both the Czech Republic and Slovakia, even though your business associates may be tardy. In Slovakia, being late for a business appointment by fifteen minutes or more is not uncommon; and in the Czech Republic, your colleagues will often apologize for being late due to any number of factors (usually traffic or general conditions). Expect open-ended situations, however (meetings can go on longer than expected, and dinners usually go on into the early morning hours). The workday usually starts early (businesses can open at 8 A.M.), but it can end early as well (workers usually go home around 4 or 5 P.M.; office staff no later than 5 to 6 P.M.). Even managers and executives are rarely in their offices after 5 or 6 P.M.

Dress

Err on the formal side, until you know to dress otherwise; this is a good rule both in social situations and at the office. You may be surprised at how informal dress is at work and how formal it is in social situations. At work, men may wear stylish suits (dark is best), white shirts, and interesting and sophisticated ties, but they also may wear slacks and a sport jacket, sometimes with a pullover sweater vest underneath the jacket (how one dresses at work is really a reflection of rank and job title, so observe carefully, and always start out dressing as if you were higher up). The long, cold winters require layers of clothing, and sweaters and vests help keep people warm throughout the workday. There probably is more fashion consciousness among Czech than Slovak men, but both Czech and Slovak women are aware of fashion. Both Czech and Slovak women often dress up for work, especially in the cities; it is fashionable, especially in summer, not to wear stockings.

On the street, informal may mean jeans and sneakers, though that is more common as clothing to wear at the gym, the beach, or while jogging (women do not wear sneakers to work); for a social gathering, informal more often than not means tastefully coordinated clothes, sometimes including a jacket and tie for men: it can also mean clean, pressed jeans and a nice dress shirt, but no sneakers or T-shirts (you may even see jeans at work, depending upon the industry, but this is not typical). "Formal" usually means formal evening wear, which is very dressy by North American standards.

Be sure to check your winter coat whenever you go into a restaurant or a theater or auditorium: it is very bad manners to carry your coat around with you in these public places (with the growing exception of movie theaters, where people roll them up and sit on them, in most cases!).

Seasonal Variations

The extremely cold and damp winter requires layers of clothes and protective boots and rain gear (which you wear over your work clothes, never in place of). Summers, though short, can be warm and sunny. Never remove your jacket or tie unless and until your Czech or Slovak colleague has done so first.

Colors

Most colors are simple, natural, and not ostentatious. Be conservative in the use of color, even with accessories: they need to blend with, not stand out from, the outfit.

Styles

Style is not critical, but a good appearance is always important. Cologne and perfume are not commonly used.

Personal Hygiene

Recognize that hot running water may be expensive, so your daily bath may have to be forsaken from time to time. However, cleanliness and neatness are highly valued.

Dining and Drinking

Mealtimes and Typical Foods

Breakfast (*snidane*) is served from about 6 to 8 A.M., and usually consists of coffee, rolls, butter, and jams. Tea and coffee are the drinks of preference. Coffee is mainly Turkish or Greek coffee, which means it is thick, dark, usually presweetened, and has lots of coffee grounds on the bottom of the cup. Be fore-warned. Tea is often drunk out of glasses. Some Czechs and Slovaks hold a cube of sugar between their front teeth and let the tea wash over it as they drink.

Lunch (*obed*) is still the main meal of the day in both rural and urban set-tings; it is served around noon to 2 P.M. during the week, and around 1 to 2 P.M. on Sundays. It usually consists of several courses, beginning with a soup, then a meat course with vegetables (potatoes, dumplings, and cabbage are every-where), bread (of all kinds), a salad (sometimes with pickled vegetables), and ending with a dessert of preserved fruit or pastries (sometimes both) and tea. Beer is served with lunch. Meat courses may include roast pork (the national dish—*veprova*), veal, or beef, either boiled or roasted. Bread dumplings (*hous-kove knedliky*) are served with almost every meal. Special foods include vege-table soups (try the beet soup, or borscht), potato pancakes, sauerkraut, goose, and sausages. Preserved, marinated, or pickled fish is often served. Fresh vege-tables and fruits are usually very hard to find most of the year, so expect canned or preserved, in most cases. Fresh salads are, therefore, a real treat—when you can get them. Desserts include pastries (turnovers, tortes, and cakes—try the famous *pischinger* torte made of chocolate meringue!), and the famous *pala-cinky* (crêpes with a fruit, nut, or chocolate sauce).

Dinner (*vecere*) is served from 6 P.M. on. It is usually just a light meal of sandwiches, soup, and pastries, especially if lunch was the main meal. If dinner is the main meal, then expect the menu to be similar to lunch (as described ear-lier), followed by Turkish coffee after dessert. Preprandials may include slivo-vitz, a plum brandy, or *becherovka*, an herbal eau-de-vie. Tea, beer, or vodka is served as the dinner drink.

Cafés are not that common (remember, there is a long winter season!), but indoor *kavárna* are as close as one comes. They serve drinks, pastries, light snacks, and the like. A *cukrárna* serves desserts and coffee. *Koliba* are fun old-fashioned taverns, usually family-run, where traditional regional ethnic food is served, in quantity. In warm weather, there are also *zahradní restaurace,* garden restaurants that are akin to outdoor beer and wine gardens. The wine garden (*vinárna*) serves wine and meals in a wine cellar atmosphere; the *pivnice,* or beer hall, does the same with beer. In a *pivnice,* find your own free table, and do not sit at a table occupied by others. Be forewarned: restaurants are rated by the numbers 1, 2, 3, and 4, but they mean exactly the opposite of the U.S. "star" system: a number 4 restaurant is the lowest class. Also, restaurants in the big cities (Prague and Bratislava, mainly) are notoriously in short supply and usu-ally overbooked: reservations are a must for anything beyond a beer hall, a wine garden, or a snack shop.

Typical Drinks and Toasting

Favorite drinks include vodka, *becherovka,* or slivovitz (all are served in shots); beer usually accompanies a meal. The beer in the Czech Republic is world famous: pilsner began in the town of Pilsen (it is generally a weaker alcoholic beer). A liquor will usually come out onto the table, along with assorted snacks, during business meetings, at virtually any time of day, including first thing in the morning. Do not drink all the liquor or beer that is offered to you, for every time you drink a glass, it will be refilled. The more you drink, the more you will be offered: know when to stop. If you don't want to drink anymore, leave your glass more than half full. If you really cannot drink at all, you'll need a very good excuse, like doctor's orders.

The most common toasts are *naz drovie* (Czech) and *naz drovia* (Slovak); both mean "to your health." Never break eye contact while making a toast, from the moment the glass leaves the table until you place it back down (blinking is allowed, however!). There can be many toasts throughout a meal; you will be expected to make one in a small group at some point, especially if you have been toasted personally or are the guest of honor. The liquors can be served room temperature or may be iced ahead of time (the most formal way to serve it); they will rarely be poured over ice.

Table Manners and the Use of Utensils

Do not begin eating until everyone has received food on their plates and the host invites you to start; this is usually done by saying, "*dobrochot.*"

Like all continental Europeans, Czechs and Slovaks do not switch knives and forks, as Americans do. The knife remains in the right hand, and the fork remains in the left. When the meal is finished, place your fork and knife together so that they are parallel on one side of the plate in a vertical position; if you cross your knife and fork over the plate, it means you are just taking a short break and have not finished yet. If you're unsure of which utensil to use, always start from the outside and work your way in, course by course. The fork and spoon above your plate are usually for dessert. Bread is usually served without butter (therefore, there will usually not be a butter knife), and there is usually no bread plate (place your bread on the side of your main plate or on the table throughout the meal).

Your hands are expected to be visible above the table: this means that you do not keep them in your lap; instead, rest your wrists on top of the table. Pass all dishes at the table to your left. If there is gravy or sauce, you can generally use your bread to soak some of it up.

Seating Plans

The most honored position is at the head of the table, with the most important guest seated immediately to the right of the host (women to the right of the host, and men to the right of the hostess). If there is a hosting couple, one will be seated at each side of the table. In keeping with the practice elsewhere on the Continent, men and women are seated next to one another, and couples are often broken up and seated next to people they may not have previously known. This is done to promote conversation, which, after all, is the main pleasure at the table. Men typically rise when women enter the room, and may or may not enter a room first when a woman is present. At the table, the oldest woman or most honored guest is served first. Remember, as is the case throughout the Continent, what the Czechs or Slovaks call the first floor is really the second floor, with the first floor usually referred to as the lobby or ground floor.

Refills and Seconds

At a private dinner party, if you do not want more food, you will really have to insist several times before the hostess will believe you. Take a little extra if you can of something you like. If you do not want more, you must leave a little food on your plate to be believed. You may always have additional beverages; drink enough to cause your cup or glass to be less than half full, and it will generally be refilled. Portions may be somewhat smaller than in the United States, but there are usually more courses, for both lunch and dinner.

At Home, in a Restaurant, or at Work

In informal restaurants, you may be required to share a table: if so, do not force conversation; act as if you are seated at a private table. Waitstaff may be summoned by making eye contact; waving or calling their names is very impolite. The business breakfast is not done here. The business lunch or dinner, depending upon how well developed your relationship is with your Czech or Slovak colleagues, is generally not the time to make business decisions. Take your cue from your Czech or Slovak associates: if they bring up business, then it's okay to discuss it, but wait to take your lead from their conversation. No gum chewing, ever, at a restaurant or on the street. No-smoking sections in restaurants are still a rarity; most people smoke throughout the meal between courses.

When you arrive at a colleague's home for a formal meal, you will be told where to sit, and there you should remain. Do not wander from room to room: much of the house is really off-limits to guests. Once you (and the group) are invited to another room, most probably the dining room, be sure to allow the more senior members of your party to enter the room ahead of you. At the table, do not presume to seat yourself, as the seating arrangement is usually predetermined. Spouses who accompany their partners on business trips are sometimes invited to attend business dinners (but usually not business lunches). Be prepared to arrive on time, and be prepared to stay late: you will insult your hosts if you end the evening too early (this means staying at least past midnight, even during the midweek). As is the case throughout much of the region (and more so the farther east you go), you might have to remove your shoes before entering a Czech or Slovak home (check to see if there are pairs of shoes lined up at the entrance to the home: if there are, it means that you should remove yours as well); be sure your socks are in good shape. You might be offered slippers to wear.

Being a Good Guest or Host

Paying the Bill

Usually the one who does the inviting pays the bill, although the guest is expected to make an effort to pay. Sometimes other circumstances determine the payee (such as rank). Making payment arrangements ahead of time so that no exchange occurs at the table is a very classy way to host. Women, when men are also present at the table, will not really be able to pay the bill at a restaurant:

if you want to, make arrangements ahead of time, and don't wait for the check to arrive at the table. The only time it is considered appropriate for a woman to pay the bill is if she is a businesswoman from abroad.

Transportation

It's a very nice idea, when acting as the host, to inquire ahead of time as to whether your guests will require transportation. If necessary, you should arrange for taxi service at the end of the meal.

You may be picked up from and taken back to your hotel by the host. Both Czechs and Slovaks are extremely warm and gracious hosts.

When to Arrive / Chores to Do

If invited to dinner at a private home, offer to help with the chores, but be prepared to be turned down at first. Ask again, and your offer will probably be accepted.

Do not leave the table unless invited to do so. When it is time to leave, always get up and shake hands with everyone: the group wave is not appreciated. If you are invited into a home, your desires become your hosts' most important concerns, so be sensitive to imposing yourself on their daily routine.

Gift Giving

In general, gift giving is common among business associates. The best gifts are useful office items, such as pen and pencil sets and nicely bound agendas. Mementos of life in the United States are very well received (towels, coffee-table books about the United States, and well-packaged gourmet foodstuffs are always appreciated). Holiday cards are very appropriate, particularly as a thank-you for your colleagues' business during the previous year, and should be mailed in time to be received the week before Christmas.

Gifts are expected for social events, especially as thank-yous for private dinner parties. The best gift in this case is a cut floral bouquet—and you should bring it along with you when you arrive. If a man is meeting a Czech or Slovak businesswoman for the first time, he should bring some flowers with him to give to her (a simple arrangement of wildflowers is best). It should always be wrapped, and you should unwrap it only in the presence of the hostess. Other good gifts would be cakes and pastries, a dessert wine or brandy, or a box of fine chocolates. Do not bring vodka, *becherovka,* or beer: your hosts already have plenty. (When traveling to this region, it may be wise to keep a bottle of Jack Daniels handy, along with a set of shot glasses—at least in the hotel or business conference room—so that you can provide drinks whenever necessary; the Jack Daniels also makes a wonderful gift because it is not easily obtainable and is a good American liquor.) If there are children in the family, it is thoughtful to bring a little something for them, such as a toy or candy, in addition to the gift for the hostess. As with other European cultures, gifts are generally opened at the time they are given and received.

Special Holidays and Celebrations

Major Holidays

Most workers get several weeks of paid vacation; July is a top vacation month. Business slows down from December 15 to January 2. Curiously, as is the case in Greek Orthodox cultures, name days (the birthdays of the saints after whom people were named) are often more important celebrations than birthdays in Slovakia.

January 1	*Novy Rok* (New Year's Day)
January 6	Epiphany (Slovakia only)
March/April	Good Friday/Easter (Slovakia only)
May 1	*Svatek prace* (Labor Day)
May 9	Liberation Day (Czech Republic only)
July 5	Saint Cyril and Saint Methodius Day (Slavic missionaries, generally regarded as the founders of the Slavic peoples)
July 6	Jan Hus Day (Czech Republic only)
August 29	National Day (Slovakia only: commemorating the uprising for independence from Czechoslovakia)
September 1	Slovak Constitution Day (Slovakia only)
September 15	Saint Maria's Day (Slovakia only; she is the patron saint of the country)
October 28	Independence Day (Czech Republic only)
November 1	All Saints' Day
December 25	Christmas (in Slovakia, December 24–26 are national holidays)

Business Culture

Daily Office Protocols

Throughout this region, office doors are mostly closed; you must knock first (this includes bathrooms) before opening doors, and when leaving rooms, close the doors behind you.

Women do not hold equal authority with men in business organizations. It is more common for women to be relegated to lower-level management and administrative support positions. It is rare (though not impossible) to see women at the highest levels of business and government.

The workday can start very early, but end around midafternoon. When making appointments, be sure to schedule them way in advance, and confirm them several times as the date and time approach. Expect some chitchat at the beginning of the meeting about nonbusiness issues, but Czechs usually move fairly quickly to substantive issues; Slovaks usually take more time. Czechs and Slovaks are eager to appear confident and competent to the Westerner, and therefore may make promises that they cannot possibly keep: be sure to confirm and inquire with independent contacts, if you can, until you are convinced of what truly can and cannot be done.

Management Styles

Privacy and individual accomplishment of one's tasks are critical. Workers provide what their bosses expect of them, and the preparation of plans, methods, and reports can be time-consuming and complicated efforts toward perfection. Gathering the information required in order to do what your boss expects from you, or creating support among your colleagues in order to accomplish a particular goal, can take a long time. All of this occurs in a formal and sometimes very rigid hierarchical structure. Titles are very important; the highest ones (e.g., vice president) are usually reserved for very senior, executive-level positions, and should not be used as casually as they are in the United States. Complimenting and rewarding employees publicly is viewed suspiciously.

Boss-Subordinate Relations

Rank most definitely has decision-making privileges. Deviating from established procedures, or not going to established authorities, typically does not get things done faster. You must get close to the decision makers, who are most often at the top; if this is your first meeting, you may not be speaking with the decision makers, but merely gatekeepers who are there to size up you and your organization, and report back to their supervisors.

Conducting a Meeting or Presentation

Meetings can, if decision makers are present, be information-sharing and decision-making forums in which all individuals are expected to contribute. Data, facts, and figures are all important, but not more important than the good feeling your Czech or Slovak associates finally have about you when you leave. Because Czechs and Slovaks have learned to deal with limited resources for so long, presentations need not be fancy, just as long as they are clear and easily understood. Presentations in English are fine, but backup documentation should be available in the local language (be especially careful that the correct language is being translated for the appropriate country).

Negotiation Styles

Both Czechs and Slovaks can display two opposing behaviors: they can play their cards close to the vest at first, not divulging information easily, and then open up as trust develops; or they can almost be effusive in their eagerness to work with you (this is because they indeed are: Western business generally means good new opportunities!). If they are in the former mode, they may appear circumspect in their communication styles, and will indicate their thoughts in indirect, associative ways; they can, however, quickly become pointedly direct as negotiations move forward. If they are in the latter mode, they will most definitely be more eager to speak openly and move the negotiations along. If you are from the West, they will assume that you have the ability to do everything you say and more, and will also assume you already have the knowledge and experience required for the work; they will also try to persuade you of the same about them, which may or may not in fact be true (you need to confirm this independently).

The first meeting is usually just a formality, with the Czechs or the Slovaks sizing up you and your organization: it will be conducted in the office. Put on a warm, dignified demeanor during the meeting. Never be condescending or offer an ultimatum; bargaining is not their style.

Contracts are serious matters to you, and should be clear, concise, and translated into both the local language and English. However, they are more likely to be viewed by Czechs and Slovaks as statements of intent (especially so in Slovakia), and when things change, good business partners are expected to accommodate the changing needs of the other; try to remain flexible with respect to the terms of the agreement when and if you need to be.

Entertaining during the course of the negotiations is important, but limit yourself only to the people you are negotiating with (or else the whole office will show up!).

Written Correspondence

Be clear, precise, and respectful in your business correspondence; don't be too flowery. Last names usually are written in uppercase; dates are given using the day/month/year format (with periods in between, not slashes); and an honorific plus a title is as common as an honorific plus the last name. The time of day is written in military style; weights and measures are metric. Monetary amounts are written so that periods break up the figures into tens, hundreds, and thousands (e.g., K10.000,00 = ten thousand krouna). You can get straight to the point in written business communications.

The Central European Cultures: Hungary

Some Introductory Background on Hungary and the Hungarians

Hungarians have a reputation of being perhaps the most formal of all the central Europeans; they also have a reputation of being fiercely independent and unpredictable. Their temper and sensitivity is as well-known as their paprika; both are hot and spicy. They pride themselves in being skilled horsemen (the people who founded the country literally rode in on horseback from the east about a thousand years ago), sportsmen, outdoors aficionados (indeed, the opportunities that the land provides is one of the main reasons why the country was originally settled, and no doubt one of the main reasons why the inhabitants have fought so ferociously to save it). The Hungarians appear to most other Europeans to be unlike them in many ways, precisely because they are indeed *not* like any of their neighbors.

As Finland is different from all of its Nordic neighbors, Hungary is different from all of its Slavic neighbors. Essentially, it is not a Slavic culture, and its people are not Slavs. The language that is spoken bears no resemblance to any of the Slavic languages spoken by Hungary's neighbors; it is a Finno-Ugric language, more similar to the Finnish and, yes, Korean language, than it is to any other European language. Like their cousins the Finns, the Hungarians moved west out of central Asia; eventually they came to settle in the agriculturally fertile valley formed by the Danube River and the Carpathian Mountains. (Curiously, the Koreans also came from the same central Asian group of peoples, only they are, in part, the descendants of those that moved even earlier east across Mongolia and on into eastern Asia.) It is said by many that even the physiognomy of the Hungarian is more Asian than it is Slavic, and that within the depths of the Hungarian soul there is preserved (no doubt in reaction to the historic struggle to maintain their land and their culture against the incursions of their neighbors) an Eastern heart.

Ethnically, most Hungarians are Magyars, and that is also what they call their language. Because of their central Asian roots, English speakers mistakenly refer to them as descendants of the central Asian Huns—hence the current name, Hungary, or Hungaria, as most Europeans refer to the country. (Attila, the great Hun leader, did coincidentally arrive in the region, but about five hundred years before the Magyars, who arrived around A.D. 900.) It is important never to confuse Gypsies with Hungarians, which sometimes is done, intentionally or not (perhaps due to the fact that the Gypsies also came from Asia into Europe, and have coincidentally influenced Hungarian and central European culture in their own ways). While Hungarians also came from Asia, they were not nomadic. Gypsies are an Aryan people; their correct name is Romany, which is the language that they speak. They were indigenous Europeans who settled in India and Persia and wandered back into Europe as a nomadic itinerant culture. The original Hungarians were Asians who came west and settled there, becoming more European as they planted their roots.

Some Historical Context

Defending their turf was not easy, as Slavs and other Europeans staked out claims to neighboring territories. Even today, it is important not to speak too much about Hungary's neighbors, as there is always talk of Slovaks from the north, Romanians and Russians from the east, Croats from the south, and Germans from the west encroaching on their lands (just as these people believe that Hungarians are coming over their borders and encroaching on their lands). As European monarchies consolidated across Europe from the fifteenth through the eighteenth centuries, Hungary became a powerful player in the region, joining forces with Austria in the eighteenth century to create one of the most powerful empires in Europe: the Austro-Hungarian Empire. The great power and wealth of the Austro-Hungarian Empire came, in part, from its victories over the equally powerful and encroaching Ottoman Empire of Muslim Turks to the east. The Austrian Hapsburgs were the western branch of this aristocratic alliance, and the Hungarians were the representatives of the eastern branch. The Hungarians learned much from their relationship with the Austrians, and are today the very proud cobearers, along with the Austrians, of the great central European aristocratic traditions that date from this time.

Modern history repeated what Hungarians have always experienced—invasion and turmoil; the demise of the empire saw the Hungarians ruled first by Germans and then Russians. In each case, the fierce, independent nature of the Hungarian never fully permitted the foreigners and their customs to take root. Today, Hungary is rapidly and smoothly emerging out from under the Soviet yoke; while the latest generation may not be completely cognizant of Western ways, they are not ignorant of Hungarian ways. This makes for a rich, complicated, formal, aristocratic, and sometimes challenging culture for outsiders.

An Area Briefing

Politics and Government

Today, Hungary is a parliamentary republic, with a prime minister and a surprisingly powerful president (while the prime minister is the head of state, the president controls the armed forces), and a unicameral legislature; it is a representative democracy, with many active political parties.

Schools and Education

The educational system today is similar to those found elsewhere in Europe. There is the equivalent of elementary, middle, and high school levels, with students, after passing a final exam, having the option to go on to a university or technical (vocational) training academies. The literacy rate is extremely high. Education under the Communists was extremely ideological and, despite efforts to promote the trades, the arts, and the sciences, lacking in comparison to Western education. Those who were lucky enough to go on to a university were generally better trained in Western concepts, but the general population was not.

Religion and Demographics

The majority of the population is Roman Catholic, but there is a significant minority composed of Protestants, Greek Orthodox, Jews, and others. Religion plays a powerful role in the lives of some people, but not with others. It is difficult to assess the importance of the Roman Catholic Church in Hungary today, as there are significant generational differences that make for different attitudes toward the church, and all other social institutions.

Men and women still fill very distinct niches in society. Women, while active in the workplace, usually do not hold important positions of authority in the Hungarian business organization. At home, they are still expected to fulfill the role of wife and mother. Again, younger Hungarians in general are split on the roles of men and women. Non-Hungarian businesswomen who visit the country must behave in a strictly professional fashion in order to be taken seriously.

Fundamental Cultural Orientations

1. What's the Best Way for People to Relate to One Another?

OTHER-INDEPENDENT OR OTHER-DEPENDENT? Hungarians are fairly individualistic; while family members and trusted friends form the social nucleus, individuals are responsible for their own affairs, often act independently, and are rewarded for independent action when it succeeds, and accept responsibility for it when it fails. The greater your status, the more you are expected to act independently; but actions must reflect well on others. There is suspicion of out-groups, which means that non-Hungarians, while being eagerly courted for quick business gains, must in the long run prove their reliability and trustworthiness for most deals to be long-lasting and beneficial.

HIERARCHY-ORIENTED OR EGALITY-ORIENTED? There is a strong need for structure and organization, with power and authority coming from above. Working in a Hungarian organization means working within a definite hierarchy, and having access to decision makers means having the ear of the top team. In social life, the rules of etiquette still require men to defer to women in public, and younger people to defer to their elders. Women are treated most chivalrously, at least by the older generation.

RULE-ORIENTED OR RELATIONSHIP-ORIENTED? The strong Western influence of secular rationality and applied method provides well-educated Hungarians with an intellectual tradition of respecting the universality of rules and systems; this is less the case with the average Hungarian on the street, who relies more on relationships with others. Systems and rules have not always worked in the Hungarian's favor, and relationships between individuals and the manipulation of rules and systems for one's benefit still play a powerful role in society. Clever Hungarians either know someone who can get them out of a jam, or help them take advantage of a favorable situation, or are themselves ingenious enough to make a situation work in their favor, despite the existence of rules that are supposed to be for the welfare and benefit of all.

2. What's the Best Way to View Time?

MONOCHRONIC OR POLYCHRONIC? Hungarians are generally monochronic. They may be slightly late from time to time, but it is important for non-Hungarians to be on time. Punctuality is valued and precision in agendas and timetables is important. Nevertheless, while this monochronism results in the imposition of the clock on daily routines, projects and planning can take an interminably long time. This is generally due to the powerful social structures, bureaucracies, and detail-consciousness that is the legacy of both the very formal Austro-Hungarian Empire and the equally powerful Soviet bureaucratic machine. While you may not be kept waiting for a meeting (be on time!), you may be kept waiting a long time for a decision or some action to be taken. Be persistent, stay in touch, keep the process going. You will be told if your Hungarian associate does not want to continue doing business with you; if you have not heard this, press on. And remember, you should arrive on time for a dinner party or any social event; anything more than five or ten minutes late is really unacceptable.

RISK-TAKING OR RISK-AVERSE? As is the case in much of the region, the answer to this one is . . . both, depending on the larger context. Hungarians are extremely eager to do business with Westerners and will promise things they cannot deliver, and propose all sorts of deals they may not be able to follow through on, in the hope of doing business with someone with resources from the outside who is willing to make an investment in Hungary. At the same time, true day-to-day business in Hungary is still encumbered by regulations, and the general mistrust between people who do not know each other can take a long time to overcome. The history of their country has also taught Hungarians to be ready at any moment to change course, be flexible, and expect the new (indeed, embrace it, if necessary), and this makes for a high tolerance for uncertainty.

PAST-ORIENTED OR FUTURE-ORIENTED? The past plays a significant role in Hungary: it is both a weight and a source of identity. It controls and limits possibilities, but it also defines who the Hungarians are. While essentially proud of their long heritage and accomplishments, Hungarians, long ago learning the virtues of adaptability and the lesson that nothing stays the same, look to the future. In fact, this optimism, or at least belief in a future that will be different from the past, distinguishes Hungarians from many of their neighbors—who also find this cultural attribute occasionally frightening.

3. What's the Best Way for Society to Work with the World at Large?

LOW-CONTEXT DIRECT OR HIGH-CONTEXT INDIRECT COMMUNICATORS?
Hungarians will say what is on their minds, and can be direct and clear in their thoughts with others; while the context is always a concern, Hungarians will generally be vibrant in their communication styles, and expect their words to be taken seriously. They will expect the same of others.

PROCESS-ORIENTED OR RESULT-ORIENTED? Subjective experience, belief, and associative judgment play a powerful role in decision making, but with younger and better-educated Hungarians, there is an appreciation for and reliance upon facts, numbers, logic, and rationalism as criteria for decision making and action.

FORMAL OR INFORMAL? Hungary is a very formal culture. While there is apparently a significant generational gap in this area, formality and the proper ways of doing things are still regarded as important. Individuals are not admired for their ability to be casual; they are admired for their ability to know and do the right thing in the right circumstance, as evidenced by their adherence to established protocol and etiquette. Hungarians are extremely sensitive to being treated disrespectfully and informally: American casualness often neglects the formality that the Hungarian requires, thereby inadvertently causing insult when one merely intends to be friendly. Be careful: always remember your "please" and "thank yous," all the time, and honor rank, status, and age.

Greetings and Introductions

Language and Basic Vocabulary

Hungarian is considered by many non-Hungarians as a difficult language to learn. Perhaps for this reason, there are many words used in Hungary today that are borrowed from other languages, especially English. However, English is not the second language of the average Hungarian: in most cases, it is German. Nevertheless, many younger and more business-savvy Hungarians are learning and speaking English. Be sure to evaluate the need for an interpreter prior to your visit.

In Hungarian, most words are strongly accented on the first syllable, and every letter is pronounced as written with the following exceptions:

- *j* is pronounced like the *y* in *yes,* or if followed by a consonant, like *yee* in *year*
- *s* is pronounced like the *sh* in *shoe*
- *cs* is pronounced like the *ch* in *cheese*
- *sz* is pronounced like the *s* in *sneeze*

Here are some basic terms.

Jó napot?	Hello (How do you do?)
jó reggelt	good morning
jó estét	good evening
jó ejszakát	good night

viszonlátásra	good-bye
kérem	please
köszönöm	thank you
köszönöm szepen	thank you very much
nincs mit	you're welcome
szivésen	don't mention it
igen	yes
nem	no
bocsánat	excuse me
Sajnalom	I'm sorry

Honorifics for Men, Women, and Children

The words for Mr., Mrs., and Miss (the honorifics) in Hungarian come after the family surname. Therefore, Mr. Bartok is Bartok-ur (*ur* is Hungarian for "Mr."). Note that since these suffixes follow the last name, they are not capitalized, and that they are sometimes attached to the name with a hyphen. Miss in Hungarian is *kisasszony* (Miss Bartok is Bartok kisasszony). If a married woman is to be shown a great deal of respect, then the honorific *asszony* is placed after her surname (even if the surname is her husband's family name); for example, Mrs. Mary Stewart would be Mary Stewart asszony. More commonly, however, married women merely take their husband's family name and add the suffix *ne* to the end of it, indicating "Mrs."; for example, Ms. Marie Lizst would be more commonly referred to as Marie Lisztne. Sometimes, among close friends and associates, the honorific may be used with the first name. Unless and until your Hungarian colleague specifically invites you to use first names, and despite how he or she might refer to you, you must always use the family name plus the correct Hungarian honorific. Children are absolutely required to be respectful when speaking with adults, and must always use honorifics.

In situations where a title is known, the honorific plus the title is usually used, either with or without the name. For casual contacts (e.g., with waiters, store help, etc.), just use the honorific without the name. It is important to greet people at work or in stores or restaurants with an appropriate greeting (see the list of Hungarian terms, provided earlier) and to say good-bye upon leaving. If you speak any Hungarian at all, it is important to use it; it will absolutely amaze and delight your Hungarian associates, and help build that all-important relationship. Do not use any other Slavic language if you speak it before first asking; use German or English instead.

The What, When, and How of Introducing People

Always wait to be introduced to strangers before taking that responsibility upon yourself. You will always be introduced to women first, then men, in descending order of age. Hungarians absolutely insist on third-party introductions whenever possible, so wait a moment before introducing yourself to a new group; in most cases, you will not have to wait long for someone to take up the cause of introducing you. Women do not necessarily rise when someone enters a room, but men always do, for both women and men. Do not presume to seat yourself at a gathering: if possible, wait to be told where to sit. Shake hands with everyone individually in a group before departing: the American group wave is definitely not appreciated, and will be taken as an insult. Once you greet someone you will encounter later that day in the same circumstances (e.g., at the office), there is no need to greet them again. Kissing is a common greeting with and between all genders (women/women or men/men or women/men) only when there is an established, familiar relationship; it usually involves two kisses (actually "air kisses"), first on the left side, and then the right. This is usually done only between very close friends, family members, and highly regarded business associates.

Physical Greeting Styles

The handshake is common. The Hungarian version is a formal, rigid single shake between two men, but not as robustly between men and women or two women. The handshake should be accompanied by the appropriate greetings (outlined earlier). Never shake hands across another pair of shaking hands (resulting in an *X,* which is considered to be bad luck). Older men may lift the hand of the woman and bring it to their lips for an "air kiss" (the lips never really touch the top of the woman's hand). Men must remove their gloves when shaking hands with women, but women do not need to remove their gloves. Smiling and other nonverbal forms of communication may not always accompany the handshake, especially between people who have not met before. Men should wait until a woman extends her hand before reaching for it, and women may take the lead in extending their hand or not; this may or may not occur, especially among older women. Eye contact during the introduction is very important, and must be maintained as long as the individual is addressing you.

The use of business cards is common; if possible, you should have yours translated into Hungarian on the reverse side. Be sure to put any advanced educational degrees and your full title or position on both sides of your business card. Such evidence of your status is very important: the Hungarians want to know who you are. Also, if your company has been around more than fifty years or so, put its founding date on the card after the company name: this indicates stability, and is impressive. Using an English-language business card, as well as speaking English and obviously being from the United States, is a real advantage in Hungary today, for you will often be given preferential treatment. Don't hide your American identity under a bushel; at the same time, be yourself, and try to display your knowledge and awareness of Hungarian customs and protocols.

Communication Styles

Okay Topics / Not Okay Topics

Okay: anything positive (as long as they bring it up first) about your home country, especially if it is the West, such as your work routines or family life. Your knowledge of and interest in Hungarian culture and history will be appreciated, although it may be dismissed at first (in fact, if you display too much knowledge, it will seem a bit strange); persist in wanting to know more, though, and you will be treated with great admiration and respect. *Not okay:* While you should not inquire about a person's occupation or income in casual conversation, this and many other aspects of your life (though not necessarily your personal life) will probably be asked of you. This is meant to get to know you, and to learn more about the United States: answer in general and in full for the greatest comfort and maximum effect (e.g., "Well, in America, the average salary for my position is ———, but you know, the average mortgage on a house is ———, and it costs about ——— to live a middle-class life"). Most Hungarians will ask a great many questions about the West, and probably offer a few opinions, as well (which may or may not be correct: remember, under the Communists, only a limited amount of very skewed information was passed along about the rest of the world to the population). Hungarians love talking about children, and you should bring pictures of your own family with you to show. Show an interest in Hungarian wines and food, and you will have plenty to talk about. Do not discuss World War II or the Holocaust, or give your opinion about Czechs, Slovaks, or any other ethnic group in the region (e.g., Germans, Hungarians, Russians, Gypsies, etc.). As should be the case everywhere in the world, be a teacher when the topic of your country comes up, and be a student when the topic of their country comes up. Generally, it is best to avoid complimenting people, as it usually strikes Hungarians as insincere and unnecessary.

Tone, Volume, and Speed

Hungarians tend to speak emotionally and directly. This does not mean that they speak loudly, however; in fact, in general conversation, they speak more softly than Westerners. It is especially important for women that they not appear loud or assertive: the traditional role of women as nurturers is still strong (despite the fact that both men and women work), and even in business settings, the woman who is perceived as aggressive loses authority. On the street, all individuals are expected to maintain decorum: loud, disruptive behavior and boisterous laughter are seen as very bad behavior, especially coming from women.

Use of Silence

There may be some, depending upon the circumstances, second language competency, the rank of those present, and the degree to which a personal relationship has been established.

Physical Gestures and Facial Expressions

Until Hungarians get to know you, they may appear to be reserved and formal one time, and emotionally assertive the next. This will even out as trust and familiarity grow. Flicking a few fingers against the neck is an invitation (usually between men) to join the person for a drink. The "okay" sign, made with the forefinger and the thumb, is generally not understood; the "thumbs up" sign is a more accepted practice. Smiling is generally not done casually: in public, with strangers, smiling is seen as odd; even greeting someone with a smile is unusual.

Waving and Counting

The thumb represents the number 1, the index finger the number 2, and so on. You may beckon someone by merely extending the index finger and raising your hand (do not wiggle the index finger). If you need to gesture for a waiter, subtly raise your hand with your index finger slightly outstretched.

Physicality and Physical Space

Hungarians tend to get slightly closer than northern Europeans; however, when two people who do not know each other meet for the first time, they stand just slightly farther apart, lending an air of formality to the greeting. Never speak to or greet anyone with your hands in your pockets: always keep them firmly to your side when standing. If men and women must cross their legs, it should never be ankle over knee (for women, the preferred style is to cross ankle over ankle). Remember, in public, formal is always better than informal: no gum chewing, *ever;* don't slouch; and don't lean against things.

Eye Contact

Eye contact should be very direct most of the time. It is important not to interpret this behavior as a way of intentionally trying to make you uncomfortable; rather, it is a sign of respect. If you look away, your behavior will say to your Hungarian colleague that you are either disinterested or rude. Either way, maintain eye contact when it is made with you, especially when making a toast. If two strangers' eyes meet and linger, it implies (romantic) interest. Women should be especially careful about making casual eye contact with men.

Emotive Orientation

Hungarians are generally emotive. Their interpersonal communication style has been described as unpredictable: it is a combination of German restraint and Latin expressiveness. It is like paprika. It slowly heats up under the surface until it erupts.

Protocol in Public

Walking Styles and Waiting in Lines

Lines are usually respected. There may be certain situations, however, where lines are ignored, such as at public bus stops. This will not generally present a challenge, however.

People stay to the right when walking on the street. Men accompanied by women, as well as the younger of two people, walk on the curbside; if more than two people are walking together, the "odd" gender is flanked by the pair from the opposite gender. When a close relationship has been established, individuals often walk arm in arm on the street, no matter their genders.

Behavior in Public Places: Airports, Terminals, and the Market

Customer service as a concept simply did not exist in eastern and central Europe during the Communist era, and even today it is less and less evident the farther east across the region you go. As employees of the state, with guaranteed jobs, store clerks simply had no motivation to be nice, let alone to serve, during the Communist days. Today, as a concept, it is catching on, but slowly. Store hours are typically not built around customer convenience (many stores are closed on weekends and most evenings—except Thursdays, usually). Personally thanking store owners, waiters, chefs, and hotel managers for their services is not the custom. As in much of Europe, if you touch the produce in food markets, you buy it; in goods stores, it may be difficult for you to return a product unless there is a flaw in it. Bargaining does not occur, in general. In most stores, you pay for the item you want first; the cashier will then give you a receipt; you then pick up the item with your receipt and leave. When you pay for something, put your money on the counter, and not in the hand of the clerk: in return the clerk will put any change down on the counter, not directly into your hand. Smoking in public places is still a common occurrence, although the Hungarians are slowly becoming aware of the need to control it. Never applaud in a church (you might go to one for a concert; it is a common form of entertainment) unless others do first. Unescorted women can expect men to approach them whenever they are in public, but rarely in restaurants.

Bus / Metro / Taxi / Car

Driving is on the right, but people pass very quickly on the left. Do not drive if you've been drinking: DWI laws are strictly enforced.

The metros shut down after midnight. Your best bet for catching a cab is at designated taxi stands. Hotels are good places, but often charge more for the same ride: a hotel surcharge is added to the meter fare, in some cases. In Budapest especially, use only taxis that have the company name and phone number on the side of the door; do not use a nontitled taxi, even if it has a taxi sign on the roof, unless you are willing to pay much more for the ride than you should. The safest thing to do is always telephone for a cab from a taxi company.

On public transportation, younger people should give up their seats to older people, and men should give up their seats to women, especially if they are pregnant or have babies or small children with them.

Tipping

A 10 percent tip is usually sufficient for restaurants and taxis; more is considered nouveau and gauche. Porters and hotel help get about one hundred forints per service rendered, theater and bathroom attendants usually the same. Restaurants may not have the 10 percent tip already included on the bill, so be sure to ask. Even if it is included, it is still appropriate to leave some odd change, bringing the total tip to about 15 percent. Include the tip when you pay the bill at the cashier: do not leave either the bill payment or the tip on the table (the bill is usually made out and left on the table when you order). You might have Gypsy musicians come and play at your table: you will be expected to tip them something (approximately two hundred forints): give it to the leader of the group as you or they leave.

Answer your telephone call by saying "*allo*." Hungarians sometimes end their phone call with a word that sounds like "pussy" in English: it is Hungarian for "kisses to you."

Punctuality

Be punctual for all business and social activities, but be prepared for things to run over their appointed end times from time to time. The workday usually starts early (businesses can open at 8 A.M.), but it can end early as well (workers usually go home around 4 or 5 P.M., office staff no later than 5 or 6 P.M.). Even managers and executives are rarely in their offices after 5 or 6 P.M.

Spa Etiquette

Hungarians have some of the world's finest natural thermal springs, especially in Budapest. The etiquette at these spas is simple: men and women usually have separate bathing areas or share a bathing area at different times: check with the spa before you go. It is rare that men and women will share a bathing area together. Some same-sex bathing areas may be reserved for nude soaking, but if you wear a bathing suit, it is okay. Bring a suit, towel, and soap along with you; you will be given a locker to change at, and you will be expected to wash off before entering the hot bath. There is no swimming or cleansing in the baths: they are thermal and therapeutic and meant for soaking only. Some have ancillary services, such as massages and hot oil rubs afterward, which are usually very inexpensive and may come as part of the therapy sessions. Stay as long as you are comfortable: there is no problem leaving a spa after even just a few minutes if you feel dizzy, uncomfortable, or too hot.

Dress

As with most things in Hungary, err on the formal side, until you know to dress otherwise; this is a good rule both in social situations and at the office. You may be surprised at how informal dress is at work and how formal it is in social situations. At work, men may wear stylish suits (dark is best), white shirts, and interesting and sophisticated ties, but they also may wear slacks and a sport jacket, sometimes with a pullover sweater vest underneath the jacket (how one dresses at work is really a reflection of rank and job title, so observe carefully, and always start out dressing as if you were higher up). The long, cold winters require layers of clothing, and sweaters and vests help keep people warm throughout the workday. There probably is more fashion-consciousness among younger Hungarians than among older people. Hungarian women often dress up for work, especially in the cities; it is fashionable, especially in summer, not to wear stockings.

On the street, informal may mean jeans and sneakers, though that is more common as clothing to wear at the gym, the beach, or while jogging (women do not wear sneakers to work). For a social gathering, informal more often than not means tastefully coordinated clothes, sometimes including a jacket and tie for men: it can also mean clean, pressed jeans and a nice dress shirt, but no sneakers or T-shirts (you may even see jeans at work, depending upon the industry, but this is not typical). "Formal" usually means formal evening wear, which is very dressy by North American standards. Be sure to check your winter coat whenever you go into a restaurant or theater or auditorium: it is very bad manners to carry your coat around with you in these public places (with the growing exception of movie theaters, where people roll them up and sit on them, in most cases!).

Seasonal Variations

The extremely cold and damp winter requires layers of clothes and protective boots and rain gear (which you wear over your workclothes, never in place of). Summers, though short, can be warm and sunny. Never remove your jacket or tie unless and until your Hungarian colleague has done so first.

Colors

Most colors are simple, natural, and not ostentatious. Be conservative in use of color, even with accessories: they need to blend with, not stand out from, the outfit.

Styles

Style is not as critical, but a good appearance is always important. Cologne and perfume are not as commonly used.

Personal Hygiene

Recognize that hot running water may be expensive in some places, so the daily bath may be forsaken from time to time. However, cleanliness and neatness are highly valued.

Dining and Drinking

Mealtimes and Typical Foods

Breakfast (*reggeli*) is served from about 7 to 9 A.M., and usually consists of coffee, rolls, butter, and jams. If there are eggs at breakfast, they are mainly softboiled. Tea and coffee are the drinks of preference. For breakfast, coffee is often Turkish coffee or espresso served with hot milk in it. Otherwise, the coffee is mainly Turkish or Greek coffee, which means it is thick, dark, usually presweetened, and has lots of coffee grounds on the bottom of the cup. Be forewarned. As an alternative, ask for a "large" coffee with milk, for a "regular" (American-sized and prepared) cup of coffee. Tea is often drunk out of glasses. Some Hungarians hold a cube of sugar between their front teeth and let the tea wash over it as they drink.

Lunch (*ebéd*) is still the main meal of the day in both rural and urban settings; it is served around noon to 2 P.M. during the week, and around 1 to 2 P.M. on Sundays. It usually consists of several courses, beginning with soup—either hot (in winter, made with beans and meat) or cold (in summer, made with fruit, like cherries), then a meat course (Wiener schnitzel or pork stew), with vegetables (potatoes, dumplings, and cabbage are everywhere), bread (of all kinds), a salad (sometimes with pickled vegetables), and ending with a dessert of preserved fruit or pastries (sometimes both) and espresso. Beer or wine is served with lunch. Meat courses may include roast pork stew (*pörkölt*), boiled or roasted veal or beef, stuffed cabbage (*töltött káposzta*), and *fátányéros* (a mixed grill of sausages, meats, and peppers, which is served with potato salad and pickles). Special foods include vegetable soups (try the cold sour cherry soup) and potato pancakes (*palacsinta,* which can be filled with fruits for dessert or meats or vegetables to accompany the main course). Preserved, marinated, or pickled fish is often served. Fresh vegetables and fruits are usually very hard to find most of the year, so expect canned or preserved, in most cases. Fresh salads are, therefore, a real treat—when you can get them. Desserts include *somola* (a kind of custard), fruit *palacsintas, retes* (strudels), and the wonderful *dobos torta* (a many-layered cake with chocolate filling). Most foods are heavy and rich, and spices—not necessarily hot ones—like paprika are very common.

Dinner (*vacsora*) is served from 7 P.M. on. In the rural areas, this is a light meal of sandwiches, soup, and pastries, especially if lunch was the main meal. If dinner is the main meal (usually in the cities), then expect to be served dishes similar to those on the lunch menu as described earlier, followed by Turkish coffee after dessert. Preprandial drinks typically include schnapps (a kind of brandy; the Hungarian schnapps, *unicom,* is made from a variety of herbs), or a Puszta cocktail (named after the open "cowboy" plains region of Hungary), made with nonsweet apricot schnapps, sweet Tokay wine, and an herbal schnapps. Tea, wine, or beer is served with dinner.

People usually meet at a café around 5 or 6 P.M. for a snack and to catch up on local events. Hungary has a wonderful variety of cafés from which to choose. An *eszpresszo* is the best place for cakes and coffees, any time of the day or night. If you are invited to a café for cakes and coffee, by all means, go. It is the standard way Hungarians socialize and catch up with the news and each other.

Besides cafés, there are a number of other fine places to eat. The standard elaborate restaurant, called an *étterem,* is usually quite large and can serve many diners at once. A *söröső* is a bar where snacks are served, along with beers and brandies. An *étel-bar* serves snacks and drinks; while a *borozó* is a bar solely for alcoholic drinks (women should not go to a *borozó* alone). A *cukrárszda* also serves desserts and coffee. (Curiously, on many menus, desserts are listed first, perhaps because Hungarians are so fond of sweets!) The *czarda* is where you will get authentic regional Hungarian cuisine and music, most of the time. Finally, the family-run establishment serving Hungarian ethnic food in quantity and at a good bargain is called either the *vendéglő* or *maszek.* Be fore-warned: restaurants are rated by the numbers 1, 2, 3, and 4, but they mean exactly the opposite of the U.S. "star" system: a number 4 restaurant is the lowest class.

Typical Drinks and Toasting

One of Hungary's favorite drinks is schnapps, served in shots; beer or wine usually accompanies a meal. Schnapps will usually come out onto the table, along with assorted snacks, during business meetings at virtually any time of day, including first thing in the morning. It may be served room temperature or ice cold. Do not drink all the liquor or beer that is offered to you, for every time you drink a glass, it will be refilled. The more you drink, the more you will be offered: know when to stop. If you don't want to drink anymore, leave your glass more than half full. If you really cannot drink, you'll need a very good excuse, like doctor's orders.

The wine in Hungary is quite good (especially Tokay, which ranges from slightly to very sweet). The most common toast is *kedves egeszsegere* (to your health). Never break eye contact while making a toast, from the moment the glass leaves the table until you place it back down (blinking is allowed, however!). There can be many toasts throughout a meal; you will be expected to make one in a small group at some point, especially if you have been toasted personally or are the guest of honor.

Table Manners and the Use of Utensils

Do not begin eating until the host invites you to and until everyone has received food on their plates, and the host invites you to start; this is usually done by saying, *"jo atvadyat."*

Like all continental Europeans, Hungarians do not switch knives and forks, as Americans do. The knife remains in the right hand, and the fork remains in the left. When the meal is finished, place your fork and knife together so that they are parallel in the middle of the plate. If you're unsure of which utensil to use, always start from the outside and work your way in, course by course. The fork and spoon above your plate are usually for dessert. Bread is usually served without butter (therefore, there will usually not be a butter knife), and there is usually no bread plate (place your bread on the side of your main plate or on the table throughout the meal). Never use your knife when eating fish unless it is absolutely necessary.

Your hands are expected to be visible above the table: this means that you do not keep them in your lap; instead, rest your wrists on top of the table. Pass all dishes at the table to your left. If there is gravy or sauce, you cannot use your bread to soak some of it up, except in family-style restaurants or less formal dinner parties at home. Before you start to eat any new course, wait for the hostess to begin, or for her to give the signal that it is okay to begin.

Seating Plans

The most honored position is at the head of the table, with the most important guest seated immediately to the right of the host (women to the right of the host, and men to the right of the hostess). If there is a hosting couple, one will be seated at each side of the table. In keeping with the practice elsewhere on the Continent, men and women are seated next to one another, and couples are often broken up and seated next to people they may not have previously known. This is done to promote conversation, which, after all, is one of the main pleasures at the table. Men typically must rise when women enter the room, and may or may not enter a room first when a woman is present. At the table, the oldest woman or most honored guest is served first. Remember, as is the case throughout the Continent, what the Hungarians call the first floor is really the second floor, with the first floor usually referred to as the lobby or ground floor.

Refills and Seconds

At a private dinner party, if you do not want more food, you will really have to insist several times before the hostess will believe you. Take a little extra if you can of something you like. If you do not want more, you must leave a little food on your plate to be believed. You may always have additional beverages; drink enough to cause your cup or glass to be less than half full, and it will generally be refilled. Portions can be hearty, and there are generally more courses than in the United States, for both lunch and dinner. Hungarians really do enjoy their wonderfully unique food.

At Home, in a Restaurant, or at Work

In informal restaurants, you may be required to share a table: if so, do not force conversation; act as if you are seated at a private table. Waitstaff may be summoned by making eye contact and saying "*kérem*"; waving or calling their names is very impolite. The business breakfast is not done here. The business lunch or dinner, depending upon how well developed your relationship is with your Hungarian colleagues, is generally not the time to make business decisions. Take your cue from your Hungarian associates: if they bring up business, then it's okay to discuss it, but wait to take your lead from their conversation. No gum chewing, ever, at a restaurant or on the street. No-smoking sections in restaurants are still a rarity; most people smoke throughout the meal between courses.

When you arrive at a Hungarian colleague's home for a formal meal, you will be told where to sit, and there you should remain. Do not wander from room to room: much of the house is really off-limits to guests. Once you (and the group) are invited to another room, most probably the dining room, be sure to allow the more senior members of your party to enter the room ahead of you. At the table, do not presume to seat yourself, as the seating arrangement is usually predetermined. Spouses who accompany their partners on business trips are usually not invited to attend meals. Be prepared to arrive on time, and be prepared to stay late: you will insult your hosts if you end the evening too early (this means staying at least past midnight, even during the midweek). As is the case throughout much of the region (and more so the farther east you go), you might have to remove your shoes before entering a home (check to see if there are pairs of shoes lined up at the entrance to the home: if there are, it means that you should remove yours as well); be sure your socks are in good shape. You might be offered slippers to wear.

Being a Good Guest or Host

Paying the Bill

Usually the one who does the inviting pays the bill, although the guest is expected to make an effort to pay. Sometimes other circumstances determine the payee (such as rank). Making payment arrangements ahead of time so that no exchange occurs at the table is a very classy way to host. Women, when men are at the table, will not really be able to pay the bill at a restaurant: if you want to, make arrangements ahead of time, and don't wait for the check to arrive at the table. The only time it is considered appropriate for a woman to pay the bill is if she is a businesswoman from abroad.

Transportation

It's a very nice idea, when acting as the host, to inquire ahead of time as to whether your guests will require transportation. If necessary, you should arrange for taxi service at the end of the meal.

You may be picked up from and taken back to your hotel by the host. Hungarians are extremely warm and gracious hosts.

When to Arrive / Chores to Do

If invited to dinner at a private home, offer to help with the chores, but be prepared to be turned down at first. Ask again, and your offer will probably be accepted.

Do not leave the table unless invited to do so. When it is time to leave, always get up and shake hands with everyone: the group wave is not appreciated. If you are invited into a home, your desires become your hosts' most important concerns, so be sensitive to imposing yourself on their daily routines.

Gift Giving

In general, gift giving is common among business associates. The best gifts are useful office items, such as pen and pencil sets and nicely bound agendas. Mementos of life in the United States are very well received (towels, coffee-table books about the United States, and well-packaged gourmet foodstuffs are always appreciated). Holiday cards are very appropriate, particularly as a thank-you for your colleagues' business during the previous year, and should be mailed in time to be received the week before Christmas. If a man is meeting a Hungarian businesswoman for the first time, he should bring some flowers with him to give to her (a simple arrangement of wildflowers is best).

Gifts are expected for social events, especially as thank-yous for private dinner parties. The best gift in this case is a cut floral bouquet—and you should bring it along with you when you arrive. It should always be wrapped, and you should unwrap it only in the presence of the hostess. Other good gifts would be cakes and pastries, a dessert wine or brandy, or a box of fine chocolates. Do not bring schnapps, wine, or beer: your hosts already have plenty. (When traveling to this region, it may be wise to keep a bottle of Jack Daniels handy, along with a set of shot glasses—at least in the hotel or business conference room—so that you can provide drinks whenever necessary; the Jack Daniels also makes a wonderful gift because it is not easily obtainable and is a good American liquor.) If there are children in the family, it is thoughtful to bring a little something for them, such as a toy or candy, in addition to the gift for the hostess. As with other European cultures, gifts are generally opened at the time they are given and received.

If you are bringing gifts to your business associates, be sure you bring enough for everyone in the office: it is more important to do that than to bring one gift for your key contact (and make sure that the gifts you give out in the office are the same for everyone—even your key contact).

Special Holidays and Celebrations

Major Holidays

Most Hungarian workers get several weeks of paid vacation; July is a top vacation month. Business slows down from December 15 to January 2. Curiously, as is the case in Orthodox cultures, name days (the birthdays of the saints, after whom people were named) are often more important celebrations than birthdays for some in Hungary.

January 1	*Új Év* (New Year's Day)
March 15	*Nemzeti Ünnep* (Revolution Day 1848)
March/April	*Húsvét Hétfo/Pünkösd Hétfo* (Good Friday/Easter)
April 4	Liberation Day
May 1	*A munka ünnepe* (Labor Day)
August 20	Saint Stephen's Day
October 23	*Nemzeti Ünnep* (Republic Day)
December 25	*Karácsony* (Christmas)
December 26	*Karácsony* (Boxing Day)

Business Culture

Daily Office Protocols

In Hungary, office doors are mostly closed; you must knock first (this includes bathrooms) before opening doors, and when leaving rooms, close the doors behind you.

Women do not hold equal authority with men in business organizations. It is more common for women to be relegated to lower-level management and administrative support positions. It is rare (though not impossible) to see women at the highest levels of business and government.

The workday can start very early and end around midafternoon, or it can go on into early evening. When making appointments, be sure to schedule them way in advance, and confirm them several times as the date and time approach. Expect some chitchat at the beginning of the meeting about nonbusiness issues; this may take some time. Hungarians are eager to appear confident and competent to the Westerner, and therefore may make promises that they cannot possibly keep: be sure to confirm and inquire with independent contacts when possible, until you are convinced of what truly can and cannot be done.

Management Styles

Privacy and individual accomplishment of one's tasks are critical. Workers provide what their bosses expect of them, and the preparation of plans, methods, and reports can be time-consuming and complicated efforts toward perfection. Gathering the information required in order to do what your boss expects from you, or creating consensus among your colleagues in order to accomplish a particular goal, can take a long time. All of this occurs in a formal and sometimes very rigid hierarchical structure. Titles are very important; the highest ones (e.g., vice president) are usually reserved for very senior, executive-level positions, and should not be used as casually as they are in the United States. Complimenting and rewarding employees publicly is viewed suspiciously.

Boss-Subordinate Relations

Rank most definitely has its privileges, especially when it comes to decision making. Deviating from established hierarchy typically does not get things done any faster. You must get close to the decision makers, who are most often at the top; if this is your first meeting, you may not be speaking with decision makers, but merely gatekeepers who are there to size up you and your organization, and report back to their supervisors. It is best to expect the utmost formality at introductory meetings.

Conducting a Meeting or Presentation

Meetings can be information-sharing and decision-making forums in which all individuals are expected to contribute. Data, facts, and figures are all important, but not more important than the good feeling your Hungarian associates finally have about you when you leave. Your presentations need to be simple and clearly understood, but they also should be formal and attractively designed. Presentations in English are fine, but backup documentation should be available in Hungarian for maximum effect.

Negotiation Styles

Hungarians can display two opposing behaviors: they can play their cards close to the vest at first, not divulging information easily, and then open up as trust develops; or they can almost be effusive and apparently very open in their eagerness to work with you (this is because they indeed are: Western business generally means good new opportunities!). If they are in the former mode, they may appear circumspect in their communication styles, and will indicate their thoughts in indirect, associative ways; they can, however, quickly become point-edly direct as negotiations move forward. If they are in the latter mode, they will most definitely be more eager to speak openly and move the negotiations along. If you are from the West, they will assume that you have the ability to do everything you say and more, and will also assume you already have the knowl-edge and experience required for the work; they will also try to persuade you of the same about them, which may or may not in fact be true (you need to con-firm this independently).

The first meeting is usually just a formality, with the Hungarians sizing up you and your organization: it will most likely be conducted in a hotel room or a hotel conference room (follow-up meetings are held in offices). Put on a warm, dignified demeanor during the meeting. Never be condescending or offer an ultimatum; bargaining is not their style.

Contracts are serious matters to you, and should be clear, concise, and translated into both Hungarian and English. However, they are more likely to be viewed by Hungarians as statements of intent, and when things change, good business partners are expected to accommodate the changing needs of the other; try to remain flexible with respect to the terms of the agreement.

Entertaining during the course of the negotiations is important, but limit yourself only to the people you are negotiating with (or else the whole office will show up!). When the deal is finally signed, throw a small party at a restau-rant or at your hotel.

Written Correspondence

Be clear, precise, and respectful in your business correspondence. Flowery and formal is fine. Last names usually are written in uppercase; dates are given using the year/month/day format (with periods in between, not slashes); and an honorific plus a title is as common as an honorific plus the last name. The time of day is written in military style; weights and measures are metric. Monetary amounts are written so that periods break up the figures into tens, hundreds, and thousands (e.g., F10.000,00 = ten thousand forints). You can get straight to the point in written business communications.

The Eastern European Cultures: Romania and Moldova

ROMANIA

Some Introductory Background on Romania and the Romanians

Romania (spelled this way today to correctly associate the country with its origins) is one of the poorest nations in Europe, and one of the most paradoxical. It is a landlocked Mediterranean culture (at least in most of the people's minds); the people seem to be Latin by nature, although Slavic by blood, which means a strong combination of the two, resulting in, among other things, a culture in many ways not unlike Italy, but with most of the people counting themselves as Eastern Orthodox (the Romanian Orthodox Church). Even the language is Latin based, but Slavic influenced, remarkably resembling the Genoese dialect of Italian. (Some say if you speak Italian, you can get by in Romanian, but the Slavic influence is strong, and speaking Italian, in fact, will not create intelligibility between yourself and your Romanian colleagues.) Bucharest, the capital, appears physically at least, to attempt a Slavic imitation of Paris, with its starlike circles and radiating boulevards (there are few honking taxis, however). The poverty of the nation, though, can be quite disconcerting for the Westerner who views it through this Latin veneer; it is never far away from you, and a challenge for both the visitor and the Romanians you will meet.

Some Historical Context

Originally settled by Dacians (the country was originally known as Dacia), the region was conquered by the Romans and has remained under Roman influence ever since; when the Roman Empire fell and the Holy Roman Empire replaced it, with Slavs moving into the region, Romania remained heavily oriented toward the West, while being significantly influenced by its Slavic captors. It would be incorrect to think of Romania as a non-Slavic culture: it is a Slavic culture with Slavic people, but one that has been superimposed onto a deeper Latin base. It is this mixture that makes Romania so very unique. Even among its own people, Romania has struggled to define itself as more or less Roman or Slavic. This problem with Romanian self-identity has been mirrored in the difficulties it has had with its neighbors, such as Moldova (for more on that country, see the end of this chapter). Earlier in this century, Romania fought with Russia against the Turks; switched sides three times during World War I, ultimately joining the victorious Allies; and participated in the German invasion of Russia during World War II, only to be swallowed up itself by the Nazi war machine. Most recently, the overthrow of the Communists and the totalitarian regime of Nicolae Ceauşescu (which devastated the economy of the country) have provided Romanians with a future as a democracy; nevertheless, the country must surmount the Communist legacy of shattered social relationships, a ruined ecology, and an unstable free market economy. The country in many ways is starting from scratch again, with the exception of the long cultural heritage that is uniquely its own.

An Area Briefing

Politics and Government

Today, Romania is a parliamentary republic, with a prime minister, a president, and a bicameral legislature. There are currently many active political parties, including the Communist Party, which, despite its horrific record in the past, still retains an allegiance among some people—no doubt due in part to its ability to provide these same people with some form of jobs, education, health care, and housing. The nation is struggling to remain on the path of democracy and an open market economic system.

Schools and Education

The educational system today is similar to those found elsewhere in Europe. There is the equivalent of elementary, middle, and high school levels, with students, after passing a final exam, having the option to go on to a university or technical (vocational) training academies. The literacy rate is about 80 percent. Education under the Communists was extremely ideological, and lacking in comparison to Western education, despite efforts to promote the trades, the arts, and the sciences. Those lucky enough to go on to a university were generally better trained in Western concepts, but the general population was not. Schools in the last few years of the Ceauşescu regime were notoriously bad institutions, not operating much above the level of day care.

Religion and Demographics

The majority of the population is Romanian Eastern Orthodox. This is a rather conservative form of Eastern Orthodox; for example, Western women who might go into a Romanian Orthodox church need to have their shoulders, arms, and knees covered. There is no significant minority of other faiths. Religion plays a powerful role in the lives of some people, but not with others. It is difficult to assess the importance of the church in Romania today, as there are significant generational differences that make for different attitudes toward the church, and all other social institutions.

Men and women still fill very distinct niches in society. Women, while active in the workplace, usually do not hold important positions of authority in business. At home, they are still expected to fulfill the role of wife and mother. Again, younger Romanians in general are split on the roles of men and women. Non-Romanian businesswomen must behave in a strictly professional fashion in order to be taken seriously.

The country's population is dramatically split between rural and urban, with the residents of Bucharest and Timisoara, for example, living rather sophisticated lives, and residents of the country regions living very conservative and tradition-bound existences, similar to those of several centuries ago.

Fundamental Cultural Orientations

1. What's the Best Way for People to Relate to One Another?

OTHER-INDEPENDENT OR OTHER-DEPENDENT? Romanians are fairly group oriented, but individuals are valued for their ability to be shrewd, clever, or wise enough to achieve things on their own. Family members and trusted friends form the social nucleus, while individuals are responsible for their own affairs, often act independently, and are rewarded for independent action when it succeeds, though they attempt to deflect responsibility either to the anonymous group or others when it fails. The greater your status, the more you are expected to act independently; but actions must reflect well on others. There is great intolerance of out-groups, which means that non-Romanians (in fact, nonmembers of any subgroup—for example, Russian-Romanians, or Moldovans), while being eagerly courted for quick business, must, in the long run, prove their reliability and trustworthiness for most deals to be long-lasting and beneficial.

HIERARCHY-ORIENTED OR EGALITY-ORIENTED? There is a strong need for structure and organization, with power and authority coming from above. Working in a Romanian organization means working within a definite hierarchy, and having access to decision makers means having the ear of the top team. In social life, the rules of etiquette still require men to defer to women in public, and younger people to defer to their elders.

RULE-ORIENTED OR RELATIONSHIP-ORIENTED? Most Romanians are focused mainly on their relationships and their own subjective interpretation of things, in order to see them through life. Rules, processes, and systems have never been particularly useful to the average Romanian, or were out of his or her power to manipulate; in fact, in most cases, such systems usually made problems in the daily life of the average Romanian. And like the Roman Catholic Church, the Orthodox Church seemed immutable in its authority, providing an important sense of stability and certainty in an otherwise dangerous and difficult world. The strong Western influence of secular rationality and applied method today provides some well-educated Romanians with additional tools of judgment, but it never weighs more heavily than the connections one has, and the subjective interpretation of the world of the individual Romanian on the street. Clever Romanians either know someone who can get them out of a jam, or help them take advantage of a favorable situation, or are themselves ingenious enough to make a situation work in their favor, despite the existence of rules that are supposed to be for the welfare and benefit of all.

2. What's the Best Way to View Time?

MONOCHRONIC OR POLYCHRONIC? Romanians, like their Latin cousins, are generally polychronic, but with strong, selective monochronic tendencies. It is important to be on time, but be prepared to wait. Punctuality is valued, but is rarely achieved. Projects and planning can take an interminably long time, or they can move very quickly, depending on whether your Romanian colleagues are really interested, see the deal in their best interest, or have to work within or have the resources to move around the interminable hierarchy and government bureaucracies. While you may not be kept waiting for a meeting (be very on time!), you may be kept waiting a long time for a decision or some action to be taken. Be persistent, stay in touch, keep the process going. You will be told if your Romanian associate does not want to continue doing business with you; if you have not heard this, press on. And remember, you can arrive about fifteen minutes late for a dinner party or any social event; be on time at theaters and concerts, though.

RISK-TAKING OR RISK-AVERSE? As is the case in much of the region, the answer to this one is . . . both. Romanians are extremely eager to do business with Westerners and will promise things they cannot deliver, and propose all sorts of deals they may not be able to follow through on, in the hope of doing business with someone with resources from the outside who is willing to make an investment in Romania. At the same time, true day-to-day business in Romania is still encumbered by regulations, and the general mistrust between people who do not know each other can take a long time to overcome. The history of their country has also taught Romanians to be ready at any moment to change course, be flexible, and expect the new (indeed, embrace it, if necessary), and this makes for a high tolerance for uncertainty. This is especially the case among the younger generation.

PAST-ORIENTED OR FUTURE-ORIENTED? The past plays a significant role in Romania, but most Romanians are eager to forget it: it is a weight they would like to lose. It controls and limits possibilities, and prevents solutions. While essentially proud of their long heritage and accomplishments, Romanians long ago learned the virtues of adaptability and the lesson that nothing stays the same, look to the future. In fact, this optimism, or at least belief in a future that can be different from the past, drives some of your Romanian associates to an overblown admiration for and desire to emulate the West.

3. What's the Best Way for Society to Work with the World at Large?

LOW-CONTEXT DIRECT OR HIGH-CONTEXT INDIRECT COMMUNICATORS? Romanians have had to learn to be circumspect with what they say, how they say it, and with whom. This is consistent with both Latin and Slavic notions of communications. Because of this high-context orientation, humor is usually context bound and therefore does not translate well: avoid it unless you are absolutely sure the context-bound nuances will be understood. Their style of communication, therefore, is soft and low-keyed as well. They will expect the same of others.

PROCESS-ORIENTED OR RESULT-ORIENTED? Subjective experience, belief, and associative judgment play powerful roles in decision making, but with younger and better-educated Romanians, there is an appreciation for and reliance upon facts, numbers, logic, and rationalism as criteria for decision making and action.

FORMAL OR INFORMAL? Romania is a very formal culture for outsiders, but once you are an insider, you will find it to be informal. While there is apparently a significant generational gap in this area, formality and the proper ways of doing things are still regarded as important. Individuals who are not known are not admired for their ability to be casual; they are admired for their ability to know and do the right thing in the right circumstance, as evidenced by their adherence to established protocol and etiquette.

Greetings and Introductions

Language and Basic Vocabulary

Romanian is a Latin language, akin to Italian and French, in many ways. In fact, the second language spoken by Romanians, if any, is usually French (many well-educated Romanians got their education abroad, more often than not in France). English is little understood except for "pop-English," which is known basically only to the young. In regions close to Austria, German is spoken, and in areas closer to Hungary, Hungarian may also be spoken. Russian may be spoken in the eastern regions (but many people avoid it, even if they know it). While the language may appear to resemble Italian and French, it has been heavily influenced by Slavic, so the pronunciation of most of the letters (like *t* being pronounced as *ts*) are like the Slavic pronunciations highlighted in previous chapters.

Here are some basic Romanian terms and their English meanings:

bună dimineata	good morning
bună ziua	good afternoon
naope buna	good night
la revedere	good-bye
Ce mai faceti?	How are you?
mulţumesc	fine, thanks
Bine, si dumneavoastra?	And you?
da	yes
nu	no
vă rog	please
mulţumesc	thank you
Poftim?	I beg your pardon? (Excuse me?)

Honorifics for Men, Women, and Children

Domnule (Mr.), *doamna* (Mrs.), and *domnisoara* (Miss) are not commonly used; instead, the last (family) surname is used, plus a title (e.g., Engineer Cipriandu). Sometimes, among close friends and associates, the honorific may be used with the first name. Unless and until your Romanian colleague specifically invites you to use first names, and despite how he or she might refer to you, you must always use the family name plus the correct Romanian honorific. Children are absolutely required to be respectful when speaking with adults, and must always use honorifics.

In situations where a title is known, the honorific plus the title is usually used, either with or without the name. For casual contacts (e.g., with waiters, store help, etc.), just use the honorific without the name. It is important to meet people at work or in stores or restaurants with an appropriate greeting for the time of day (see the list of Romanian terms provided earlier) and to say good-bye upon leaving, although you should not expect to be acknowledged all the time. If you speak any Romanian at all, it is important to use it; it will absolutely delight your Romanian associates, and help build that all-important relationship, although you will also need to explain, being a foreigner, how it is that you know the language (they may be suspicious of your occupation). Do not use Italian or any Slavic language if you speak it before first asking; use French or try English instead (the latter, although it is not well known, will mark you as a Westerner, and that will give you preferential treatment).

The What, When, and How of Introducing People

Always wait to be introduced to strangers before taking that responsibility upon yourself. You will always be introduced to women first, then men, in descending order of age. Always greet wives first in any group, if they are introduced to you as such. Romanians absolutely insist on third-party introductions whenever possible, so wait a moment before introducing yourself to a new group; in most cases, you will not have to wait long for someone to take up the cause of introducing you. Women do not necessarily rise when someone enters a room, but men always do, for both women and men. Do not presume to seat yourself at a gathering: if possible, wait to be told where to sit. Shake hands with everyone individually in a group before departing: the American group wave is definitely not appreciated, and will be taken as an insult. As opposed to common practice in other parts of Europe, in Romania, every time you meet someone, you shake their hand, even if you have already done so earlier in the day. Kissing is a common greeting with and between all genders (women/women or men/men or women/men) only when there is an established, familiar relationship; it usually involves two kisses: (actually "air kisses"), first on the left side, and then the right. This is usually done only between very close friends, family members, and highly regarded business associates, but it can be done with great vitality.

Physical Greeting Styles

The handshake is common. The Romanian version is a series of formal, solid shakes between two men; it is not as robust between men and women or two women. The handshake should be accompanied by the appropriate greetings (outlined earlier). Never shake hands across another pair of shaking hands (resulting in an *X*), which is considered bad luck. Older men may lift the hand of the woman and bring it to their lips for an "air kiss" (the lips never really touch the top of the woman's hand). Men must remove their gloves when shaking hands with women, but women do not need to remove their gloves. Smiling and other nonverbal forms of communication may not always accompany the handshake, especially between people who have not met before. Men should wait until a woman extends her hand before reaching for it, and women may take the lead in extending their hand or not; this may or may not occur, especially among older women. Eye contact during the introduction is very important, and must be maintained as long as the individual is addressing you.

The use of business cards is very common (take plenty with you); if possible, you should have yours translated into Romanian on the reverse side. Be sure to put any advanced educational degrees and your full title or position on both sides of your business card. Such evidence of your status is very important: the Romanians want to know who you are. Also, if your company has been around more than fifty years or so, put its founding date on the card after the company name: this indicates stability, and is impressive. Using an English-language business card, as well as speaking English and obviously being from the United States, is a real advantage in Romania today, for you will often be given preferential treatment. Don't hide your American identity under a bushel; at the same time, be yourself, and try to display your knowledge and awareness of Romanian customs and protocols.

Communication Styles

Okay Topics / Not Okay Topics

Okay: anything positive (as long as they bring it up first) about your home country, especially if it is in the West, such as work routines or family life. Your knowledge of and interest in Romanian culture and history will be appreciated, although it may be dismissed at first (in fact, if you display too much knowledge, it will seem a bit strange); persist in wanting to know more, though, and you will be treated with great admiration and respect. It is perfectly all right to inquire about a person's family or career, but be careful to do so only if you know that the individual can answer proudly. Many personal questions will probably be asked of you. This is meant to get to know you, and to learn more about America: answer in general and in full for the greatest comfort and maximum effect (e.g., "Well, in the United States, the average salary for my position is ———, but you know, the average mortgage on a house is ———, and it costs about ——— to live a middle-class life"). Most Romanians will ask a great many questions about the West, and probably offer a few opinions, as well (which may or may not be correct: remember, under the Communists, only a limited amount of very skewed information was passed along about the rest of the world to the population). Show an interest in Romanian wines and food, and you will have plenty to talk about. *Not okay:* Do not discuss World War II, the Holocaust, the news about orphans and AIDS, the Moldavan problem, or other ethnic groups in the region (e.g., Germans, Hungarians, Russians, Gypsies, etc.). As should be the case everywhere in the world, be a teacher when the topic of your country comes up, and be a student when the topic of their country comes up. Compliments are generally well received, and not an embarrassment for Romanians.

Tone, Volume, and Speed

Romanians tend to speak softly, calmly, and in a low tone, especially at first with strangers. It is especially important for women that they not appear loud or assertive: the traditional attitude toward the role of women is strongly held (despite the fact that both men and women work), and even in business settings, the woman who is perceived as aggressive loses authority. On the street, all individuals are expected to maintain decorum: loud, disruptive behavior and boisterous laughter are seen as very bad behavior, especially coming from women.

Use of Silence

There may be some, depending upon the circumstances, although the pacing of speech is similar to Latin cultures, and silence is usually not a concern.

Physical Gestures and Facial Expressions

Romanians are physically emotive (this is probably a result of the Latin and Slavic influences), and this is especially true once they are comfortable with you. Flicking a few fingers against the neck is an invitation (usually between men) to join the person for a drink. The "okay" sign, made with the forefinger and the thumb, is generally not a good sign to use; the "thumbs up" sign is more acceptable. The *figa* sign (putting the thumb between the first and second finger in a fist) is considered obscene. Many of the Romanians' gestures and facial expressions are similar to the Italians', including the "horn" sign, the upwardly moving elbow with a fist, the drooping eyelid, and the tapped elbow (see the chapter on Italy). Smiling is generally not done casually: in public, with strangers, smiling is seen as odd.

Waving and Counting

The thumb represents the number 1, the index finger the number 2, and so on. You may get someone's attention by merely extending the index finger and raising your hand (do not wiggle the index finger). If you need to gesture for a waiter, subtly raise your hand with your index finger slightly outstretched. If you want to beckon someone to come over, raise your hand palm down and make a back-and-forth scratching motion with your four fingers.

Physicality and Physical Space

Romanians tend to get slightly closer than northern Europeans; however, when two people who do not know each other meet for the first time, they stand just slightly farther apart, lending an air of formality to the greeting. Never speak or greet anyone with your hands in your pockets: always keep them firmly to your side when standing. If men and women must cross their legs, it must never be ankle over knee (for women, the preferred style is to cross ankle over ankle).

Remember, in public, formal is always better than informal: no gum chewing, *ever;* don't slouch; and don't lean against things.

Eye Contact

Eye contact will be very direct most of the time. It is important not to interpret this behavior as a way of intentionally trying to make you uncomfortable; rather, it is a sign of respect. If you look away, your behavior will say to your Hungarian colleague that you are either disinterested or rude. Either way, maintain eye contact when it is made with you, especially when making a toast. If two strangers' eyes meet and linger, it implies (romantic) interest. Women should be especially careful about making casual eye contact with men.

Emotive Orientation

Romanians are generally very emotive; their interpersonal communication style is similar to Latin expressiveness.

Protocol in Public

Walking Styles and Waiting in Lines

Lines are usually respected. This will not generally present a challenge, however. People stay to the right when walking on the street. Men accompanied by women, as well as the younger of two people, walk on the curbside; if more than two people are walking together, the "odd" gender is flanked by the pair from the opposite gender. When a close relationship has been established, individuals often walk arm in arm on the street, no matter their genders.

Behavior in Public Places: Airports, Terminals, and the Market

Customer service as a concept simply did not exist in eastern and central Europe during the Communist era, and even today it is less and less evident the farther east across the region you go. As employees of the state, with guaranteed jobs, store clerks simply had no motivation to be nice, let alone to serve, during the Communist days. Today, as a concept, it is catching on, but very slowly. Store hours are typically not built around customer convenience (many stores are closed on weekends and most evenings—except Thursdays, usually). Personally thanking store owners, waiters, chefs, and hotel managers for their services seems strange to them as it was not the custom under the Communists. As in much of Europe, if you touch the produce in food markets, you buy it; in goods stores, it may be difficult for you to return a product unless there is a flaw in it. Bargaining does not occur, in general. If you are identified as being from the West, you may be given a different price than the locals get: to avoid this, go with a Romanian colleague, if you can, or politely ask to see a record in the store indicating the price of the item. In most stores, you pay for the item you want first; the cashier will then give you a receipt; and then you pick up the item with your receipt and leave. When you pay for something, put your money on the counter, not in the hand of the clerk; in return, the clerk will put any change down on the counter, not directly into your hand.

Smoking in public places is still a common occurrence, although the Romanians are slowly becoming aware of the need to control it. Never applaud in a church (you might go to one for a concert; it is a common form of entertainment) unless others do it first. Unescorted women can expect men to approach them whenever they are in public, but rarely in restaurants.

Bus / Metro / Taxi / Car

Driving is on the right, but people pass very quickly on the left. The saving grace is that there simply are not that many vehicles on the road; still, those that are on the road act as if they own it. Do not drive if you've been drinking: DWI laws are strictly enforced.

The metros shut down after midnight. Your best bet for catching a cab is at designated taxi stands (hotels are good places, but often charge more for the same ride: a hotel surcharge is added to the meter fare, in some cases).

On public transportation, younger people should give up their seats to older people, and men should give up their seats to women, especially if they are pregnant or have babies or small children with them.

Tipping

A 12 percent tip is usually sufficient for restaurants and taxis; more is considered nouveau and gauche. Porters and hotel help get about thirty to forty lei per service rendered, theater and bathroom attendants usually the same. Restaurants usually have the 12 percent tip already included on the bill, but it's okay to ask to make sure. Even if it is included, it is still appropriate to leave some odd change, bringing the total to about 15 percent. Include the tip when you pay the bill at the cashier: do not leave either the bill payment or the tip on the table (the bill is usually made out and left on the table when you order).

On the telephone, answer your call by saying *allo*. Telephone service may be sporadic, and your ability to remain patient with the overworked telephone operators, who probably do not speak English, will be rewarded by being eventually connected. Have someone nearby who can place the call for you in Romanian.

Punctuality

Be punctual for all business and social activities, but expect to wait, and anticipate all sorts of possible delays. The workday usually starts early (businesses can open at 8 A.M.), but it can end early as well (workers usually go home around 4 or 5 P.M., office staff no later than 5 or 6 P.M.). Even managers and executives are rarely in their offices after 6 P.M. There is usually half a day of work on Saturday morning, as well.

Dress

Err on the formal side, until you know to dress otherwise; this is a good rule both in social situations and at the office. You may be surprised at how informal dress is at work and how formal it is in social situations; sometimes jeans and a nice, neat dress shirt, with or without a sport jacket, will do just fine at work or for a social occasion at home. Romanians are very casual at home (but that does not mean sneakers or T-shirts are okay at the dinner table). At work, men may wear stylish suits (dark is best), white shirts, and dark ties, but they also may wear slacks and a sport jacket, sometimes with a pullover sweater vest underneath the jacket (how one dresses at work is really a reflection of rank and job title, so observe carefully, and always start out dressing as if you were higher up). Romanian men wear hats . . . always; remember to remove your hat as soon as you come indoors, for it is considered very rude to keep it on. The long, cold winters require layers of clothing, and sweaters and vests help keep people warm throughout the workday. Romanian women often dress up for work, especially in the cities; it is fashionable, especially in summer, not to wear stockings.

On the street, informal may mean jeans and sneakers, though that is more common as clothing to wear at the gym, the beach, or while jogging (women do not wear sneakers to work). For a social gathering, informal more often than not means jeans and a dress shirt or a blouse. You do not need to dress formally for a dinner at someone's home, and no formal dress code exists for the theater and concerts (a jacket and tie will do just as well as a tuxedo; this is the dressiest you'll ever need to get). Be sure to check your winter coat whenever you go into a restaurant or theater or auditorium: it is very bad manners to carry your coat around with you in these public places (with the growing exception of movie theaters, where people roll them up and sit on them, in most cases!).

Seasonal Variations

The extremely cold and damp winter requires layers of clothes and protective boots and rain gear. Summers, though short, can be warm and sunny. Never remove your jacket or tie unless and until your Romanian colleague has done so first. In the office, Romanian men sometimes wear short-sleeved shirts in the summer without jackets (take your cue from them).

Colors

Most colors are simple, natural, and not ostentatious. Be conservative in the use of color, even with accessories: they need to blend with, not stand out from, the outfit.

Styles

Style is not critical, but a good appearance is always important. Cologne and perfume are not commonly used.

Personal Hygiene

Recognize that hot running water may be expensive, so your daily bath may have to be forsaken from time to time depending on where in Romania you are. However, cleanliness and neatness are highly valued.

Dining and Drinking

Mealtimes and Typical Foods

Breakfast (*micul dejun*) is served from about 7 to 9 A.M., and usually consists of rolls, butter, and jams. Coffee is enjoyed in the morning, but is not as common as tea. The coffee is mainly of the Turkish or Greek variety, which means it is thick, dark, usually presweetened, and has lots of coffee grounds on the bottom of the cup. Be forewarned. Tea sometimes is drunk out of glasses. Some Romanians hold a cube of sugar between their front teeth and let the tea wash over it as they drink.

Lunch (*dejun*) is still the main meal of the day in both rural and urban settings; it is served between noon and 2 P.M. during the week, and between 1 and 2 P.M. on Sundays. It usually consists of several courses, beginning with soup—either hot (in winter, made with beans or meat) or cold (in summer, made with fruit, like cherries), then a fish or stew course with vegetables (potatoes, dumplings, and stuffed cabbage), bread, sometimes pickled vegetables, and ending with a dessert of preserved fruit. Wine or water is usually served with lunch. At dinner, or a more formal lunch, appetizers of feta cheese, meatballs, or pickled vegetables might be served. Special Romanian meat dishes include *mititei,* a grilled, skinless sausage (very spicy!), and *sarmala* (stuffed cabbage). *Mămăgliă* (a side dish similar to cornmeal) is served with everything. Typical desserts include baklavas and *palacsinkas* (pancakes sweetened with preserves).

Dinner (*masa de seara*) is served from 7 P.M. on. In the rural areas, this is usually a light meal of noodles, cheese, salad (if available), and yogurt, especially if lunch was the main meal. If dinner is the main meal (usually in the cities), then expect to be served dishes similar to those on the lunch menu as described above, followed by Turkish coffee after dessert, and brandy. There may or may not be predinner drinks at a formal dinner (if there are, they will probably be a local *schnapps* or a white Romanian wine).

Typical Drinks and Toasting

The most common toast is *no roc* (good luck), or *salut* (to your health). The drink will be brandy or a Romanian wine or beer (the brandy will be drunk in shots at once). The wine or beer will accompany the meal.

Schnapps will usually come out onto the table, along with assorted snacks, during business meetings at virtually any time of day, including first thing in the morning. It can be served at room temperature. Do not drink all the liquor or beer that is offered to you, for every time you drink a glass, it will be refilled. The more you drink, the more you will be offered: know when to stop. If you don't want to drink anymore, leave your glass more than half full. If you really cannot drink, you'll need a very good excuse, like doctor's orders.

The wine in Romania varies in quality: you may or may not luck out.

Never break eye contact while making a toast, from the moment the glass leaves the table until you place it back down (blinking is allowed, however!). There can be much toasting throughout the meal, and when it is possible, glasses should be clinked. You will be expected to make a toast in a small group at some point during the meal, especially if you have been toasted personally or are the guest of honor.

Table Manners and the Use of Utensils

Do not begin eating until the host invites you to.

Like all continental Europeans, Romanians do not switch knives and forks, as Americans do. The knife remains in the right hand, and the fork remains in the left. When the meal is finished, place your fork and knife parallel together vertically in the middle of the plate. If you're unsure of which utensil to use, always start from the outside and work your way in, course by course. The fork and spoon above your plate are usually for dessert. Bread is generally served without butter (therefore, there will usually not be a butter knife), and there is often no bread plate (place your bread on the side of your main plate or on the table throughout the meal). Salad, when available, is served with the main course on the same plate.

Your hands are expected to be visible above the table: this means that you do not keep them in your lap; instead, rest your wrists on top of the table. Neither do you keep your napkin in your lap: it is always kept on the table. Pass all dishes at the table to your left. If there is gravy or sauce, you can generally use your bread to soak some of it up.

Seating Plans

The most honored position is at the head of the table, with the second most important guest seated at the opposite end of the table. If there is a host and hostess, one usually sits immediately to the right of the honored guest, who is seated at the opposite end of the table from the other host (women to the right of the host, and men to the right of the hostess). In keeping with practice elsewhere on the Continent, men and women are seated next to one another, and couples are often broken up and seated next to people they may not have previously known. This is done to promote conversation, which, after all, is the main pleasure at the table. Men typically must rise when women enter the room, and may or may not enter a room first when a woman is present. At meals, the oldest woman or most honored guest is served first. Remember, as is the case throughout the Continent, what the Romanians call the first floor is really the second floor, with the first floor usually referred to as the lobby or ground floor.

Refills and Seconds

At a private dinner party, if you do not want more food, you will really have to insist several times before the hostess will believe you. Take a little extra if you can of something you like. If you do not want more, you must leave a little food on your plate to be believed. You may always have additional beverages; drink enough to cause your cup or glass to be less than half full, and it will generally be refilled. Portions are generally smaller than in the United States, but there are usually more courses, for both lunch and dinner. It is a great honor (and sometimes at considerable cost to the host) to be invited to dinner at a Romanian home, so be sure to sample and eat most of everything: it was made for you.

At Home, in a Restaurant, or at Work

In informal restaurants, you may be required to share a table: if so, do not force conversation; act as if you are seated at a private table. Waitstaff may be summoned by making eye contact and saying "*va rog*"; waving or calling their names is very impolite. The business breakfast is not done. The business lunch or dinner, depending upon how well developed your relationship is with your Romanian colleagues, is generally not the time to make business decisions. Take your cue from your Romanian associates: if they bring up business, then it's okay to discuss it, but wait to take your lead from their conversation. No gum chewing, ever, at a restaurant or on the street. No-smoking sections in restaurants are still a rarity: most people smoke throughout the meal between courses.

When you arrive at a Romanian colleague's home for a formal meal, you will be told where to sit, and there you should remain. Do not wander from room to room: much of the house is really off-limits to guests. Once you (and the group) are invited to another room, most probably the dining room, be sure to allow the more senior members of your party to enter the room ahead of you. At the table, do not presume to seat yourself, as the seating arrangement is predetermined. (This is important in Romania, for while the meal may be informal, the etiquette surrounding it generally is not, since Romanians pride themselves on being Eastern Latins.) Spouses who accompany their partners on business trips are usually not invited to attend meals. Make sure you arrive on time, but be prepared to leave no later than 11 P.M. As is the case throughout much of the region (and more so the farther east you go), you might have to remove your shoes before entering a home (check to see if there are pairs of shoes lined up at the entrance to the home: if there are, it means that you should remove yours as well); be sure your socks are in good shape. You might be offered slippers to wear.

Being a Good Guest or Host

Paying the Bill

Usually the one who does the inviting pays the bill, although the guest is expected to make an effort to pay. Sometimes other circumstances determine the payee (such as rank). Making payment arrangements ahead of time so that no exchange occurs at the table is a very classy way to host. Women, when men are present at the table, will not really be able to pay the bill at a restaurant: if you want to, make arrangements ahead of time, and don't wait for the check to arrive at the table. The only time it is considered appropriate for a woman to pay the bill is if she is a businesswoman from abroad.

Transportation

It's a very nice idea, when acting as the host, to inquire ahead of time as to whether your guests will require transportation. If necessary, you should arrange for taxi service at the end of the meal.

You may be picked up from and taken back to your hotel by the host.

When to Arrive / Chores to Do

When you arrive for a dinner in a private home, be sure to thank the hostess for the invitation as soon as you get there and present her with your gift. Offer to help with the chores, but be prepared to be turned down at first. Ask again, and your offer will probably be accepted.

Do not leave the table unless invited to do so. When it is time to leave, always get up and shake hands with everyone: the group wave is not appreciated. If you are invited into a home, your desires become your hosts' most important concerns, so be sensitive to imposing yourself on their daily routines.

Gift Giving

In general, gift giving is common among business colleagues. The best gifts are useful items such as pen and pencil sets and nicely bound agendas. Mementos of life in the United States are very well received (towels, coffee-table books about the United States, and well-packaged gourmet foodstuffs are always appreciated). Given the climate of scarcity in Romania, almost anything that you can bring along from the West will be appreciated: toys, perfumes, cosmetics, kitchenware, cigarettes, cigars, office supplies, personal items, jeans, CDs, and so on. The gifts should not be ostentatious, but they must be useful. (Remember to keep some smaller items handy throughout the day, such as a ballpoint pen or a pack of cigarettes; they can go far in getting someone's assistance, or to keep things flowing smoothly.) Holiday cards are not usually exchanged.

Gifts are expected for social events, especially as thank-yous for private dinner parties. The best gift in this case is a cut floral bouquet—and you should bring it along with you when you arrive. It should always be wrapped, and you should unwrap it only in the presence of the hostess. Other good gifts would be wine, cakes and pastries, a dessert wine or brandy, a box of fine chocolates, or any of the items mentioned earlier. If there are children in the family, it is thoughtful to bring a little something for them, such as a toy or candy, in addition to the gift for the hostess. As with other European cultures, gifts are generally opened at the time they are given and received.

If you are bringing gifts to your business associates, be sure you bring enough for everyone in the office. Most Romanians need and appreciate something from the West (but your key contact deserves something special, in addition, from simple kitchen utensils to clothes to office supplies).

Special Holidays and Celebrations

Major Holidays

Most Romanian workers take their vacations during July, if they can. Business slows down from December 15 to January 2. This being an Eastern Orthodox culture, name days (the birthdays of the saints after whom people were named) are often more important celebrations than birthdays.

January 1–2   New Year's (the celebration takes place over two days)
March/April   Good Friday/Easter
May 1–2   Labor Day (the celebration takes place over two days)
December 1   Romanian National Day
December 25   Christmas

Business Culture

Daily Office Protocols

In Romania, office doors are mostly closed; you must knock first (this includes bathrooms) before opening doors, and when leaving rooms, close the doors behind you.

Women do not hold equal authority with men in business organizations. It is more common for women to be relegated to lower-level management and administrative support positions. It is rare (though not impossible) to see women at the highest levels of business and government.

The workday can start very early and end around midafternoon, or it continues on into early evening. When making appointments, be sure to schedule them way in advance, and confirm them several times as the date and time approach. Expect some chitchat at the beginning of the meeting about nonbusiness issues; this may take some time. Romanians are eager to appear confident and competent to the Westerner, and therefore may make promises that they cannot possibly keep: be sure to confirm and inquire from independent contacts, if available, until you are convinced of what truly can and cannot be done. Do not travel to Romania without many of the little gift items mentioned earlier to help smooth your way daily.

Management Styles

Privacy and individual accomplishment of one's tasks are critical. Workers provide what their bosses expect of them, and the preparation of plans, methods, and reports can be time-consuming and complicated efforts toward perfection. Gathering the information required in order to do what your boss expects from you, or creating consensus among your colleagues in order to accomplish a particular goal, can take a long time. All of this occurs in a formal and sometimes very rigid hierarchical structure. Titles are very important; the highest ones (e.g., vice president) are usually reserved for very senior, executive-level positions, and should not be used as casually as they are in the United States. Complimenting and rewarding employees publicly is viewed suspiciously.

Boss-Subordinate Relations

Rank most definitely has its decision-making privileges. Deviating from established hierarchy typically does not get things done any faster. You must get close to the decision makers, who are most often at the top; if this is your first meeting, you may not be speaking with decision makers, but merely gatekeepers who are there to size up you and your organization, and report back to their supervisors. It is best to expect the utmost formality at introductory meetings. If a man is meeting a Romanian businesswoman for the first time, he should bring some flowers with him to give to her (a simple arrangement of wildflowers is best).

Conducting a Meeting or Presentation

Meetings can be information-sharing and decision-making forums in which all individuals are expected to contribute. Data, facts, and figures are all important, but not more important than the good feeling your Romanian associates finally have about you when you leave. Your presentations need to be simple and clearly understood, but they also should be formal and attractively packaged. Presentations in English are fine, but backup documentation should be available in Romanian for maximum effect.

Negotiation Styles

Romanians can display two opposing behaviors: they can play their cards close to the vest at first, not divulging information easily, and open up as trust develops; or they can almost be effusive in their eagerness to work with you (this is because they indeed are: Western business generally means good new opportunities!). If they are in the former mode, they may appear circumspect in their communication styles, and will indicate their thoughts in indirect, associative ways; they can, however, quickly become pointedly direct as negotiations move forward. If they are in the latter mode, they will most definitely be more eager to speak openly and move the negotiations along. If you are from the West, they will assume that you have the ability to do everything you say and more, and will also assume you already have the knowledge and experience required for the work; they will also try to persuade you of the same about them, which may or may not in fact be true (you need to confirm this independently).

The first meeting is usually just a formality, with the Romanians sizing up you and your organization: it will most likely be conducted in a hotel room or a hotel conference room (follow-up meetings are held in offices). Put on a warm, dignified demeanor during the meeting. Never be condescending or offer an ultimatum; bargaining is not their style.

Contracts are serious matters to you; they should be clear, concise, and translated into both Romanian and English. However, they are more likely to be viewed by Romanians as statements of intent, and when things change, good business partners are expected to accommodate the changing needs of the other; try to remain flexible with respect to the terms of the agreement.

Entertaining during the course of the negotiations is important, but limit yourself only to the people you are negotiating with (or else the whole office will show up!). When the deal is finally signed, throw a small party at a restaurant or at your hotel.

Written Correspondence

Be clear, precise, and respectful in your business correspondence. Flowery and formal is fine. Last names usually are written in uppercase; dates are given using the day/month/year format (with periods in between, not slashes); time is written in military style; weights and measures are metric; and an honorific plus the title is as common as an honorific plus the last name. Monetary amounts are written so that periods break up the figures into tens, hundreds, and thousands, and a comma separates the lei from the bani (i.e., L10.000,00 = ten thousand lei). You can get straight to the point in written business communications.

MOLDOVA

Moldova, formerly known as Moldavia (or the Moldavian Republic) when it was a part of the Soviet Union, is now an independent nation. We are referring to it here because the culture is very similar to Romania's: in fact, until the recent Soviet experience, most Moldovans considered themselves to be Romanians, and that is at the heart of the difficulty in Moldova.

Historically, most of what now constitutes the country was culturally, if not politically, Romanian, yet, because of the Russian occupation in the eastern part of Moldova, there has always been a severe division between Moldavian Romanians and their Russian cousins east of the Dnieper River. Severe and sometimes catastrophic conflicts erupted between these groups. As the Russians claimed the region, especially during the recent Communist period, this ancient rivalry was resurrected. In fact, during the Soviet era, the Russians attempted to perpetrate the myth that there was a separate and unique Moldavian culture and country when, in fact, Romanian Moldovans associated themselves with Romania, and Russian Moldovans associated themselves with Russia. Most recently, when the Soviet empire collapsed, Romanian Moldovans initially acted to reincorporate Moldova back into Romania, but Russian-affiliated Moldovans threatened to establish their own republic east of the Dnieper, essentially dividing the nation. The decision was made not to run the risk of another devastating conflict, and the compromise solution was an independent state, neither Russian nor Romanian.

Practically speaking, however, Romanian and Russian Moldovans live in two different worlds, and the first thing to do in Moldova is establish whether you are working with Romanians or Russians. Then behave accordingly. The other major consideration in Moldova is that it is a very poor country with a notoriously vicious history. Unfortunately, those historic passions could easily erupt again. It is an unstable environment, in which powerful subjective opinions, ancient clannish relationships, and alliances determine decisions and actions.

The Eastern European Cultures: The Southern Slavs

SLOVENIA, CROATIA, SERBIA, BOSNIA, MONTENEGRO, MACEDONIA, ALBANIA, AND BULGARIA

The countries of the former Yugoslavia and the Balkans share many customs in common, while experiencing enormous cultural conflicts arising from different languages and religious roots. The countries in this region are Slovenia, Croatia, Serbia, Bosnia, Montenegro, Macedonia, Albania, and Bulgaria. For this reason, we will outline the general southern Slavic traditions and customs that can be found throughout all the countries in the region, and then discuss some country-specific variations.

Some Introductory Background on the Southern Slavic Region and the Southern Slavs

The area that comprised the former Yugoslavia and the Balkans lies on one of the world's great cultural fault lines; great cultural plates collide here, from east to west, west to east, and south to north. There is an ancient collision of languages and religions, dating back in some cases thousands of years. The peoples of this region have been in close and mostly hostile proximity with each other for so long that they know each other well, and have—at least superficially—adopted many cultural behaviors of the other. A generalized set of customs and attitudes serves the foreigner well, since the same attitude and behavior, in many cases, will suffice in all countries. Yet underneath this surface familiarity are profound divisions that revolve primarily around religion and politics, differences that have fueled vicious hatred and misunderstanding for centuries; the world outlooks may be the same, but politics and religion in this region often turn familiarity into violence. We will both look at the pan-Southern Slavic behaviors that are appropriate for the foreigner in day-to-day life in most all the countries and provide some cautionary notes regarding the fundamental differences that lie just below the surface like land mines, ready to trap the unsuspecting and well-meaning foreigner in a quagmire of misunderstanding and bad feelings.

Some Historical Context

A Serbian colleague of mine once became quite passionate about the way his homeland was misunderstood in the West. "If it weren't for the sacrifice of my ancestors," he said, "there would not have been a Renaissance in Italy, the Enlightenment would never have come to western Europe, and America probably would never have come to be." This may sound preposterous to our minds; however, in Serbia, and throughout the region, there is a strong and endlessly remembered history. My colleague was referring to the fact that Serbs had been in the front line of the defense against the Islamic Turks invading Europe. It is his contention that Serbia held the gates closed as late as the 1700s, and by so doing, allowed the West to flourish. Croats, of course, say the same, but add that they had the greater burden, having had to pick up the pieces when the Serbs failed, and yet having to struggle against them as well. The debates about the role of these nations in Europe's larger experience are endless, of course, as is the debate around who sacrificed more and whose fault it was that this should have been the case.

Let's outline the cultural situation: all countries in the region speak a form of Serbo-Croatian (with the exception of Bulgaria and Albania, which have their own languages) that is, for the most part, mutually intelligible by all (despite the refusal of one group to use the "other's" language). However, in Slovenia and Croatia, Serbo-Croatian is written in the Latin script, because the culture is Western and Roman Catholic, the result of these peoples having aligned themselves historically with Rome. Serbia, along with Serbian parts of Macedonia, have their own version of Serbo-Croatian, which is written in the Cyrillic script of the East, for these cultures are Eastern and Orthodox (the Serbian Orthodox Church and the Macedonian Orthodox Church), having historically aligned themselves with Constantinople. (It should be no surprise that the major Croatian ally in Europe is Germany, and the main Serbian ally is Russia.) Complicating this situation is the fact that while both Croats and Serbs (and most everybody else in the region at one time or another) battled the invading Islamic Turks several times, there was a considerable period of history where Islam made important inroads into the region. The Kosovo province of southern Serbia, for example, is predominantly Muslim Albanian, yet is claimed by Serbia precisely because it is the site where Serbian nationalism (against invading Muslims) was born centuries ago. Albania and Bosnia are predominantly Muslim countries (in both countries, the natives converted to Islam; in Albania, the indigenous people were descendants of the ancient Mediterranean Illyrian peoples, and there was no subsequent forced reconversion; but in Bosnia, there was forced reconversion, in part because Bosnians were seen by their neighbors as more like them, and those Muslims who did not reconvert back to Christianity in Bosnia are particularly disliked by both the Croats and the Serbs).

Macedonia is perhaps the most culturally complex country in the region. Bordered as it is on all sides by competing neighbors, it is amazing that Macedonia has retained its sovereignty. Southern Macedonia is the northern part of a larger region called "Macedonia," whose southern part is in northern Greece: the Greeks, therefore, are very wary of their northern neighbors in Macedonia calling their country the same name as a part of Greece, and believe that this is just the first step in Macedonia's efforts to retake northern Greece (something that was done many times in the past, beginning with Alexander the Great). Greeks refer to the country of Macedonia, therefore, as the Republic of Skopje (referring to the capital city of the country). Many Bulgarians in the eastern section of Macedonia want to unite with Bulgaria, making other Macedonians nervous that the eastern part of their country will be annexed by that neighboring country. Serbian Macedonians in the north see that part of the country as Serbian territory, and other Macedonians are equally nervous that this will cause Serbia, currently in a fairly aggressive mode, to claim northern Macedonia. Finally, western Macedonians are mainly Albanian (Muslim), and are hounded to leave Macedonia by many other Macedonians fearful of an Albanian effort to incorporate Kosovo and western Macedonia. The name *Macedonia* itself is the source of the word *macaroni,* originally meaning a mishmash, or a mixed combination.

Finally, there is Bulgaria, an Orthodox country unique to the region in that it has historically been insulated from some of the fiercest internecine battles because the Bulgarians, not being Latin-influenced like their northern Romanian neighbors, and definitively not being Greek, like their southern neighbors, were isolated between mountains, far from the concerns of their surroundings. They are a steadfast, agricultural people, with a low-key, commonsense, hardworking, no-nonsense approach to the world.

An Area Briefing

Politics and Government

Unless you haven't read a newspaper in the last ten or twenty years, it should come as no surprise that the southern Slavic region is politically and economically in a state ranging somewhere between difficult and disastrous. Slovenia (capital, Ljubljana), being the most northern and the most heavily influenced by the West (Italy and Austria mainly), is perhaps the most stable, and approaching the most democratic, with an elected legislature and a prime minister, and a Western-influenced, educated business population. Slovenes speak English and German as second languages and have the reputation of being sophisticated businesspeople. Croatia (capital, Zagreb) and Serbia (capital, Belgrade) are in an on-again, off-again state of conflict, with governments that are only nominally representative; Bosnia (capital, Sarajevo) has essentially been reduced to an administrative unit of the United Nations; Macedonia is held together by U.S. and UN troops; and Albania is in complete economic and political disarray.

Religion and Demographics

The religious divisions as discussed are profound, and even if these divisions no longer define the behaviors and relationships between individuals, families, towns, and nations, they did at the beginning of the repeated cycles of violence and misunderstanding that have in themselves become reasons for continued violence, vendetta, and mistrust. When society is functioning, women and men usually have strictly defined gender roles; women are subordinate to men in business and social affairs, and men are subordinate to women in affairs of the home and family.

Fundamental Cultural Orientations

1. What's the Best Way for People to Relate to One Another?

OTHER-INDEPENDENT OR OTHER-DEPENDENT? Within groups, there is strong loyalty; there is an intense need to define individuals in terms of being either inside or outside the group. As an outsider, your loyalty will be tested: do not make a point of doing business with the out-group. Clans, in fact, and the associated vendettas and anarchic rule that they exercise, have been the dominant way of civic life in much of Albania (especially in the rugged mountain north).

HIERARCHY-ORIENTED OR EGALITY-ORIENTED? There is a strong need for structure and organization, with power and authority coming from above. Most organizations that function have very rigid chains of command; having access to decision makers means having the ear of the top team. In social life, the rules of etiquette still require men to defer to women in public, and younger people to defer to their elders.

RULE-ORIENTED OR RELATIONSHIP-ORIENTED? Relationships define reality in this very unstable environment. A Serb once commented to me that he was sure democracy would never succeed in his country because people were being asked to trust in the one thing that historically they could never trust in and which would in the end always be seen as yet another foreign invasion: a democratic system. He went on to say that the only thing the average Serb could rely on was his relationship with trusted family and friends, and that the obligations inherent in this relationship would outlive any foreign idea. Right and wrong, good and bad, what to do and what not, all are determined by the subjective interpretation of reality based on how it affects the personal relationships of the individuals involved and how such relationships can, in turn, impact the situation.

2. What's the Best Way to View Time?

MONOCHRONIC OR POLYCHRONIC? The region is mainly polychronic and more so the farther south you go through the Balkan Peninsula. Slovenians are fairly monochronic, in both their social and business dealings (you should arrive pretty much on time for business meetings and for social dinners); as you move through Croatia and Serbia, and in Macedonia and Bulgaria, time becomes much more fluid, and meetings and dinners alike may be delayed by between fifteen and thirty minutes; the golden rule is to arrive on time, and be prepared to wait.

RISK-TAKING OR RISK-AVERSE? Throughout much of the region, the answer to this is . . . both. When people are extremely eager to do business with Westerners, they will promise things they cannot deliver and propose all sorts of deals they may not be able to follow through on, in the hope of doing business with someone with resources from the outside who is willing to make an investment in their country. When one has nothing to lose, it is easy to take risks.

At the same time, true day-to-day business is still encumbered by regulations and wars, and the general mistrust between people who do not know each other can take a long time to overcome. History has taught these people to be ready at any moment to change course and be flexible, but to initially resist anything new and different. There may be some softening in this attitude among the younger generation (this still remains to be seen, especially as they themselves get older).

PAST-ORIENTED OR FUTURE-ORIENTED? The people of this region are very fatalistic and superstitious, more so as you move from north to south. The past is the reason for the actions of the present, and there often is little belief that the future will be anything else but a replay of the past, unless and until the "other" changes his ways. There is a strong resistance to see oneself and one's country as part of the problem and a powerful tendency to shift blame to the other for the problems of the moment; this is true individually and, often, as a culture, throughout the region.

3. What's the Best Way for Society to Work with the World at Large?

LOW-CONTEXT DIRECT OR HIGH-CONTEXT INDIRECT COMMUNICATORS? Because the situation will so powerfully control what people can safely say and do, we have to say that these cultures are primarily high-context. Remember, however, that these peoples, as we have seen with most Slavs, can alternately be open, direct, blunt, and forthright (especially Bulgarians, who have a reputation for appearing the most "Russian" of all these southern Slavs) and equally reserved, playing things very close to the vest, and secretive.

PROCESS-ORIENTED OR RESULT-ORIENTED? Subjective experience, belief, and associative judgment play the more powerful roles in decision making, although to be fair, among the better educated, there is an appreciation for and reliance upon facts, numbers, logic, and rationalism as criteria for decision making and action.

FORMAL OR INFORMAL? Again, due to context, both value systems are held in the region: southern Slavs can be open, spontaneous, and informal as well as formal, closed, and reserved, while waiting to see the outsider show respect for their customs and manners.

Greetings and Introductions

Language and Basic Vocabulary

The primary language throughout the region is Serbo-Croatian, with Bulgarian and Albanian, both Slavic languages, spoken in those two countries. Insofar as the people of this area are concerned, however, it is a name used only by foreigners, for in Serbia, the people speak Serbian, and in Croatia, the people speak Croatian, and so on. Serbo-Croatian is really a combination of many different dialects, and speakers in one country will pretend not to understand you if you use the Serbo-Croatian dialect of another country. For the most part, it is generally intelligible throughout the region. German is the main second language in the north (if German doesn't work in the south and east, try Russian). English is not well known outside Slovenia.

Here are some basic terms in "generic" Serbo-Croatian (since Serbo-Croatian uses both the Latin and Cyrillic script, we will simply spell out the phonetic pronunciation here):

dobro yootro	good morning
dobro vaychah	good evening
zbogom	good-bye
eezvenitsah	excuse me
molim	please
chvalah	thank you (Note: in Bulgaria, use the French *merci*)
molim	you're welcome
da	yes
ne	no
gospodeen	Mr.
gospodjo	Mrs.
gospodjice	Miss

Honorifics for Men, Women, and Children

Gospodeen (Mr.), *gospodjo* (Mrs.), and *gospodjice* (Miss) are commonly used. Sometimes, among close friends and associates, the honorific may be used with the first name. Unless and until your colleague specifically invites you to use first names, and despite how he or she might refer to you, you must always use the family name plus the correct honorific (the switch to first names might occur quite quickly). Children are absolutely required to be respectful when speaking with adults, and must always use honorifics.

In situations where a title is known, the honorific plus the title is usually used, either with or without the name. For casual contacts (e.g., with waiters, store help, etc.), just use the honorific without the name. It is important to meet people at work or in stores or restaurants with an appropriate greeting for the time of day (see the list of Serbo-Croatian terms above) and to say good-bye upon leaving, although you should not expect to be acknowledged all the time. If you speak any of the local language at all, it is important to use it; it will absolutely delight your associates, and help build that all-important relationship, although language is a strong identifier of what group you are from or sympathize with, and you will be branded by it. You will also need to explain, being a foreigner, how it is that you know the language (they may be suspicious of your reasons to be in the country).

The What, When, and How of Introducing People

Always wait to be introduced to strangers before taking that responsibility upon yourself. You will always be introduced to women first, then men, in descending order of age. Always greet the wives first in any group, if they are introduced to you as such. In this suspicious climate, third-party introductions are preferred whenever possible (especially in business settings), so wait a moment before introducing yourself to a new group; in most cases, you will not have to wait long for someone will take up the cause of introducing you. Women do not necessarily rise when someone enters a room, but men always do, for both women and men. Do not presume to seat yourself at a gathering; if possible, wait to be told where to sit. In Slovenia, Croatia, Bosnia, Macedonia, and Serbia, you do not shake hands with people when departing—only upon arrival (with everyone; leave no one out). You do not need to shake someone's hand again the same day after you have already done so earlier. Kissing is a common greeting with and between all genders (women/women or men/men or women/men) only when there is an established, familiar relationship; it usually involves two kisses (actually "air kisses"), first on the left side, and then the right (note: kissing is not typical in Slovenia).

Physical Greeting Styles

The handshake is a series of formal, solid shakes between two men; it is not as robust between men and women or two women. The handshake should be accompanied by the appropriate greetings (outlined above). Older men in the north may lift the hand of a woman and bring it to their lips for an "air kiss" (the lips never really touch the top of the woman's hand). Men must remove their gloves when shaking hands with women, but women do not need to remove their gloves. Smiling and other nonverbal forms of communication may not always accompany the handshake, especially between people who have not met before. Men should wait until the woman extends her hand before reaching for it, and women may take the lead in extending their hand or not; this may or may not occur, especially among older women (Muslim women typically do not extend their hands to men). The use of the left hand is particularly discouraged in Bosnia, Albania, and other Muslim areas (where it is considered the "unclean" hand by some), and in these areas women may or may not feel comfortable extending their hands to men at all. Eye contact during the introduction is very important, and must be maintained as long as the individual is addressing you.

The use of business cards is very common (take plenty with you); if possible, you should have yours translated into the local language on the reverse side. Be sure to put any advanced education degrees and your full title or position on both sides of your business card; these marks of your status are very important. Also, if your company has been around more than fifty years or so, put its founding date on the card after the company name: this indicates stability and is impressive. Using an English-language business card, as well as speaking the language and obviously being from the United States, is a real advantage in this region today, for you will often be given preferential treatment. In general, don't hide your American identity under a bushel, at least with the general populace (officials are something else! The prevailing attitude toward Americans—and other non-Balkans—however, can change dramatically in response to current political and military events, so it is important to keep your ear to the ground on this issue all the time). At the same time, be yourself, and try to display your knowledge and awareness of local customs, current events, and protocols.

Communication Styles

Okay Topics / Not Okay Topics

Okay: anything positive (as long as they bring it up first) about your home country, especially if it is the West, such as work routines or family life. Your knowledge of and interest in local culture and history will be appreciated, although it may be dismissed at first (in fact, if you display too much knowledge, it will seem a bit strange; locals simply do not believe Americans or Westerners in general have any real appreciation for the history of the region); persist in wanting to know more, though, and you will be treated with great admiration and respect. It is perfectly all right to inquire about a person's family or career, but be careful to do so only if you know that the individual can answer proudly. Many personal questions will probably be asked of you; as a Westerner, you will be the object of everyone's attention wherever you go. This curiosity reflects their desire to get to know you, and to learn more about the United States: answer in general and in full for the greatest comfort and maximum effect (e.g., "Well, in the United States, the average salary for my position is ———, but you know, the average mortgage on a house is ———, and it costs about ——— to live a middle-class life"). Show an interest in local wines and food, and you will have plenty to talk about. *Not okay:* Do not discuss World War II, the Holocaust, or other ethnic groups in the region. As should be the case everywhere in the world, be a teacher when the topic of your country comes up, and be a student when the topic of their country comes up. Compliments are generally well received and not considered embarrassing.

Tone, Volume, and Speed

There is a tendency to speak softly, calmly, and in a low tone, especially at first with strangers. It is especially important for women that they not appear loud or assertive; the traditional attitude toward the nurturing role of women is strongly held (despite the fact that both men and women work), and even in business settings, the woman who is perceived as aggressive loses authority. On the street, all individuals are expected to maintain decorum; loud, disruptive behavior and boisterous laughter are seen as very bad behavior, especially coming from women.

Use of Silence

There may be some, depending upon the circumstances, although the pacing of speech is similar to other cultures in the region. Bulgarians may employ slightly more silence in their speech patterns, depending upon the context.

Physical Gestures and Facial Expressions

People in this region can be very physical, especially once they become comfortable with you. Flicking a few fingers against the neck is an invitation (usually between men) to join the person for a drink. The "okay" sign, made with the forefinger and the thumb, is generally not a good sign to use; the "thumbs up" sign is more acceptable. The *figa* sign (putting the thumb between the first and second finger in a fist) is best avoided, as it is considered obscene by some, but not by others (not for Bulgarians, for example, where it means "nothing"). The use of the left hand is discouraged, as it is considered the "unclean" hand by some: this is especially the case in Bosnia, Albania, and other Muslim areas. Additionally, the "V for victory" sign is usually associated with some political party or other throughout the region, so avoid using it. Smiling is generally not done casually: in public, with strangers, it is seen as odd; even greeting someone with a smile is unusual. In Bulgaria, the Western up-and-down head nod indicating "yes" actually means "no," and the Western side-to-side head shake indicating "no" actually means "yes." These gestures are usually not as pronounced in Bulgaria, and are often very confusing for Westerners.

Waving and Counting

The thumb represents the number 1, the index finger the number 2, and so on. You may get someone's attention by merely extending the index finger and raising your hand (do not wiggle the index finger). If you need to gesture for a waiter, subtly raise your hand with your index finger slightly outstretched. If you want to beckon someone to come over, raise your hand palm down and make a back-and-forth scratching motion with your four fingers.

Physicality and Physical Space

People in this region tend to get slightly closer than northern Europeans. Never speak to or greet anyone with your hands in your pockets; always keep them firmly to your side when standing. If men and women must cross their legs, it must never be ankle over knee, (for women, the preferred style is to cross ankle over ankle). Showing the sole of one's shoe to another person is generally regarded as rude, and is very much an insult in Muslim areas such as Bosnia and Albania. Additionally, in Muslim areas of the region, women need to dress modestly, covering their arms, legs, and head when in public. It is important in Muslim areas that men *never* touch a woman in public—even in greeting. Remember, formal is always better than informal: no gum chewing, *ever;* don't slouch; and don't lean against things.

Eye Contact

Eye contact will be very direct most of the time. It is important not to interpret this behavior as a way of intentionally trying to make you uncomfortable; rather it is a sign of respect. If you look away, your behavior will say to your colleague that you are either disinterested or rude. Either way, maintain eye contact when it is made with you, especially when making a toast. If two strangers' eyes meet and linger, it implies (romantic) interest. Women should be especially careful about making causal eye contact with men, and men should be especially careful about making eye contact prior to being introduced to a Muslim woman.

Emotive Orientation

The people of this region are generally very emotive; their interpersonal communication style is very expressive (generally less so, at first, for Bulgarians).

Protocol in Public

Walking Styles and Waiting in Lines

Lines are usually respected, and people stay to the right on the street, but both become less important as you move south through the region. There may be certain situations, however, where lines are ignored, such as at public bus stops. This will not generally present a challenge, however.

Men accompanied by women, as well as the younger of two people, walk on the curbside; if more than two people are walking together, the "odd" gender is flanked by the pair from the opposite gender. When a close relationship has been established, individuals often walk arm in arm on the street, no matter their genders.

Behavior in Public Places: Airports, Terminals, and the Market

Customer service as a concept simply did not exist in eastern and central Europe during the Communist era, and even today it is less and less evident the farther east across the region you go. As employees of the state, with guaranteed jobs, store clerks simply had no motivation to be nice, let alone to serve, during the Communist days. Today, as a concept, it is catching on, but slowly. Store hours are typically not built around customer convenience (many stores are closed on weekends and most evenings). As in much of Europe, if you touch the produce in food markets, you buy it; in goods stores, it may be difficult for you to return a product unless there is a debilitating flaw in it. Bargaining is a way of life in the markets, and in most stores. If you are identified as being from the West, you may be given a different price than the locals get: to avoid this, go with a native colleague, if you can, or politely ask to see a record in the store indicating the price of the item. In most stores, you pay for the item you want first; the cashier will then give you a receipt; and then you pick up the item with your receipt, and leave. When you pay for something, put your money on the counter, not in the hand of the clerk; in return the clerk will put any change down on the counter, not directly into your hand. Smoking in public places is still a common occurrence, including the developed areas of Slovenia and the touristic Adriatic coast. Never applaud in a church (you might go to one for a concert; it is a common form of entertainment) unless others do it first. Unescorted women can expect men to approach them whenever they are in public, including restaurants. The best thing is to be with another female friend, look busy or preoccupied, and when approached, ignore the advance. This usually works, as the male and female roles in this play are well known by all local actors, and the lines and appropriate responses are well rehearsed.

Bus / Metro / Taxi / Car

Driving is on the right, but people pass very quickly on the left; in fact, the way people drive in this region is described more often than not as chaotic. The saving grace is that there simply are not that many vehicles on the road; still, those that are on the road act as if they own it. Do not drive if you've been drinking: DWI laws are strictly enforced. The political difficulties make driving here nearly impossible; there will be checkpoints all along the way, and unless you know where you are going, you could be heading into dangerous areas.

Public transport usually shuts down after midnight in those towns that have it (current situations make such transport erratic, and perhaps dangerous, at other times, as well). Your best bet for catching a cab is at designated taxi stands (hotels are good places, but often charge more for the same ride: a hotel surcharge is added to the meter fare, but in all cases, be sure to negotiate the fare when you first get into the cab).

On public transportation, younger people should give up their seats to older people, and men should give up their seats to women, especially if they are pregnant or have babies or small children with them.

Tipping

A 10 percent tip is usually sufficient for restaurants and taxis; more is considered nouveau and gauche. Porters and hotel help get about the equivalent of US $0.50 per service rendered; theater and bathroom attendants usually receive the same. Restaurants usually have the 10 percent tip already included on the bill, but it's okay to ask to make sure. Even if it is included, it is still appropriate to leave some odd change, provided the service was worth it. Include the tip when you pay the bill at the cashier: do not leave either the bill payment or the tip on the table (the bill is usually made out and left on the table when you order). Answer your telephone by saying "allo." Telephone service may be sporadic, and your ability to remain patient with the overworked telephone operators, who probably do not speak English, might be appreciated with the connection you seek. Have someone nearby who can place the call for you in the local language.

Punctuality

Be punctual for all business and social activities, but expect to wait, and anticipate all sorts of possible delays. The workday usually starts early (businesses can open at 7 A.M.), but can end early as well (workers usually go home around 2 or 3 P.M., office staff no later than 4 or 5 P.M.). Even managers and executives are rarely in their offices after 5 P.M. There is usually half a day of work on Saturday mornings, as well.

Dress

Err on the formal side, until you know to dress otherwise; this is a good rule both in social situations and at the office. You may be surprised at how informal dress is at work and in social situations: sometimes clean, pressed jeans and a nice neat dress shirt, with or without a sport jacket, will do just fine at work or for a social occasion at home. Southern Slavs, of course, are very casual at home (but that does not mean sneakers or T-shirts are okay at the dinner table). At work, men may wear suits (dark is best), white shirts, and ties, but they also may wear slacks and a sport jacket, sometimes with a pullover sweater vest underneath the jacket (how one dresses at work is really a reflection of rank and job title, so observe carefully, and always start out dressing as if you were higher up). If you wear a hat, always remember to remove it as soon as you come indoors; it is very rude to keep it on. The long cold winters require layers of clothes, and sweaters and vests help keep people warm throughout the workday.

On the street, informal may mean jeans and sneakers (women do not wear sneakers to work); for a social gathering, informal more often than not means jeans and a dress shirt or a blouse. You do not need to dress formally for a dinner at someone's home, and no formal dress code exists for the theater and concerts (a jacket and tie will do; that is the dressiest you'll ever need to get). Be sure to check your winter coat whenever you go into a restaurant or theater or auditorium: it is very bad manners to carry your coat around with you in these public places (with the growing exception of movie theaters, where people roll them up and sit on them, in most cases!). If you are visiting a church, women need to cover up their arms, legs, and neck; having a head covering handy for women in church is a good idea, as well. Men need to wear long-sleeved collared shirts when visiting churches.

If you are visiting a mosque, you will be required to take your shoes off. Some mosques offer slippers to wear instead, and if you are not properly attired, some will also provide you with a long robe to wear. In mosques, women and men are usually segregated. Do not attempt to visit a mosque on Fridays, when services are usually held (the Muslim Sabbath is Friday), unless you are Muslim. Muslim women cover their heads, arms, and legs in public, and Western women visiting Muslim areas need to mirror this modesty.

Seasonal Variations

The extremely cold and damp winter requires layers of clothes and protective boots and rain gear. Summers, though short, can be warm and sunny. Never remove your jacket or tie unless and until your colleague has done so first. In the office, men sometimes wear short-sleeved shirts in the summer without jackets (take your cue from them).

Colors

Most colors are simple, natural, and not ostentatious. Be conservative in the use of color, even with accessories: they need to blend with, not stand out from, the outfit.

Styles

Style is not critical, but a good appearance is always important. Cologne and perfume are not commonly used. Men often have facial hair in the form of mustaches.

Personal Hygiene

Recognize that hot running water is expensive and unavailable at times, so your daily bath may be forsaken for awhile. However, cleanliness and neatness is highly valued.

Dining and Drinking

Mealtimes and Typical Foods

Breakfast (*doručak; zakuska* in Bulgaria) is served from about 7 to 9 A.M., and usually consists of coffee, rolls, butter, jams, and tea or coffee. *Burek* is a favorite breakfast staple: it is a cheese pie often served with yogurt (the yogurt in the region is often made from goat's milk and is unsweetened or flavored, so you may want to put some jam or honey in it). The coffee is mainly of the Turkish or Greek variety (but it is always referred to nationalistically; for example, as Bulgarian coffee, or Serbian coffee), which means it is thick, dark, usually presweetened, and has lots of coffee grounds on the bottom of the cup. Be forewarned: tea sometimes is drunk out of glasses. Some locals hold a cube of sugar between their front teeth and let the tea wash over it as they drink.

Lunch (*riča; bet* in Bulgaria) is still the main meal of the day in both rural and urban settings; it is served around 2 P.M. during the week, and around 2 or 3 P.M. on Sundays. It usually consists of several courses, beginning with soup—either hot (in winter, made with bean or meat) or cold (in summer, made with fruit, like cherries), then a fish or stew course with vegetables (potatoes, dumplings, and stuffed cabbage), bread, sometimes pickled vegetables, and ending with a dessert of preserved fruit. Wine, beer, or water is usually drunk with lunch. At dinner, or a more formal lunch, there can be preprandial drinks, cheese, and prosciutto (*pršuta*), then soup. In this part of the world, salad follows the soup and precedes the main course. Then there is dessert, then coffee with postprandial drinks.

Dinner (*večera; vecherya* in Bulgaria) is served late, starting from about 9 P.M. In the rural areas, dinner is usually a light meal of noodles, cheese, salad (if available), and yogurt, but it can also be another major meal with a hearty main dish, such as cabbage and meat.

A common local tradition is to start a meal with something sweet: this is not dessert, but a way to get the appetite going. This predinner treat usually consists of very sweet preserved fruits or compote in a thick, sweet, honey-type syrup. You are served this from a jar with a long spoon; you dip the spoon into the jar and remove a spoonful of the preserved fruit. Eat it off the spoon, then take a drink of the cold water that is served along with it. Just one spoonful is enough. A preprandial drink usually follows.

Regional Differences

In the north, in Slovenia and Croatia, cheese and other dairy foods are featured, along with soups (in fact, almost every meal in Slovenia includes a soup course). As you move along the coast, the food appears very Adriatic, almost Italian, in nature. In Serbia, cabbage and meats such as beef and pork are widely used. The Muslim countries (and Bulgaria) turn to lamb and mutton (as pork is prohibited by Muslim tradition). The food in Macedonia and Bosnia has been heavily influenced by Greek and Turkish cooking, including the wonderful sweet desserts, such as Turkish delight and Greek baklavas; it is also the spiciest in the region. Yogurt is used throughout the region in all dishes, from appetizers right on through dessert, and the staples are cabbage, potatoes, and rice. Bulgarians emphasize the use of yogurt and grains in many of their dishes. Note that when you see "toast" on a menu, it means a grilled sandwich of some kind, usually cheese (i.e., the bread is toasted).

Café life is common along the touristic Dalmatian coast and as one heads south through the region (*kafić,* or cafés, also serve lots of hard liquor and snacks). In addition to full-service restaurants (more common along the coast and in the major cities in the form of *riblji,* or fish restaurants), there is the *čevabdžinica,* a kind of full-service, fast-food place, serving only meats. *Pivnica,* more common in Slovenia and Croatia, are beer halls where wine and other drinks are also served, and *slastičarna* or *poslastičarnica* (*slatkarneetsa* in Bulgaria) are the ubiquitous ice cream and pastry shops of the region. Also in Bulgaria are *mehnahna,* gathering places that serve light meals, drinks, and lots of local color and hospitality.

Typical Drinks and Toasting

The most common toast is *nazdroyeh* (to your health). The drink will be either a plum brandy (*šlivovitz*) or *rakia,* more of a liqueur. These drinks are meant to be taken in shots (with the exception of Bulgaria, where the slivovitz, after the introductory shot, is more often sipped, not gulped, along with the food). Wine or beer will typically accompany the meal.

These liquors may be served, along with assorted snacks, during business meetings at virtually any time of day, including first thing in the morning. Do not drink all the liquor or beer that is offered to you, for every time you drink a glass, it will be refilled. The more you drink, the more you will be offered: know when to stop. If you really cannot drink, you'll need a very good excuse, like doctor's orders.

Never break eye contact while making a toast, from the moment the glass leaves the table until you place it back down (blinking is allowed, however!). There can be much toasting throughout the meal, and when it is possible, glasses should be clinked. You will be expected to make a toast in a small group at some point during the meal, especially if you have been toasted personally or are the guest of honor. Slivovitz and brandies are usually served at room temperature.

In Muslim cultures, alcoholic beverages may not be served among devout faithful (alcohol is prohibited by Islamic tradition). This is more or less observed in these regions, according to individual preference, so take your cue from your colleagues. Where this religious injunction is observed, tea, coffee, water, or fruit juice is typically served in place of the alcohol.

Table Manners and the Use of Utensils

Do not begin eating until the host invites you to.

Like all continental Europeans, locals do not switch knives and forks as Americans do. The knife remains in the right hand, and the fork remains in the left. When the meal is finished, place your fork and knife together so that they are parallel and lie vertically across the middle of the plate, fork tines left of the knife. If you're unsure of which utensil to use, always start from the outside and work your way in, course by course. The fork and spoon above your plate are usually for dessert. Bread is usually served without butter (therefore, there will usually not be a butter knife), and there is usually no bread plate (place your bread on the side of your main plate or on the table throughout the meal). A substantial quantity of bread is consumed with every meal. Salad, when available, is served with the main course on the same plate.

Your hands are expected to be visible above the table: this means that you do not keep them in your lap; instead, rest your wrists on top of the table. In Bulgaria it is especially important never to rest your elbows on the table. Neither do you keep your napkin in your lap: it is always kept on the table. Pass all dishes at the table to your left. If there is gravy or sauce, you can generally use your bread to soak some of it up, but not with your hands; put the bread on your plate, then move it around in the gravy with your fork, then eat it.

Throughout the region, particularly in Bulgaria, there may be significantly less talking at the table during the meal than in the West: you are there to enjoy the food. However, conversation revives dramatically over coffee and drinks, and after dinner: for this reason, plan to stay for a long time after the meal (several hours is not uncommon).

Certain foods, especially in the south and in the Islamic countries, may be eaten with the fingers of the right hand, without cutlery (these usually are cheese and rice ball specialties). Take your cue from your host; when you see him or her doing this, follow along.

Seating Plans

The most honored position is in the middle of the table; as the guest of honor, you will probably be seated there, although the hosts will usually be at either end of the table. Genders are more likely to be seated together in this part of Europe than in western Europe, with women on one side and men on the other. In some conservative Muslim homes, women and men may eat separately, with the men being served first. Men typically must rise when women enter the room, and may or may not enter a room first when a woman is present. At meals, the oldest woman or most honored guest is served first. Remember, as is the case throughout the Continent, what the locals call the first floor is really the second floor, with the first floor usually referred to as the lobby or ground floor.

Refills and Seconds

At a private dinner party, if you do not want more food, you will really have to insist several times before the hostess will believe you. Take a little extra if you can of something you like. If you do not want more, you must leave a little food on your plate to be believed. You may always have additional beverages; drink enough to cause your cup or glass to be less than half full, and it will generally be refilled. Portions may be larger than in the United States; there are also more courses, for both lunch and dinner. It is a great honor (and sometimes at great cost to the host as well) to be invited to dinner at someone's home, so be sure to sample and eat most of everything: it was made for you.

At Home, in a Restaurant, or at Work

In informal restaurants, you may be required to share a table: if so, do not force conversation; act as if you are seated at a private table. Waitstaff may be summoned by making eye contact and raising your hand slightly; waving or calling their names is very impolite. The business breakfast is not known. The business lunch or dinner (if there is one), depending upon how well developed your relationship is with your colleagues, is generally not the time to make business decisions. Take your cue from your local associates: if they bring up business, then it's okay to discuss it, but wait to take your lead from their conversation. No gum chewing, ever, at a restaurant or on the street. No-smoking sections in restaurants are still a rarity: most people smoke throughout the meal between courses.

When you arrive at a colleague's home for a formal meal, you will be told where to sit, and there you should remain. Do not wander around, even if the home (an apartment in most cases) is rather small. Once you (and the group) are invited to another room, most probably the eating area in or near the kitchen, be sure to allow the more senior members of your party to enter the room ahead of you. At the table, do not presume to seat yourself, as the seating arrangement is usually predetermined. Spouses who accompany their partners on business trips are usually not invited to attend meals at restaurants, but will be, in most cases, for those given at homes. Be prepared to arrive slightly later as you move south through the region: be on time in Slovenia, five minutes late in Croatia, ten minutes late in Serbia and Bosnia, fifteen minutes late in Bulgaria, and twenty minutes late in Macedonia and Albania. And be prepared to stay late and long. As is the case throughout much of the region, you might have to remove your shoes before entering a home (check to see if there are pairs of shoes lined up at the entrance to the home: if there are, it means that you should remove yours as well); be sure your socks are in good shape. You might be offered slippers to wear.

Because of the early business hours, workers usually have lunch at home and take a siesta or small nap afterward. The second half of the day for those employees who return after lunch then begins around 4 or 5 P.M.

Being a Good Guest or Host

Paying the Bill

Usually the one who does the inviting pays the bill, although the guest is expected to make an effort to pay. Sometimes other circumstances determine the payee (such as rank). Making payment arrangements ahead of time so that no exchange occurs at the table is a very classy way to host. Women, if men are present at the table, will not really be able to pay the bill at a restaurant: if you want to, make arrangements ahead of time, and don't wait for the check to arrive at the table. The only time it is considered appropriate for a woman to pay the bill is if she is a businesswoman from abroad, and even then it will be a very difficult thing to do.

Transportation

It's a very nice idea, when acting as the host, to inquire ahead of time as to whether your guests will require transportation. If necessary, you should arrange for a car at the end of the meal.

You may be picked up from and taken back to your hotel by the host.

When to Arrive / Chores to Do

When you arrive for a dinner in a private home, be sure to thank the hostess for the invitation as soon as you get there and present her with your gift. Offer to help with the chores, but be prepared to be turned down at first. Ask again, and your offer will probably be accepted.

Do not leave the table unless invited to do so. When it is time to leave, it can take a long time to say good-bye. In most cases, hugs and kisses will be the farewell (not a handshake).

If you are invited into a home, your desires become your hosts' most important concerns, so be sensitive to imposing yourself on their daily routines.

Gift Giving

In general, gift giving is very common among business associates. The best gifts are useful items, such as pen and pencil sets and nicely bound agendas. In fact, having small gifts available to dispense to people you meet throughout the day helps to keep things moving smoothly: a ballpoint pen or a pack of cigarettes can go far in getting someone's assistance. Mementos of life in the United States are very well received (towels, coffee-table books about the United States, and well-packaged gourmet foodstuffs are always appreciated). Given the climate of scarcity throughout the region, almost anything that you can bring along from the West will be appreciated: toys, perfumes, cosmetics, kitchenware, cigarettes, cigars, office supplies, personal items, jeans, CDs, and so on. The gifts should not be ostentatious, but they must be useful. Holiday cards are not usually done since they carry no intrinsic value (except in more urban areas in the north).

Gifts are expected for social events, especially as thank-yous for private dinner parties. The best gift in this case is a cut floral bouquet of an odd number of flowers (not thirteen; it is bad luck). Never bring chrysanthemums, lilies, or gladioli, as they are used at funerals and religious events; also avoid red roses, for they signify romantic intent. Make sure you bring it along with you when you arrive. The bouquet should always be wrapped, and you should unwrap it only in the presence of the hostess. Other good gifts would be wine, cakes and pastries, a dessert wine or brandy, a box of fine chocolates, or any of the items mentioned above. If there are children in the family, it is thoughtful to bring a little something for them, such as a toy or candy, in addition to the gift for the hostess. As with other European cultures, gifts are generally opened at the time they are given and received.

If you are bringing gifts to your business associates, be sure you bring enough for everyone in the office. Most anything—from simple kitchen and household appliances to clothing to office supplies—from the West is usually appreciated by all (but your key contact deserves something special, in addition).

Special Holidays and Celebrations

Major Holidays

Most workers in this region take their vacations during July, if they can. Business slows down from December 15 to January 2 for Catholics, from December

20 to January 6 for Orthodox Church members, and for the entire month of Ramadan (on the lunar calendar, anywhere from mid-December through early March) for Muslims. Ramadan is a holy month celebrating Muhammad's divine inspiration, and Muslims do not eat, drink, or smoke during the day during this period: it would be impolite to do the same in front of them during this time. In Eastern Orthodox cultures, name days (the birthdays of the saints, after whom people were named) are often more important celebrations than birthdays. Each country now has its own national day celebration, which is more or less observed by the populace, depending on their ethnic association.

March 1 marks the beginning of an unofficial celebration of spring. In Bulgaria (and in other parts of the region), good luck charms are exchanged (usually in the form of red and white silk strings).

January 1	New Year's Day
January 7	Orthodox Christmas
March/April	Good Friday/Easter (different for Catholics and Orthodox Church members by about one week)
March 8	Woman's Day
May 1	Labor Day

Business Culture

Daily Office Protocols

Office doors are mostly kept closed; you must knock first (this includes bathrooms) before opening doors, and when leaving rooms, close the doors behind you.

Women do not hold equal authority with men in business organizations (except perhaps in Slovenia, in certain situations). It is more common for women to be relegated to lower-level management and administrative support positions. It is rare (though not impossible) to see women at the highest levels of business and government.

The workday can start very early and end around midafternoon. When making appointments, be sure to schedule them way in advance, and confirm them several times as the date and time approaches. Expect some chitchat at the beginning of the meeting about nonbusiness issues; this may take some time. The locals are eager to appear confident and competent to the Westerner, and therefore may make promises that they cannot possibly keep: be sure to confirm and inquire of independent sources, if available, until you are convinced of what truly can and cannot be done. Do not travel to the region without many of the little gift items mentioned above to help smooth your daily way.

Management Styles

Privacy and individual accomplishment of one's tasks are critical in the north, less so as you move south. Workers provide what their bosses expect of them, and the preparation of plans, methods, and reports can be time-consuming and complicated efforts toward perfection. Gathering the information required in order to do what your boss expects from you, or creating consensus among your colleagues in order to accomplish a particular goal, can take a long time. All of this occurs in a formal and sometimes very rigid hierarchical structure. Titles are very important; the highest ones (e.g., vice president) are usually reserved for very senior, executive-level positions, and should not be used as casually as they are in the United States. Complimenting and rewarding employees publicly is viewed suspiciously. In Muslim countries, it is important to expect, and allow for, daily prayer times. Muslims pray for a few moments five times each day (upon rising, at noon, at mid-day, at sunset, and at night) and appreciate a private area in which to pray. Prayer rooms are typical accommodations for Muslim employees in most work establishments in the region.

Boss-Subordinate Relations

Rank most definitely has its decision-making privileges. Deviating from established hierarchy (either formal or informal) typically does not get things done any faster. You must get close to the decision makers, who are most often at the top; if this is your first meeting, you may not be speaking with decision makers, but merely gatekeepers who are there to size up you and your organization, and report back to their supervisors. It is best to expect utmost formality at introductory meetings. If a man is meeting a local businesswoman for the first time, he should bring some flowers with him to give to her (a simple arrangement of wildflowers is best).

Conducting a Meeting or Presentation

Meetings can be information-sharing and decision-making forums in which all individuals are expected to contribute. Data, facts, and figures are all important, but not more important than the good feeling your local associates finally have about you when you leave. Presentations need to be simple and clearly understood, but they also should be formal and attractively packaged. Presentations in English are fine, but backup documentation should be available in the local dialect for maximum effect. Get a good local translator to work for your side: do not depend on the meeting translator provided by your hosts.

Negotiation Styles

In this region, there are two opposing negotiating behaviors: the locals can play their cards close to the vest at first, not divulging information easily, and open up as trust develops; or they can almost be effusive in their eagerness to work with you (this is because they indeed are: Western business generally means good new opportunities!). If they are in the former mode, they may appear circumspect in their communication styles, and will indicate their thoughts in indirect, associative ways; they can, however, quickly become pointedly direct as negotiations move forward. If they are in the latter mode, they will most definitely be more eager to speak openly and move the negotiations along. If you are from the West, they will assume that you have the ability to do everything you say and more, and will also assume you already have the knowledge and experience required for the work; they will also try to persuade you of the same about them, which may or may not in fact be true (you need to confirm this independently).

The first meeting is usually just a formality, with your colleagues sizing up you and your organization: it will most likely be conducted in a hotel room or a hotel conference room (follow-up meetings are held in offices). Put on a warm, dignified demeanor during the meeting. Never be condescending or offer an ultimatum. Contracts are serious matters to you; they should be clear, concise, and translated into both the local language and English. However, they are more likely to be viewed by the locals as statements of intent, and when things change, good business partners are expected to accommodate to the changing needs of the other; try to remain flexible with respect to the terms of the agreement.

Entertaining during the course of negotiations is important, but limit yourself only to the people you are negotiating with (or else the whole office will show up!). When the deal is finally signed, throw a small party at a restaurant or at your hotel. In Serbia and Bulgaria, expect to see the influence of the Russian behaviors identified in the Russian section; expect more Greek-like behavior in Macedonia and Albania.

Written Correspondence

Be clear, precise, and respectful in your business correspondence. Flowery and formal is fine. Last names usually are written in uppercase; dates are given using the day/month/year format (with periods in between, not slashes); time is written in military style; weights and measures are metric; and an honorific plus the title is as common as the honorific plus the last name. Monetary amounts are written so that periods break up the figures into tens, hundreds, and thousands (i.e., D10.000,00 = ten thousand dinar). You can get straight to the point in written business communications.

Addresses in Serbia and points south are usually written as follows:

Line 1: Country and postal code
Line 2: City
Line 3: Street address
Line 4: Name

The Eastern European
Cultures: Russia

Some Introductory Background on Russia
and the Russians

Even with the breakup of the Soviet Union, Russia is still the world's largest
nation, and one of the most heterogeneous (curiously, along with the United
States). Despite the enormous numbers of minorities still represented within its
borders, this is predominantly a Slavic nation, ironically named after the Norse
term for people from the east (*Rus*). The great Rus consolidated themselves
again and again, ultimately creating a greater culture that now spans, both geographically and historically, east and west, Europe and Asia. While creating
their great culture, the Rus also created a great dilemma for themselves: an
identity that is neither East nor West, and yet very definitely both at the same
time. It is the source of the brooding, the introspection, the apparently endless
cycles of despair and exuberance, of iron authoritarianism and anarchic freedom, of expansive grandiosity and self-defeating inferiority that has historically
defined the classic Russian psyche. This is the wellspring of the Slavic soul, of
the great challenge to the West, of the door to the East.

Being so much each other's balance, Russia and the United States in many
surprising ways mirror each other, and historically and culturally, precisely
because of their different paths, the two countries share similar historical
moments. Both are massive heterogeneous cultures, sometimes locked in fierce
competition, both striving to define the nature of modern man and to move their
respective societies forward through the twenty-first century. As we have seen
elsewhere, the icons of a culture often serve as metaphors for understanding it;
and the icon for Russia would be the famous matrioska doll. What appears on
the surface as grandiose and large is in fact a cover for a smaller, more hidden
layer, which in turn covers a smaller, more hidden layer, which hides yet
another, and another. The exterior is bold and outsized, but it hides a sacred,
precious core within.

This image is also reflected in the timeless Russian mir, or village (the same
word means "peace"), which is the source of the collective nature of the Russian soul, and which provided, among other things, the cultural receptivity to
Communist theory, allowing the great Marxist experiment to root first in the rich
soil of feudal Russia, and not in the industrial cities of capitalist Great Britain
as Marx predicted. The ancient mir was the root of Russianness: it needed first

and foremost to be protected and defended. Against the treacherous climate. Against marauding outsiders. Against the strangers in the next mir. All individual residents of the mir had to subordinate their personal individual goals to the overriding collective goal for mir survival. The center was sacred, and each layer out, each kilometer from the heart, was a defensive line, culminating finally in the outside perimeter, where the mir's face, like the outer matrioska doll, met the outside world. The Russian bear is king in his cave, and patrols the perimeters keeping the outsiders away. Russian defensiveness is a way to constantly patrol the borders, secure the perimeter, and protect the sacred inner center; Russian aggressiveness therefore is often an effort not to aggrandize at first, but to create security zones so that the outside is farther away from the sacred center.

One of the great paradoxes and sources of tension for the Russian is the degree to which one can both keep the outsider away from the center and incorporate and learn from the outsider, as well. (The American parallel of this problem is to what degree "Americanness" changes in relation to the new cultures that the United States must constantly receive and incorporate.) All great Russian leaders struggle with the dilemma of keeping both the East and West at bay, and yet learning from and incorporating the best of what both could provide into the developing Russian state. From Peter the Great to Catherine the Great, from Nikita Khrushchev to Boris Yeltsin, the tension between protecting the mir and allowing the fruits of the outside world into the cave, is always a delicate balancing act. Non-Russians must appreciate that history continuously tips the scales one way or the other, and in most all cases, against the Russians sooner or later, for no culture can be either one or the other without first being itself. Non-Russians must recognize that Russians may act and sound and dress like Westerners, but they are not. Russians went from bitter feudalism to Communism: the experiences that made the West the West never rooted into the Russian heartland. Despite Napoléon and the proactive efforts of Russians to embrace the best the West had to offer, the risk was ultimately always too great, the price too high. The West was always destroying what it didn't understand, and Russia was always having to sacrifice what it merely wanted to improve upon. Russians are not Western, nor are they Eastern; yet their Orientalism shames them in the eyes of the West, and their Westernness keeps them from participating fully and constructively with their Asian cousins. The European republican revolutions never occurred in Russia. The Enlightenment did not happen in Russia. The Renaissance never reached Russian soil. The Russian experience, to the contrary, is oriental, byzantine, mysterious, irrational, orthodox, a source of self-pride, self-loathing, openness and retreat; at the same time, it produced the many-layered, ambivalent personal Russian soul and the complex and matrioska-like society of today.

Some Historical Context

Today, we are dealing with a culture in the throes of massive self-reconstruction: the best and worst of Russian complexity is evident in all moments of life and work in Russia today. If the system is unstable and unreliable, it gives one the chance, at least, to see the Russian culture, for all its glorious, multilayered complexity, laid bare and apparent. In a sense, this is the best time to be in Russia, for it is Russia at its rawest, protecting the mir while trying again to find a way to safely bring the world in, and safely coexist in turn, with the rest of the world.

Russia stands today, at the beginning of the twenty-first century, having to deal with the crushing fact that what it spent most of the twentieth century trying to accomplish turned out not to be a very good idea after all; and while Communism did lift the country out of fifteenth-century feudalism, there was no infrastructure—political, social, economic, educational, or otherwise—that would enable the country to join the twentieth century without lockstep authoritarianism to keep everything in place. The Nazis provided the excuse, and Joseph Stalin did the rest. Between World War II and Stalin, Russia lost millions of its most talented people. And now, in its efforts to reconstruct itself, after casting off what it finally could not bear, it is struggling in its attempts to reform its economy, stabilize its society, and provide for its people at least what they had under Communism while attempting to create a representative republic, with no historic democratic traditions to draw from. This may not be possible. But this is a very good time to examine the many layers of the matrioska.

An Area Briefing

Politics and Government

Ostensibly, Russia is technically a federal republic, with a representative government consisting of a legislature and a prime minister, plus a president. The Communist Party is technically outlawed (although there is great pressure from many former Communists to reinstate Communist practices in the hope that many of the things that people have lost in the tumult over privatization may be recovered through the reinstatement of socialist policies; for many, privatization merely meant the accumulation of much wealth by a few at the expense of the masses, a situation that was supposedly a main reason for the Communist revolution against the czars in the first place). As we know, the stability of the government and the entire electoral process in Russia is very fragile. Now that the Soviet Union is no longer, many of the states that were former members are free and independent nations, and that has put considerable pressure on the many ethnic nationalities and associated states within the Russian Federation to also secede. However, despite the independence movements within Russia itself, the Russian Federation is, at this moment, holding. The former Soviet states that, along with Russia comprised the USSR are now, with the exception of the three Baltic states of Estonia, Latvia, and Lithuania, members of the Confederation of Independent States (CIS), a loose alliance promoting cooperative trade and mutual assistance.

Schools and Education

The educational system, like all institutions in Russia, is in massive flux today. The truth is, the Communist system was as successful in establishing effective schools and universities as it was successful at most everything else. It provided access to schools for masses of people who previously went unschooled, but the schooling was technical at best, dripping in ideology, and did little to advance the development of the rational in the face of the medieval. This change is only today slowly occurring, and most school systems, like most state-run systems in the current state of collapse and reinvention, are poor. A generation has been lost. Most Russians you will meet, young and old alike, are simply not trained to employ scientific rationalism to the same degree as subjective intuition; their images of the West are still rather skewed, and their knowledge of the rest of the world still severely warped, by decades of dogma. They are intensely curious, however, about the west, and will be so about you.

Religion and Demographics

The Russian Orthodox Church, (and myriad other faiths to varying degrees, including Islam, Protestantism, and Judaism), is resurgent in a land that was legally atheistic before the Soviet fall. Russian Orthodoxy is particularly mystical and conservative, an example of which are the Old Believers, who hold on to some of the original rites that were subsequently renovated by the modern Orthodox Church in the thirteenth century. It remains to be seen whether the church will continue to play a stabilizing force in the otherwise very unstable social climate, for while many people did find their way back to religion, many have not, and have put their energies into trying to revive the Communist welfare state.

Women and men traditionally had different roles in Russian society, and today women do not hold equal positions of authority at work (despite the theoretical egalitarianism of women and men that began under the Communists). Russia is a very macho culture, and women are seen as subordinate to men in the social structure. Non-Russian businesswomen today need to have their credibility established prior to their visit, and must behave in a strictly professional fashion in order to be taken seriously; even then, it will be a significant and ongoing struggle.

Unlike other eastern European countries, there does not appear to be a real and significant difference in fundamental values between the younger generation and the older one. There are specific regions within Russia that are quite unique and different from the rest of the country.

Fundamental Cultural Orientations

1. What's the Best Way for People to Relate to One Another?

OTHER-INDEPENDENT OR OTHER-DEPENDENT? Family and friends are everything: the in-group with which you are associated determines your field of vision and requires your loyalty, while out-groups tend to be avoided and are met, at first, with caution at best, and suspicion at worst. This means that you may or may not be received warmly. Once a decision has been made about you, however, there will be no doubt: you will be hosted lavishly (and at their own great sacrifice, in most cases) or rejected out of hand. Nevertheless, this concern for others, for membership in a greater family (your own, the neighborhood, the church, etc.), does not preclude individual responsibility for what happens in one's life. The struggle for the Russian is to find a way to gain greater individual responsibility in a world where decisions that control one's life are often still made by greater powers and where the expectation that anything different will happen is more often than not fulfilled; this results in a rejection of personal responsibility when events go bad, and a drive for personal power (sometimes at the expense of others, rules, morality, etc.) when an opportunity appears.

HIERARCHY-ORIENTED OR EGALITY-ORIENTED? There is a strong need for structure and organization, with power and authority coming from above. There is great distrust over many Western ways of doing things, of empowering individuals, for in the Russian experience, empowered individuals merely enslaved others. Under Communism, from their perspective, the state made sure that no one person had more than anyone else. Of course, everyone recognizes that the system became thoroughly corrupt; however, many view the chaos of the moment as something far worse—the same corruption prevails, but there is no structure at all to guarantee the people anything.

Working in a traditional Russian organization means working within a definite hierarchy, and having access to decision makers means having the ear of the top team (group orientation usually means that there may be more than one individual identified as the decision maker). Even in the very bureaucratic Soviet structure, the decision maker at the top always solicited input from the group below, in a kind of upward consensus building, before issuing his fiat.

RULE-ORIENTED OR RELATIONSHIP-ORIENTED? Rules can be complex (especially when working with government agencies) and bothersome, but they are always subordinate to the individual relationships one has with powers that may be able to overcome the rules. Clever Russians either know someone who can get them out of a jam, or help them take advantage of a favorable situation, or are themselves clever enough to make a situation work in their favor, despite the existence of rules that are supposed to be for the welfare and benefit of all. The Russian experience has been that official rules were never designed for the benefit of all, and that systems and processes mainly benefited only those who instituted them, leaving most others to fend for themselves. And while in much of eastern Europe there may be some valuing and understanding of how individuals can benefit from the universal application of rules and systems, in Russia, rules and systems are applied for the benefit of the state (the modern-day mir), not individuals; individuals need to find a way through or around the rules on their own. Russians will more easily rely on their subjective notions of right and wrong and their personal relationships to control their lives than they will on processes, rules, and systems. It's not that they don't understand it (although that might in some cases be part of it); it's that it simply doesn't count in their experience.

2. What's the Best Way to View Time?

MONOCHRONIC OR POLYCHRONIC? Polychronic. Everything, including schedules, agendas, and deadlines is subordinate to raw hierarchical power, and one's ability to harness such power through relationships for one's own benefit. The

Russian day begins rather early, but from that point on, it can be difficult to predict when things will start and stop with certainty. Agendas can be changed quickly, last-minute adjustments are common, and while things may start on time, they may not end on time. In fact, business meetings and social events both seem to be open-ended affairs. Be punctual, but stay flexible.

RISK-TAKING OR RISK-AVERSE? Here is that Slavic duality again: seize an opportunity when you see it or make it, for it may not come again, and there is often little to lose; at the same time, one must be careful not to take any action that may jeopardize one's situation, or the situation of others (especially one's family), any further. The former approach usually leads to quick and sudden risk taking, while the latter usually results in a slow and plodding movement toward a specific goal. You will see both mind-sets in Russia, to the extreme. Under the Communists, there was great fear to say and do anything without being absolutely certain that it was safe, according to your superior, to do so. As a result, things today can move remarkably slowly, and while decisions are being made by other powers, your immediate contact might be stalling and equivocating. As the market economy (and shadier versions of it) develops, however, there is increased risk taking, and as long as people prosper or get away with it, it continues. Working in Russia, you will feel both approaches at different times, and to prepare yourself to respond to either—to both the eager Russian who has an opportunity too good to be true, and to the Russian who demands more and more information without making a decision or giving anything up—requires some substantial pre-trip homework, time, a thick skin, and stamina.

PAST-ORIENTED OR FUTURE-ORIENTED? The past plays a significant role in Russian society: it is both a weight and a source of identity. It controls and limits possibilities, but it also defines who the Russians are. Russians believe that if individuals are to have any control over what happens to them, they must struggle, in all ways possible, against impossible odds—and society, as it has been structured, cooperates with this expectation. There is great acceptance of the fact that much of what will happen is beyond the control of mere individuals, even powerful ones, and that ultimately God (at least among the Orthodox) is the source of all events. It has been said that no people can endure and suffer like the Russian people.

3. What's the Best Way for Society to Work with the World at Large?

LOW-CONTEXT DIRECT OR HIGH-CONTEXT INDIRECT COMMUNICATORS? You will see both; under Communism, Russians had to live their day-to-day lives being very careful about what was said: one's life, and those of one's loved ones, was at risk. Consequently, they can be very circumspect about what they say, and speak metaphorically and symbolically. There is much reliance on nonverbal forms of communication as a result of this. At the same time, Russians can also speak their minds very directly, especially when prompted emotionally, which happens all too frequently given their comfort with making and expressing decisions intuitively.

PROCESS-ORIENTED OR RESULT-ORIENTED? Subjective experience, belief, and judgment are probably more important than evidence and logic. Russians admire the intellectual developments of the West, but do not trust them. Therefore, while facts and figures, proof and logic count, they rarely tip the scale against feeling, intuition, and associative experience. This will make for a repetitive kind of bargaining, which will have little impact on the outcome, the outcome instead being determined by other factors, such as decision makers and conditions or situations beyond your control.

FORMAL OR INFORMAL? Russian society is both formal and spontaneous. The people can be overwhelmingly warm and generous, informal and inclusive. At other times, they can be formal, prescriptive, and demanding to the letter. In negotiations, for example, it will be essential to read and sign a "protocol," a written statement taken at the end of practically every meeting to indicate both side's agreement to what was discussed. Nevertheless, this need for absolute detail is ignored when it comes to the final contract, which, although needing to be as absolutely ironclad and watertight as one can make it, is often ignored over time, due to the fact that circumstances change, and what might have been possible on the day the contract was signed is, in fact, no longer the case down the road. These contradictory spontaneous and formal behaviors can reveal themselves either positively or negatively in both social and business situations. Russian formality requires, for example, that guests drink considerable vodka; it usually leads to great informality (if done well), but is itself a formal requirement. Russians have a term for not knowing the formalities, not knowing how to behave: *nyekulturny* (uncultured). Nevertheless, the rules are expected to be known (the important ones are reviewed below).

Greetings and Introductions

Language and Basic Vocabulary

Most older Russians do not speak English, although many younger Russians do (English is required in all schools, and is taught beginning at around the fourth grade). However, many Russian businesspeople do speak some English (often good enough to comprehend, if not to speak). Depending on the person with whom you are speaking, they may also speak German, a local or regional language, or even French.

Slavic languages are pronounced just as they are written, often with the elimination of unpronounced vowels. When written, however, there are some differences between the Slavic languages and English pronunciations, which are outlined in the previous chapters on Slavic culture. It will be useful to become familiar with the written Cyrillic alphabet in order to identify words, particulary in signage, when in Russia.

Here are some basic Slavic phrases, written phonetically:

dobrayee ootrah	good morning
dobriy dyehn	good afternoon
dobriy vyechyeer	good evening
spahkoynigh nochyee	good night
dah sveedahneeyah	good-bye
da skorigh vstryechchyee	see you later

etah . . .	this is . . .
gahspadeen	Mr.
gahspahzhah	Mrs.
gahspahzhah	Miss
ochyeen preeyatnah pahznakomitsah	pleased to meet you
Kahk dyehlah?	How are you?
spahseebah khahrasho	very well, thank you
Ah oo vahss?	And you?
pryeekrahsnah	fine
spahseebah	thank you
prahsteetyee	excuse me

Honorifics for Men, Women, and Children

Russians generally have three names: the first name is their given name, the last name is their father's family name, and the middle name is a version of their father's first (given) name. This middle name is known as the patronymic, and since this is what is different for Russians, we will focus on the use of the patronymic here. For a man, the patronymic is the father's first name with the suffixes *-vich* or *-ovich* added, which mean "son of" (for example, "Ivan Pavlovich Smirnoff" means "Ivan, son of Pavel Smirnoff"); for a woman, the patronymic is also the father's first name, but with the suffixes *-a* or *-ova* added, which mean "daughter of" (for example, "Beata Pavlova Smirnoff" means "Beata, daughter of Pavel Smirnoff"). When spoken to, in either case, a person is referred to most formally by their first name plus their patronymic plus their last name; as one becomes more familiar with people, one can refer to them by their first name plus their patronymic. Only people who are very intimate friends or relations refer to one another by only the first name. The honorifics *gaspodin* (Mr.), or *gaspazhah* (Mrs. or Miss) are not generally used among Russians, and are usually used by Russians only for foreigners. It is appropriate, therefore, as a foreigner, to refer to your Russian colleague by either *gaspodin* or *gaspazhah* plus the last (family) name, as we do in the West. You may also refer to them with the most formal use of their three names. If using their full names with patronymics, you do not need to use the honorifics. Do not use only the first name and patronymic unless and until invited to do so, and never use only the first name, as these last two versions are informal and very familiar.

Married women take their husband's last name, but indicate their gender by changing the last letter when it is a vowel (which it almost always is) into an *a* (or adding *a* to the last name): for example, Ivan Pavlovich Smirnoff's wife, the former Maria Ivanova Karnovsky, is referred to as Maria Ivanova Smirnova after their wedding (she may choose to also retain her maiden name, which gives her four names, her husband's family name coming last: Maria Ivanova Karnovsky Smirnova).

Children in Russia are absolutely required to be respectful when speaking with adults, and must always use honorifics, although they are usually referred to by an amazing array of diminutives and nicknames.

In situations where a title is known, the honorific plus the title is usually used, either with or without the name, especially when spoken by foreigners. For casual contacts (e.g., with waiters, store help, etc.), just use *gaspodeen* without the name. It is perfectly appropriate, when meeting someone, to simply state your family name without any additional greeting (Russians will most likely do this). The old term *tovarisch,* meaning "comrade," is out of fashion now: it was popular in the Communist days, but it should no longer be used, even if it is employed in reference to you. If you speak any Russian at all, use it; it will absolutely delight your Russian associates, who will want to know how you came to learn it. Be ready, however, to switch to English, especially among those learning it, because they will want to practice with you.

The What, When, and How of Introducing People

Always wait to be introduced to strangers before taking that responsibility upon yourself. You will always be introduced to women first, then men, in descending order of age. Russians are most comfortable with a third-party introduction whenever possible, so wait a moment before introducing yourself to a new group; if, after a few minutes, no introduction is forthcoming, go ahead and do the honors yourself. Women do not necessarily rise when someone enters a room, but men always do, for both women and men. Do not presume to seat yourself at a gathering: if possible, wait to be told where to sit. Shake hands with everyone individually in a group before departing: the American group wave is not appreciated. Once you greet someone you will encounter later that day in the same circumstances (e.g., at the office), there is no need to greet them again. Kissing is a common greeting with and between all genders (women/women or men/men or women/men) once you have established a familiar relationship; it usually involves three "air kisses," first on the left side, and then the right, and then on the left again. Sometimes two men or two women will kiss each other on the lips to express real closeness, familiarity, and sincerity. This is usually only between very close friends, family members, and highly trusted business associates. Do *not* initiate such familiar greetings yourself.

Physical Greeting Styles

The handshake is common. The Russian version is a firm grip with several quick shakes between two men; between men and women or two women, the handshake is much softer. It should be accompanied by the appropriate greetings (outlined above), and may be accompanied by a kiss or an embrace. The eastern European tradition of men occasionally lifting the hand of a woman and bringing it to their lips really does not exist anymore in Russia, as it was associated with the prerevolutionary monarchy, and therefore fell out of favor. Men must remove their gloves when shaking hands with women, but women do not need to remove their gloves. Smiling and other nonverbal forms of communication may not always accompany the handshake, especially between people who have not met before. Men should wait until a woman extends her hand before reaching for it, and women may take the lead in extending their hand or not; this may or may not occur, especially among older women. Between women, the older woman extends her hand first. Eye contact during the introduction is very important, and must be maintained as long as the individual is addressing you.

The use of business cards is common; if possible, you should have yours translated into Russian (with Cyrillic text) on the reverse side. Be sure to put any advanced educational degrees and your full title or position on both sides of your translated business card. Such emblems of your status are very important:

Russians want to know who you are. When handing out your translated card, present it so that the side printed in Russian is readable. Beware, though, that you may not necessarily receive a business card in return: they are not as easily printed in the East, and are not as readily available. If this happens, it is perfectly okay to write names and contact information down on a piece of paper after handing out your card.

Communication Styles

Okay Topics / Not Okay Topics

Okay: anything positive (as long as they bring it up first) about the similarities and differences between Russia and your home country. Your knowledge of and interest in Russian culture and history will be appreciated, although it may be dismissed at first. (In fact, if you display too much knowledge, it will seem a bit strange; besides, Russians simply won't believe you if you try to persuade them that you like Russia, especially if you are from the West. At the same time, don't complain about Russia, for it will not be appreciated.) *Not okay:* While you should not inquire about a person's occupation or income in casual conversation, this and many other aspects of your life, both general and personal, will probably be asked of you. This is meant to get to know you, and to learn more about America: answer in general and in full for the greatest comfort and maximum effect (e.g., "Well, in America, the average salary for my position is ———, but you know, the average mortgage on a house is ———, and it costs about ——— to live a middle-class life"). Do not be evasive: Russians will press you for details. Do not discuss World War II (most every Russian family lost members in the war), the czar and the monarchy, the Holocaust, and ethnic minorities, or give your opinions about religion. One should be careful about comparing Moscow and Saint Petersburg: the two, like Rio de Janeiro and São Paulo, New York and Los Angeles, or Rome and Milan, are locked in competition, which sometimes gets less than friendly. Be careful of compliments: Russians are suspicious of them, charmed by them, and obligated by them. If you are in someone's home, for example, and you admire something, it might be thrust upon you as a gift at the end of the evening (and it may be something your Russian hosts can ill afford to part with); instead, try making your compliment without involving yourself (e.g., "Vases as beautiful as that one are usually found in museums in the United States," instead of, "I love that vase over there").

Tone, Volume, and Speed

Russians tend to run the gamut from soft, almost reticent speech, to full-blown dramatic walkouts. As a result, the Russian communication style is totally context-determined. Westerners should speak softly, slowly, and calmly whenever possible, appearing neither to be ruffled nor intimidated by displays of Russian emotion, or the lack thereof. It is not considered disrespectful and immature to raise one's voice, if the occasion demands it. Even though the traditional attitude toward the role of women in Russia is strongly held, the woman who is perceived as aggressive and strong has as much (or perhaps more) authority than a man.

Use of Silence

There may be some silence, depending upon the circumstances, although more often than not, if a Russian is uncomfortable he or she will say so; Russians usually do not remain silent for long.

Physical Gestures and Facial Expressions

When first meeting someone new, Russians may appear to be reserved and formal. This will change rapidly as trust and familiarity grow, which they will accelerate quickly in order to feel comfortable. There are many nonverbal behaviors that are the result of many factors, including, under the Communists, the inability to say directly what needed to be said. Medieval superstitions have also worked their way into the nonverbal language. Flicking a few fingers against the neck is an invitation (usually between men) to join the person for a drink of vodka. Whistling is considered bad luck, especially in theaters (don't "whistle" your approval of the performance) or inside the home (it will cause all wealth to disappear). If you do something wrong, are responsible for a problem, find yourself with a problem, or are at the mercy of someone else, spit three times over your left shoulder (this keeps the devil in these situations from coming closer). Knock three times on wood to bring good luck; and as a guest, sit down for a few seconds just before ever leaving someone's home. Any of the typical Western hand gestures (such as the "okay" sign, made with the thumb and the forefinger, and the *figa* sign, made by placing the thumb in between the index finger and the second finger) are considered very rude. Avoid showing the soles of your shoes to anyone (don't sit ankle over knee); it is considered rude. For this and other reasons, you might take your shoes off when entering a Russian home—your cue is if you see shoes lined up at the door—and sometimes even museums (in this case, they will give you slippers to wear). The American "thumbs-up" sign is okay.

Waving and Counting

The thumb represents the number 1, the index finger the number 2, and so on. It is insulting to beckon someone with the forefinger (instead, turn your hand so that the palm faces down and motion inward with all four fingers at once). If you need to gesture for a waiter, subtly raise your hand with your index finger slightly outstretched.

Physicality and Physical Space

Russians like to stand about a hand's-length closer to the other person than North Americans are accustomed to, and this happens almost instantly. On lines, people will be standing directly behind and in front of you, almost touching. It is very *nyekulturny* to speak with your hands in your pockets: always keep them firmly to your side when standing. If men and women must cross their legs, it must never be ankle over knee (for women, the preferred style is to cross ankle over ankle). Remember, in public, formal is always better than informal: no gum chewing, *ever;* don't slouch; and don't lean against things. It is especially important always to take your hat and coat off when entering a public building. Heating in Russian public buildings is usually quite good, so you'll broil unless you do so, anyway; in concert halls, for example, it is absolutely essential to always check your coat and hat at the wardrobe and do not carry it with you (very *nyekulturny*!).

Eye Contact

Eye contact will be direct most of the time. It is important not to interpret this behavior as a way of intentionally trying to make you uncomfortable; rather, it is a Russian sign of respect. If you look away, your behavior will say to your Russian colleague that you are either disinterested or rude. Either way, maintain eye contact when it is made with you, especially when making a toast. If two strangers' eyes meet and linger, it implies romantic interest; women should be especially careful about making casual eye contact with men. If a Russian squints his or her eyes, it means he or she is disinterested in either you, what you are saying, or both.

Emotive Orientation

Russians are generally not shy about their feelings. There will be much emotiveness, loudness, hand gestures, and the like. In public, however, it is *nyekulturny* to be loud, boisterous, and disturbing, even among people who know each other.

Protocol in Public

Walking Styles and Waiting in Lines

Lines are something that Russians, from the Communist days, are used to. Even in today's privatized economic climate, there may be lines. Lines are usually respected, sometimes not. It often depends on the flow of information about the availability of the goods one is waiting in line for. There will also often be more than one line that you will be required to get on in order to obtain some item or service: usually you get on a line to pay, then another to select the item, then another to actually collect it. Lines are usually not respected at public transportation facilities: there, people generally jostle and elbow for position. It is considered appropriate for people to stay to the right on the street. In Russian Orthodox churches, there generally are few pews; most people stand, walk around, and mingle (in hushed tones) during services.

Behavior in Public Places: Airports, Terminals, and the Market

Customer service as a concept simply did not exist in eastern and central Europe during the Communist era, and it exists minimally in Russia today. As employees of the state, with guaranteed jobs, store clerks simply had no motivation to be nice, let alone to serve, during the Communist days. And the scarcity of goods merely complicated the problem. Store hours are typically not built around customer convenience (stores are closed on Saturdays, open on Sundays and some evenings—especially Wednesday, usually, but close around 5 P.M. all other days) and may be erratic. As in much of Europe, if you touch the produce in food markets, you buy it; in goods stores, it may be difficult for you to return a product unless there is a flaw in it. You will be recognized as a foreigner, and you will be amazed at how prices will change upward as soon as you arrive: ask your neighbor on line the price they are willing to pay for the item, if this bothers you. Bartering is a way of life (that's one of the reasons you should bring lots of western items with you) for goods that are scarce; get used to it, for it will get you what you want more quickly than rubles (which vary in value from very deflated to almost worthless). Your use of hard currency, such as dollars, will be sought, and you must evaluate these situations carefully; changing money on the street is absolutely a bad idea (even friends will want to help you do this, and their motives are not always bad, since Russians live this way daily, but you should resist), but having U.S. dollars available to purchase goods will open doors instantly for you. You are expected (and encouraged) to bargain in the markets, in general (but not in large stores with listed prices). Smoking in public places is still a common occurrence, although the Russians are slowly becoming aware of the need to control it.

Bus / Metro / Taxi / Car

Don't drive in Russia. Checkpoints still abound on the roads (in the past, people needed papers permitting them to travel from one city to another), and the highways can be in terrible condition. Drunk driving is a problem; moreover, most Russians drive as if they own the entire road within a circumference of fifty feet surrounding the vehicle. Driving is on the right. If you are driving, put all personal items, including the windshield wipers and detachable antennas, away before leaving the car or else they won't be there when you return. Although pedestrians technically have the right of way, people drive as if cars do; however, public transport definitely always has the right of way. Most drivers do not turn on their lights at night (it is thought to blind the oncoming drivers).

The metros shut down after midnight. Your best bet for catching a cab is at designated taxi stands (hotels are good places, but often charge more for the same ride: a hotel surcharge is added to the meter fare). In some cases, convincing taxis to stop and take you in the first place is an art, best accomplished by offering a pack of American cigarettes in addition to the fare. It's a good idea to negotiate the fare before the ride begins; don't depend on the meter, whether it's working or not.

Bring food and water on board a commuter train if your trip is a long one, as there may not be a café car. Despite trends to the contrary, on public transportation, younger people should give up their seats to older people, and men should give up their seats to women, especially if they are pregnant or have babies or small children with them.

Tipping

Originally illegal, today the tip (of about 9 to 10 percent) is typically incorporated into the price, but any service is usually best acknowledged with a few loose coins plus "bartered items." Cigarettes, CDs, personal care items, ballpoint pens, tea, and coffee are the best tips for any service, including waiters, taxi drivers, theater attendants, and porters.

Punctuality

Be punctual, but expect delays—sometimes notorious delays—due either to the unexpected, or simply due to the needs of daily life. Expect open-ended situations (meetings can go on longer than expected, and dinners usually go on into the early morning hours). The Russian workday usually starts early (businesses can open at 8 A.M.), but ends late (workers usually go home around 4 P.M., office staff usually no later than 5 P.M.). Even managers and executives are rarely in their offices after five o'clock. However, many Russian women go food shopping after work, which often includes waiting on long lines. The Russian workweek often includes Saturday morning.

Dress

Err on the formal side, until you know to dress otherwise; this is a good rule both in social situations and at the office. You may be surprised at how informal dress is at work and in social situations. Do not expect people to be fashionably dressed: scarcity, along with a lack of awareness of Western styles, has reduced most Russians to wearing functional clothes. It is *nyekulturny* to wear anything at work that is loud or looks trendy: slacks, a sport jacket, a white shirt, and a dark tie, with or without a sweater vest, is often the attire. Depending on the position or job, you might see businesspeople in suits and ties; or you might see workers in jeans and a sweater. The long, cold winters in Russia require layers of clothes, and sweaters and vests help keep people warm throughout the workday. The well-heated public buildings allow you to layer off clothes as you settle in during the winter (and layer on in the spring and early fall, when the heat goes off, but can still be a bit chilly inside). Alternately, on those rare sunny and warm days, Russians will peel off clothes just as quickly (no nudity, though, except on specifically marked gender-separated beaches along the Black Sea). On the street, informal may mean jeans and sneakers; for a social gathering, informal more often than not means the same clothes one wore to work. Women must wear a long-sleeved garment, a long skirt below the knees, and a head covering (scarf or hat) when visiting a Russian Orthodox church.

Seasonal Variations

The extremely cold and damp winter requires layers of clothes and protective boots, hats, and rain gear. Never remove your jacket or tie unless and until your Russian colleague has done so first.

Colors

Most colors are simple, natural, and not ostentatious. Be conservative in the use of color, even with accessories: they need to blend with, not stand out from, the outfit.

Styles

Style is not critical, but a good appearance is always appreciated. Cologne and perfume are not commonly used. As in most Slavic cultures, men may have facial hair (usually in the form of a mustache).

Personal Hygiene

Recognize that hot running water in some places may be expensive, so your daily bath may have to be forsaken from time to time.

Dining and Drinking

Mealtimes and Typical Foods

Breakfast (*zahvtrahk*) is served from about 7 to 8 A.M., and usually consists of breads, butter, jams, sometimes hot cereal (*kasha*), and eggs (usually soft-boiled); remember, the shortages of food are difficult to predict, so restaurant menus are unreliable. Check with the waiter or the management to see what is available. Tea (*cha*) is the drink of preference for most meals (usually served at the end of the meal, not during), and in between. Tea is often drunk out of glasses. Some Russians hold a cube of sugar between their front teeth and let the tea wash over it as they drink.

Lunch (*ahbyed*) is still the main meal of the day in both rural and urban settings; it is served around noontime during the week, and around 1 or 2 P.M. on Sundays. It usually consists of three courses, beginning with appetizers such as pickled vegetables and preserved fish (herrings or sardines), then moving on to soup (usually borscht or cabbage soup), and a main course of noodles and/or potatoes and meat, if available. Chicken is made any number of ways: fried, baked, in cream sauce (Kiev), or served *satsivi* (with a spicy nut sauce), or *tkemali* (with a sweet and spicy fruit sauce). Beef is often regally served Stroganoff style. Bread (*kleb*) is available throughout the meal (and often with vodka, in order to absorb the alcohol and help make the drinking last longer). Desserts are usually fruit (fresh if available, preserved if not). Beer (or sometimes kvass, low-alcohol beer) or vodka is drunk with lunch.

Dinner (*oozhin*) is usually served from 6 to 8 P.M. or later. If lunch was the main meal of the day, dinner is usually just a light meal of sandwiches, sausages, cheese, and potato or beet salad. Beer or vodka may be served before, during, and after; tea is usually served after.

If you have a chance, try caviar in Russia: there are many different types, and it is as available as other foods (which may or may not be frequent). When hosting guests, Russians will often begin the meal with tasty snacks called *zakuzki,* which are served often on white bread (it is considered the finest bread). When there are lots of them, they may end up to be the entire meal.

Cafés are not common (remember, there is a long winter season!), and good restaurants require reservations (and sometimes a bribe of some sort) a long time ahead. Most of the restaurants are in hotels, and may or may not be good. Avoid public cafeterias (*stolovaya*) and food stalls on the streets (even though the broiling meats—shish kebabs, usually—smell good, it may not be a good idea, from a health standpoint, to eat even cooked food from the street). There are small, snack-type places that sell specialty food items: eat there only if they look clean and attractive. *Pelmeni* stands sell *pelmeni* (small stuffed dumplings), sausage bars (*sosisochnaya*) sell sausages, and *blinnaya* sell blinis or pancakes with all sorts of toppings. *Konditerskaya* sell baked goods and cookies (some specialty baked good stores sell only bread). Ice cream can be purchased almost everywhere in special shops called *morozhenoye* (Russians love ice cream year-round).

Typical Drinks and Toasting

The most common toast is *na zdrovia* (to your health). The Russians' favorite drink is vodka, which is served before a meal begins, during all meals, and at all social events. It will usually come out onto the table, along with assorted snacks, during business meetings at virtually any time of day, including first thing in the morning. Vodka is best iced ahead of time (the most formal way to serve it); it will rarely be poured over ice. Drink it in one gulp, or shot. Do not drink all the vodka that is offered to you, for every time you drink a glass, it will be refilled. The more you drink, the more you will be offered: know when to stop. If you really cannot drink, you'll need a very good excuse, like doctor's orders. Always take some bread after each drink: you'll need it. If you drink too much, you can always have *kfir,* or buttermilk, which the Russians drink for hangovers.

Never break eye contact while making a toast, from the moment the glass leaves the table until you place it down again (blinking is allowed, however!). There can be many toasts throughout a meal; you will be expected to make one in a small group at some point during the meal, especially if you have been toasted personally or are the guest of honor (always try to say a few words in Russian: it is very much appreciated).

Table Manners and the Use of Utensils

Do not begin eating until all the guests have received food on their plates and your host invites you to begin; this is usually done by saying, "*Pree yat na vah appeteetah.*"

Like all continental Europeans, Russians do not switch knives and forks, as Americans do. The knife remains in the right hand, and the fork remains in the left. When the meal is finished, place your fork and knife across the plate horizontally, facing left; this indicates that you are done. If you're unsure of which utensil to use, always start from the outside and work your way in, course by course. The spoon above your plate is usually for dessert. Bread is usually served without butter (therefore, there usually will not be a butter knife) and there usually is no bread plate (place your bread on the side of your main plate or on the table throughout the meal). Your setting will include a small plate for *zakuzki* (if there is only a *zakuski* plate, you will know that appetizers will make up the meal), a vodka shot glass, a water glass, and a wine glass. The wine in Russia is usually sweet and drunk only with dessert.

Your hands are expected to be visible above the table: this means you do not keep them in your lap; instead, rest your wrists on top of the table. Pass all dishes at the table to your left. If there is gravy or sauce, you can use your bread to soak some of it up. You will be expected to eat all the bread you take throughout the meal: it is considered bad luck, *nyetkulturny,* and wasteful not to eat all the bread you take.

Seating Plans

The most honored position is at the head of the table, with the most important guest seated immediately to the right of the host (women to the right of the host, and men to the right of the hostess); if there is a hosting couple, one will be seated at each side of the table. In keeping with the practice elsewhere on the Continent (in formal situations), men and women are seated next to one another, and couples are often broken up and seated next to people they may not have previously known. In informal situations, the sexes may be seated together. Men typically must rise when women enter the room, and may or may not enter a room first when a woman is present. At meals, the oldest or most honored guest is served first. Remember, as is the case throughout the Continent, what the Russians refer to as the first floor is really the second floor, with the first floor usually referred to as the lobby or ground floor.

Refills and Seconds

At a private dinner party, if you do not want more food, you will really have to insist several times before the hostess will believe you. Food will usually be passed around on a platter, several times, if necessary. Take a little extra if you can of something you like. If you do not want more, you must leave a little food on your plate to be believed. You may always have additional beverages; if you drink enough to cause your cup or glass to be less than half full, it will generally be refilled. Portions are generally similar in size to those in the United States, but there can be more courses, for both lunch and dinner, and Russians are extravagant hosts.

At Home, in a Restaurant, or at Work

In informal restaurants, you may be required to share a table: if so, do not force conversation; act as if you are seated at a private table. Waitstaff may be summoned by making eye contact; waving or calling their names is very impolite. The business breakfast is unheard of, but drinks and snacks at meetings in offices are very common, even first thing in the morning. The business lunch or dinner, depending upon how well developed your relationship is with your Russian associates, is generally the time to seal a deal, not to make decisions, negotiate, or get to know each other. (It will be difficult to do any business dining, for getting reservations at restaurants can be difficult, and restaurants are where celebrations occur, not negotiations.) Don't chew gum, ever, at a restaurant or on the street. No-smoking sections in restaurants do not exist (Russians smoke constantly throughout the meal).

When invited to a Russian colleague's home for a formal meal, you will be told where to sit, and there you should remain. Do not wander around, even though most homes are very small, cramped apartments. If your hosts do move you from one room to another, allow the more senior members of your party to enter the room ahead of you. Once at the table, do not presume to seat yourself, as the seating arrangement is usually predetermined. Spouses who accompany their partners on business trips are often invited to attend meals at homes, if you let it be known in the course of conversation that your spouse is with you (be diplomatic). Plan to arrive about 7 P.M. or so (do not be too late for meals at someone's home), and be prepared to stay late: you will insult your hosts if you end the evening too early (this means staying at least past midnight, even during the midweek); eat slowly, plan to spend the whole night. You might need to remove your shoes before entering a Russian home (check to see if there are pairs of shoes lined up at the entrance to the home: if there are, it means you should remove yours as well); be sure your socks are in good shape. You might be offered slippers to wear.

Being a Good Guest or Host

Paying the Bill

Usually the one who does the inviting pays the bill, although the guest is expected to make an effort to pay. Sometimes other circumstances determine the payee (such as rank). Making payment arrangements ahead of time so that no exchange occurs at the table is a very classy way to host. Women simply do not dine alone in Russia, and never pay the bill when invited out. It will be insulting to your male guests if you even attempt to make payment arrangements ahead of time.

Transportation

It's a very nice idea, when acting as the host, to inquire ahead of time as to whether the guests will require transportation. If necessary, you should arrange for taxi service at the end of the meal.

In Russia, you may be picked up from and taken back to your hotel by the host.

When to Arrive / Chores to Do

Russians are extravagant hosts, and will sacrifice much to make sure there is an abundance of food for you. If invited to dinner at a private home, offer to help with the chores, but expect to be turned down at first. Ask again, and your offer will probably be accepted. Do not leave the table unless invited to do so. When it is time to leave, always get up and shake hands with everyone: the group wave is not appreciated. But it is possible that you will be asked to spend the night, as well. Recognize that this will probably require some member(s) of the family to sleep on the floor or the couch. Remember, if you are invited into a home, your desires become your hosts' most important concerns, so be sensitive to imposing yourself on their daily chores, and be willing to help out with the most difficult ones (such as the daily food shopping, cleaning, etc.).

Gift Giving

In general, gift giving is common among business associates, and the best gifts are useful office items, such as pen and pencil sets or nicely bound agendas. This is especially appreciated at New Year's time. Mementos of life in the United States are very well received (towels, coffee-table books on the United States, and well-packaged gourmet foodstuffs are always appreciated).

Holiday cards are not very appropriate, because they carry no intrinsic value of their own.

Gifts are expected for social events, especially as thank-yous for private dinner parties or overnight stays at someone's home. The best gifts in these cases are items for personal use (shampoo, cologne, perfumes, CDs, clothing—jeans, tights, sweatshirts, T-shirts—cigarettes, etc). Avoid flowers: they are useless and too symbolic. Other good gifts would be cakes and pastries, good wine (bring several bottles, so that one may be used with the meal, and the others by the hosts later), a box of fine chocolates, or preserved fruits. Do not bring only vodka alone: there is usually already plenty. If there are children in the family, it is thoughtful to bring a little something for them, such as a toy or candy, in addition to the gift for the hostess. Unlike other European cultures, gifts tend to be accepted and opened later (not in the presence of the giver); in addition, there may not be great enthusiasm shown for receiving the gift, but be assured it is valued (an acknowledgment of the gift in the form of a card or letter is not customary). Because useful gifts can also appear as philanthropy, be tactful, and use an excuse, if necessary (your company provides you with more of these items than you can personally use, etc.). It is bad luck to give a pregnant woman a baby gift until after the baby is born.

Special Holidays and Celebrations

Major Holidays

Most Russian workers get several weeks of paid vacation; August is a leading vacation time. Business slows down from December 15 to January 6, and Holy Week is sometimes a more difficult time to accomplish work than Christmas (in Russia, as is the case with all Eastern Orthodox cultures, Easter is more important than Christmas). Moreover, as is also the case in Orthodox cultures, name days (the birthdays of the saints after whom people were named) are often more important celebrations than birthdays among the observant; still, for most Russians, the secular birthday is still more important. They may celebrate both.

January 1	*Noviy God* (New Year's Day; a major celebration)
March/April	Good Friday (for observers only; not a national day)
March/April	*Pasha* (Easter; for observers only; not a national day)
March 8	*Zgenskiy Den'* (Women's Day)
May 1–2	*Pervoe Maya* (May Day)
May 9	*Den' Pobedi* (Victory Day; celebrating Russia's defeat of Nazi Germany)
October 7	*Den' Konstituzzii* (Constitution Day)
November 1	All Saints' Day (observers only; not a national day)
December 25	*Rozgdestve* (Christmas; observers only; not a national day)

Business Culture

Daily Office Protocols

In Russia, office doors are mostly closed; you must knock first (this includes bathrooms) before opening doors, and when leaving rooms, close the doors behind you.

Women do not hold equal authority as men in business. It is more common for women to be relegated to lower-level management, worker, or administrative support positions. It is rare (though not impossible) to see women at the highest levels of business and government.

The Russian workday can start early, and may end around late afternoon. When making appointments, be sure to schedule them way in advance, and confirm them several times as the date and time approach. Delays can be very frustrating, especially when working with government officials and offices. Expect some chitchat at the beginning of the meeting about nonbusiness issues, but Russians usually move fairly quickly to substantive issues. Communications may be very difficult: the phone systems are ancient, and each former "official" had his or her own number, usually a single phone, which only they answered. You may or may not ever get the direct number, so it may or may not be possible to reach him or her. Copiers, computers, and fax machines are unreliable and may not be easily accessible: bring whatever documents you need with you. Because workers were, in the past, guaranteed jobs no matter how badly they did them, and because anyone could be untrustworthy, you must anticipate non-cooperation, negativity, and suspicion from all contacts other than those you are working with directly (and from them as well, until you have established a relationship and mutual need).

Management Styles

Basic Western business concepts are still new ideas for most Russians. This means that ideas such as proprietary rights, motivation, profit, loss, pricing, accountability, and individual reward all may be new, suspect, and misunderstood. Consider providing important information and informal education as part of your work in Russia. Privacy and individual accomplishment of one's tasks are not known, as individuals were not held accountable for the success or failure of a project, and project goals were set according to authoritarian demand, not the marketplace. Traditionally, under Communism (and harkening back to previous small-business ventures in Russia), superiors had authority over their subordinates, and while ultimately responsible for a decision, involved most individuals below them in their unit (or a structural task unit, STU—a cog in a huge, state-run, quantity-oriented operation) in a consensus-building process of inquiry and information gathering. After several consultations with subordinates, senior managers then made final decisions, and all involved lockstepped in obedience to those decisions. Today, the process and the results are essentially still the same, but the hierarchies are less dominated by the state.

Titles in Russia are very important; the highest ones (e.g., vice president or director) are usually reserved for very senior, executive-level positions, and should not be used as casually as they are in the United States, although the authority and responsibility of the title may not be understood. Complimenting and rewarding individuals publicly is viewed suspiciously. Do not expect Russians to work after-hours on weekends or during vacation time (when they are, if privileged to be able to do so, at their dacha, or country bungalow).

Boss-Subordinate Relations

Rank most definitely has its decision-making privileges and perquisites. Deviating from the proper channels typically does not get things done any faster, and historically has been a very dangerous thing to do. In the Communist system, bosses were also government agents. Today, you must get close to the decision makers, who are most often at the top of former state-run organizations; if this is your first meeting in Russia, you may not be speaking with decision makers, but merely gatekeepers who are there to size up you and your organization, and report back to their supervisors. Be sure you are dealing, whenever possible, with real decision makers. One way to ensure this is to be sure that you have plenty of the right kind of contacts prior to your trip, with well-detailed agendas made up with their buy-in and understanding ahead of time. If you are dealing with new *biznis* people (usually younger and entrepreneurial), or older former state officials, be sure you do your homework and get unbiased information about their reputations and their credibility. Russians will often make unfounded guarantees to get your investment and their veracity may in fact be questionable.

Conducting a Meeting or Presentation

Meetings can, if decision makers are present, be information-sharing and decision-making forums in which all individuals are expected to contribute. Data, facts, and figures are all important, but not more important than the good feeling your Russian associates finally have about you when you leave. Because Russians have learned to deal with limited resources for so long, presentations need not be fancy, as long as they are clear and easily understood. Presentations in English are fine, but backup documentation should also be in Russian. Be sure you have your own translator: do not depend upon the interpreter provided for the meeting by the Russian side.

Negotiation Styles

Russians can display two opposing behaviors: they can play their cards close to the vest at first, not divulging information easily at the beginning, and open up as trust develops; or they can almost be effusive in their eagerness to work with you (this is because they indeed are: Western business generally means good new opportunities!). If they are in the former mode, they may appear circumspect in their communication styles, and will indicate their thoughts in indirect, associative ways; they can, however, quickly become pointedly direct as negotiations move forward. If they are in their latter mode, they will most definitely be more eager to speak openly and move negotiations along. If you are from the West, they will assume that you have the ability to do everything you say and more (and consequently ask for much), and will also assume that you already have the knowledge and experience required for the work; moreover, they will try to persuade you of the same about them, which may or may not in fact be true (you need to confirm this independently).

The first meeting is usually just a formality, with the Russians sizing up you and your organization (and you sizing up their credibility, as well): it will be conducted in the office. Put on a warm, firm, nonaggressive, dignified demeanor during the meeting. Horse trading and a win/lose approach are what Russians expect. You can expect all sorts of delay tactics, emotional outbursts, pressures, and threats. Resist such tactics and negotiate from mutual benefits, search for mutual needs. Russians are great "sitters"; bureaucracies and a polychronic sense of time can create interminably lengthy negotiations. This is especially challenging when one has return air tickets (and Russians can use this as a pressuring tactic to force you to concede to their demands). The seating arrangement at the negotiating table usually puts the decision maker in the center at one side of the table, flanked by his or her aides in descending order of rank, and you and your team should sit (or be seated) in a mirror image of your Russian associates on the opposite side of the table. Contracts are serious matters: they should be clear, concise, and translated into both Russian and English. Once signed, they are viewed as inviolate (although situations will develop in the future that will require future meetings to adjust the contract). Therefore, all written documentation is very important, and copious notes should be taken throughout every meeting. The Russians will sometimes insist on this (it usually takes the form of a "protocol"; at the end of each meeting, the protocol is read, everyone agrees on it, and it is signed).

Written Correspondence

Be clear, precise, and respectful in your business correspondence; you can be flowery in the intent, but be very specific in the details. Last names usually are written in uppercase; dates are given using the day/month/year format (with periods in between, not slashes); time is written in military style; weights and measures are metric; and an honorific plus the title is as common as an honorific plus the last name. Monetary amounts are written so that periods break up the figures into tens, hundreds, and thousands (i.e., R10.000,00 = ten thousand rubles). Addresses in Russia are in reverse order from those in the West: the first line is the country (Russia), the second line is the city, the third line is the street address, and the last line is the name of the individual. Mail is usually not opened by anyone (including secretaries) other than the person it is addressed to; this can cause delays. You can get straight to the point in written business communications.

The Eastern European Cultures: Ukraine and Belarus

Note: The countries of Ukraine and Belarus share many cultural traditions with Russia. For this reason, the discussion that follows will refer to the essential general Slavic cultural patterns described in the preceding chapter on Russia, with additional variations that are specific to Ukraine and Belarus.

UKRAINE

Some Introductory Background on Ukraine and the Ukranians

For starters, the country is called "Ukraine" (or as other Europeans refer to it, "Ukrainia"), not "the Ukraine" (to do so demeans the independent status of the country, making it sound too much like a section of greater Russia, which it most definitely is not). The word in Ukrainian means "borderland," and in many ways Ukraine has stood as the border between Europe and Asia for both Europeans (mainly Poles and Lithuanians in the fourteenth century) and Asians (first the Mongols in the twelfth century, later the Turks in the fifteenth century). Ukrainians are definitely not Russians, and will object to any attempt to conflate the two (although there are many Russians living in Ukraine, and they do view themselves as Russian Ukrainians, complicating the matter). But Ukrainians *do* see themselves as members of a distinct European culture in the third-largest country in Europe.

The topography of the country has played a major role in its history, which, in turn, has played a major role in defining its culture. For one thing, it is mainly flat, and very fertile. This makes it a coveted prize for any marauder going east or west across it—and makes it easy to travel across, as well. No natural defenses exist, so it is simple for powerful neighboring armies to sweep across it. If you use the former Soviet Union as a reference point, Ukraine is located in the south. The climate is warmer (in fact, southern Ukraine was used as a vacation spot for Russians), resulting, according to some, in a different temperament among the people. These topographical and climatic factors resulted in an agricultural system that did not base itself on communal defense, as the Russian mir did. Hence, there was far less subordination of individual will in the Ukrainian experience, resulting in a less group-oriented culture than Russians.

If Russians are complex, conflicted, introspective, and defensive, Ukrainians are clearer, happier, outgoing, and romantic—as one visitor put it, they are "softer." They do not question their identity, which is an essential characteristic of the Russian. If there is a particularly Slavic burden Ukrainians do carry, it is the fact that they see themselves as protectors of the heart of the Slavic faith, and essentially the original bearers of Slavic Eastern Orthodoxy. Before there was Moscow, there was Kiev (capital of Ukraine), and Christianity, in the form of Eastern Orthodoxy, first came to all the Slavs, including Russians, from Constantinople by way of Kiev in the ninth century.

Some Historical Context

Being as vulnerable as they were to outside invasions, and being the people who brought Orthodoxy to the Slavic world, Ukrainians see themselves as historic defenders of the faith. Early in the medieval period, Poland overran Ukraine, attempting to replace Orthodoxy with Catholicism; after the Poles, Lithuanians (at one time in a Lithuanian-Polish empire in the fourteenth century) attempted to do the same. After both had failed at trying to establish Roman Catholicism, Ukrainians had to defend themselves against Turks and Islam in the fifteenth and sixteenth centuries. Finally, in the twentieth century, Ukrainians had to defend themselves against the Russians, with whom they aligned themselves at first in an effort to strengthen their stand against the Turks; once aligned, the Russians viewed Ukraine as within their sphere of influence, and brought both authoritarian rule and atheism under their Communist system, making Ukraine the breadbasket for all the Soviet empire. The nuclear disaster at Chernobyl only added to the miseries that Ukrainians have endured. Today, as in the past, Ukraine is struggling to maintain its independence, overcome its difficult history, and establish a stable economy.

An Area Briefing

Religion and Demographics

It is important to recognize that the most recent Russian domination of Ukraine has changed the demographic face of the country. About one-third of the people in Ukraine speak Russian, and most of these identify themselves as Russians. These Ukrainians often do not see Ukraine as a separate nation, but prefer to think of it as an area of Russia. Non-Russian Ukrainians, born as such in Ukraine, often refuse to speak Russian and struggle to maintain their Ukrainian culture. This is a very sensitive issue in Ukraine, and a delicate one for foreigners to get involved with.

Like Russia, Ukraine is a macho culture, although women are not quite as subordinate to men. Generational differences within Ukraine are generally not as severe an issue as the Russian-Ukrainian ethnicity split.

The historic struggle to maintain Eastern Orthodoxy against the incursions of Western Catholics (led by the Cossacks, originally a Ukrainian peasant group, and subsequently challenged by and ultimately appropriated by the Russians) has resulted in an intransigent, almost fundamentalist devotion among the faithful, with the Ukrainian Orthodox Church being one of the most deeply symbolic, ritualistic, and mystical of all the Orthodox Churches; alternately, the struggle has also resulted in the presence of Catholicism (the two groups often do not get along: Poles and Lithuanians brought their Catholicism through the work of proselytizing Jesuits, and even today, Catholics and Jesuits are scorned and feared by the Ukrainian Orthodox faithful), and the unique Uniate Church, which follows Eastern Orthodox rites but accepts the authority of Rome, formed, understandably enough, as an effort to bridge the gap between the Catholic and Orthodox Churches in Ukraine.

Fundamental Cultural Orientations

1. What's the Best Way for People to Relate to One Another?

OTHER-INDEPENDENT OR OTHER-DEPENDENT? Ukranians have far greater individual responsibility and decision-making authority at any level they may be at in society than their Russian cousins. The welfare of the group, of course, as represented by the extended family, is the reason for much individual action, but responsibility for things, for better or for worse, rests far more with the individual and his or her immediate family than with the larger group.

HIERARCHY-ORIENTED OR EGALITY-ORIENTED? The need for structure, hierarchy, and organization is strong, and Ukrainians find their strength in their church and the deeply personal role played by each individual as they take their place in society, the world, the universe. There is a deep, almost mystical, sense of the connectedness between individual Ukrainians and the cosmos, and this makes Ukrainians immensely proud of their culture. There is a greater equality between women and men than exists in Russia, and there is deep respect for women and their maternal role in society. There are many women in the workplace, and they may hold equal positions with men in some cases.

RULE-ORIENTED OR RELATIONSHIP-ORIENTED? There is a developing sense of the importance of universally applied rules, systems, and processes, and a lessened fear of being victimized by them than exists in Russian culture. Nevertheless, who you know may be more important than relying on the rules and systems. In the face of the challenges to their existence, there is a strong nationalism that is often a criteria against which judgments are made and action taken.

2. What's the Best Way to View Time?

MONOCHRONIC OR POLYCHRONIC? Like Russia, Ukraine is polychronic, but essentially because it was and still is mainly an agricultural country running on agricultural time, and less because of the Communist influence.

RISK-TAKING OR RISK-AVERSE? There is a very conservative aspect to Ukrainian nature, no doubt the result of the combination of historical experience, rural values, and the strong Eastern Orthodox religion. Ukrainians need a lot of information before a comfort level is reached in order to take action.

PAST-ORIENTED OR FUTURE-ORIENTED? Ukrainians get their pride from their past accomplishments, and their ability to move forward into the future in many ways will be a measure of their ability to harness the energy they get from their traditional values. There is no one clear plan for the future, but there is almost universal agreement in celebrating the past.

3. What's the Best Way for Society to Work with the World at Large?

LOW-CONTEXT DIRECT OR HIGH-CONTEXT INDIRECT COMMUNICATORS? Ukranians are essentially intuitive, almost poetic people, but not in the over-the-top emotive Russian way; this makes for a gentle form of communication, where context does supply much of the message, but where the message is also almost always delivered with concern for its impact on the other.

PROCESS-ORIENTED OR RESULT-ORIENTED? Ukranians are perhaps less associative than their Russian cousins, but certainly heavily influenced by the very overwhelming subjective experiences that they, as individuals, families, and a society, have experienced in the recent past.

FORMAL OR INFORMAL? Ukranians are a far more consistently informal and spontaneous people than their Russian cousins, but they tend to be reserved at first, and relax a little later.

Greetings and Introductions

Language and Basic Vocabulary

The Ukrainian language is similar to Russian, and many Russians and Ukrainians can communicate with each other; however, there is a reticence among non-Russian Ukrainians to use Russian, and a tendency to use Russian among Russian Ukrainians: this is a constant strain on society. The Ukrainian language is heavily influenced by the Polish and Lithuanian languages; Russian essentially is not. If there is a second language of choice, it probably is German or English, although there will be few speakers of either. Here are some basic Ukrainian terms and their English meanings:

dobrihy rahnok	good morning
dobrihy dehn	good day
dobrihy vehcheer	good evening
pro-shoo	please
dya kooyoo	yes, thank you
dya kooyoo nee	no, thank you

peh-reh pro shoo yoo excuse me
do po bah-chehn nya good-bye

Honorifics for Men, Women, and Children

A Ukrainian variation here is in the name: if the family name ends with *-enko* (*-enka* is the ending for a woman), there is a very good chance the individual is Ukrainian and not Russian.

Physical Greeting Styles

A Ukrainian consideration here would be regarding the translation of your business card: if you have already translated your cards into Russian on the reverse side, it might be better to use a nontranslated card than cards translated into Russian. Cards printed in English or specifically translated into Ukranian are best.

Communication Styles

Okay Topics / Not Okay Topics

You should be particularly concerned in Ukraine with identifying the background of your Ukrainian colleague before launching into discussions of Russians, Ukrainian nationalism, and the like. *Not okay:* Topics to avoid include World War II, the Holocaust, Catholics, Lithuanians, Jesuits, and Poles, and Chernobyl. Ukrainians, unlike Russians, will not disbelieve you if you express an interest in and a liking for their country and their ways. They admire the West, and will be curious about you, your life in the West, and aspects of Western politics, economics, and culture, but will also want to show you the best they have to offer.

Tone, Volume, and Speed

Ukranians are, in the main, a soft-spoken people. Their speech is slow, careful, considerate, and, in a way, poetic.

Physical Gestures and Facial Expressions

Ukrainians use the *figa* gesture (the thumb placed between the index and middle fingers with the hand in the shape of a fist): it means "zero," and is a way of indicating that nothing is available. It is not vulgar (although many of the other gestures already noted still are). Other Russian gestures previously noted apply.

Emotive Orientation

In general, Ukranians are more subdued than their Russian neighbors.

Dress

Seasonal Variations

There is a long summer and a warm, wet spring. Along the Black Sea coast, resort dress is the rule.

Dining and Drinking

Ukranian dining is similar in many ways to Russian dining, except that the food can include many more fresh vegetables and fruits, especially in season.

Typical Drinks and Toasting

There is a uniquely Ukrainian liqueur called *medikva,* which is made from honey: it will be offered to you after meals, and sometimes before. After toasting and dining, dancing and singing usually ensues, and you will be expected to join in the fun. Go ahead and sing a song in English: if Ukrainians know it, they'll join in; even if they don't know it, they're just as likely to join in. As with Russians, there will usually be two bottles of clear liquid on the table: one is vodka, the other is mineral water and they are often unlabeled. Once a bottle is opened, it is usually not resealable, so it must be drunk down completely. Consider carefully!

Special Holidays and Celebrations

Major Holidays

The Eastern Orthodox (Julian) calendar is in force in Ukraine, so the dates of major religious festivals, which are important celebrations there, are different from similar celebrations in the West (such as Christmas and Easter). Easter and the accompanying Holy Week are far more important than Christmas, and special foods (such as an Easter bread baked with a hard-boiled egg and a coin in the center) celebrate the holiday. Again, name days are generally more important celebrations than birthdays.

January 1	New Year's Day
January 7	Eastern Orthodox Christmas
March 8	International Women's Day
May 1	Solidarity Day/May Day
May 9	Victory Day (end of World War II)
August 24	Independence Day

Business Culture

Expect to do a lot of business entertaining in Ukraine; more restaurants are available than in Russia, and people are more inclined to hold meetings over drinks. Don't be surprised to find your final negotiations occurring over lunch or dinner. Take your cue from your Ukrainian colleagues. Ukrainians, once they identify you as a Westerner, will want to impress upon you the benefits of doing business with them and not the Russians: if you can demonstrate that you are not doing business with Russia, and only with them, this will take you far—as long as you are not dealing with Russian Ukrainians.

BELARUS

As a nation, Belarus is a very new idea. The Belarusians are culturally very similar to Russians. Informally known as White Russians, with their capital in Minsk, they have historically been compliant to the will and culture of their Russian cousins in Moscow. This does not mean that they do not seek their own identity; but the history of the people has been one of heeding the will of powerful leaders, and this has led to Russian domination more often than not. For much of its history, the country has aligned itself with Moscow for protection, although culturally, because of it agricultural base, Belarusians are more like their Ukrainian neighbors. The religion is primarily Eastern Orthodox. The language is similar to Russian, as well.

Perhaps the one aspect of Belarusians that sets them apart for foreigners is their personal affability and informality: you will probably be invited into their homes almost immediately, introduced to the family, expected to be friends with their friends, and feasted, often at great personal sacrifice. Once a solid personal relationship is established, business usually proceeds, although Belarusians must contend with the remnants of their former authoritarian government and economic system, and thus negotiate and conduct business in ways similar to Russians—with equally frustrating results for Westerners. Despite their informality socially (which is absolutely essential in order to create the personal relationship needed to get any business arrangement going), their desire for absolute (authoritarian) certainty makes for a very detail-conscious and red-tape-driven business environment (bring lots of documentation, and ask for the same).

Index